COMPREHENSIVE INTELLECTUAL CAPITAL MANAGEMENT

COMPREHENSIVE INTELLECTUAL CAPITAL MANAGEMENT

Step-by-Step

Nermien Al-Ali

WILEY

John Wiley & Sons, Inc.

For general information on our other products and services, or technical support, please contact
our Customer Care Department within the United States at 800-762-2974, outside the United
States at 317-572-3993 or fax 317-572-4002.

Wiley also publishes its books in a variety of electronic formats. Some content that appears in
print may not be available in electronic books.

ISBN: 0-471-27506-9

Printed in the United States of America

10 9 8 7 6 5 4 3 2 1

To my parents, Fatmeh and Afeef Al-Ali,
for opening the gates of knowledge for me
and enlightening my mind and soul.
I owe them more than my life.

To John Hutson for believing in me
and supporting my intellectual quest.

About the Author

Nermien Al-Ali began her Intellectual Property (IP) career as the Managing Attorney of the IP Department of one of Egypt's leading international business law firms, Ibrachy & Dermarkar. Then she counseled multinational clients on local and international IP laws and treaties. Her business experience encouraged her to embark on researching models for managing IP and other intellectual capital, leading to her teaching career. Through extensive research in the emerging field of intellectual capital management (ICM), Professor Al-Ali designed and teaches a course on ICM as a business management approach for the management of human capital, knowledge and intellectual property in the new economy at Franklin Pierce Law Center. It is not only the first course of its kind to be offered at a U.S. law school, but one that offers a comprehensive approach for understanding the emerging field of ICM—hence her Comprehensive Intellectual Capital Management (CICM) model. *(www.ipmall.fplc.edu/hosted_resources/Al-Ali/home.htm).*

Contents

Foreword

By Gordon Smith

From the Rust Belt[1] to Silicon Valley—the business world has made that conceptual journey, like it or not. And whether we are managers of business, investors, employees, or professionals who toil in support of business, we all have a different understanding of what that journey meant, because it affected our lives differently.

This book examines that journey and focuses on some intriguing challenges that we face in this new business world.

Let's remember what was rusting in the Rust Belt. It was the tangible infrastructure of companies whose products and services were no longer competitive in world markets. The blast furnaces went cold and the rolling mills became silent, but these assets were once the driving forces within the companies that exploited them. Whoever owned these huge, immovable physical assets owned the earning power of the business. Innovation was captured in the machines and in the process, and management's job was to extract maximum capacity from machines and labor.

The reader of this book will come to understand that the profits of today's businesses are driven by intangible assets, not "bricks". Around the abandoned-in-place mills have sprung up centers of high technology—profitable businesses with no specialized tangible assets, but with highly specialized and valuable intangible ones. New career paths have emerged and enterprise has created products and services unknown to us just a few years ago.

Now it is true that intangible assets have been a part of enterprise ever since the first person discovered how to chip a spear point and kept the knowledge to himself. It is the magnitude and importance of this type of property that has mushroomed in our lives. Few foresaw the Internet-spawned bubble of e-commerce businesses that were dubbed "the New Economy" and, to be sure, they were prime examples of enterprises with no "bricks". This phenomenon did not create the change we discuss, however, it merely accelerated it.

Today's business managers are beginning to understand that the "care and feeding" of these intangible assets is crucial to their "bottom line" and to the long-term growth of their business. These assets are *mission-critical* and managements that ignore them do so at their peril. Everyone needs to learn new skills, because there has been a rapid, but evolutionary, change in the character of business and in the character of the capital tools employed in an enterprise. This book focuses on the critical management skills that must be developed and used in the stewardship of the "new" assets.

This book will introduce the reader to a new business lexicon. As the word "snow" is insufficient to convey appropriate nuances to expert skiers, the descriptor "intangible assets" lacks the precision necessary to permit the rigorous analysis and appropriate exploitation of its elements, and so the reader is introduced to the concept of *intellectual capital*. The study of intellectual capital (described in various ways) has been going on with some intensity for several years, and analytical constructs have been advanced by business managers, business writers, consultants, and academicians. During that time several concepts have been introduced, among them Knowledge Management (KM), Intellectual Asset Management (IAM), Innovation Management (IM), and

---

[1] A coined phrase, referring to the heavy-industry areas of the upper Midwestern United States in the 1970s

Intellectual Capital Management (ICM). Observers in this field are forgiven if they express some confusion about the meaning of these terms. In this book, however, Ms. Al-Ali introduces the *Comprehensive Intellectual Capital Management* approach, and the reader will find that her presentation greatly helps to explain and sort out the diversity of terms and acronyms. She has aggregated these seemingly disparate concepts in understandable fashion, and illustrated with real-world examples of how corporate managers have applied intellectual capital management principles to improve profitability.

This is a book for managers who want to be at the cutting edge, for those early in their careers who seek a challenging new path, and for the CEO's of the world who have their eye on the future.

GORDON V. SMITH

Sanibel, Florida

Preface

This book marks an important stage in my professional life. In one way it may seem a digression from my profession as an attorney, but on second thought it seems that everything that I have been doing in the past seven years of my professional life were leading to this book. Being a business lawyer, I came to appreciate that my corporate (mostly multinational) clients need to manage intellectual assets in a more systematic way. Many legal audits I performed boiled down to advising on ways that management can implement to better protect and leverage their intellectual assets and knowledge resources. With that in mind I embarked on my LLM with one main end goal—first to learn best practices in this area (by learning from the best—Pierce Law's international reputation is what brought me to the small town of Concord, New Hampshire) and then to develop models that systematically manage intellectual assets.

Soon after, I discovered that intellectual assets (or property) management is only one part of the equation for managing all of a business's intellectual resources or capital. My research expanded beyond an LLM, and that was when the support of the progressive dean and faculty of Pierce Law proved invaluable. The dean, John Hutson, adopted and financially supported my research and course development, which expanded beyond IP law and management into the related disciplines of knowledge and intellectual capital management as well. His futuristic vision of the role of IP lawyers in the knowledge economy fueled this venture.

This book grows out of my professional experience for the past seven years and my intensive research for the past three years, and from teaching intellectual capital management courses to law students, attorneys, IP managers, and business executives who come to Pierce Law. The book is directed at the manager who needs to develop pragmatic approaches and systems for the management of intellectual resources and capital. It is also written for the general reader who needs to appreciate the emerging field of intellectual capital management (ICM) with a methodical approach. It is hoped that this book will advance both academic and applied research and experimentation in this field and contribute to its modest literature in this area.

From the beginning of this journey, besides financing my research, Dean John Hutson's support and encouragement were instrumental in carrying me through tough times. Being the place it is, the support of the whole community at Pierce Law—faculty, staff, and students—sustained me through the longest working hours (practically all waking hours) of my professional life: smiles, caring, and cheering by Jan Neuman, Pilar Silva, Puala Jewell, Brian Daniels, Peter Husak, Amy Cutler, Debbie Beauragard, Sharon Callahan, Terry Cromwell, Donna Garofoli, and by faculty members—Professors Karl Jorda, Bill Hennessey, Susan Richey, Bill Murphy, and John Orcutt.

Special thanks are due to Professors Thomas Field, Ronald Neary, and Jon Cavicchi, and to the Access Services Supervisor Roberta Woods. At the early stages of my research, the intellectual discourse with Tom Field not only enhanced my appreciation of the significance of IP and its relation to market value, but also helped validate many of my green ideas. Field's recognition of ICM as the "science of the future" and advocacy for the inclusion of my ICM course in Pierce Law's curriculum were two milestones that supported me immensely in my challenging quest. For that I am forever grateful.

Special thanks are due to Roberta Woods for editing and commenting on parts of the book, but more importantly for her great friendship and support, stirring in me "grim determination (GD)" whenever my zeal flattened.

Special thanks are due to Ron Neary for his review of my first outline, which helped me clarify my overall methodology in approaching the subject; and to Jon Cavicchi for sharing with me his knowledge of patent mining tools and for his continuous gracious support.

At the early stages of my intellectual journey, I was fortunate to meet a number of pioneering business executives who expanded and deepened my understanding of ICM. I am particularly grateful to David Near, the Director of Business Excellence at Dow Chemical, and Jan Hoffmeister, Skandia's VP of ICM, for sharing with me their experience and the challenges they meet in managing IC. The meeting of our minds on a number of ICM issues and approaches was not only thrilling to me but also indicative of the business viability of many of my ideas. Meeting Alex Bennet, the then Deputy CIO of the U.S. Navy, at a later stage refined my approach to knowledge management, and gave me a live example of a relentless agent of change.

I was also fortunate to benefit from the experience of pioneers in the legal world who expanded my understanding of the use of intellectual property strategies, marrying them with business strategies, and, most importantly, keeping the marriage happy. In particular I mention Bahy Elibrachy, Managing Partner of Ibrachy & Dermarkar; Russell Barron, of Foley & Lardner and Chairperson of INTX; and Ronald Myrick, Chief IP Counsel of General Electric. I also mention Gordon Smith, President of AUS, Inc. and adjunct professor at Pierce Law, who expanded my understanding of IP valuation and commercial assessment. To Professor Smith, I also express my deep gratitude for his thoughtful encouragement and for writing the foreword to this book.

My students, who ranged from second-year law students to IP professionals and attorneys to business executives, have greatly contributed to this book through their research projects, professional experience, and outstanding intellectual discourse. To them I am indebted.

My heartfelt thanks are due to my parents, Fatmeh and Afeef Al-Ali, and to Nesrien, Haytham, and Khaled Al-Ali, and to Dodo and Basha Mahmoud for their unconditional love and support, without which none of this would have been possible. My special thanks goes to everyone at John Wiley & Sons who worked on this book: particularly Susan McDermott and Jennifer Gaines for their patience and kind support. Finally, a word of thanks to Pierce Law's Dean and community for making my intellectual journey a very enjoyable one. I hope your journey reading this book will be equally enjoyable and rewarding.

NERMIEN A. AL-ALI

Concord, New Hampshire
September 9, 2002

Part One

Intellectual Capital Management

Part One introduces the reader to the world of intellectual capital by first examining the main dynamics that affect competition in the knowledge economy. Exploring these dynamics from multiple perspectives, intellectual capital is uncovered as the driving force behind competition in the knowledge economy. Chapter 1 demonstrates that intellectual capital is the main driver behind mergers, start-ups, innovation, and hence business performance. As such, developing intellectual capital management as the core organizational competency is the formula of success. This, however, is a very general statement, and therefore Chapter 1 breaks this into a number of organizational competencies comprising knowledge, innovation and intellectual property management, creating the right culture for intellectual capital management, and synchronizing different programs into a comprehensive intellectual capital management system.

Before this part proceeds with the "how," it examines the classifications and models that emerged to define, recognize, and measure intellectual capital. Despite the great insight provided by the intellectual capital model, which to date has been the basis of all efforts and models to manage intellectual capital, it falls short of providing business with pragmatic practices and applications. Building on the intellectual capital model and expanding it immensely, the author develops the Comprehensive Intellectual Capital Management (CICM) model outlined in Chapter 4, after examining the question of IC reporting in Chapter 3.

The CICM model is designed to manage all forms of intellectual capital at three stages—knowledge, innovation, and intellectual property management. Though the latter two stages have been established for decades, they are presented under the light of the IC concept and combined with the new discipline of knowledge management to create the CICM model. Chapter 4 presents an overview of the CICM model and outlines its pragmatic features, and thus serves as a gate to Part Two.

1

Intellectual Capital Management and the Knowledge Economy

INTRODUCTION

Exponential growth of information in the knowledge economy focuses attention on the importance of managing knowledge in organizations. So-called learning organizations, those that recognize the value of knowledge within their organizations, can grow and prosper through knowledge management (KM). Much has been written on the subject of KM and the learning organization. An equal number of writings similarly addressed intellectual property (IP) and its potential in securing a competitive advantage and generating revenue. Indeed, it is no secret anymore in the business world that IP can on its own be the core business asset, which underscores the importance of intellectual asset or intellectual property management (IAM/IPM). Little, if any, has been written about the correlation between KM and IAM/IPM and how an organization can use both management approaches to implement an integrated program or system for the total management of its intellectual capital and resources. KM and IAM/IPM are not one and the same despite many similarities in their basic precepts. KM relates to the creation of value, the harvesting of ideas, the mining of employee brainpower, and the conversion of tacit knowledge into explicit knowledge that the organization can codify and transfer. IAM/IPM relates to the maximization of value, the licensing of know-how, patents and trademarks, and the use of IP to gain a competitive edge, enter new markets, establish strategic alliances, and generate revenue.

Proponents of each management approach admit the benefits of the other management approaches to the bottom line, yet fail to see the connection or the interplay between them. It is true that for some industries, one approach may seem more important than the other. Nonetheless, for any organization to succeed in the knowledge economy, it is essential that it adopt both management approaches to some extent, as each deals with complementary strategic needs. What some organizations fail to see is that KM and IAM/IPM are essential components for the total management of an organization's intellectual capital.[1]

Focusing on one approach to the exclusion of the other would result in a waste of management and financial resources, and the polarization of the management philosophy of the enterprise. This in turn will result in desynchronization between the departments within an organization as well as conflict between the proponents of the different approaches. Attempting to combine both approaches is not the solution. At best, such a combination would be artificial, resulting in disoriented processes and a dysfunctional system.[2] This is because each of these management approaches has a different function, namely, creation versus extraction of value, and to combine them an organization should implement another intermediary management approach: innovation management (IM).

The only way to work with intellectual capital management (ICM) as a coherent discipline and approach is to understand the relation between the three management approaches (KM, IM, IAM/IPM) and how each affects the bottom line and facilitates the management of the whole organization. This is what this book is all about. It presents an approach developed for the total strategic management of an organization's intellectual capital throughout the entire enterprise and at every stage of development of the intellectual capital. The Comprehensive Intellectual Capital Management (CICM) approach is designed to overcome the limitation of any one discipline in the field of ICM, while taking advantage of what each discipline has to offer in creating and sustaining an organization's[3] competitive advantage.

Traditionally, and to date, ICM as a discipline has been divided among IP lawyers and professionals, business managers and consultants, and accountants. Intellectual property professionals call it IAM or IPM (used interchangeably), and limit their attention to the knowledge assets that can be codified and legally protected. They mainly focus on business strategies and techniques that enhance the commercial exploitation of the IP in question. Those with human resources and information technology (IT) backgrounds, however, prefer to call it KM and focus on sharing knowledge that an organization has both in its practices and databases, and that it knows is stored in employees' and customers' heads. Research and development (R&D) and product development people focus mainly on managing the innovation and research process to produce the most efficient results, while accountants mainly experiment with designing metrics to measure IC to enable better investment decision making.

But is ICM new? Since the 1950s, managers from various disciplines have developed a number of management models and approaches to strategically manage intellectual capital, in search of a competitive advantage. R&D management, human resource (HR) management, total quality management (TQM), just-in-time (JIT), and, more recently, conversation management are all approaches attempting to manage one form or another of IC. In today's ICM terms, R&D manages human and process capital, HR manages human capital, both TQM and JIT manage process and structural capital.[4] So what else does ICM has to offer?

The thesis of this book is that ICM should be seen as a total approach to strategic business management and not merely a compilation of all the previous approaches purporting to manage different types of IC—an approach that purports to manage the organizational wealth of the whole enterprise, 80 percent of which is now intangible. The fact that 80 percent of corporate wealth in America and other developed economies is intangible makes ICM not a mere method or collection of processes to manage one resource of the enterprise, but an approach for the management of the entire enterprise.

Comprehending ICM as a coherent discipline with all this diversity may seem impossible. It would require the expertise of the multidisciplines involved: business, law, technology, accountancy, and industrial psychology. But bringing all these perspectives under a coherent model is not the main challenge confronting ICM. The challenge is to understand the interplay between them and bring them together in an effective way to enable an organization to realize, manage, and leverage its intellectual capital effectively.

The CICM approach integrates the three management approaches—KM, IM, IAM/IPM—while recognizing that each has unique objectives, processes, strategies, and tools. One of the functions of this book, and perhaps the most important one, is to present the CICM approach as an evolutionary stage of strategic business management for the knowledge economy. *Comprehensive Intellectual Capital Management: Step by Step* will demonstrate with practical examples that to create and extract value from organizational intellectual capital, and create and sustain competitive advantage, an organization needs to adopt ICM as its modus operandi, rather than implement separate programs limited to one or a few divisions.

Part One introduces ICM in a way that the business reader can understand. It explains the relationship between IC and market value, business growth, stock price, and overall competitive performance. Use Chapter 1 to understand the challenges that face your business in the new economy, the competitive dynamics that your business is subject to, and the solutions that ICM can provide for capitalizing on your business innovative power. Real-world examples are used to demonstrate the real value of IC and its relation to market capitalization. Chapter 2 defines what IC is and the models that emerged to explain how value is created from its management. This chapter will also cover the crucial issues relating to measurement of intellectual capital, and the systems that emerged for this purpose, while Chapter 3 will deal with the issue of IC reporting and future trends. Suggestions for a reporting model will also be presented. Part One will conclude with an overview of the CICM model, and the framework it sets for managing IC under three stages of knowledge, innovation, and IP management.

Part Two presents the disciplines of knowledge, innovation, and IP management under the IC concept. Two case studies are presented in Part Two: Dow Chemical and Skandia—companies that implement models of comprehensive intellectual capital management. These companies have been chosen for their pioneering work in the field of intellectual capital management as well as in their respective industries. The case studies aim to provide businesses with practical guidance on how Dow and Skandia mastered ICM with demonstrated benefits. A case study of the U.S. Department of the Navy will also be used to demonstrate mastering knowledge management.

Part Three takes the business reader into step-by-step application of practical techniques, processes, and strategies for managing intellectual capital using the CICM model. Chapters 11 through 13 will present a detailed account of the three stages of the CICM model, for managing IC under knowledge, innovation, and IP management stages. Each of these chapters commences with defining the management objectives that should be targeted for each of the stages, which in turn informs what returns to expect, and what indicators to monitor. But not every organization can implement the three stages of ICM to the fullest degree. For one thing, this will place considerable demand on resource allocation when maybe it is not the right time to introduce change. More importantly, this may not be what is required in view of the strategy of the business. Nonetheless, it is essential that management understand that the three stages reinforce each other and that implementation of a program or effecting certain changes under one of the stages will affect programs and changes under the other. Chapter 14 presents the variables that should be taken into consideration in implementing the CICM model, as well as suggestions on how to devise a phased-out plan that takes into account budgetary constraints and strategic objectives. Chapter 14 also presents a diagnostic tool, the Intellectual Capital Grid, that a business can use to assess its needs in terms of ICM initiatives, where it is, where it needs to be, and how to get there.

Because this book is written for the general reader, no more than the general knowledge of business management and of intellectual property is assumed. To be able to fully appreciate and later implement an ICM model, a deeper knowledge is needed. Therefore, the book includes a number of appendices: a mini MBA (Master of Business Administration) presenting basic business management concepts, and a mini MIP (Master of Intellectual Property)[5] presenting requisite knowledge of intellectual property law.

INTELLECTUAL CAPITAL AND BUSINESS VALUE— THE HIDDEN RESOURCE

What is intellectual capital and how is this "capital" used or converted into business value and profits? The IC of an organization comprises such intangible resources and assets that an organization can use to create value by converting it into new processes, products, and services.

Though there is no solid consensus on what IC is, there is wide agreement on its definition.[6] It is the knowledge, experience, and brainpower of employees as well as knowledge resources stored in an organization's databases, systems, processes, culture, and philosophy.[7]

Business has always relied on its intangible resources, along with tangible and capital resources, to create value and achieve the organization's goals. Business performance and success depend on how well an organization manages its resources. Formerly, business resources comprised 80 percent of tangible and capital resources, with intangible assets making up around 20 percent. Gradually, this changed with intangible assets reaching 80 percent of the assets of most organizations by 1999. Though a widely declared observation, it is important to explain how the 80 percent is calculated.

The 80 percent figure is calculated by considering the divergence between the market and book values of an organization, known as *market capitalization*. Though market capitalization is not a phenomenon specific to the knowledge economy, it has escalated in the knowledge economy to reach unprecedented multiples of the book value. Market and book values are never identical,[8] but in the knowledge economy staggering market capitalization figures sent many writers in search for the hidden resource that is creating such huge market values. So what does the book value communicate?

Book values of publicly traded companies mainly reflect the value of tangible and capital assets of the company. Sometimes the book value reflects some of the intangible assets of the company under the heading of goodwill. This is hardly an accurate reflection of the value of intangible assets as it is created to balance the books following an acquisition.[9] The market value of the company reflects the value of a hidden resource that is recognized and valued by the market, including but not limited to the company's reputation, innovativeness, technological prowess, and brand equity. These and other attributes like a company's culture make up the intangible resources of a company. Market capitalization only reflects such resources that can create value (i.e., the company's intellectual capital).[10]

To arrive at an approximation of the value of a company's IC, subtract the book value of a company—the total of its tangible and capital resources—from its market value. For example, Microsoft's book value (total assets minus total liabilities) on March 31, 2001, was $54.3 billion. This included $1.4 billion in goodwill and $277 million in intangible assets. Its market capitalization (number of outstanding shares multiplied by stock price), however, amounted to approximately $301 billion. Subtracting the net book value and that of reported intangible assets results in a staggering figure of $248.4 billion. If we agree that this is the value of Microsoft's intellectual capital, then it makes 82.4 percent of the company's total assets.

Carrying out similar calculations on other companies, it is noted that IC makes up around 80 percent of the Standard & Poor's (S&P) 500 companies, with an average market capitalization rate of 6.5.[11] Of course, the 80 percent figure may be higher in high-tech industries or dot-coms where intellectual capital may reach over 90 percent of the corporate value. Think of Amazon, for example. One would think that this percentage would drop when it comes to more traditional or low-tech industries, but the best-performing companies in all industries show similar results. Ford's IC amounted to 83 percent of its total assets based on its market capitalization value of March 31, 2001.

Studying market capitalization rates[12] by reference to industry in 1995, Sveiby found that industries heavily dependent on IC like companies in the pharmaceutical and business services industries are valued at multiples of their book value. In contrast, companies that mainly manage tangible assets like those in traditional manufacturing and real estate industries have market values that are close to their book values.[13] Interestingly, the best-performing companies in any industry still display high market capitalization rates regardless of their industry. Sveiby compares two steel companies, Nucor and Bethlehem. He notes that though both companies have nearly the same annual revenue of $1.3 billion, Bethlehem is valued by the market close to its book value. Nucor, however, is valued by the market at around four times its book value. Sveiby attributes this to Nucor's mini mill technology and its "management approach that releases the competence of its employees"[14]—in short, its IC and its ability to effectively manage it.

In an economy where IC forms the majority of an organization's resources and assets, it is essential to develop ways to identify and manage it. According to IC theorists, intellectual capital is made up of three main components: human capital, customer capital, and structural capital. The first represents employee knowledge, competency, and brainpower. Customer capital represents relations with customers, suppliers, and distributors. Structural capital designates the organizational systems, culture, practices, and processes.[15]

Human, customer, and structural capital have always been part of the intangible resources of business. To say that organizations have to allocate more resources for the management of IC now because it makes up 80 percent instead of 20 percent of organizational resources does not adequately explain how that would impact business performance in the knowledge economy. Generally speaking, business performance in any industry is affected by an organization's business processes, the capability of its employees, and its understanding of customers' needs. The knowledge intensity of these three pillars of business performance, however, proliferates in the knowledge economy to such an extent that an organization that neglects managing knowledge and other forms of IC risks dissipating its most valuable business resources and assets. The fact that these resources are intangible raises the question whether they can be managed under the traditional management approaches, which evolved for managing tangible and capital resources. As will be shown later in this chapter, the management of IC requires the development of specific competencies. But first, let's look at how business processes, employee roles, and customer needs have been transformed by the knowledge economy.

THE KNOWLEDGE ECONOMY—THE MAIN CULPRIT

The knowledge economy has transformed business processes by elevating the role of innovation as the core production process and the main enabler of business success. As a result, the role of the employee also changed. Employees in the knowledge economy are required to do brainwork most of the time to incorporate knowledge into new applications and innovate new products, processes, and services. To a great extent the knowledge intensity of business processes and the workforce is brought about by an increased demand in the market for knowledge. The customers of the knowledge economy are knowledge thirsty, creating more demand for knowledge-intensive products. Knowledge gets cycled and recycled through the innovation process to make new products, which in turn increase the body of knowledge that gets fed again into the production process as illustrated in Exhibit 1.1.

Business Processes and the Fast Lane of Innovation— Join It or Pull Off the Highway

In the industrial economy, organizations were able to secure a strong competitive position for a greater number of years. Once a competitive position was secured, organizations then created and maximized value through a process of optimization (or economizing). Organizations that performed well were those that optimized their production process by shortening the time of production, improving the quality of the end product, and reducing the number of employees

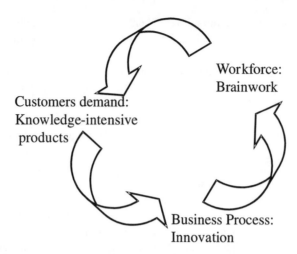

EXHIBIT 1.1   The Cycle of Knowledge, Innovation, and Production

assigned to any single task. Value creation then was dependent more on an organization's indus-trial capability and capital budgeting—its tangible and financial assets.

In the knowledge economy this is not the case anymore. For one thing, to maintain a compet-itive position, regardless of its strength, for a long period of time is not possible with the short life cycles of knowledge and the high rate of innovation. Though optimization, as a process, is equally important in the knowledge economy, it alone cannot create or maximize value. The only way to create value in the knowledge economy is by adopting innovation as the core business process. An organization's ability to create value depends on its innovation process, its intellec-tual resources, and the creativity of its workforce—its intellectual assets.

Innovation has been an important driver since the dawn of humanity, but now it is the main driver of business performance. The knowledge economy is all about the speed with which mar-kets and business embrace and create change.[16] It is about the creation and production of new knowledge and new applications of old knowledge to deal with short—or much shorter compared to that under the industrial economy—product life cycles. Knowledge and intellectual resources are not only the raw materials for production, but once developed into defined methods become the main process of production as well (hence the innovation process).

A new computer game, for example, has the same tangible material used in older products. The tangible material is abundant and is not critical to the product. The most important and valu-able raw material that goes into the production of the computer game, however, is intangible. Art-work, graphics, ideas, and the technology are what makes it all happen and distinguish one game from another.

The extensive use of intangibles as raw resources is not limited to the high-tech, chemical, and consumer products industries. Organizations in traditional industries found it hard to succeed without a strong commitment to innovation as well. Organizations in traditional industries are continually pushed into this fast lane of innovation. While new technological applications have presented them with new challenges, they have also opened a world of opportunities.

In one of the most traditional industries, oil, British Petroleum was able to use technological advances to innovate its drilling activities. As a result, the company invented the *smart drill*, which in turn reduced the company's production costs and enabled it to produce new products that emit fewer pollutants into the atmosphere.

In the steel industry, organizations that innovate are able to excel, while others just struggle to survive. Faced with the danger of extinction, Norton Steel innovated the way it makes and sells steel. The company survived tough economic times by incorporating its customers' input into the composition of the steel it produces. Coming from its customers, knowledge, like iron, became a raw material and, like steel, became a product.

With intellectual resources forming the majority of the required raw materials for production, the knowledge economy has created a demand for new ideas that can be processed through innovation into new products and services. But machines do not produce ideas. Even artificial intelligence computer engineers have not been able to create a computer that can think like a human brain. Until they succeed, if ever, the human mind is the primary machine that organizations need to generate new knowledge and innovation.

Employees—The Knowledge Processors

New industries have emerged and some have been transformed by the knowledge economy, but the whole workforce has undergone a metamorphosis as well. The majority of the workforce in most industries in developed economies is comprised of knowledge workers—workers who apply their brainpower and skills to process information into applicable knowledge to make new products. The knowledge economy gives real meaning to the business motto "Our people are our most valuable assets." Because the generation of new knowledge and innovation creates value, organizations need employees who can process the vast body of information available into applicable knowledge. And employees need to be enabled, or to use a term more in vogue, *empowered,* to activate their ideas and creativity.

This is in sharp contrast to the profile of the ideal worker of the industrial economy. The ideal worker then was one who operated machines in the most efficient way on a production line. That is not to say brainpower was unimportant in the industrial economy, which created some of the greatest inventions. Brain work, however, was limited to those who worked primarily in R&D laboratories, engineering, or marketing departments. Not only was brain work limited within an organization to certain departments and sometimes to certain employees in that department, but also the demand for innovation was much lower.

Having a limited number of brain workers will not work in an economy where you need 3,000 ideas to get one commercially successful product,[17] and where you have to plan for the maturing of your products shortly after launching them. The organization needs the contribution of every mind it has access to, in order to meet the high demand for new ideas, or it will run out of raw resources. The ideal worker now is one who innovates, brainstorms ideas, shares knowledge, thinks, contemplates, and experiments. It is not enough to limit the innovative activity to the R&D department any more. A good idea from the marketing department or administrative staff may save the organization a substantial amount of time and money, which will be detailed later on in Chapter 7. A vital component in employee job descriptions now includes terminology for the creation, application, transfer, and commercialization of knowledge.

In the industrial economy, salaries and wages were considered a production cost and knowledge and training were provided only on a need basis. This is strikingly different from what business now demands from its workforce, and in turn what the knowledge worker expects from the workplace. Salaries and wages are now seen, at least by some, to be more of an investment in one of the most important intellectual resources of the enterprise. As such, learning, continuous training, and development becomes an essential tool in building strategic competencies.

Whether in the industrial or the knowledge economy, people are people. In the former, management concerned itself with machines more than with people to optimize production.

Machines that could be operated easily were the main tools of production. Though machines are still very important in the knowledge economy, the main tool of production now is the human mind, a "machine" that operates under a chaotic set of rules, if any. Generally speaking, operating even the most complicated of machines is possible. They come with instructions; human minds don't. How do you make minds work or stop? How do you maintain and improve them?

As if that was not enough complexity for business managers in the knowledge economy to deal with, minds do not come alone. Minds come with hearts and aspirations, and offer another challenge for management: how to motivate knowledge workers to innovate? How to manage the social aspects of knowledge creation while maintaining efficiency? All this means that not only are the raw materials intellectual, but also the production process is dependent on intellectual processes. In the knowledge economy, the demand for the new and sophisticated is very high. This is because both consumers and customers have also been transformed by the knowledge economy.

The Knowledge-Thirsty Customers

Customers now more than ever want what is new and innovative. The increase in technological awareness of customers created more needs for businesses to satisfy. More than ever, customers need to be connected, informed, entertained, and provided with "emotional" value.

There are numerous examples of ordinary products and goods that have been transformed to meet technological needs. In the auto industry, for example, manufacturers also realized they needed to deliver more in emotional value to consumers. Many automobile manufacturers have made substantial investments in making their cars more interesting to the buyer. Customers want a car that is "cooler," like the new Volkswagen Beetle with its bright colors and bud vase or one that has seats that can be removed for a quiet day in the wilderness.

Customers and consumers also want to have an input in the development of new products and services. Given the value of such input, many organizations adapted to receive and accommodate it. Consumers asked: Can this mobile phone show me e-mail messages? Can I activate my home alarm from a distance? Can you prescribe this medicine for my condition? Although customer input was valuable in the industrial economy, in the knowledge economy customers look at knowledge as a commodity where the more they can get the better.

These differences between industrial and knowledge economies in the nature of the raw materials, the need for speedy innovation, the sophistication of customers and consumers, and the transformation of the role of the workforce have affected business management in the knowledge economy in many respects. But the real question is: Do these differences require the development of a new business management approach?

DOES A NEW ECONOMY REQUIRE A NEW BUSINESS MANAGEMENT APPROACH?

Are the new features of the knowledge economy sufficient for us to claim that there is a "new" economy that is subject to "new" rules, and which requires different business management approaches and procedures? Many have argued that the knowledge economy is subject to new rules.

According to Brian Arthur of the Santa Fe Institute, it is an economy of increasing rather than diminishing returns. Once a product is adopted as the market standard, the cost of reproduction and production of new versions becomes minimal while the profits multiply.[18] Is that a phenomenon that is limited to the high-tech industry, and thus may be an accurate description of the wealth of companies like Microsoft, IBM, Apple, and Netscape but not companies in other industries?

Granstrand argues that it is not, and that in the knowledge economy a new form of capitalism emerged—*intellectual capitalism.* When intellectual resources are increasingly the source of economic wealth, they become the main driver of the knowledge economy, while the tangible and financial resources become of a lesser importance for success.[19] Whether or not we agree with Granstrand that the knowledge economy is subject to a new form of capitalism, it is evident that there has been a change, at least in the way that the most successful organizations now describe and envision themselves.

DuPont describes its work as "delivering the miracle of science," while Dow Chemical sees its mission as "driving value from our intellectual assets." Ford advertises, "We have a passion for better ideas," while General Motors professes, "Technology is a significant enabler for us to meet our vision." And British Petroleum proclaims, "Our business is about discovery." How is it that organizations now see themselves differently?

Regardless of the view taken and the degree of importance attributed to the role of IC for competitive performance, it is undeniable that business now is subjected to disruptive and turbulent waves brought about by an innovation- and knowledge-intensive economy. It is an economy that is different because the production processes are different, the customers are different, and the workers are different. All these differences require a business management approach that accommodates the peculiar nature of IC and differentiates between its various forms.

In fact, business management in the knowledge economy has undergone a number of substantial changes reflected in how organizations now structure themselves and reorganize their business. These changes are not based on a specific methodology or a theoretical framework, but to a great extent stem from organizations' need to better manage their IC. That being said, there is one common thread that permeates all these changes—namely, that they are all based on and driven by the dynamics of intellectual capital (IC-enabled dynamics). Following is an outline of these dynamics and how they influenced organizational design, management and leadership styles, and business strategy and growth.

IC-ENABLED DYNAMICS AND TRANSFORMATION OF BUSINESS MANAGEMENT: THE MANAGEMENT OF MINDS

> The single greatest challenge facing managers in the developed countries of the world is to raise the productivity of knowledge and service workers. The challenge, which will dominate the management agenda for the next several decades, will ultimately determine the competitive performance of companies.
>
> —Peter Drucker[20]

In the industrial economy, machines—being nonhuman—were both predictable and easily operable. That all changed with the knowledge economy, in which the main machine or tool of production is the human mind. Business leaders in the new economy will no doubt agree that it is difficult, maybe even impossible, to manage minds. Perhaps managers should not even try because any attempt to control a mind may stifle its creativity, an essential enabler of innovation. Left to its own rhythm, a mind may produce nothing more than whimsical ideas much like a walk with Alice in Wonderland, never to come back again. While that may be good for some industries that offer the magic of Wonderland as their main product line, or what Disney calls "the magic of Disney," other industries need to have a systematic way to manage or attempt to manage these mind machines.

Another potential problem is control. In order to control something, you need to own or possess it. But when it comes to minds, an organization can never do that, because minds are possessed by human beings, or knowledge workers. Even with the best of intentions, one might wonder how much of his or her mind a knowledge worker can control. How to motivate and guide the thought processes of knowledge workers has been the subject of many disciplines: philosophy, psychology, epistemology, and anthropology, to name a few. So how can the business leader in this economy manage these "machines" to ensure productivity?

Organizations in the industrial economy were designed to maximize value extraction from an organization's industrial capability. Organizational boundaries were well defined and the chain of command and authority was clear. Innovation and research were functions of R&D or the new product development department, where a clear research agenda was identified. Workers in this department had it as their job to innovate. Others had different work to do: to market, to legalize, to sell, to lead, and so on. Top management was the source of ideas that revitalized business and made it succeed and grow, while the workers primarily performed the tasks assigned to them or written in their job descriptions.

Great ideas in the industrial economy were initiated and implemented by business leaders, and legacies were created. Henry Ford, for example, conceptualized the $5.00 a day wage and an economical automobile his workers could afford. Sears & Roebuck extended services to U.S. farmers in remote areas and established the company as the provider of *well*-priced quality goods. Legendary leaders with new good ideas, and workers following in his or her steps is no longer the ideal model. For one thing, one idea is not enough. Ideas are contagious in this age, and competition quickly adopts an idea unless it is novel and patented. The demand for new ideas supplied by one or even a whole R&D department is now uneconomical and insufficient.

More raw ideas and innovative resources are required. Once new ideas are supplied, more minds are required to sift and process them into new products, processes, and services. It has been claimed that it takes 3,000 good ideas to have four research or product development projects, and only one of these four will be commercially successful.[21] If this is true, then that means the more new ideas generated the higher the probability of market success. If innovation is initiated at the top of the organization, then not only will the number of ideas be meager but the value of these ideas will be doubtful as well. This is because those at the top are not necessarily the ones in constant contact with customers, and thus possess the knowledge about market trends and customer needs.

To grow, organizations need a structure that allows for the creation of new knowledge and generation of ideas from the frontlines. Innovation needs to be a bottom-up–driven activity that travels through as few layers as possible. This also requires fewer horizontal boundaries between departments, divisions, and business units so that the organization can benefit from the mix of expertise and richness of knowledge that each brings from his or her own perspective. This can hardly be achieved through a command line management style. Other styles need to be developed to accommodate IC-enabled dynamics as well.

Take for example Asea Brown Baveri[22] (ABB), the U.K. giant of 60 businesses, 6000 profit centers in 1300 operating companies, and $30 billion annual revenue. ABB's success can be attributed to a great extent to its management style, symbolized by the 30-30-30-10 rule, which ABB's leadership applies to existing and acquired businesses. The rule provides that 30 percent of employees are kept at top management, 30 percent at middle management, 30 percent on the frontline management and 10 percent are laid off. The point is to push down as many managers as possible and thus to push decision making further down where actual contact with the market, and hence innovation, occurs. At ABB, "frontline managers are now entrepreneurs driving a bottom-up process; middle managers are coaches, leveragers, and developers of the organization; and top managers are institution builders and creators of the organization's values and purpose."[23]

In the industrial economy the majority of management resources and expertise are focused on managing the production line and ensuring that assigned tasks are performed as efficiently as possible. Management style was linear at best and less complicated, as displayed in Exhibit 1.2. The core of business management under this system is capital budgeting, in which the emphasis is on cost reduction and efficiency. Under this system, measurement of performance is mainly quantitative, where a break in the production line and its effect on the final output is ascertainable. Units of cost, time, and sales are thus effective metrics to measure the success of a certain project and inform future investment decisions.

In the knowledge economy, the production flow is strikingly different. Business management is no longer focused on managing predictable, controllable production lines but must pay attention to rather complex human and knowledge systems and relations. What business needs to manage is the process of knowledge creation and innovation as well as the resultant intellectual products or products of the human mind. At best, this creates an environment of organized chaos, in which the role of management is transformed from a supervisory to an inspirational role. The core of business management under this system is knowledge accumulation to enable innovation, production, and business growth. Under this system, the metrics are performance measures, many of which are qualitative. This creates the need for management to consult a set of measures and outcomes that are not as predictable or controllable.

Overall, the variables that management needs to consider in order to leverage organizational IC have changed. More importantly, the profiles of the good manager and the good leader have also changed. Management genius and excellence now are demonstrated by those who know how to motivate and inspire knowledge workers so that more ideas are produced. Leadership success is possible only when the leader creates a culture of trust wherein workers at all levels and in various departments share their knowledge—sideways, top-down, and bottom-up.

Managers and leaders need to have a nose for good ideas and a gut-feeling indicator that detects good projects. Again, determining what is a good idea depends on the manager's experience, hunch, or previous training—in short, tacit knowledge. The more the leadership and managerial role changed the more the organizational structure and communication patterns changed to allow for collaboration sideways, vertically, and between individuals. This gave rise in some organizations to new top managerial positions: for example, the chief knowledge officer (CKO), and VP of intellectual capital management (VP of ICM),[24] who are particularly focused on development and management of knowledge and IC.

The creation of such new positions, though necessary for the development and advance of ICM in the whole organization, are not enough to enable an organization to extract the maximum

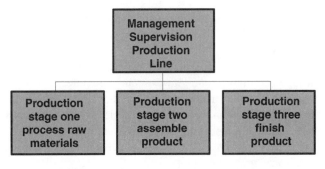

EXHIBIT 1.2   Production Flow: Linear

value of its IC. The whole organization needs to adapt to the IC-enabled dynamics, which transformed the organizational design of the most successful knowledge organizations.

IC-ENABLED DYNAMICS AND TRANSFORMATION OF ORGANIZATIONAL DESIGN

The Democratic Organization—Fewer Layers and More Ambassadors

> On the Eve of 2000, the structure of most industries looks very different than it did fifteen
> years ago.
>
> —Science Technology and Economic Policy Board[25]

With the growing demand for new ideas, an organization needs the ideas of employees everywhere in the organization, not only in the R&D department. The increased importance of communication for the transfer of knowledge made it essential for organizations to implement an IT
infrastructure that provides means and channels of communication if the motivation is there. To
compete effectively, most organizations implemented an infrastructure to facilitate the collection
and processing of knowledge and ideas for their incorporation in new forms.

Idea banks, intranets, networking, and brainstorming sessions became part of the modus
operandi of businesses in most industries today. It is the infrastructure brought about by the
knowledge economy. Those organizations that did not have such an infrastructure were pushed to
change. Xerox, for example, after discovering how its technical reps solved more problems by
merely sharing their stories with each other in the coffee room, provided them with radiophones
to share their ideas about the problems while in the field.

But IT is only one part of the transformation that the knowledge organization needs to go
through. IT can, in the right culture, facilitate knowledge transfer between various departments
(i.e., sideways). However, more structural reform is necessary if knowledge is to be shared
upward and downward as well. As a result, organizations found the need to delayer to reduce the
number of layers that information, knowledge, and decisions have to traverse.

Dow Chemical delayered 9 layers and reduced its layers to 5 from 14, and thus created a more
flattened structure. A flattened structure is more effective for the transfer and sharing of knowledge across geographical, departmental, and hierarchal boundaries. ABB, for example, has only
four layers.

A very interesting structure is one that Harley Davidson Inc. adopted to reinvent itself. Harley
Davidson changed its pyramid hierarchical structure to three circles called "the Create Demand
Circle, the Produce Products Circle, and the Support Circle." The three circles overlap and intersect, representing the integration among the marketing, sales, manufacturing and engineering,
and administrative and support functions at the various intersections. In addition, there is a fourth
circle where the three circles intersect that consists of seven executives—the CEO and managers
elected by their peers from the three circles.[26]

Organizations started to flatten their structures, promote boundaryless flow, and provide the
tools to enable real-time communication. However, any structure, no matter how flexible, will
become rigid with time. A flexible structure alone is not enough. The continuous movement of
personnel and the formation and dissolution of communities of practice are necessary to keep the
structure alive and act against stagnation. In addition, knowledge sharing should be tied to
employees' jobs or practice to prevent employees from perceiving knowledge sharing as a sense-
less social activity or, worse, a waste of time.

Savvy organizations have addressed the problem of stagnating structures by developing communities of practice (CoPs) and communities of interest (CoIs).[27] CoPs are groups of people coming together to share and learn from one another in a specified area of practice (or interest for CoIs) tied to a strategic objective. CoP membership spans vertical, horizontal, and geographic boundaries and sometimes includes external parties (from outside the organization). CoPs range from being formal to informal, temporary to permanent but, most importantly, fuel the organic evolution of groups regardless of the fixed structure, and irrespective of how flexible it is.

The second problem precluding knowledge sharing stems from the social and human nature of knowledge sharing and transfer. Employees need an environment of trust in order to feel comfortable in sharing their knowledge, and they need to see its value in getting the job done. Raising awareness about the value of IC for organizational success, and changing the organizational culture to make it acceptable to socialize, are only one part of the solution.

This is why many organizations included knowledge sharing in job descriptions and tied it to their compensation and reward systems.[28] More importantly, some organizations created new positions at middle and frontline management levels to raise employee awareness and implement programs that enable effective management of intellectual capital. As a result, many organizations incorporated in their job designs intellectual capital "ambassadors" (Skandia), knowledge managers and engineers (the Navy), and intellectual asset managers (Dow).

These ambassadors may be organized in teams like Dow's Intellectual Asset Management Teams, in a separate business unit like DuPont's Intellectual Asset Management Business, an independent company like BellSouth Intellectual Property Management Co., or as individuals like Skandia's Navigator Ambassadors. Some organizations, like the U.S. Navy, went as far as developing new career paths for knowledge management.[29]

Regardless of the way they are organized, these ambassadors are entrusted with facilitating knowledge transfer in the whole organization and finding ways to develop and leverage the organization's IC. Or, as DuPont puts it in the mission statement of its intellectual asset management business, "to get paid for what we know as well as what we make." They are ambassadors because they work beyond business and departmental boundaries and focus on the good of the whole enterprise, advocating ICM at all levels.

The intellectual capital concept[30] has changed not only the way organizations are evolving internally and in relation to their employees but also in the way organizations grow and compete. Increasingly in the knowledge economy, IC-enabled dynamics shape business growth strategies.

IC-ENABLED DYNAMICS AND TRANSFORMATION OF BUSINESS GROWTH STRATEGIES

Business growth in the knowledge economy has been characterized by exponential growth in the service sector/industry; proliferation in the rate of mergers, acquisitions, and strategic alliances; and the rise of the start-up business model. Examination of each of these characteristics, and the growth strategies of the knowledge economy, will show how they are driven by and based on IC-enabled dynamics.

Diversify into the Business of Service: The High-Growth Sector

In 1999, the service sector generated three-quarters of the U.S. gross domestic product (GDP) and employed 80 percent or more of the workforce.[31] The situation is not much different in other developed economies. Organizations, regardless of the industry they are in, have found it necessary to diversify into providing services and solutions, along with manufactured goods. Whether supplying computers, cars, apparel, or kitchen appliances, the organization will not be able to retain customers for long unless it also provides service. Service can be provided as an ancillary product to the main product lines, or it can be the basis of an independent business for providing solutions to a certain segment of customers. Once organizations master manufacturing and other technical processes, they can grow by offering their expertise in the form of professional/technical service. Employing this strategy has proven to create high growth rates for many mature lines of business.

It seems to be the only survival/growth[32] strategy for mature lines of business and for traditional industries. Diversification into provision of services, such as customer services, finance, maintenance, training, and consulting, have offered the most profitable growth area for conglomerates and those in mature businesses or industries. This is because knowledge, as a commodity, never really matures. Its continuous change and development through circulation internally and externally makes it both a limitless resource and a renewable product.

General Electric (GE) adopted this strategy early on, and has demonstrated how service provision can offer the highest return to an organization. It was so successful that GE continues to acquire service companies to solidify its market position. In 2000, GE Capital announced that it would acquire Franchise Finance Company for $2.2 billion and merge it with its commercial equipment financing business to become the nation's biggest commercial lending operation. GE's finance leasing business has grown to encompass 90 equipment types, ranging from airplanes to much smaller equipment and machines.

Another example is Boeing.[33] In 2000, Boeing suffered from a plateauing of its profits and growth. The company adopted GE's strategy of diversifying into the service sector, by creating and providing a variety of services to its customers. Boeing started with providing maintenance and repair services for the airplanes it sold to its airline customers. Then, Boeing provided a service of training pilots on the use of the planes it made. With the need for increased security, Boeing now offers security training for pilots to cope with hijacking attempts. With stagnation in the aircraft industry and the pressure from its main competitor, Airbus, diversification into the service industry offered Boeing the best survival and growth strategy.

Even in businesses that are not as mature and where new processes or products are developed on a continuous basis, provision of service is a proven revenue generator. An example from the chemical industry is Dow Chemical (Dow). Dow Contract Manufacturing Services (CMS), a business formed in 1995, offers solutions and advice to manufacturing customers on process development and optimization. CMS is not a totally new business, as it has been providing custom manufacturing solutions for more than 20 years for Dow subsidiaries. Now these solutions are offered to companies outside Dow. After having excelled in a certain manufacturing process, CMS offers its know-how and expertise to customers. In an interview with then Director of Business Excellence, David Near, Mr. Near explained that "this business offers manufacturers state-of-the-art processes as well as technical assistance and advice on which processes are more suitable for the client's needs, market, size, and strategy. Dow still maintains its competitive advantage by developing advanced and improved processes at the same time for its own use."[34]

For Dow and other organizations employing this strategy, the interest lies not only in the financial revenue stream but the intellectual revenue as well.[35] Intellectual revenue is realized by directly or indirectly receiving input from customers on how to improve existing, or develop new, products.[36] Thus, the need to grow through service provision is not merely to implement a successful business strategy but to tap into customers' (suppliers, consumers, and distributors) IC. This provides businesses with a source of competitive advantage that should not be overlooked.

The need to connect with customers as an enhancer and supporter of an organization's IC is better portrayed in the high-tech industry. Even in the high-tech industry with its fierce price wars and quick pace of innovation, service is a source of both growth and stability. Technologically sophisticated customers of the knowledge economy will display higher loyalty rates to an organization if they are served and more involved in the development of the product. This brings us to the second IC-enabled business growth strategy.

Growth Through Mergers, Acquisitions, and Strategic Alliances: To Merge or Not to Merge

The sustenance and development of IC is closely related to the creation and maintenance of competitive advantage in the knowledge economy. The speed with which an organization would need to develop its IC to respond to market changes and challenges has increased in most industries. This led many organizations to consider mergers and strategic alliances to fortify the base of their intellectual capital and resources.

At no time has business witnessed such an upsurge in the number and value of mergers and acquisitions like the past decade. In 2000, in the United States alone there were around 7,739 deals worth about $1.2 trillion. Though over half of these deals were in the telecom and technology sector, other sectors and industries accounted for a disproportionate number of deals.[37] Indeed, this phenomenon is global with acquisitions crossing borders for better companies and better deals. A study by KPMG International has shown that the United States ranked second following Germany, which came first in foreign business acquisitions of $209 billion. As a cross-border buyer, the United States ranked third, spending $95 billion after the United Kingdom's $254 billion and France's $113 billion.[38]

The reason for this trend is that sometimes to secure the IC necessary for the desired or projected rate of growth, the level of your internal development and maximization of IC may be too slow or uncertain. To cope with this problem, companies get IC from the market or partner with another organization to share it. Mergers and acquisitions have always provided a route for growth, but in the new economy we have seen phenomenal proliferation in mergers and acquisitions—so much so that it has been called *merger mania*. The main driver of these mergers is the need to grow the IC base and maintain its depth and breadth.[39]

This explains why the most vibrant merger activity has been reported in the high-tech industries where the pace of change and the complexity of the technology sometimes drive organizations to merge or perish. Take the pharmaceutical industry, for example, which worked with 40 proteins as the basis for new drugs for decades. After the discovery of the human genome, suddenly a virtually unlimited reservoir of material for innovation, some 200 proteins, was made available. The raw materials of innovation are abundant, limitless, and, primarily, yet to be explored. That in and of itself may be a persuasive reason not to merge. However, organizations have discovered that their intellectual capabilities were not sufficient to tackle the wealth of new knowledge.

New knowledge is in many ways still virgin and requires a very strong IC to be processed before it can be the basis of any useful invention. Thus, pharmaceutical companies found themselves in great need of trained human minds, or human capital, and proven ways of extracting and processing knowledge. The only sound business decision was to merge one or more of their businesses with that of their competitors.

The most recent merger, and maybe the largest in the pharmaceutical industry, was that of Pfizer and Warner-Lambert. Pfizer paid $90 billion in February 2000 to acquire Warner-Lambert Company. Pfizer CFO David Shedlarz said at the time, "Certainly, the impact on intellectual capital and knowledge is one of the critical things we are trying to achieve." He declared the goal of the merger was to "create a new competitive standard in developing a breadth and depth of research capability."[40] Wall Street saw a winner in the marriage of the two pharmaceutical giants. Combined, they will grow faster (24 percent annually) than either could alone (20 percent annually).[41]

Similarly, in the computer industry, major companies are constantly on the lookout for small companies with solid IC to acquire. The AOL acquisition of iAmaze and Quack.com in October 2000 upgraded AOL's site graphic and audio capability. What AOL, Pfizer, Hewlett-Packard (HP), and other major players are buying with their mergers and acquisitions is brainpower.

There is another strategic reason for such acquisitions. Acquisitions allow an organization to maintain market leadership and create more entry barriers to competition. This type of growth strategy should be exercised with discretion as not to subject the organization to anti-trust allegations as in the case of Microsoft. Microsoft's obsession with buying every smaller company that has promising IC brought its practices under judicial scrutiny.

The rate and complexity of mergers and acquisitions sometimes makes it difficult to know who owns what and when. Take the AOL–Time Warner merger with possibilities of having AT&T becoming a party in the deal. In July 2000, there were major discussions between AT&T and AOL Time Warner to merge their number 1 and number 2 performing cable television companies. AT&T declared its intention to spin off its cable company first, then merge it with Time Warner Cable. What makes the alliance landscape between these two companies more complicated is that AT&T owns 25.5 percent of Time Warner Entertainment as well.

While it seems intuitive that this is only happening in the high-tech industries where new knowledge and inventions have made organizations doubt the efficacy of their intellectual capability to face new challenges and the resultant change, that is not true. Mergers are widespread even in traditional industries in which the combined intellectual capability is of equal strategic importance. For example, Devon Energy Corporation set out to buy the Canadian natural gas producer Anderson Exploration Ltd. in September 2001 for $3.4 billion, to become the largest independent producer of oil and gas in North America. Three weeks earlier it announced its acquisition of Mitchel Energy & Development for $3.1 billion.

Even when organizations do not want to get on the merger and acquisition radar screens, they are entering into more strategic alliances than ever, sometimes even with their own competitors, to help each other survive. The two competitors Visa International and MasterCard International found they had to collaborate to develop an Internet technology for making secure credit card payments. While the deal resulted in cost savings for both companies, the main driver was to combine their IC to provide a solution to a problem that threatened the market share of both.

It is the IC-enabled dynamic of networking and interaction that is changing the way organizations are behaving. Consequently, both the volume of strategic alliances and their frequency have multiplied in the knowledge economy. At no time was the competitive landscape as tangled as it is now. Determining who competes with whom and where requires a lot of research to uncover.

Because IC is what drives mergers, the alliance between the acquirer and acquired IC is what makes or breaks a merger. Intellectual capital misfits have been reported to be the primary reason behind failed mergers where major financial losses have been sustained. In the example of Med-Partners Inc. and PhyCor Inc., two physician practice management companies spoiled their $6.25 billion merger as a result of IC misfits. The two companies found that they not only could not integrate their computer systems but that their respective approaches to business were different in a number of key areas. In short, their business philosophy and cultures were different to the point of defying the streamlining required for a merger despite the great potential in cost reduction as a result of the merger.

The need to have the right IC, including business approach, culture, and people, promoted the start-up business model as one of the main models in the knowledge economy. That development is also one brought about by IC-enabled dynamics.

Growth and the Start-Up Business Model: The Idea Incubators

Start-ups have operated in the knowledge economy as technology or idea incubators, wherein a technology is tested and developed by a highly motivated, culturally aligned, and dedicated group of people. The trend has been to clone a start-up company somewhere in a garage until the technology has developed to a stage where it can be commercialized and marketed. Once that happens, the start-up company can be offered publicly or becomes an interesting target for big, established companies looking for more IC to solidify their position.

There is no doubt that the rise in the number of high-tech start-ups is a phenomenon enabled by the IC dynamics of a group of entrepreneurs. The promise of such IC and what it can deliver have resulted in the rise of venture capital funds to a staggering $5 billion in 1999.[42] Despite the slowdown in funding Internet or dot-com companies, the funding of biotech, software, and computer chip companies continues at an increasing rate.

But why start-ups? Is it because of the old-time proposition that smaller companies are more innovative? Real-life situations have proven the contrary. The most innovative companies nowadays are of the giant size, like 3M, IBM, Dow, DuPont, and Microsoft to name a few. What is it, then, in the structure of start-ups that makes them more attractive to innovators who prefer not to join one of the major companies instead? Is it that kindred innovative spirits prefer to choose whom to work with and to keep control over their project development? But most research labs in companies and universities provide considerable autonomy to their innovators. What then is so special about the start-up business model?

The answer may be in the fact that start-up businesses are less controlled by bureaucratic structures. Even an innovative company like IBM professes to be highly bureaucratic. David Snowden, the U.K. Director of IBM's Institute of Knowledge Management, explained how the United States and other governments like to work with IBM "because it makes them feel non-bureaucratic" in comparison.[43] It is interesting that this bureaucracy stops at the research lab doors. Researchers at IBM are known to have a lot of time to play as well as work on assigned projects. When a group of IBM researchers wanted to see the effect of laser beams on a human wounded finger, their curiosity then led them to wonder about the effect of laser beams on dead cows' eyes. From this creative play, the application of lasers to eye surgery was discovered.

So start-ups are less bureaucratic, and innovation thrives in a liberal environment. But that's not all. Start-ups have a very loose and flat organizational structure. Idealab, like most start-ups, has a physical layout that reflects its organizational structure. Idealab employees work in an open space— a 50,000-square-foot, one-level building with very few walls. The office of Bill Gross, the CEO, is in the center with concentric circles around it; the innermost circles represent early-phase start-ups. There is an egalitarian environment, with people actively interacting with each other. As businesses grow, those that reach a size of around 70 employees are spun off and moved to another building.[44]

Above all, the start-up business model has relaxed financial objectives—at least at the start-up and preliminary phases—thus freeing intellectual and management resources to focus on innovation goals. The vision and mission statements of such companies are not like the ordinary "we want to be the best" or "the leader in the market" statements. Instead, they have a shared, sometimes undeclared, vision/mission of "changing how people do things," and of "introducing new disruptive technologies." It is that vision—the culture it creates, the loose structure, the dedication and teamwork it inspires, and the innovation that results—that makes the start-up business model a success (or sometimes a failure). This is because breakthrough innovation is both a high-return and high-risk business.

Major organizations (companies and universities) adopt the start-up business model either internally or externally to capitalize on the innovativeness of their people. 3M's[45] model is an example of an internal application in which managers and technical employees are allowed 20 percent of their time and financial resources to experiment with new ideas. If successful, the same manager is allowed to establish, and possibly run, an independent business and have equity shares in it.

Other organizations adopted the model externally by creating venture capital units or companies with the goal of investing in noncore technologies developed by their own employees.[46] Xerox and Lucent Technologies each formed venture capital companies, to finance start-ups coming out of research done at Xerox's Palo Alto Research Center (PARC) and Bell Labs, respectively. Both Xerox and Lucent learned the hard way that to develop core technologies alone is to drive out innovation and profit. Xerox lost its PC prototype to Steve Jobs of Apple Computer. Lucent drove a key researcher with his transistor technology out of the company. The researcher and his technology later formed the basis of Intel. Now both companies' venture capital funds spin out dozens of start-ups annually, some very successful.

This also explains why companies always spin parts of their business as separately traded entities wherein a "child" has developed a distinct IC warranting its independence from the "parent." Companies are spinning off both business divisions and independent companies. Kodak spun off Eastman Chemical, which originally was a business division of Kodak producing film developing chemicals. Getting better and better at it what it does, Eastman Chemical was spun off and expanded the offering of its products to customers other than Kodak.

The preceding section shows how business growth strategies have been triggered and affected by the need to acquire greater brainpower (or other types of IC), incubate, or spin off new forms of knowledge in a certain area. This not only affected growth strategies, but it transformed the art and science of strategic business management as a whole, by inducing the business community to recognize IC as the primary source of competitive advantage. This brings us closer to the thesis of this book—ICM is not a mere business practice or process, but an approach based on the core precepts of strategic management, with particular emphasis on the needs of organizations in the knowledge economy. The next section explains how, and proposes that to effectively compete in the knowledge economy organizations need to develop at least one ICM competency.

THE REQUIRED COMPETENCIES IN THE KNOWLEDGE ECONOMY: TOWARD STRATEGIC INTELLECTUAL CAPITAL MANAGEMENT

To generate new knowledge and apply it in new ways, or simply to innovate, is the main competence an organization needs in the knowledge economy to create and sustain a competitive advantage. To create and sustain a competitive advantage that is unique to your organization is the quest of strategic management. The SWOT (strengths, weaknesses, opportunities, and threats) analysis, developed by Ken Andrew of Harvard Business School in the mid-1960s, is the essence of strategic planning. Considering the organization's strengths and weaknesses, top management can strategize how to lead the organization to exploit opportunities and deal with threats. The SWOT analysis has been dominated until very recently[47] by Michael Porter's five forces model. Porter explains that five factors determine the threats and opportunities faced by an industry. These factors include the bargaining power of customers, the bargaining power of suppliers, the threat of new entrants, the threat of substitute products, and, finally, the nature and strength of rivalry in a particular industry. According to Porter, there are three generic strategies for competitive positioning[48]: cost leadership (offering a lower-cost product), differentiation of products (unique features commanding a price premium), or market focus (specializing in a certain product market segment).[49]

In contrast to the five forces theory, the resource-based approach directs the organization's attention inward and applies the SWOT analysis to its capabilities. This approach asserts that organizations have unique resources, capabilities, and endowments, including intellectual and other capabilities; reputation; and relations that stem from the history and culture of each organization. Those resources, capabilities, and endowments that have a strategic importance and cannot be imitated or replicated by the competition are the source of competitive advantage. Based on this view the generic strategy is to identify your organization's unique strategic resources and decide in which markets and analogous markets these resources can be effectively capitalized.[50] According to this theory, financial and physical assets do not provide an organization with a competitive advantage.

In the knowledge economy the resource-based view of the organization gave birth to the knowledge-based view where these resources, capabilities, and endowments are knowledge intensive. Strategic management under this approach entails the identification of unique intellectual and knowledge resources and capabilities and utilizing them in target and analogous markets. The main point is that a competitive advantage comes from within the organization and is not one that is created by balancing some external market or industry forces. It follows that strategic management involves organizational soul-searching as well as understanding the market.

The main goal of course is to create and sustain a competitive advantage that is hard for competitors to imitate and eventually creating strong entry barriers in the way of competition. This explains why the value of intellectual property is appreciated more in the knowledge economy. First, it is well grounded in the organization, being the product of its collective brainpower, internal practices and routines, and business philosophy. As such, its uniqueness is not limited to the legal rights accorded by the patent, trademark, or copyright, but rather the technology, the brand, or the creativity that underlies each of these respective properties. Thus, the intellectual property is only the tip of the iceberg. The source of the competitive advantage is not IP per se, but the knowledge, brainpower, practices, and systems that give birth to them.

Of course, for some industries—generally service industries—IP is not the most effective generator of entry barriers to the competition. Even when it comes to R&D- or patent-intensive industries, it is not the quasi-monopoly afforded by IP that enables the achievement of a competitive advantage. To a great extent, that depends on other capabilities like time to market and creating new uses for the technology in related markets. The aggregate of these capabilities, including the ability to acquire IP, is what forms an organization's unique mix of IC and hence the basis of its competitive advantage—one that cannot be imitated by the competition.

One intellectual asset, however, does not offer a competitive advantage, but rather the unique combination of such assets. Increasingly, organizations, regardless of industry and strategy, gain a competitive advantage by having one or more of the following: a strong brand that commands customer loyalty and a price premium,[51] a demonstrated research capability with new products in the pipeline, strong IP rights that create high entry barriers for competition and huge licensing revenue,[52] or a reputation for having and keeping creative and innovative people.[53]

How to manage IC to achieve a competitive advantage is the mission of strategic management in the knowledge economy. The main question is: What are the core competencies that an organization should develop to effectively manage IC for maximum value? Therefore, the dynamics of competitive performance in the knowledge economy are IC enabled. An organization's ability to compete is now dependent on how well top management identifies, manages, and leverages the organization's IC. In particular, it depends on one or more of the following competencies:

- Speed with which the organization can acquire and apply knowledge (knowledge management)

- Ability to anticipate change in the market and respond to it (innovation management)
- Ability and speed to protect and leverage intellectual capital (IPM)
- Ability to assess the organization's values and culture, and to adopt the culture that supports and fosters effective knowledge, innovation, and IP creation and management
- Ability to coordinate, oversee, and synchronize organization-wide practices and programs related to all of the above through strategic alignment (CICM).

Part Two will outline the requirements for establishing a system for the management of knowledge, innovation, and IP, under the comprehensive intellectual capital management (CICM) model I developed. But before getting into the CICM model, the competencies required for managing IC effectively are explained.

Knowledge Management—Increasing Your Organizational IQ

Knowledge management is the first competency that an organization needs to develop for the management of IC. Knowledge management constitutes the ability of an organization to learn, to remember what it learned, and to leverage what it learned internally and externally—internally by transferring it to different workers and departments, and externally by sharing it with suppliers, distributors, partners, and customers. In short, it enables an organization to leverage its knowledge to improve its overall performance. Knowledge management's critical importance lies in building the platform of knowledge on which innovation and other core business processes are launched and fortified. A weak knowledge management system or infrastructure would result in the waste of the knowledge resources of the organization, affecting the efficiency of its operations and processes and the leveraging of its employees' brainpower.

British Petroleum (BP) leadership, a pioneer in knowledge management, transformed the entire organization to a "big brain," boosting its overall performance extensively by implementing a progressive knowledge management program. In 1990, BP was suffering from the plummeting of its stock price after having grown in both size and operations. Downsizing and cost cutting in many operations, as well as top management promotion of knowledge sharing, did not help. It was not until 1995, when John Brown was appointed as CEO, that knowledge management was taken to another level, both on the strategic and operational planes, becoming a way of doing business at BP.[54]

Summarizing its knowledge management strategy, BP professed that collaboration between employees to transform personal into organizational knowledge is what makes "the bigger brain that is BP." BP innovated and implemented a number of programs on the operational level designed to make knowledge sharing the job of every employee and division, realizing great profits. Estimated profits from BP's knowledge management skyrocketed to $800 million to date.[55] In one instance, BP showed a saving of $50 million just by transferring best practices on how to drill new sites. Knowledge management in BP moved from being a mere program or philosophy to a core competence that translated into a formidable competitive advantage.

But to manage knowledge alone is not enough. No organization can win by brains alone. What is also needed is a system that manages the output of brains to transform it into new products and services. This brings us to the second competency required for ICM—the systemization of innovation as the core business process of the organization.

Innovation Management—Systematize Your Collective Thinking

To innovate is to apply knowledge to new situations, producing new solutions, services, processes, and products. Innovation is about change—responding to and creating change. It is about evolution and revolution, evolving into higher and newer planes, and leaping onto another wave of technology. Innovative organizations are futuristic, daring, and pioneers of social change. To be innovative, it is not enough for organizations to respond to changing market forces or trends as they appear. They must be able to predict, foresee, or even create change. No organization can see the future; no organization should try, but it should at least monitor possible sources of change in technology and in the market constantly. To do that, it is important that the organization emancipates the innovative ability of its employees to boost its collective innovative power. Knowledge management is certainly a powerful enabler, but the organization needs to systemize the innovative activity as the core business process as well.

Innovation management is a key core competency in an economy where cycles of change are more recurrent. As a core competency, it involves the ability to embrace and create change, take risks, accept failure as part of the experimentation process, and get from product concept to market in the shortest time. All these capabilities should translate into a new product development process that capitalizes on a pool of employee-, and customer-, generated ideas. Organizations need to listen to their employees, who are in constant contact with the market and customers. The speed with which organizations capture, leverage, and implement new ideas of their employees may be of critical importance in the knowledge economy where ideas are contagious.

Consider the experience of Encyclopedia Britannica. Britannica continued producing their leather-bound encyclopedia volumes after the market was ready to purchase the same data in another medium—compact discs. Microsoft seized the opportunity and produced their own encyclopedic CDs, Encarta, for less than a tenth of the price. The market, preferring the fractional price and the added convenience of digital, searchable encyclopedic CDs, forced Britannica into bankruptcy. As a matter of fact, Britannica saw this coming. Britannica included a CD with its last leather-bound volumes, but the organization's resistance to change caused it to cling to the old way of doing things instead of embracing change and moving forward. No matter what Britannica's reasons were, it is evident that the organization's system of innovation failed to prepare it for change. Being innovative involves having the system to transform ideas into marketable products as much as having the right ideas to start with.

Losing a chance to capitalize on employees' ideas may result not only in an economic loss but also in loss of an opportunity that may take years, if ever, to come again. The Silicon Valley legend of Xerox and Steve Jobs, demonstrates this in a striking manner.

The legend goes like this: Steve Jobs, the CEO of Apple at the time, on a visit to Xerox's Palo Alto Research Center (PARC) sees a prototype of the mouse and the PC preface. He borrowed these ideas and established the PC world as we know it today, making billions for Apple and securing other business opportunities for years after that. Of course, Jobs and Apple did so much more than borrow Xerox's ideas to launch us into the PC world. For one thing, the prototype Steve Jobs saw at PARC was a very early and expensive version of what we know today as the mouse. However, it all started with an idea and a prototype that Xerox failed to develop and it was up to the next entrepreneur to seize the moment—exactly like the Britannica example, though Xerox legend has more to it.

Xerox did not fail to innovate or convert its employees' ideas into product concepts and prototypes. Xerox, however, failed to acquire the adequate IP protection to secure exclusive commercialization rights. Had Xerox obtained the right patent(s) on their prototype, Steve Jobs's borrowing would have cost Apple dearly. Apple would then have to design around such patents, which would have raised Apple's development costs and, most importantly, deprived Apple of the market leadership position. Intellectual property rights are critical when used as competitive and commercial tools. An organization that operates in patent-intensive (R&D), trademark-intensive (consumer products and service), and copyright-intensive (entertainment) industries needs to develop IP management as well as a core competency. To that we now turn.

Intellectual Property Management—Protect or Lose

To protect ideas, expressions, and other intellectual capital, organizations have to manage their IP, because until protected, ideas and expressions are the property of no one. The speed and comprehensibility with which an organization moves to protect a good idea sometimes can be critical. This is true now more than ever with the Internet's super highway enabling ideas to travel at high speeds.

With competitive intelligence and monitoring of market trends, the same idea may be developed almost simultaneously by two or more organizations. The only organization that can maximize its capitalization of the idea is the one that has adequately protected it. But not all ideas can be protected by patents, as many will not satisfy the stringent patent requirements. Still, a trademark or other form of IP can protect most ideas. That is where IP management helps an organization decide on the suitable protection to set up legal traps around its competitive territory.

Developing IP management as a core competency involves much more than securing the right legal protection. It involves adopting the suitable IP strategy for competitive positioning, and exploitation of the IP rights in integrated markets. IBM is a company that developed IP management as a core competency. IBM first adopted a very aggressive patenting strategy, where inventions are patented regardless of whether they fall in a core technological area or not. To enable this strategy, IBM made licensing of noncore as well as core technologies its business. Patenting widely, IBM innovated a system of licensing in which reverse engineering is used to detect infringements of its patents and subsequently seeking licensees. In a decade, IBM raised its licensing revenue from $90 million to $1.5 billion.

Organizational Culture—The Main Enabler

The previously mentioned competencies cannot be developed without the support of the right organizational culture. Many surveys and reports[56] have shown how the best knowledge, innovation, and IP management programs fail because of an adverse organizational culture. Organizational culture is the set of shared unspoken values that stem from the organizational philosophy and history, and affect its behavioral patterns. It implicitly defines and affects the way business is done and the attitude of management and other employees. It was discovered that whenever an organization's culture is contrary to the values presented by a new initiative or program, the latter fails, sometimes even before it is fully launched.

For example, a culture that is permeated by top management's apathy toward employees' new ideas defeats all attempts to push innovation down in the organization, despite the best efforts of top management to communicate that they had a change of heart. No matter how many speeches top management gives to communicate their change of heart, entrenched organizational culture infuses a contrary message that defeats the initiative. If that culture conveys the message that to come up with new ideas is to be "a troublemaker," then no attempt by top management to champion this behavior will work unless clear steps are taken to change the culture. The impact of culture is so strong because it is rooted in an organization's "subconscious."[57]

Culture is like the physical body's defense system, which is activated whenever a foreign object enters the body. The body fires out its fiercest antibodies to destroy the object, with some bodies being more sensitive than others. This is done without any control from the conscious mind. The same can be said of organizational behavior. Prior to introducing any change that is contrary to the existing culture, management needs to assess the existing and desirable cultures. In Chapter 10, ways in which management can assess and change its organizational culture are explored, among other changes that an organization has to undertake before embarking on implementing an ICM program.

Being deeply entrenched in the organization, a positive culture and philosophy is a core competency that can hardly be replicated by the competition. Culture also enables the development of knowledge, innovation, and IP management as core competencies. Every organization needs to develop culture as a core competency, but the same is not true for the other mentioned competencies. The reason is that each of these competencies predominantly relates to the management of a particular form of IC (knowledge resources, innovation processes, or IP), which is not necessarily the main driver of value in a particular industry. For example, the crucial importance of managing patents for technologically intensive industries, or managing brands for consumer products companies, is not matched in the service industry where knowledge management is king.

That being said, each organization will still need to develop all of the ICM stages (for the management of knowledge, innovation and IP) to leverage its IC to the maximum. The ability to determine the level to which each of the stages should be developed, and the coordination between the stages, is an organizational competency in its own right.

Comprehensive Management of Intellectual Capital—Orchestrate Your Music

Despite the fact that an organization's industry, strategy and stage of development are what shape the form and features of its ICM program, each organization still needs to have a comprehensive IC strategy. By comprehensive I mean a model for the management of IC over the business cycle of value creation as explained in Chapter 4. The need of every organization for such a comprehensive model, regardless of its situational requirements, stems from the strategic questions that top management have to deal with in the knowledge economy, in order to create a competitive advantage. In a knowledge- and innovation-intensive economy, or, as I call it, one driven by IC-enabled economic dynamics, the art of strategic management involves the following questions:

- What do we know and need to know? How are we going to acquire the knowledge resources needed to attain the desired competitive/strategic position? Do we develop such resources internally through knowledge sharing and transfer or externally through acquisition and partnerships? (Questions that pertain to the realm of knowledge management)
- How are we going to utilize our brainpower to create our competitive advantage? By incremental or radical innovation? (Questions that pertain to the realm of innovation management)
- How are we going to use our IC muscle to compete in existing and new markets? (Question that pertain to the realm of IPM)
- And, finally, what is the IC strategy that will enable us to sustain our competitive advantage? (Questions that pertain to the ICM model)

The IC strategy should aim at creating a balance between the need of establishing a comprehensive model to manage IC while at the same time customizing it to the organization's situational requirements. The challenge in managing IC is that if top management does not understand the nature and value of IC, how to create, extract, and maximize such value, then they would not fully appreciate whether they have the resources necessary to make a success of a new strategy. One of the main problems when it comes to managing IC is that ICM models lack a clear methodical basis, and hence provide only partial solutions. This is in part due to the fact that to date ICM models have been developed "by practitioners without an academic theoretical basis."[58]

This book presents a comprehensive model for the management of IC called the CICM model. While the model does not venture into an academic search for a new strategic management theory, it presents a methodical basis for making sense of all the approaches that have emerged under the banner of ICM. The model is designed to be customized through three dimensions: intellectual value drivers of a particular industry, organizational culture, and business strategy. An understanding of the type and nature of IC that drives value creation and maximization in a specific industry is essential to effective customization of CICM. An important dimension to consider is the organizational culture and management style dynamics. No model of ICM can be implemented without thorough and careful attention to the organizational context. In addition, the CICM model incorporates a diagnostic tool that enables organizations to assess and prioritize their short- and long-term needs for the various stages of ICM. The model will be presented in Part Three. Before we get to the CICM model, it is necessary to lay a foundation for it by examining the modest amount of literature on IC.

NOTES

[1] *Intellectual capital* is used as a generic term to denote all intellectual resources (e.g., knowledge and information databases), assets (e.g., processes), and properties (e.g., patents and trademarks) that an organization owns, controls, or has access to.

[2] See, for example, Sproule & Sullivan, "Case History: Integrated IP Management," *Les Nouvelles,* June 1999, p. 70. The article reveals the problems resulting from implementing two separate programs for knowledge and intellectual property management.

[3] The term *organization* will be used throughout the book to refer to corporations, publicly traded companies, government agencies, and nonprofit organizations.

[4] Pfeffer and Sutton report that only one out of five TQM initiatives succeed, while 70 percent of reengineering efforts fail. See J. Pfeffer & R. Sutton, *The Knowing Doing Gap* (Boston: Harvard Business School Press, 1999), p. 2.

[5] Master of Intellectual Property is the only graduate degree offered in the United States and the world to nonlawyers. The degree was first offered in 1983 by Franklin Pierce Law Center as part of its graduate program. Today, the program attracts over 100 students nationally and internationally, including government officials and business executives in addition to lawyers and law students.

[6] See L. Edvinsson and M. Malone, *Intellectual Capital: Realizing Your Company's True Value by Finding Its Hidden Brainpower* (New York: Harper Business, 1997), p. 146. The authors give credit for the creation of this model to Hubert St. Onge, Charles Armstrong, Gordon Petrash, and Leif Eduinsson.

[7] In some definitions of *intellectual capital,* intellectual property is included mainly as part of the structural capital since it is owned by the organization. Other writers, however, either do not mention intellectual property or limit it to being a legal instrument. The meaning of the term *intellectual capital* and how it emerged and evolved is covered in Chapter 2.

[8] The divergence between market and book values could be explained to some extent by the fact that some of the depreciated assets on the books may still be appreciated by the market. Sveiby demonstrates in his article [K. E. Sveiby, "Measuring Intangibles and Intellectual Capital," in Morey, Maybury, and Rhuraisingham (eds.), *Knowledge Management: Classic and Contempo-*

rary Works (Cambridge: MIT Press, 2000), pp. 337–354] that publicly traded companies since the 1920s had market capitalization values higher than their book values. The difference is that market capitalization amounted only to 187 percent of the book value then, and it was not until the late 1980s/early 1990s that this rate jumped to over 500 percent of the book value.

[9] In an increasing number of cases the price paid for the acquired company exceeds many times the book value of the acquired company. To balance the books the difference is reported under "goodwill" in the books of the acquiring companies. Goodwill reflects the value of some of the acquired company's intellectual capital. Internally developed intellectual assets, however, cannot be reported in the books under the current accounting system. This will be discussed further in Chapter 3.

[10] Some writers use the terms *intangible resources* and *intellectual capital* as synonymous. I differentiate between the two since, though all intellectual capital is intangible, not all intangible resources can be used to drive value in every industry. Thus, the term *intellectual capital* refers to such intangible resources that drive value in a particular industry or organization.

[11] See, for example, ITWorld.com article at *www.itworld.com/Man/2698/CIO010315lev/*.

[12] Book to market value ratio.

[13] K. E. Sveiby, *The New Organizational Wealth: Managing and Measuring Intangible Resources* (San Francisco: Berrett-Koehler Publishers, 1997), pp. 6–7.

[14] *Id.*

[15] Supra note 6.

[16] Take the Internet, for example. In around five years it transformed consumer expectations and the way business is done, and created new markets—maybe even a new industry.

[17] This figure is reported in a recent study using data from venture capitalists and the patent literature mentioned in P. Norling, "Structuring and Managing R&D Work Processes: Why Bother?", *CHEMTECH*, October 1997, p. 1. Other studies mentioned in Chapter 6, however, mention that it takes four to six new product development projects to have a commercial success. The divergence may be explained by reference to raw ideas (the first figure) as opposed to product concepts (the second figure).

[18] Brian Arthur, "New Economics for a Knowledge Economy." In Ruggles & Holtshouse (editors), *The Knowledge Advantage* (U.K., Oxford: Capstone, 1999), pp. 195–212.

[19] Ove Granstrand, *The Economics and Management of Intellectual Property* (Northhampton, MA: Edward Elgar, 1999), pp. 10–12.

[20] P. Drucker, "New Productivity Challenge," *Harvard Business Review,* November–December 1991.

[21] Supra note 17.

[22] A group of Swedish, Swiss, Finnish, and U.S. companies that have been integrated into a global leader in the electro-technical field.

[23] Christopher Bartlett, "The Knowledge Based Organization". In Ruggles & Holtshouse (editors), *The Knowledge Advantage* (Oxford, U.K., Capstone 1999), p. 116. Also see p 110–117 for a detailed description of the ABB model.

[24] The first such positions created were those of intellectual capital director at Skandia in early 1990s and that of organizational learning director at the Imperial Bank of Canada.

[25] Board on Science, Technology and Economic Policy (STEP), "Securing America's Industrial Strength," *STEP,* 1999, p. 2.

[26] Gina Imperato, "Harley Shifts Gears," *Fast Company,* June–July 1997.

[27] One very good example of the use of CoPs is provided by Siemens. A multinational with around 500,000 employees worldwide in 190 countries, Siemens uses CoPs to overcome the bureaucracy and rigidity entailed by its size and vast operations, and to mine its rich human capital. More about CoPs and CoIs and the companies that use them will be explained in Chapter 5 on knowledge management.

[28] An example here is PricewaterhouseCoopers, which ties promotion of its managers to their knowledge sharing activities. Indeed, this is common in other consulting businesses as well where sharing of knowledge is essential for the organization to remain competitive.

[29] More about this in Chapter 6.

[30] In this book, I use this term to denote the new role that intellectual capital plays in the knowledge economy as the core generator of organizational competitive advantage.

[31] Supra note 27.

[32] I call it survival/growth strategy because without growth an organization will eventually die or be relatively dormant.

[33] Credit for comments on Boeing goes to a research project by a group of my students: Susan Lesmerises, Mathew Borick, and Bryan Erickson, Fall 2001.

[34] Interview with David Near, the then Director of Business Excellence, May 2001.

[35] Originally an idea developed by Karl Erik Sveiby, a pioneer IC theorist. Sveiby explains how intangible (as he prefers to call them) revenues that a business gains from its customers are very valuable for its growth (discussed in Chapter 2).

[36] Throughout the book, the word *products* is used to denote services, processes, solutions, and manufactured goods.

[37] See *www.mergerstat.com* and *www.webmergers.com.*

[38] KPMG International Report, 2000, available at *www.mergerstat.com.*

[39] The "depth" of the IC base relates to the specialized knowledge and expertise in core areas, while "breadth" relates to new knowledge across a number of core and noncore areas.

[40] Mintz, S. L., "What's a Merger Worth," *CFO Magazine* (April 1, 2000).

[41] *Id.*

[42] "Innovation in Industry," U.S. Patent Law, February 20, 1999, p. 13.

[43] Comment made in presentation by David Snowden at the Intellectual Capital Congress, McMaster University, Canada, January 17, 2002.

[44] See A. Hargadon and R. Sutton, "Building An Innovation Factory," 78 *Harvard Business Review* 157, 2000, p. 162.

[45] One of the leading global companies with over 60,000 products, $15 billion in annual sales, and operating in 60 countries, 3M is known for its high innovativeness with more than 30 percent of its products being introduced in the last four years. Since 1948, 3M leadership has believed that only through empowering their employees can they be an innovative company.

[46] This will be discussed further in Chapter 8.

[47] For a review of the development in strategic management theories, concepts, and applications, see M. Porter, *Competitive Strategy* (Boston, MA: Free Press, 1980), and R. Rumelt, D. Schendel, & D. Teece, *Fundamental Issues in Strategy* (Cambridge: Harvard University Press, 1994).

[48] These will be explored further in Chapter 7.

[49] M. Porter, *Competitive Advantage: Creating and Sustaining Superior Performance* (New York: The Free Press, 1985), pp. 11–26.

[50] D. Teece, G. Pisano, and A. Sheun, "Dynamic Capabilities and Strategic Management." In M. Zack (editor), *Knowledge and Strategy* (Stoneham, MA: Butterworth-Heinemann, 1999), p. 77.

[51] For example, Coca-Cola Company, whose trademark is valued at $47 billion in 1997. The value of the trademark stems from consumers' loyalty to the brand.

[52] For example, IBM multiplied its patent licensing revenue from $90 million in 1990 to around $1.5 billion in 2001.

[53] For example, 3M and Microsoft.

[54] Supra note 4, pp. 217–222.

[55] Douglas Weidner, Knowledge Management Workshop, KM Conference, April 22, 2002.

[56] See, for example, a survey done by Ernst & Young in Rudy Ruggles, "The State of the Notion: Knowledge Management in Practice," *California Management Review* 40, Summer 1998, p. 83.

[57] It is not new that organizations are referred to in psychological terms. Many theories look at organizations as living entities that not only grow and evolve but also have a personality. See, for example, Bennet, A., "Managing Change in a Knowledge Environment," (unpublished) in which the author mentions the id and the ego of organizations. Also interesting is W. Bridges, *The Character of Organizations: Using Personality Types in Organization Development* (Palo Alto, CA: Davies Black Publishing, 2000), in which the author applies Jungian archetypes of personality to organizations.

[58] See J. Roos, G. Roos, L. Edvinsson, and N. Dragonetti, *Intellectual Capital: Navigating in the New Business Landscape* (New York: New York University Press, 1998), p. 24. Also see K. E. Sveiby, "Measuring Intangibles and Intellectual Capital." In Morey, Maybury, and Rhuraisingham (editors), *Knowledge Management: Classic and Contemporary Works* (Cambridge: MIT Press, 2000), pp. 337–338.

2

The Intellectual Capital Model

Most organizations have adapted or transformed their management styles and business models to manage intellectual capital (IC) and respond to the IC-enabled dynamics of the knowledge economy. Many of these organizations have done it without even realizing that they are adopting an intellectual capital management (ICM) approach. A top executive of a leading consumer products company, whose name is withheld, commented that his company is not interested in ICM. "Show me the money," he said. "All I see are the circles and pyramids that ICM people draw in conferences." What this executive did not realize is that he was already managing IC in one way or another on a daily basis to make money. If it weren't for this executive's daily reliance on his gut feeling and tacit knowledge to manage his employees' innovation, the company he works for wouldn't be a market leader. If the company's employees did not care about the management of customer and structural capital, it wouldn't invest millions of dollars in its interactive Web site to solicit consumers' feedback 24 hours a day, seven days a week.

Successful managers and businesses have been managing intellectual capital one way or another all along, whether consciously or intuitively. This however, does not mean that they have an ICM program or strategy. Managing IC as a matter of common business sense is not sufficient for the development of ICM as an organizational competency. It is only when a management style moves from being intuitively applied to a planned and systemized process that it can be perfected. Only then can it be substantially transformed from being an art to becoming a science. Once it transitions into a science, it becomes testable, measurable, more predictable, and, most importantly, repeatable. Though organizations that apply ICM advance this goal, there is still a long road of experimentation and applied research ahead for the emerging field of ICM to become more of a "science."

One of the established precepts of ICM to date, however, is dividing IC into human, customer, and structural capital—what I will call the IC model. Before examining the "circles and pyramids" of the IC model, and why they are so frustrating to many executives, let's consider what's in a name.

WHAT'S IN A NAME?—DEFINING THE TERMS

How we define something impacts the way we perceive it, and the way we perceive it in turn affects how we deal with it. Terms have meanings and connotations that trigger impressions and expectations with a number of underlying assumptions. What we call intangible assets or hidden resources will have practical implications on how they are identified and managed. At this writing, there is still disagreement as to how to define and classify an organization's intangible assets. Even after apparent consensus on the use of one term over another, producing a definition of the term sets off a chain reaction of explanations about it. As it stands today, academics and practitioners use the term *intellectual capital* more consistently to refer to the intangible assets that a business can use to create value.

Replacing the word *capital,* the word *assets* has also been used. Sometimes the words are used interchangeably, and other times "assets" refers to specifically identified items of IC such as best practices or patents. Despite general acceptance of the terms *capital* and *assets,* these terms generate controversy because they have distinct definitions in the context of financial accounting.

The generally accepted meaning of the term *asset* refers to items that are both ascertainable and transferable. The problem is that intellectual capabilities, with the exclusion of intellectual property (IP), are not readily ascertainable or transferable. Human intellectual resources, whether originating in an employee or a customer, defy ownership by a business, are not transferable, and fall out of the realm of "assets," in the strict sense of the word. Even when it comes to IP, the uncertainty that surrounds its value makes describing it as transferable assets questionable. Moreover, the fact that IP can lose its value if mismanaged, infringed, or invalidated makes its value, even if it is ascertainable, elusive.

The term *capital* may seem less problematic. Capital is defined as "accumulated goods devoted to the production of other goods," or "accumulated possessions calculated to bring in income."[1] Assuming that the words *goods* and *possessions* include intangibles, the term *capital* implies that such goods can be used to create value and are not necessarily transferable. Unlike tangible goods, however, defining or measuring the perceived value of intangible goods is problematic, since there is no market for it until after it is transformed into a marketable product. Furthermore, the term *capital* becomes more objectionable when used to refer to human resources, since a business can never really own or possess employee brainpower or customers' relations, though it presumably has access to both.

Regardless of the foregoing arguments against the use of the term *capital,* it seems to be accepted by a majority of practitioners in the field, perhaps because the term triggers images of economic value, liquidity, money, moneymaking potential, and investment potential. It also implies flow and flexibility.

The other term used to refer to intangible resources and capabilities is *intellectual.* Though apparently less controversial, one might ask if we are limiting our ability to perceive intangible resources and capabilities by limiting them to what is intellectual? In other words, can the term *intellectual* include such capabilities and resources that are not, strictly speaking, intellectual? For example, does it include the emotional intelligence of a team and its leader, an essential factor for the success of the project? Does it include interpersonal qualities, like the ability to lead, inspire, and initiate trust, essential for effective knowledge sharing? Does *intellectual* include the shared values and culture an organization has built through the years? Strictly speaking, it does not.

By defining intangible resources as intellectual capital, is our pool of resources restricted to only those produced by the left rather than the right side of the brain, or the mind as opposed to the heart? Wouldn't the term exclude tacit knowledge, which is formed from intuition and gut feeling? Indeed, the term *intellectual capital* needs to be stretched to new semantic boundaries if it is to include all that is also a right brain, heart or gut, activity.

As with any other body of knowledge, those skilled in it usually define the terms and the underlying assumptions. Similarly, practitioners in the field of ICM have expanded the meaning of the term *intellectual capital* to include other intangible assets that are not intellectual, and to broaden the meanings of the words *assets* and *capital* beyond their meanings as financial accounting terms.

Skandia, a Swedish financial and insurance services company and a pioneer in the field of ICM, first coined the term *intellectual capital.* In its first IC supplement to its annual report of 1994, the term referred to all intangible resources that the organization has including human, process, and organizational capital. Leif Edvinsson, the architect of Skandia's model, defines intellectual capital as the collective sum of knowledge of an organization's members and their transformation of this knowledge into intangible assets, later equating IC with any intangible asset that is used to create value.[2] In other words, IC comprises all resources, capabilities, relations, and networks, whether intellectual like knowledge and ideas, or emotional and interpersonal like attitude, culture, and values, that enable an organization to create and maximize value.

A definition of intellectual capital is an essential step in recognizing what we are talking about. But to manage intellectual capital, we need more than definitions. We need frames of reference that enable us to understand, locate, and collectively refer to various forms of intellectual capital. Such frames of reference serve two main functions. First, they create a conceptual context necessary for the recognition of invisible assets. Second, they provide an operational context in which to define the scope of objectives that can be achieved from the management of these assets. A function closely connected to the second function of defining management objectives is to provide a platform for designing measurements. The following discussion examines the most popular IC classification models (the circles) and their measurement systems.

FRAMES OF REFERENCE—THE IC MODEL AND THE THREE CIRCLES

The most popular model, called the IC model, classifies IC into human, customer, and structural capital.[3] *Human capital* includes employee competency, skills, brainpower, and tacit knowledge. *Customer capital* includes customer relations, feedback, input as to the product/service, suggestions, experience, and tacit knowledge. Customer is defined broadly to include suppliers, distributors, and other players who can contribute to the value chain. *Structural capital* is the organizational knowledge contained in databases, practices, know-how, and culture. It stands for all organizational capabilities that enable it to respond and meet market needs and challenges. Other three-circle models have been developed that identify other forms of IC in the circles. Haanes and Lowendahl[4] categorize intangible resources into competency and relational assets. Relational capital refers to relations and reputation and thus corresponds with customer capital. Competency is defined as the ability to perform a given task both at the individual and organizational level closely corresponding to the human, and structural capital in the IC model.[5]

But it is not all circles. Karl Erik Sveiby introduced the first classification of intangible assets in the late 1980s while working as a consultant for the KONRAD group of Sweden. Sveiby developed the invisible balance sheet, which he uses to explain that an organization's tangible and financial assets reflected in the balance sheet are sustained and supported by intangible assets.[6] These intangible assets, as Sveiby prefers to call them, comprise internal structure, external structure, and competency. In essence, the internal and external structures correspond to structural and customer capital, while competency corresponds to human capital. However, a closer look at Sveiby's model shows distinctions in his model that are not addressed by the other three circle models.

Though Sveiby defines individual competency as the collective skills, experience, education, and social skills of all the employees in an organization, he makes a distinction between "professional" and "support" employees. Only the former type of employees contribute to the organization's individual competency capital, while the latter are part of the internal structure. He explains that professional employees plan, produce, or process new products and solutions, so that their level of competency represents the collective organizational knowledge and expertise. Support employees, however, are those who perform general management administration, accounting, personnel services, and other activities that relate to supporting the organization's operations. Other models in which human capital encompasses the knowledge and expertise of all employees do not draw the distinction between employees' knowledge. Still, the distinction may be important, as Sveiby shows, to measure variables in the performance of both the professional and the support staff.

Further, Sveiby fits different types of IP under different forms of IC. He includes patents as part of the internal structure, along with concepts, models, information technology (IT) and administrative systems, routines, internal networks, and culture. Internal structure is owned by the organization, even though it has been created and updated by the support staff. In Sveiby's classification, patents are part of the internal structure, since they enable an organization to use and commercialize a particular technology, while trademarks are included as part of the external structure, since they are used to identify the source of a product or service to customers and build goodwill.

While the classification of trademarks as part of the external structure makes sense, grouping patents in the internal structure limits their use to an enabling technology. There is little doubt that with exponential growth in technology licensing, patent and know-how or trade secrets are used to build networks and alliances with external partners including suppliers and competitors. This means that patents should be seen as part of both the external as well as internal structures. The importance of grouping patents as part of the external structure cannot be overstressed because it directs the attention of management to maximize their exploitation in related markets through licensing and cross-licensing, which may be adversely affected if only seen as a technology for internal use.

Copyrights are not mentioned by Sveiby; however, using the same analogy, it seems plausible to suggest that copyrighted works that enable production, like software products, are part of the internal structure, while those used in advertising and promoting the corporate image are part of the external structure. Sveiby's classification scheme is one of the few models that recognizes and categorizes IP in the IC model. Other models hardly pay any attention to IP, thereby reducing it to merely a legal instrument. In that respect, Sveiby's system provides a more comprehensive view of IC.

Sveiby applies insightful analysis into the external structure by distinguishing between image-enhancing customers and other customers. Image-enhancing customers are leaders in their industries. Their good reputation rubs off on the organization. By endorsing the organization's products and indirectly training its professional employees, these customers bring a valuable stream of intangible revenue. Although image-enhancing customers are probably limited to the service sector, the idea of intangible revenue applies to all industries.

No matter which of the models you adopt to define intellectual capital, the differences will be minor. All models stress that the most important feature of the IC model is to understand how value is created. The interaction and transformation of IC from one form to another, or from one circle to another, creates value and enables an organization to extract maximum value from its IC. That's where the "pyramid" comes into play.

VALUE CREATION—THE COMING OF THE PYRAMIDS

According to the IC model, to create value from managing IC, it is essential to transfer individual knowledge, or human capital, into organizational knowledge and practices (i.e., structural capital) that can then be passed on to customers in the form of new products and services. This in turn will expand the organization's customer base and market share and maximize the intangible

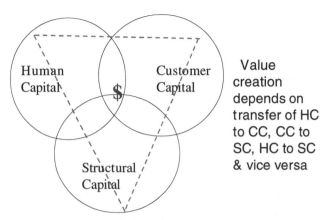

EXHIBIT 2.1   Value Creation Under the IC Model

revenue from these customers. The value creation/maximization cycle is the most important cycle for a business because it provides the key to achieving greater return on investment (ROI). It follows that the key is not to be found in the three circles but in the triangle that denotes the value platform,[7] illustrated in Exhibit 2.1.

The principle underlying the value platform is that value does not reside in the development of one form of IC but in the transfer of one form to another, and hence the relationship between them. This means the focus should not be on the management of the individual forms of IC but rather the interrelationship between them, since strengthening one strengthens the other and vice versa. One way of managing this interrelationship is that developed by Skandia.

SKANDIA'S NAVIGATOR AND THE HUMAN FOCUS

Leif Edvinsson, newly appointed as Skandia's director of ICM in the early 1990s, found the triangle insufficient to unlock the value of IC. Instead, Edvinsson developed a system he called "the Navigator," using a "house" depiction to explain the relationship between the various forms of IC as shown in Exhibit 2.2. Though based on the three circles classification model, Edvinsson developed a unique classification system for it. He broke structural capital into smaller components, customer and organizational capital, wherein organizational capital includes process and innovation capital.[8]

With IC broken down into smaller parts, Skandia recognized that value is created by the flow between the parts.[9] Based on this more detailed classification of IC, Skandia's Navigator showed that creation of value from IC depends on navigating the organizational strategy through five focuses—financial, human, process, renewal, and development. Under the Navigator, the human focus drives financial results and future growth, since it is the only one that enables interaction between the other focuses.

Human focus (i.e., employees) transforms customer input and knowledge into new processes and products through innovation, and sets in motion the renewal and development of the organization, which in turn leads to positive financial results. Employees also build and develop organizational capital by creating business processes and routines as well as intellectual assets that are owned by the organization. The Navigator model places most of the emphasis in the value

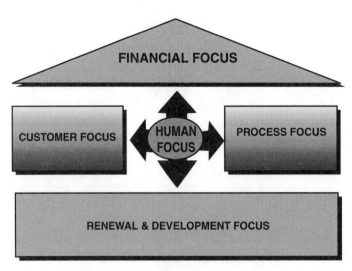

EXHIBIT 2.2   The Skandia Navigator

creation cycle on human capital as the generator and facilitator of value. Although this model and the value platform principle make sense, they fail to provide more than general guidance to management on how IC can be managed for value creation.

Andriessen[10] challenged the IC model classification and its underlying premise about the role of IC in value creation. Instead, Andriessen applies the core competency theory advanced by Prahalad and Hamel[11] to the IC concept to explain that breaking IC into its component parts in the way suggested by the IC models ignores the fact that the value of an organization's IC lies in its unique grouping of the various forms of IC under a single core competency.

THE CORE COMPETENCY PRINCIPLE AND VALUE CREATION

Andriessen contends that using IC models that classify capital into generic forms that are applicable to all organizations, makes all organizations look the same and hence, does not enable strategic planning based on the unique and different combinations of IC that a particular organization has. Andriessen prefers to classify IC as a unique bundle of intangible assets that make up a core competency, where an organization usually has somewhere between 8 and 10 competencies.

According to this classification model, a core competency is made up of the following forms of IC—processes, employee skills and tacit knowledge, organizational endowments, collective values, technology, and explicit knowledge. Endowments include what the organization inherits from the past, including brand image, networks of suppliers, and customers. Value creation under this model depends on the flow of IC in relation to each of the organization's core competencies. The strength of a core competency is assessed according to five criteria. These criteria assess the value a core competency adds to customers, the competitive edge it gives an organization, the future potential it has, the number of years it can be sustained by creating entry barriers, and how firmly it is anchored in the organization.[12]

Andriessen's model enables an organization to see IC more as a group instead of individual separate units, or, in his words, "to see the forest, not the trees." Again, one wonders if it gives more than general guidance as to the way IC should be managed for value creation. Like the value platform and Skandia's Navigator, the core competency model asserts that value creation is the result of the combination and interaction of the various forms of IC.

THE IC MODEL, CORE COMPETENCIES MODEL, AND MANAGEMENT

Further analysis of the IC and core competency models' view of value creation reveals that they are polarized approaches. While the IC models focus on separating the individual forms of IC to determine the effect of investing in one form over the other in the value creation cycle, the core competency model suggests the various IC forms should be managed as one cluster. Value is created not through transfer between the generic forms of IC but such transfer that occurs in the context of a core competency. Thus, the focus of this model is on unifying the various forms of IC under a common core competency, where the degree of value creation is measured as the resultant strength of the competency as a whole.

Though the IC models' approach may seem divisive, they serve to provide insight into the potential value that each form of IC contributes to an organization. They offer a generic approach to the classification of IC, identifying the genre of each form of IC and its unique features and needs. Classification is based on the source of the IC. Expertise, attitude, and creativity come from the human mind and psyche, and thus are grouped under human capital. Any intangibles that originate from interaction with the market and customers are grouped under customer, external, or relational capital. Finally, those developed or owned by the organization as part of its operations and processes are grouped under structural, organizational, or internal capital.

Such systems allow management to focus ICM practices and address the development of each form of intellectual capital. But the question remains as to *how* to invest in human capital, customer capital, and structural capital to create value for the whole organization? The IC models are too vague to guide management as to the objectives they should aim for in managing each form of IC. While the models inform management that competitive performance is dependent on the development of IC, when it comes to *how,* it offers merely broad terms and generalizations. Satisfy your employees and customers, transfer human knowledge into structural/organizational knowledge, and your organization's profits will increase. Such vagueness may explain why skepticism surrounds the IC model.

The core competency model appears to be more attractive since it implies that IC should be developed in the context of the whole. The stronger the competency becomes, the more likely it is that the organization is effectively leveraging the underlying IC. As the core competency model points out, the strength of an organization's IC lies in its unique combination of IC to form a core competency and not in having strong forms of IC per se. From this premise, to effectively manage IC, the various forms must be observed in action.

A core competency may include each of the various identified forms of IC, but they are developed by the organization as a bundle of assets relating to one core competency. As a bundle, it may make it easier for organizations to identify their IC and define their management objectives under a strategy of developing specific core competencies. Despite the clarity that this model offers, it risks hindering the natural or organic development of IC to the extent of limiting the potential of growth and value creation stored in it. For this reason, the core competencies model focuses on the development of structured, defined core competencies instead of developing IC forms as an organizational resource that could give birth to new noncore businesses.

Learning from IBM, 3M, Xerox, Apple, Lucent, and Intel

To clarify this point, consider an organization that sees itself as an innovator, not in particular core areas, but in all areas. As in the examples of Xerox and Apple, and Lucent and Intel, a narrow focus on core business caused Xerox and Lucent to miss out on financially lucrative opportunities. What if an organization wants to allow development in noncore areas even though it does not intend to solidify the underlying IC into any of its core competencies? Organizations that adopt this strategy as one of their growth strategies have reaped great benefits as a result. One outstanding example is found in IBM.

Over the years, IBM has developed numerous noncore technologies and subsequently offered them for licensing. As a result, IBM generated over $1.5 billion in revenue from annual licensing fees. IBM's strategy may not be the ideal strategy for other organizations, but it is certainly one of the most important strategies of the knowledge economy. It is a strategy behind the success of 3M, Intel, Lucent, Xerox, and others. A strong focus on core competencies in total disregard to other capabilities that an organization's IC may enable it to develop is to waste and undercapitalize the intellectual resources of the organization.

Recognition—The First Step in Managing IC

Both approaches, however, are useful when it comes to recognizing where to find IC in the organization and what to call it, and thus serve the conceptual context. When it comes to the operational context, however, the IC model offers only general guidelines as to management of IC, while the core competencies model limits what management can do in developing IC. A classification model for IC defeats its purpose if it does not provide clear objectives for ICM and how to achieve them. Classification is but an artificial grouping, and when it comes to IC, it should enable their effective management. The real question, therefore, is to what extent do these models enable effective management of intellectual capital? Hence the "so what?" test.

The recognition of IC under any model serves to create enterprise-wide awareness of the importance of IC in sustaining the present and future competitive performance of a business. Proponents of IC models single-handedly established and advanced the field of ICM by providing a conceptual context that enabled us to see and understand the underlying invisible assets of an organization. Understanding and awareness alone can improve the innovative power of an organization.

For one thing, the invisible asset is now visible, and management decisions to invest in it will not be viewed with extreme skepticism or utter cynicism. Once recognized, returns from investing in IC can be monitored. Intellectual property has long been recognized for its business value from goodwill built with customers to royalty income and entry barriers constructed by IP that bar the path of competitors. Yet other forms of IC have not proven their worth as much as IP has. The IC models have advanced our ability to appreciate the value of the more hidden or softer forms of IC.

However, when it comes to creating an operational context, something more is needed. What is needed is a measurement system that enables management to monitor the effects of IC-related activities in creating value for the organization. To manage is to measure, and no management system can be effective without some measures that provide insight into the outcome of management's efforts. Managers need a methodological way to determine whether IC programs, practices, and systems are working and how well they are working.

MEASURING INTELLECTUAL CAPITAL

How do you measure intellectual capital? How do you measure something that is invisible, contained inside the human brain, databases, processes, culture, and products? Quite simply, you don't. The goal of IC measurement is not to determine how much knowledge or IC you have by counting the number of computers or key employees, but how effective the organization is in creating value from it. The key to IC measurement is to measure the effectiveness of various forms of IC in achieving the organization's goals, in enhancing its innovative and competitive ability, and in renewing and growing its IC. Performance measurement, which originated early in the twentieth century, provided a suitable framework for most of the IC measurement models.

Generally speaking, the role of measurement is to provide a framework to focus attention on the thing you intend to monitor. For example, consider a set of bathroom scales. A person who constantly weighs himself on the scales can, as a result of that behavior, alter his eating habits. As such, measurement offers management a powerful tool that can influence organizational behavior and action. The axiom "what gets measured gets managed" is slightly skewed. The truth is *what gets measured gets noticed* by top and senior management and, as a result, something gets done about it. Therefore, it is important that only the key success enablers get monitored and measured.

To measure performance in all areas, management would necessarily be spread too thinly across an organization, thereby sapping the human resources of management, which would result in confusion and a blurred sense of direction throughout the organization. Management has been dissatisfied with the use of financial measures per se to monitor business future performance. For some, they hardly monitor the characteristics that create an organization's competitive advantage. Financial measures (e.g., ROI) are too general to indicate the areas that management should focus on to drive future competitive performance. Because financial measures are retrospective in nature, they also fail as predictors of current problems the organization is facing. Since the beginning of the industrial revolution, management recognized that financial reporting offers too little, too late and developed performance measures.[13] The oldest are found in the manufacturing industry. Its "units per hour" indicator measured production performance. Hotels and hospitals used bed occupancy rate, while universities reported their graduate employment rate.

All these measures of performance look at the outcome of past performance to guide the improvement of future performance. Performance measures can be qualitative or quantitative, short or long term, in-process or end-result based, or some combination of all. To date, all performance measures have been developed to assess one form or another of IC, but some are more closely aligned to the IC concept, or were developed with the IC concept in mind.

One of the earliest attempts to measure human capital preceded the emergence of the IC concept. In the 1970s, the Human Resources Costing and Accounting measures attempted to measure employee contribution and competencies in dollars. The attempts failed. Performance measures designed to measure process capital were also developed, prior to the IC concept, with the total quality management (TQM) movement in the 1980s. These systems attempted to measure the continuous performance of production and other business processes using quality and reduction of error as the yardstick. TQM met with considerable success.

Customer satisfaction is another measure of IC. Believing that customer satisfaction is the best indicator of customer loyalty and repeat business, many businesses and organizations developed ways to measure customer satisfaction. In Sweden, the first Customer Satisfaction Barometer was issued in 1989. Other countries in Europe and the United States followed suit and issued customer satisfaction indexes to monitor customer satisfaction in different industries.[14]

These measurement attempts fall short of creating a comprehensive system based on the IC model to monitor and track value creation from ICM. Though all forms of IC should be monitored for enhanced business performance, organizations need to focus their attention and resources on managing and measuring only those IC items that are critical for their success. To aid management with this role, a number of IC measurement systems emerged in the 1990s, some of which are based on the IC models discussed earlier. These include the Balanced Scorecard

(BSC), the Intangible Asset Monitor (IAM) developed by Sveiby, and the Skandia Navigator (the Navigator).

Most of the IC measurement systems discussed in this chapter have been designed for the internal purposes of an organization, namely, strategic planning, management control, resource allocation, and raising awareness of the value of IC. Nonetheless, a number of these and other measurement systems also have external purposes, mainly reporting to external stakeholders on IC. Emphasis in this chapter will be placed on such models, or parts thereof, designed for internal purposes, while those used for external purposes are addressed in Chapter 3.

IC MEASUREMENT SYSTEMS—WHAT THEY HAVE IN COMMON

All the IC measurement systems have some features in common. They all tie the choice of metrics to the strategy of the organization and are situation or organization specific. To measure IC without focus is an impossible, though theoretically attractive, endeavor. Focus is introduced by first identifying, and later monitoring, factors that are critical for the organization to meet its strategic goals. The IC measurement systems become a tool to implement strategy and convert the organization's vision into action by zeroing in on what needs to be done and how to accomplish it.

Consequently, the process for choosing indicators or metrics used by the measurement systems is similar and follows these general steps:

1. Use one of the IC models or adopt some classification of IC.
2. Identify the assets that will be monitored under each of the classes by determining the desired outcomes.
3. Determine the key success factors (KSFs) that will enable the attainment of the desired outcomes, and link them to financial performance.
4. Design indicators that monitor the KSFs.
5. Measure and track the indicators over a defined period of time.
6. Review and adjust.

In addition, all of the models stress that their real value lies in the message that management sends out to internal and external stakeholders on the value of the organization's IC and its capability to succeed in the future. The message is that financial measures alone do not reflect the real value of the organization or reflect its ability to perform and succeed. Using measures that monitor levels of employee competency, process or operational effectiveness, and customer satisfaction over and above financial measures sends the message that management is serious about leveraging the organization's IC.

Finally, all the measurement systems discussed here stress that despite the great value of and need for IC measurement systems they should not be used as control mechanisms or tied to employee evaluation or appraisals. Measures, no matter how balanced, are still subjective. Strict adherence and dependence on them when it comes to the management of human capital can stifle employee innovation and undermine morale.

The similarities of the systems makes one wonder how they are different. The U.S. Navy in its knowledge management model allows the use of any measurement system, presumably because of their striking similarities. The difference the Navy introduces is in defining what should get measured instead of how, as explored in Chapter 5. Nonetheless, looking at the development and purpose behind these systems highlights their different approaches. Differing approaches of these systems make them attractive to different types of organizations, which are distinguished by industry, size, and culture.

IC MEASUREMENT MODELS—AN OVERVIEW

First introduced in 1992 by Kaplan and Norton, the *BSC model* offers a balanced way to view business performance. The balance is achieved by considering the customer, internal business processes, and learning and growth perspectives over and above the financial perspective. In contrast to the BSC model is Sveiby's *IAM model.* While the BSC is presented as a complementary tool to the financial measurement system that acknowledges IC value, the IAM model shows a new way of doing business by focusing on the dynamics of IC development.

Sveiby identifies the outcomes that an IC management system should aim to achieve— namely, efficiency, stability, and growth—and thus focuses the use of indicators on monitoring these three dynamics under each form of IC. He both challenges the presupposed assumptions of the financial measurement system and applies these assumptions to IC.

Based on the BSC model, Skandia developed the *Navigator measurement system.*[15] Unlike the BSC model, the Navigator has a separate focus area for employees, called the human focus. But the difference goes much deeper. Like the IAM model, the Navigator is designed and implemented inside Skandia as a robust model aimed at changing the way business is done and not merely to complement the financial measurement system. The Navigator is not only a measurement system but forms the core of Skandia's business model. Each of the measurement systems has a leading proposition that affects the way it is designed and used. Following is a critical examination of each system.

The Balanced Scorecard

The leading proposition of the BSC model is that to fly an airplane, one indicator is not enough. Pilots need a complete control panel with indicators that measure various aspects of flight, such as altitude, temperature, and speed, to provide them with critical information as to the airplane's situation and performance in flight. The same is true for strategic planning. Financial measures provide insight into the "economic consequences of past actions,"[16] but can hardly predict the organization's capability to perform in the future. Though important, they are not by themselves sufficient. Dependence on financial measures alone is as dangerous as flying a plane with only one gauge. The BSC model attempts to present a balanced view of organizational performance by focusing on nonfinancial measures of performance as well. These measures are intended to focus the attention of top management on business factors that are critical to the success of the business, and hence are indicators of future performance.[17]

Under the BSC model, these factors fall under four perspectives: financial, customer, internal business process, and learning and growth. Each perspective presents an area where strategic focus should be directed. They all come together in the strategic planning phase in which an organization asks, "According to our future vision, how must we differentiate to shareholders (financial perspective) and customers (customer perspective) with internal processes (internal business process perspective) and with our ability to grow (learning and growth perspective)?"[18] Answers to this general question should lead to defining the critical success factors that will enable the organization to meet its strategic objectives under each of the perspectives by implementing various projects or initiatives. Indicators and measures are then created to monitor the progress of these initiatives to enable the organization to develop and implement its strategic plan by taking it to the operational level.[19]

At the operational level, focus seems to fragment over individual programs and processes; nevertheless, the organization should attempt to maintain a full "balanced" view of their performance. This balanced view is maintained by looking at the perspectives as a whole, as in the airplane control panel analogy. "Like a flight simulator, the scorecard should incorporate the complex set of cause-and-effect relationships among the critical variables, including leads, lags, and feedback loops, that describe the trajectory, the flight plan, of the strategy."[20] Two principles are incorporated in the BSC model that enable this holistic view, and the creation of a "connected BSC."

First, the BSC model incorporates measures that monitor cause-and-effect relationships between the various perspectives. Such measures try to monitor the effect that performance under one critical variable affects another variable in the same or another perspective, linking performance under all perspectives together. For example, improving employee satisfaction under the internal business perspective impacts customer satisfaction under the customer perspective, which in turn influences customer loyalty, which is eventually reflected in market share—the financial perspective.

Second, the BSC model incorporates measures to monitor both outcomes (lagging indicators) and performance drivers (leading indicators).[21] This is designed to assist management in focusing on both results of past action and drivers of future performance to have a more connected view.

Financial Perspective.[22]   In general, the strategic focus of the financial perspective is to determine how the organization should appear to its shareholders in order to achieve financial success. The strategic objectives are to increase profitability and generate cash flow. The main goal of measurement is to focus on measuring the contribution of the business strategy to the bottom line. Under this perspective, typical indicators include operating income, return on capital (asset or equity), and economic value added. This is the least controversial of all perspectives as it relates to measures and indicators that have been designed long ago or are based on them. The only difference is that now they are linked to other perspectives.

Customer Perspective.[23]   The strategic focus of the customer perspective is to determine how the organization should appear to its customers in order to achieve its vision. The strategic objectives are to identify the customer and market segments the business will compete in and the value propositions a business proposes to deliver. This defines the scope of measurement. What are needed here are measures that evaluate performance in the identified segments by reference to the value propositions that a business makes. Under this perspective, the typical indicators include customer satisfaction, retention rate, new customer acquisition, and market share in identified segments.

The definition of *customer* in the BSC model is much narrower than that developed by the IC concept, and excludes distributors, partners, and suppliers. In that respect, it does not accommodate the need, in the knowledge economy, to expand the definition of customers to include the various networks that an organization needs to achieve market success. The BSC customer perspective is limiting, despite the fact that it purports to measure the same indicators as the other systems.

Internal Business Process (IBP) Perspective.[24]   The strategic focus of the IBP perspective is to determine the business processes an organization must excel at to satisfy both its shareholders and customers. The strategic objectives are not merely to identify existing internal business processes, but also to identify new ones that may have the greatest impact on customer satisfaction and deliver greater financial returns to shareholders. Internal business processes are defined widely to include "long-term value creation wave" or innovation processes, and "short-term value creation wave" or production and other operations, and postsale services. Because these processes have different needs, they require separate treatment. The BSC model deals with them separately, which amounts to the creation of subperspectives. These subperspectives make the IBP perspective the most complex.

For the innovation process, the BSC model indicates that management should choose measures that enable a business to identify future customer preferences and deliver new products that satisfy such preferences. Typical indicators include percentage of sales from new products, new product introduction compared to competitors, time to develop next generation, and time-to-market.

For the operations process, management should focus its measures on the efficient, consistent, and timely delivery of products and services to customers. For this process, the authors suggest the use of many traditional indicators that have been developed to measure cost, quality, productivity, and cycle time.

For the postsale services process—which includes warranty, repair, and customer service—management should choose measures that ensure reliable, effective, and speedy service to customers. Typical indicators include time (response time to complaints), quality, and cost (number of customers handled on a service call).

When it comes to the service industry the authors add more measures designed to quantify how well the IBPs fare in delivery of service. Typical indicators include "long waiting times, inaccurate information, access denied or delayed, request or transaction not fulfilled, financial loss for customer, customer not treated as valued, and ineffective communication."[25]

Measures for operations and postsale service processes have been developed and experimented with by business for decades. Some are more recent than others, but they all attempt to measure efficiency and effectiveness against some action-oriented goals and are, therefore, easier to develop. It is only when they attempt to measure customer satisfaction, for example, that business needs to be more creative. Though this is not mentioned by the authors as one of the typical indicators under the customer perspective, it still seems an important indicator for the postsale service process. Even when it comes to the typical indicators relating to the innovation process, the ones chosen by the BSC model seem to relate to the new product development process and do not consider factors like employee empowerment or the motivation to innovate. This is partly considered, however, under the next perspective.

Learning and Growth Perspective.[26]   The strategic focus of the learning and growth perspective is to determine how the organization will sustain its ability to change and respond to change. The strategic objective here is to fill the gaps identified under the customer and internal business process perspectives in people, systems, and organizational procedures so that the organization can achieve long-term growth and improvement. In this respect, this perspective brings together measures that also may come under other perspectives. The goal of measurement here is to monitor how well the organization is building its infrastructure to facilitate learning and growth.

The authors divide the typical indicators under this perspective into three forms. There are indicators for people to monitor learning (e.g., employee satisfaction, retention rate, training, and skills); indicators for monitoring the IT system's efficiency, and provision of critical information to employees on the frontline to enable effective decision making; and indicators to monitor procedures to ensure that employees are motivated, empowered, and aligned with the organizational strategy.

It is interesting that under this perspective the authors focus on monitoring aspects that fall into the definition of human capital under the IC concept. The authors explain that under this perspective an organization can focus on development of its employees by identifying the core competencies the organization needs to meet its growth goals.

Is It Only a Control Panel of Measures?   According to the BSC Collaborative, in 2001, 40 percent of *Fortune* 500 companies in the United States had adopted the BSC model.[27] Despite its wide acceptance, the BSC model has been criticized on a number of grounds.

One criticism is the model's overreliance on measures. This is particularly true where measures are tied to employee evaluation and bonuses. Bonuses for branch managers of Citibank branches in California have been tied to BSC measures. The performance of each branch manager was evaluated as "below par," "par" or "above par," even though it is clearly stated in the company manual that lacking an objective indicator for people performance, evaluation and bonuses will be based on the subjective judgment of the branch manager's superior.[28]

Pfeffer and Sutton warn against such practices, citing a similar BSC implementation at a financial institution where the superior's evaluation of branch managers was conducted through quarterly meetings where they merely sat down and talked for half an hour. A branch manager who trained his team members and helped them move up was evaluated as "par" because he failed to retain talent in his team.[29] The branch manager was frustrated by the evaluation and could not understand how his performance could be evaluated as "par" when he was developing talent in the division as a whole. Such use of measurement has an adverse effect on employee morale, satisfaction, and loyalty. On a similar note, Sveiby expresses frustration with executives from the United States and Australia who approach him to implement his model to gain "control" of their employees.[30]

Furthermore, overreliance on measures of any type in ICM hampers the application of tacit knowledge and wisdom. With heavily regulated measures, management is limited in its use of tacit knowledge, as it must justify its decisions by reference to measures. These problems can be avoided simply by not tying measures to performance, and by using measures as a guide rather than a straitjacket. However, problems with the BSC model go deeper.

Because the BSC model is not based on an IC model, it can be implemented under any business model. As such, it is based on the assumption that to enhance future performance in the new economy all an organization needs to do is to widen and balance its perspectives to include non-financial perspectives. Though useful in bringing some forms of IC to the attention of top management through the strategic planning phase, it fails to challenge or transform the underlying business management model. In that respect, the BSC model seems to be more suited to organizations that are not ready to transform the way they do business but still want to find a way to recognize and measure IC. It is important to understand that if the organization's business model accommodates the IC concept, then the BSC model is as good as any other IC measurement system. Otherwise, the traditional business management model of control will permeate the BSC model and eventually render it yet another control mechanism.

Another criticism of the BSC model, which applies to the other IC measurement systems as well, is its complexity and the time and cost required for its implementation compared to its "low ease of use."[31] The complexity and difficulty lie in the choice of effective measures. Roos et al. explain that for performance measures to be effective they have to be reliable and consistent with the actions of the unit, and with the short- and long-term goals of the whole organization.[32] Finding measures that are specific to the unit, yet general enough to reflect the strategy of the organization, and that incorporate long- and short-term views seems to be too optimistic. Consider the example of the branch manager discussed earlier; although he was losing talent on his team, he was developing human capital for other divisions, units, and the organization as a whole. This may be the reason the BSC model's authors stress the need to apply the model as a guide, not a full-blown plan.

Moreover, it may be a stretch to say that the BSC model creates an IC language in an organization. Even though it imparts IC jargon, its implementation does not require an underlying IC model. Challenging traditional business models and transforming an organization's understanding and resultant management of IC is what Sveiby sets out to achieve with his IAM model.

The Intangible Asset Monitor—IC Measurement Is Not a Science But a Language

Sveiby's pioneering contribution to the field of ICM is in challenging the assumptions that form the basis of financial measurement. He digs deep to examine value judgments that are traditionally used to describe financial measures as objective, and nonfinancial ones as subjective. He explains that financial measures only seem objective because they are widespread and have been in use over long periods of time. As a result, standards have been set and defined and hence, enjoy a certain degree of consistency and comparability. Standards define the set of assumptions on which a measurement system is based and impart an element of objectivity. What proves Sveiby's point is that such nonfinancial measures like the number of units produced per hour or room occupancy rate seem more objective when compared with the relatively recent ones like employee and customer satisfaction rates.

Sveiby resists expressing performance measures whenever possible in monetary units. He explains that financial measures use money simply as a "proxy for human effort."[33] What financials try to measure is the efficiency of the organization in using its capabilities regardless of what it produces. Thus, though monetary measures are suitable in some situations, like in the ROI ration, other nonmonetary units may be more effective in expressing the efficiency of the organization in using its capabilities, especially the intellectual ones, or as Sveiby prefers to call them, *intangible assets.* Therefore, Sveiby explains, proxies other than money are needed to measure intangibles[34] through the development of performance measures (e.g., units per hour). One problem identified by Sveiby is that despite the development of measures, they were not developed by academics and thus lack a coherent theoretical framework that fits the knowledge economy.[35] Sveiby attempts to develop such a framework by providing insight into what he calls *intangible revenues* and the nature of investment in intangible assets.

A third tendency that Sveiby strongly warns against is the use of performance measures to monitor employee performance. According to Sveiby, use of such measures to "control subordinates" is the "legacy of a long passed industrial era."[36] This will only stifle the employee's capacity to create and adversely affect performance. Alternatively, to monitor the performance of employees and the organization as a whole, Sveiby designed the IAM model, to create a new language that informs management of what to focus on.

In conceiving the IAM model, Sveiby examined the goals of financial measurement systems to determine yardsticks for IC measurement. Financial measures, according to Sveiby, attempt to measure the efficiency of the organization in general. Similarly, the IAM model attempts to measure intangible assets by a standard of efficiency. The degree to which an organization can sustain its performance in a certain area is its stability/risk standard. The third standard is that of growth/renewal, which indicate performance in areas of growth.

The three standards—efficiency, stability/risk, and growth/renewal—are then applied to the three forms of IC in Sveiby's model, namely, external structure, internal structure, and competency. The crossover between these forms and the three standards creates a matrix of nine cells, where a few measures are chosen under each cell. Because the IAM model aims to create a new language, Sveiby favors the use of one to two indicators in each cell. Though the indicators should be designed to reflect the strategy and goals of each organization, Sveiby provides a view of some typical measures, which follow.[37] It should be noted, however, that Sveiby's examples are based on the service industry and hence some of the examples do not apply to other industries.

External Structure.   Measuring external structure under the three standards will enable an organization to monitor its performance in relation to customers and other external players. First, the growth standard measures the increase of business from existing customers, while renewal focuses on growth resulting from innovating new products, gaining new customers, or entering new markets. Under this criterion, Sveiby includes "image-enhancing customers" as a measure that introduces intangible revenues into the business.

Efficiency is measured in terms of profitability and sales per customer. Sveiby explains that costs and profitability are usually monitored in reference to products or functions and not customers, despite the fact that 80 percent of customer sales are not profitable. Again, this seems to be specific for the service industries, though it may also be applied to customer service segments in other industries.

For stability, the IAM model includes indicators like a customer satisfaction index, the proportion of business from big customers, and the frequency of repeat orders. All are designed to show the level of risk associated with the customer base.

Internal Structure.   Measuring internal structure involves monitoring the support structure, taking into consideration general management, administration, accounting, personnel, maintenance, information systems, and other routine operations. Indicators showing how investment in new systems, such as IT systems, improves performance monitor growth of the internal structure. Internal structure can be calculated as the increase in percentage of sales or percentage of value added. Celemi,[38] a Swedish company that produces learning products, expresses product research and development in terms of a percentage of value added as another indicator. Under renewal, the typical indicator is percentage of products introduced in the last few years. IAM adds to this the number of new processes implemented regardless of their size to show that new processes are being developed without any assessment of their value.

For efficiency, the IAM model looks at the proportion of support staff to the total number of employees. Sveiby explains that by monitoring the change in this percentage, an organization can monitor efficiency. However, without tying this indicator to the size of operations, it is unclear how it can reflect efficiency. Nonetheless, as shown in Celemi's 1995 Annual Report, explanations are necessary to interpret these indicators by reference to other changes in the company. For example, in 1995, Celemi's Annual Report compared two indicators under this cell, explaining that though the change in proportion of administrative staff increased by 4% compared to 1994, the rate of sales per administrative staff declined by 20%. Celemi explains that because the company is growing in size, they recently employed a large number of administrative staff personnel that have yet to jump the learning curve before their efficiency goes up. This shows why explanations are necessary to interpret these indicators. It is not far-fetched that, with time, management will become more conversant in the new language, not needing to look at such interpretations to understand how IC is performing.

For stability, Sveiby suggests adding a "values and attitude measurement" that indicates the culture of the organization and how pleasant the workplace is. Celemi opted not to use such an indicator in its reports. It is doubtful that the culture factor can be dealt with as part of a measurement system.[39]

Instead, Celemi uses other IAM indicators in this cell, namely, support staff turnover and the "rookie ratio" (the ratio of staff employed in the last two years). The latter is used as an indicator for stability as it typically takes two years before new recruits are accustomed to the internal structure or the way the organization does business, and thus are able to sustain and improve it.

Competency. Measuring competency under the IAM model is limited to indicators that measure the competency of "professional" employees as Sveiby defines them. Sveiby hints that though the competency of outside experts and suppliers is not included as part of the organizational competency, that may change as organizations become more "virtual."[40] To measure competency, the IAM model presents innovative and radical indicators. As mentioned earlier, it is in the area of measuring human capital, as opposed to the measurement of processes and technology systems, that innovation is needed. The first thing the IAM model demonstrates is how to classify competencies in an organization according to areas of expertise, then apply the suggested indicators to measure the level of competency according to the three standards. For competency, Sveiby goes against his own advice of limiting the number of indicators in each cell to one or two and uses four to six for each cell.

Under growth and renewal the number of years in the profession are measured to monitor experience, level of education, competency-enhancing customers (based on the same concept as image-enhancing customers), training and education costs, competency index, and diversity. The last three indicators are the most innovative. The competency index attempts to create a comparable generic measure of competency by multiplying years in the profession by years employed in the organization by the level of education. Sveiby explains that once these data are collected, management can then use statistical methods to track how the index develops in various fields of expertise through time.

Competency turnover compares the competency (calculated as number of years in the profession) of those who left the organization with that of new professionals, to assess the gain or loss in years of experience in the competency of the organization. This indicator limits the definition of competency to the years of experience; however, experience cannot necessarily be equated with competency.

The third indicator looks at the percentage of women who are professional employees. Research has shown that a higher percentage of professional women in an organization translates into a more innovative workforce. This indicator has been used by a number of Skandia companies. For efficiency, the IAM model divides the number of professionals in the organization by the number of employees,[41] which is called the leverage effect, value added (or profit) per employee and per professional.

For stability, the IAM model measures the average age, seniority, or years with the same organization; relative pay position compared to other organizations in the industry; and professional turnover rate. According to Sveiby, older people are more stable than their younger counterparts in that they tend to stay with an organization longer. However, this indicator should be used with care, as an increase in average age would also indicate a decrease in drive. Like the turnover rate,[42] average years should be kept in balance.

Talking IC? The use of standards of efficiency, stability, and renewal in the IAM model outlines the factors that should be monitored to measure IC, and thus provides structured guidance to management on the purpose and benefits of working with a measurement system. It provides different lenses through which to see measurement and imparts more significance into the quest of developing measures. These models do not merely measure human, customer, or organizational capital in the abstract, but rather measure whether the IC of the organization is being managed in a way that ensures increased organizational efficiency, stability, and growth. Over time standards help to streamline the activity measured and build consistency on what is being measured. Departments or units in an organization are assessed, as much as possible, on the same factors. Whether this is credible or not is a question that requires more research before it can be answered. Still, assessing divisions on the same measurement criteria or through use of the same indicators is not something that Skandia gives priority to in its measurement system; which it sees as a big experiment.

The Navigator—Do Not Plan, Navigate

The leading feature of Skandia's Navigator is its flexibility. The companies that comprise the Skandia Corporation, maybe even departments in these companies, are not required to adopt a set form or number of measures. They are not even required to report on the same indicators from year to year, because the Navigator is primarily seen as a navigation tool and not one that provides detailed implementation guidelines. Despite its pioneering work and leadership in measuring IC, Skandia still believes in the value of learning through taking an experimental approach. Nevertheless, the Navigator is adopted widely across Skandia and has been incorporated in the MIS system of Skandia under the Dolphin system.

Skandia applies the BSC idea to the Navigator by applying measures to monitor critical business success factors under each of five focuses: financial, human, process, customer, and renewal. Under the Navigator model, the measuring entity—whether the organization or individual business units or departments—asks the question, "What are the critical factors that enable us to achieve success under each of the focus areas?" Then a number of indicators designed to reflect both present and future performance under these factors are chosen.

Edvinsson explains[43] that the measuring entity may also have a different starting point by asking, "What are the key success factors for the measuring entity in general?" The entity then asks, "What are the indicators that are needed to monitor present and future performance for the chosen success factors?" Once these are determined, as many measures as necessary are chosen to monitor them. Finally, these measures are examined and placed under the five focuses depending on what they purport to measure.

For example, SkandiaLink asked senior managers to identify five separate key success factors for the company in 1997. These included establishing long-term relationships with satisfied customers, establishing long-term relationships with distributors (particularly banks), implementing efficient administrative routines, creating an IT system that supports operations, and employing satisfied and competent employees. Each of these "success factors" generated a set of indicators, and a total of 24 were selected for tracking. For the satisfied customer factor, for example, this generated the following indicators:

- Satisfied customer index
- Customer barometer
- New sales
- Market share
- Lapse rate
- Average response time at the call center
- Discontinued calls at the call center
- Average handling time for completed cases
- Number of new products[44]

These indicators are then grouped under the various focuses. As key success factors change, the overall set of indicators for a certain period (strategic phase) that the Navigator model monitors also changes. Not only does the Navigator allow this high level of flexibility in the choice of indicators from time to time, but it also encourages individual employees to express their goals and monitor their own and their team's performance.

In one example, the Navigator model was used by Skandia's corporate IT to monitor its vision of making IT the company's competitive edge. To that end, the IT department used the following measures: Under the financial focus, the department measured return on capital employed, operating results, and value added/employee. The customer focus looked at the contracts that the department handled for Skandia-affiliated companies. The indicators included number of contracts, savings/contract, surrender ratio, and points of sale. The human focus tracked number of full-time employees, number of managers, number of female managers, and training expense/ employee. Under the process focus the department measured the number of contracts per employee, administrative expense/gross premiums written, and IT/administrative expense.[45]

In Skandia's IC Supplement, published in 1994,[46] each of Skandia's companies reported and monitored a different set of indicators reflecting the strategies and key success factors of each. The number of indicators under each focus and the factors that each company attempted to monitor were different, with the exception of recurring generic indicators like customer and employee satisfaction. But even with generic measures, the same measures were not used consistently. For example, two out of five companies looked at employee turnover, as an indicator of employee satisfaction under the human focus, while the other companies focused on the number of full-time employees in addition to or instead of training hours. As a result, the number of indicators generated for the whole organization was enormous.

Compared to the BSC model, where the measures are more or less prescribed, the Navigator's underlying philosophy allows for multiple variations. The underlying philosophy is to provide the highest level of flexibility within a defined framework. Skandia wants the Navigator to be a tool for plotting a course rather than a detailed guideline. The details can be filled in later as management steers the business toward meeting its strategic goals. Being flexible and idiosyncratic to the needs of the measuring unit, the Navigator ensures that the whole organization talks IC, while at the same time allowing each measuring unit to develop its own dialect.

Despite inconsistencies and the huge number of indicators generated,[47] Skandia automated the Navigator, through the Dolphin system, and incorporated it into its management information system (MIS). With time the Dolphin system will probably lead to streamlining the various "navigators," and give rise to a more consistent set of indicators through sharing and communication. It seems that Skandia is serious about communication despite the inconsistency of the measures used; to an extent that it reported these measures to external stakeholders. In 1993, Skandia appointed an IC (as opposed to financial) controller to "systemically develop intellectual capital information and accounting systems, which can then be integrated with traditional financial accounting."[48] Though IC reporting requires more consistent measures, or a well-defined model, Skandia appears determined to balance between its desire to provide transparency on how their organization is being run while continuing to experiment with the Navigator.

THE VALUE OF IC MEASUREMENT SYSTEMS— WHERE DOES ALL THIS LEAVE US?

The IC measurement systems all serve, in their unique ways, to ground ICM in the everyday reality of business and to monitor the achievement of projected goals. Over time, this can transform organizational behavior and routines and equip top and frontline management to appreciate the value of IC both internally and externally. But the question remains: Does the IC model offer more than the creation of a new IC vocabulary? Does it provide more than the general contention that management should give more attention to the development of their IC? Does the IC model provide guidance as to how IC can be managed in a business to yield results, beyond general propositions?

Visiting S.A. Armstrong Limited, Charles Armstrong[49] showed me a desk pad depicting a three-circle IC model. Everyone in the company has access to this pad. He explained how distributing the pad to all employees makes them feel their input is welcomed and valued (transfer of human to structural capital), and that they should tap into customer knowledge to perfect their work (transfer of customer to human to structural capital), which affects the overall culture and management of the company. But when it came to the measurement system that Mr. Armstrong developed (attempting to measure the flows of value creation), he explained that it is impossible to implement. (On a humorous note, Mr. Armstrong made the remark that I am welcome to apply for a patent on the method.)

The IC models at best provide a tool to communicate the importance and value of IC throughout the organization, but fail to provide any guidance to business leaders and managers on how IC should be managed. It is true that the measurement systems took the IC model from the theoretical to the practical level by defining the outcomes and results that managers should aim for in managing IC. That may suffice if managing IC is considered as a defined procedure directed at achieving particular results, but it certainly is not sufficient to guide the development of a model for business management in the knowledge economy where IC makes 80 percent of business value. Attempting to define and manage IC without putting it in the context and reality of business management reduces the IC concept and models to an academic pursuit. ICM should be at the crux of business management and not a mere management tool. For that to happen, a comprehensive approach that matches between the elementary functions of business management and ICM is essential, hence the comprehensive approach to intellectual capital management (CICM), outlined in Chapter 4. But first let's explore the question of IC reporting.

NOTES

[1] *Merriam-Webster Collegiate Dictionary,* available online at *www.m-w.com.*

[2] J. Roos, G. Roos, L. Edvinsson, and N. Dragonetti, *Intellectual Capital: Navigating in the New Business Landscape* (New York: New York University Press, 1998), p. 27.

[3] See L. Edvinsson and M. Malone, *Intellectual Capital* (New York: Harper Business, 1997), p. 146. The authors give credit for the creation of this model to Hubert St. Onge, Charles Armstrong, Gordon Petrash, and Leif Edvinsson.

[4] Haanes, K. and Lowendahl, B., "The Unit of Activity: Towards An Alternative to the Theories of the Firm," in Thomas, et. al. (eds), *Strategy, Structure and Style* (New York: John Wiley & Sons, Inc., 1997).

[5] Margaret Blair and Steven Wallman, *Unseen Wealth: Report of the Brookings Task Force on Understanding Intangible Sources of Value,* 2000, Appendix A "Human Capital Sub-Group Report," available at *www.brook.edu/es/research/projects/intangibles/doc/sub_hcap.htm.*

[6] K. E. Sveiby, *The New Organizational Wealth: Measuring and Managing Intangible Resources* (San Francisco: Berrett-Koehler Publishers, 1997). Also see *www.sveiby.com.au/articles/emergingstandard.html.*

[7] Supra note 3.

[8] Supra note 3, pp. 34–52.

[9] Roos et al. at p. 54 develop a table that lists 49 "flows" of value from one form of capital to another. The various types of capital listed including competency, attitude, intellectual agility, relationship, organizational, renewal and development, and financial.

[10] D. Andriessen, "Weightless Wealth: Four Modifications to Standard IC Theory," *Journal of Intellectual Capital,* Vol. 2 No. 3, pp. 204–214. Also see D. Andriessen and R. Tissen, *Weightless Wealth* (Upper Saddle River, NJ: Prentice Hall, 2001).

[11] C.K. Prahalad and G. Hamel, "The Core Competence of the Corporation," *Harvard Business Review,* May–June 1990, p. 79. Prahalad and Hamel explain that organizations usually possess five to ten core competencies, which determine the sources available to them to introduce new products or enter new markets. They contend that corporations should be guided by an understanding of their core competencies when devising their growth and innovation strategies.

[12] *Id.*

[13] For more on performance measures, see R. Eccles, "The Performance Measurement Manifesto," *Harvard Business Review,* January–February 1991, p. 131. Also refer to Chapter 5 for the Navy's system of performance measures for knowledge management.

[14] European Organization and C. Fornell, "A National Customer Satisfaction Barometer: The Swedish Experience," *Journal of Marketing,* 1992, pp. 6–21. Also see *American Customer Satisfaction Index* (ACSI), established in 1994 by the National Quality Research Center of the University of Michigan.

[15] Skandia designed the Navigator as a comprehensive model for the management of intellectual capital. The measurement system is only part of it. For the purposes of this chapter, only the measurement system of the Navigator will be explored. Chapter 9 will examine Skandia's ICM model as a whole.

[16] R. Kaplan and D. Norton, *The Balanced Scorecard: Translating Strategy into Action* (Boston: Harvard Business School Press, 1996), p. 25.

[17] *Id.,* p. 7.

[18] *Id.*

[19] Though the authors stress that their model is one for strategic implementation and not strategic formulation, it is hard to see how asking the posed questions would not satisfy both functions.

[20] Supra note 14, p. 30.

[21] *Id.*

[22] *Id.,* pp. 25–29.

[23] *Id.*

[24] *Id.,* pp. 92–123.

[25] *Id.,* p. 120.

[26] *Id.,* pp. 92–123.

[27] R. Kwon, "A Strategic Measure of IT Value," *Baseline,* October 2001.

[28] Simmons, R. and Davila, A. "Citibank: Performance Evaluation," Harvard Business School Case # 198-048. (1997).

[29] J. Pfeffer and R. Sutton, *The Knowing–Doing Gap* (Boston: Harvard Business School Press, 1999), pp. 149–150.

[30] K.E. Sveiby, "Measuring Intangibles and Intellectual Capital," in Morey, Maybury, and Rhuraisingham (editors), *Knowledge Management: Classic and Contemporary Works* (Cambridge: The MIT Press, 2000), pp. 337–354.

[31] Supra note 2, p. 22.

[32] *Id.*

[33] Supra note 28, p. 343.

[34] K.E. Sveiby, "The Intangible Assets Monitor," 1997, available online at *www.sveiby.com.au/ articles/IntangAss/CompanyMonitor.html.*

[35] *Id.*

[36] Supra note 28, p. 352.

[37] For all the measures mentioned, see Sveiby, "Measuring External Structure," *www.sveiby.com. au/articles/MeasureExternalStructure.html;* "Measuring Internal Structure," *www.sveiby.com. au/articles/MeasureInternalStructure.html;* and "Measuring Competency," *www.sveiby.com.au/ articles/MeasureCompetency.html.*

[38] Celemi is a Swedish company in the area of learning products. Celemi has been using the IAM model to report on its intellectual capital to its shareholders since 1990.

[39] To the contrary, I believe culture warrants separate thorough treatment, as will be explained in Chapter 10, since one needs to understand the culture before attempting to monitor it for positive change.

[40] A tendency that a number of organizations are moving to and will move to as the Internet and networking change the way business is done and organizations envision themselves. An example of such a business model is that developed by Cisco Systems, Inc. For more information see, Nolan, R., Porter, K. and Akers, C., "Cisco Systems Architecture: ERP and Web-Enabled IT," Harvard Business School Case # 301-099, 2001.

[41] Sveiby claims this shows how important professionals are to the firm, which can be compared with other companies or other areas in the same company. Celemi opts not to use this measure in its IAM. See Sveiby, *Measuring Competency,* supra note 34.

[42] *Id.* Sveiby explains that a "very low turnover rate (below 5%) suggests a stable but not dynamic situation. A very high turnover rate (above 20%) usually suggests that people are dissatisfied."

[43] Supra note 2, pp. 70–71.

[44] *Id.*

[45] *Visualizing Intellectual Capital in Skandia,* Supplement to Skandia's Annual Report, 1994. (Not all departments reported under all five focuses.)

[46] *Id.*

[47] The compilation of indicators for all of Skandia may amount to 164 or more indicators. Edvinsson undertakes research attempts to compile these measures. In L. Edvinsson and M. Malone, *Intellectual Capital: Realizing Your Company's True Value by Finding Its Hidden Brainpower* (New York: Harper Business, 1997), p. 164, Edvinsson explores the use of a "coefficient of intellectual capital." In J. Roos, G. Roos, L. Edvinsson, and N. Dragonetti, *Intellectual Capital: Navigating in the New Business Landscape* (New York: New York University Press, 1998), Edvinsson and others explore the creation of of indices to enable comparisons over time between the various indicators.

[48] R. Lusch and M. Harvey, "The Case for an Off-Balance-Sheet Controller," *Sloan Management Review,* Winter 1994, pp. 101–105.

[49] Charles Armstrong is the President of S.A. Armstrong Limited, a Canadian manufacturing company, and one of the authors of the IC models.

3

Intellectual Capital Reporting

THE LIMITATION OF FINANCIAL REPORTING

> [O]ur current system—through its continual devotion to a traditional "reliability" standard—is actually producing less-reliable information, if viewed as the total picture.
> —Steven Wallman, Former US Securities Exchange Commissioner[1]

Financial reports and statements are far from accurate in communicating the real value of the enterprise and its future performance potential. Companies that are publicly traded are valued by the market at multiples of their book value, sometimes as high as 20 times. Of course, a percentage of this market value can be attributed to market emotion and error. But when nearly 80 percent of corporate business assets are made of intellectual capital, and where financial reports report only on the 20 percent tangible assets, one starts to wonder about the accuracy and efficacy of these reports in reflecting the value of the enterprise and its future performance potential. Analysts, investors, CFOs, and accountants have all developed, in their own way, analytical tools and techniques to overcome its limitations. For internal management purposes, performance measures have played a major role in overcoming these limitations. Analysts developed analytical tools to value a company performance beyond financial results, taking into consideration factors like leadership, human resources, patents, brands, and specialized workforce. In addition, many companies, to reduce the amount of analysts and market speculation, voluntarily disclose information about their strategy, management objectives, and key success factors in supplements to their financial reports.

Lacking a formal standardized system for reporting on IC, investors, analysts, and companies will remain captive to this game of speculation and incomplete and inconsistent disclosures. In the industrial economy, this related only to around 20 percent of business assets, and thus was not a significant component that warrants changing or challenging the 500-year-old accounting system. But when IC forms 80 percent of corporate America and corporate wealth in developed economies, creating formal standards becomes of significant importance both from a micro- and macroeconomic perspective. At the micro level, lacking consistent procedures and standards to report on IC leads to confusion, dissipation of intellectual resources and assets for lack of management focus, and overemphasis on short-term financial gains rather than long-term and sustained performance. At the macro level, it creates confusion as to the actual state of the economy as there is no accurate reflection or measure of the wealth of corporations.

One of the reasons frequently cited against reporting externally on IC is the risk that such information may be competitively harmful to the reporting company. However, imposing such reporting on all publicly traded companies would probably reduce this risk considerably. This is because such companies will be reporting the same type of information under the same standards, and will thus be subject to the same consistent and comparable measures. In fact the increasing voluntary disclosures made by companies to report on their IC in annual reports, in the United States and

Europe, reflects their dissatisfaction with the existing reporting model to communicate their real value to stakeholders. But voluntary disclosure alone cannot be the solution, particularly when the comparability of such disclosures is negligible.

Indeed, it seems that the risks created by not reporting on IC outweigh by far the risks posed to the competitive position of the company. Consider this situation for an example. Companies have bitterly found how their stock prices can suffer if they miss their price/earning ratio's projections even slightly. This happens despite the fact that they may be doing extremely well given the market conditions. The reason behind this is not that investors are emotional, but simply that in the absence of better measures, investors and some analysts take that slightest miss to mean a weakness in the company's competitive position and management ability. If analysts and investors had better indicators of the company's future earning potential then they would be in a better position to make more informed decisions, and thus not merely react to short-term results.

There is no doubt that reporting on the critical intellectual drivers of value is of utmost importance to both the company and the economy as a whole. One of the major hurdles hampering the development of IC reporting, however, is the mystification surrounding the subject. In the United States, both the Securities and Exchange Commission (SEC) and the Financial Accounting Standards Board (FASB)[2] examined and confirmed the need for IC reporting.[3] Both have concluded, however, that before setting any standards, time should be allowed for IC reporting models to develop beyond their current rudimentary state. The case is very similar in other developed economies, and despite the large number of studies and reports on the subject to date no standardized model has emerged. Part of the mystification is caused by the divergent accounting approaches that developed to deal with IC reporting. Not only have two divergent approaches emerged to deal with IC reporting but there are variances in dealing with different types of IC under each of the approaches.

ANALYZING IC REPORTING INITIATIVES—
THE TWO APPROACHES

The first approach to IC reporting incorporates reporting on limited and defined items of IC as part of the financial accounting system. Under that approach there is a potent inconsistency in reporting on acquired as opposed to internally developed intellectual assets, creating even more confusion and unbalanced treatment. Despite this, the first approach fits with the 500-year-old tradition and thus is one which allows slow yet sure adjustment of some of the limitations of the financial reporting system. The problem, however, is that these changes are not based on a well-thought-out methodology, or review of the accounting/reporting system but rather are spurred by market and investors' pressures.

The second approach goes beyond the traditional accounting system and develops a new language to report on IC. Being a new language, the second approach suffers from inconsistency in definitions and choice of measures, and built-in idiosyncrasies caused by lack of agreed-upon standards. The following is an examination of these two approaches.

The First Approach—IC Reporting in Financial Statements

In the United States and other developed economies, certain types of IC have made it into the financial reports. To date the most tangible forms of IC, also known as hard assets—intellectual property or structural capital— are the ones that made this leap. Still, reporting on a collection of "soft" IC or assets is allowed by reporting on acquired goodwill. Some changes have happened in the United States in 2001 to distinguish between the two—the identifiable intangible assets and the general pool of intangible assets that can be grouped as goodwill—again only in relation to acquired assets. Now corporations in the United States are required not only to report on the acquired intangible assets and goodwill but to reevaluate them periodically. This has directed top management attention to the role of IC reporting in the United States, as now they have to continually assess the value of at least their acquired IC. The divergence in dealing with acquired and internally developed IC remains one of the main malfunctions of this approach. Let's have a closer look.

Acquired Intangible Assets.   Financial Accounting Standard (FAS) No. 141 (Business Combinations) and FAS No. 142 (Goodwill and other Intangibles), effective June 30, 2001, introduced the following changes:

- Eliminated pooling of interests requiring companies to report on all acquired intangibles.
- Eliminated the amortization[4] of goodwill. Goodwill now should be examined and separated from identifiable intangible assets (e.g., brands, patents and contractual agreements). Goodwill comprises all other unidentifiable elements that enhance the future earning potential of the company (e.g., corporate image and customer loyalty). Goodwill should then be allocated to a reporting unit where its value should be subject to impairment tests[5] on an annual basis, or completely written off, whenever circumstances warrant such adjustment.
- Identifiable intangible assets[6] are separated and treated according to their useful lives. Assets with indefinite life are to be treated similarly to goodwill, while those with a definite useful life are to be amortized over their useful life. Both types should be allocated to a reporting unit, and in the latter case impairment tests are carried whenever circumstances warrant, to adjust for changes in the value or the useful life.

The new rules are promising, as the accounting community is increasingly acknowledging the need for transparency in relation to merger transactions which are arguably driven by the need to strengthen the IC of the enterprise. The rules, which are similar to standards developed by the International Accounting Standards Committee (IASC), coupled with the lack of reporting on similar IC assets just because they are developed internally, rather than acquired, may grievously misrepresent the value of the IC base of the enterprise. Reporting only on acquired items of IC while failing to report on similar internally developed items will not only deepen the disparities between the actual and reported value of the enterprise, but may also result in an erroneous valuation of the enterprise. This risk is multiplied even further by disparities created by the rules pertaining to reporting on internally developed intellectual assets, as outlined next.

Internally Developed Intangible Assets.   Internally developed intangible assets are treated differently under accounting rules and standards. Investments in the development of intangible assets and IC are generally treated as costs that should be written off as incurred, a method referred to as *expensing.* Seen as a business expense rather than investment in assets, expenditures on developing intangible assets suffer under the constant pressure on organizations to cut their business expenses and show short-term profits. If seen as investment, then such costs can be accounted as assets on the basis that they will create future value (generate revenue or save cost) over their useful lives, a method referred to as capitalizing. The strong contrast in the accounting principles as they stand now is that acquired intangibles are capitalized (and hence amortized over their useful life) while their internally developed counterparts have to be expensed.

The rationale of the FASB behind this differential treatment is the uncertainty involved regarding returns from developing intangible assets. Opinion No. 17 provides that the cost of developing intangible assets may be capitalized only if the period of expected future benefits can be determined. FASB Statement No. 2 took the position that research and development (R&D) costs should be expensed based on the high degree of uncertainty and the lack of causal relationship between R&D costs and the benefits received. FAS No. 86 on the other hand modifies this slightly when it comes to computer software programs and provides that costs can be capitalized after the technological feasibility[7] of the software has been established, and be amortized on a product-by-product basis over the useful life. It is hard to see why the same standard cannot be applied to development of other intangibles upon establishing their technological or market feasibility.

The latter is the position taken by the IASC and a number of European accounting standards boards. For example the Netherlands allows the capitalization of both research and development costs while New Zealand allows the capitalization of development costs only. Germany on the other hand requires the expensing of both. It is worth noting that both Australia and the United Kingdom allow for the capitalization of the costs of brand development, unlike the United States.

The importance of IC, or as the FASB calls it intangible assets, to the performance of the company is clearly demonstrated by the various assets that forced their way into financial statements. It is true that to a great extent the most tangible forms of IC, also called hard assets—intellectual property or structural capital—are the ones that made this leap. Still, the preservation of goodwill as a collection of soft IC or assets, despite the strict scrutiny of corporate acquisitions—provided by the requirement of separating goodwill from identifiable intangible assets and reevaluating its value—is a positive indication. The rules, however, create confusion and inconsistency by treating identical items of IC differently based on whether they are internally developed or acquired, and whether R&D relates to software or other technology. The question also still remains on the viability of financial reporting to reflect the value of human and customer capital to the organization's future earning potential. The rules developed under the first approach not only fall short of reporting on all types of IC but they also confuse IC reporting by mixing and matching depending on the pressures of the time instead of developing a comprehensive approach. That is when initiatives developed under the second approach come in with attempts to develop new methodologies to address the dilemma of IC reporting. To that we now turn.

The Second Approach—Separate IC Reporting Models

The various measurement systems that have been developed for internal management and tracking of IC, discussed in Chapter 2, have been used in some cases to externally report on IC. This was made through incorporating IC supplements to the annual reports. Skandia's Navigator and Sveiby's Intangible Assets Monitor have both been used for that purpose. The authors of the Balanced Scorecard (BSC) have also remarked that the BSC can be used for that purpose as well. Despite the attraction of these various models in providing a high degree of transparency as to the organization's operations, IC wealth and its management goals and procedures, they hardly provide a common standard for IC reporting. This is because all these systems are situation specific, and are thus idiosyncratic to the needs, strategic objectives, and performance goals of the measuring unit. When it comes to the Navigator, for example, this is evident from the fact that companies in the Skandia group differ as to the indicators they monitor depending on the critical success factor identified for each business. The same is true of the BSC, where the authors repeatedly stress that indicators should be devised in accordance with strategic goals. Thus, unless performance goals and strategic goals can be normalized across industries and companies, it is hard to see how these measurement models can be used for IC reporting.

The concept and practice of developing performance measures provides a firm basis for the development of IC reporting models, provided standard performance goals that are common within and across industries can be identified. This is the basis of the IC reporting model that I developed and present at the end of this chapter. But for now, let's look at the various attempts in the United States and around the globe to develop formulae, indicators, and systems to report on IC. A nonexhaustive list of examples is presented.

THE U.S. EXPERIENCE

Science and Technology Indicators

Developed by the Technology Administration of the Department of Commerce, the science and technology indicators monitor and report on various indicators in the fifty states. These indicators include input measures that stimulate science and technology like funding in flows, human resources, capital investments and business assistance; and outcome measures that report on the high-tech intensity of the state's business base, and other outcome measures (e.g., patents, earnings, and workforce employment). These reports are made available to states to consult for their economic development plans, and also to investors and the general public.

New Economy Index

Similar to the science and technology indicators, the Progressive Policy Institute developed the New Economy Index, which compares between states according to a number of measures including the level of education of the workforce, the numbers employed in high-tech sectors, the number of patents issued, and others. These findings are used to influence the formulation of economic policies.

CHI Research

A private company that developed indicators to report on the technological prowess of companies by analyzing patent data, CHI has created a number of indicators to measure patent citations and technology cycle times, and to create the innovation index. The same measures are developed for countries in specific technological areas. These indicators are used by many analysts and investors to compare between various companies.

The Knowledge Scorecard

A method developed by Baruch Lev, New York University professor of accounting and finance, and Marc Bothwell, portfolio manager at Credit Suisse Asset Management to estimate overall return on IC, or what the authors call knowledge assets. The method is based on a number of assumptions. First, that physical and financial assets produce an annual after-tax return of 7 percent and 4.5 percent, respectively. Second, the remaining earnings after discounting those related to tangible assets can be attributed to knowledge assets with a discount rate of 10.5 percent. Calculating return on knowledge assets, the method uses an average of actual earnings for three past years and stock analysts' forecasts of earnings for three years into the future. The authors use this method to evaluate the knowledge capital of companies and industries. Though this method is based on the simple formula used by IC theorists (i.e., Intellectual Capital = Market capitalization − net book value), it adds another layer of accuracy. Similar methods of calculation include Tobin's Q formula by Nobel Prize winner James Tobin of Yale University, and NCI Research Calculated Intangible Value (CIV) formula.[8]

THE EUROPEAN EXPERIENCE

Swedish Companies

Skandia is the prime example of a Swedish company that reports annually on its IC. In addition, there are a number of companies that employ Sveiby's Intangible Asset Monitor to report on their IC annually. A prominent example is Celemi, which started reporting on its IC in 1995.[9]

Danish IC Statements

The Danish Ministry of Trade and Industry, in cooperation with 17 Danish companies, issued guidelines for IC statements (ICSs) to encourage companies to report on their IC. The ICS comprises the following parts:

1. *The knowledge narrative.* Describes how the company has organized its knowledge resources to meet the needs of its customers. This includes the company's vision, mission, and value proposition.
2. *Management challenges.* Derived from the knowledge narrative, and describes the challenges that management faces in developing knowledge resources in connection with customers, employees, processes, and technologies.
3. *The reporting part.* Describes the initiatives and actions taken to address management challenges, and reports on their progress through figures, indicators and charts. Four areas should be covered:

   - Actions that are important from a customer perspective
   - Actions vis-à-vis employees
   - Processes that are crucial to the defined actions
   - Technologies that are important to the defined actions

Though the indicators used in the samples provided in the guideline are very similar to those developed by Skandia and Celemi, two models for reporting are provided. Model A reports on customers, employees, processes, and technologies of the organization as a whole with indicators to reflect their strength, renewal, and growth. Model B uses indicators that show progress under each of the defined action areas (addressing a certain management challenge), and provides indicators across customers, employees, processes, and technologies focuses.

THE CANADIAN EXPERIENCE

Total Value Creation (TVC) Method

Developed by the Canadian Institute of Chartered Accountants, TVC is a method to calculate the present value of future value streams using discounted cash flow techniques. Though the method is not new its application is, since TVC is applied to events and not transactions as the norm is for financial reports. TVC includes four parts to report on an organization's value creation potential:

1. An organization's strategy for creating and realizing value
2. An event-driven discounted cash flow of expected future value streams
3. A report on the organization's capacity to generate the expected value streams (capacity consists of capabilities, infrastructure and networks)
4. A report to shareholders on the financial and nonfinancial value streams

It is not clear what the definition of *event* is and, like other models discussed, the TVC is still experimental.

GLOBAL INITIATIVES

The Global Reporting Initiative (GRI)

The GRI is an initiative of the Coalition for Environmentally Responsible Economies in partnership with the United Nations Environment Program to develop guidelines for reporting on the economic, environmental, and social performance of companies. Though focused on environmental and social issues, many of the indicators developed report on various aspects of IC (e.g., those relating to employee productivity and turnover).

If successful, the GRI's initiative may provide a model for global IC reporting.

Organization for Economic Cooperation and Development (OECD)

The OECD organized a symposium on Intellectual Capital Reporting in June 1999, where a number of countries and organizations presented models for reporting on IC.[10] For the most part, these presentations are based on performance measures, where indicators to measure the various forms of IC were developed. Among the presenters was KPMG of the Netherlands, basing its measuring model on Andreissen's model of IC, outlined in Chapter 2. There was no follow up to the Symposium, and it is still to be seen if the OECD will take a more active role in IC reporting.

SUGGESTIONS FOR DEVELOPING
A UNIVERSAL IC REPORTING MODEL (UICR)

Before any progress can be made in relation to IC reporting it is important to determine which of the approaches to IC reporting is more feasible or acceptable. Experimentation under each of the approaches may also be undertaken, to compare their effectiveness, provided it is clear which approach is adopted. It seems that regulatory or standard-setting bodies favor the first approach for the gradual and slow pace of change that it involves and hence lower risk for stock markets. However, as explained previously, it lacks a clear methodological framework and may backfire by creating confusion and misrepresentation of the enterprise's value. IC theorists and practitioners seem to favor the second approach for its focus on intellectual value drivers of every enterprise in the knowledge economy. Nonetheless, the rudimentary state of research and experimentation based on the second approach, and hence the high level of risk involved, vitiates its present viability. That being said, the second approach still presents more promise for the development of a universal (i.e. comparable, reliable and consistent) IC reporting model.

The universal model presented here is based on the following propositions:

- Perceptions of value have differed in the knowledge economy, where more emphasis is placed on an organization's ability to innovate and manage IC than its ability to acquire and manage tangible assets.
- Despite the fact that the main intellectual drivers of value are different for different industries and organizations, a number of value drivers are common to all in the knowledge economy. These include: the strength of the organization's IC (the source of its livelihood and competitive ability); the percentage of value that can be attributed to IC; and demonstration of management ability to leverage IC.
- Indicators can be developed to monitor the common main value drivers described above, within and across industries.

A number of indicators can be developed for each of the common value drivers as follows:

COMMON VALUE DRIVERS	INDICATORS
Human capital and how it is being leveraged (Innovation Index)	Idea Generation Rate Idea Implementation Rate Internal Profitability Rate External Profitability Rate Growth Potential Rate (based on all the above)
Organizational knowledge (process capital) and how it is being leveraged (Renewal Index)	Time To Market, % of Revenue of Products introduced in the last 2 years, Customer Response Rate, % of Time and Revenue for Renewal
Intellectual property and how it is being leveraged (Intellectual Property Index)	IP Capitalization Rate (either Total Brand Equity, Patent/Trade Secret Capitalization Rate, or Copyright Diversity Rate)

The indicators enumerated here can be used to communicate an enterprise's innovation, renewal (or growth), and IP capabilities and potential. Reporting on the human capital (or brainpower) through idea generation and implementation rates, and the benefits realized as a consequence, would reflect an organization's brainpower and how it is leveraging human capital by converting ideas into solutions. Reporting on process capital would show the potential and rate of an organization's growth and renewal through use of metrics that measure its responsiveness to its market (customers), the time it invests to grow and the resultant renewal rate. Finally, reporting on an organization's rate of capitalization related to its IC would show the potential and success of a company to capitalize on its intellectual property after it is acquired. Different forms of intellectual property are important to different industries, hence the differentiation between patents, trademarks and copyrights related rates. The IP capitalization rate aims to streamline the differentiated rates to reflect an organization's ability to capitalize on its intellectual property regardless of form and across industry.

These indicators present a road map wherein a lot of streets and alleys are yet to be identified and named. The search still continues and it is far from complete. Nonetheless, that road map is introduced to show that developing a standard universal IC reporting model is feasible. IC is the most valuable asset in the knowledge economy, and it is time that there is a model that reports on how organizations are leveraging their IC. That is where the future lies. The present efforts, however, should be focused on developing models for managing IC beyond their rudimentary state, hence the CICM model introduced in the next chapter.

NOTES

[1] Wallman, S., "The Importance of Measuring Intangible Assets: Public Policy Implications," in Imparato, N. (ed.), *Capital for Our Time* (Stanford University, California: Hoover Institution Press, 1998), pp. 181–187, at p. 187.

[2] A private national nonprofit organization that sets standards and rules for the U.S. private sector in relation to corporate reporting.

[3] See Upton, W., "Special Report on Business and Financial Reporting: Challenges from the New Economy" (FASB, April 2001), p. 29–58. Also see, Blair, M. and Wallman, S., "Unseen Wealth: Report of the Brookings Institute Taskforce on Understanding Intangible Sources of Value" (Brookings Institute, 2000).

[4] An accounting term that is equivalent to *depreciation,* but used in relation to intangible assets.

[5] To perform an impairment test, a reporting unit has to check at least at the end of each financial year its value and write off any such amounts that are above the fair value (market value) of the reporting unit. Adjustments should be made if the fair value is less than the carrying value of the entire reporting unit. The first step is to allocate the excess to identifiable intangible assets other than goodwill. Any excess of the fair value over the allocated amounts is then the implied value of the goodwill. The value of the goodwill should then be compared to the carrying value of the acquired goodwill, and reduced by the amount of the excess over the implied value.

[6] Defined as those that can be separately sold, transferred, licensed or exchanged and those obtained through contractual or other legal rights. It is clear that intellectual property and related rights are the IC that fit this definition. All other IC is lumped under the general term of goodwill.

[7] Defined as the stage where the "enterprise has completed all planning, designing, coding, and testing activities that are necessary to establish that the product can be produced to meet its design specifications including functions, features, and technical performance requirements."

[8] For more on these two methods see Thomas Stewart, "Trying to Grasp the Intangible," *Fortune,* October 2, 1995.

[9] For copies of Celemi's IC reports, see *www.celemi.com.*

[10] For a copy of the various presentations, see *http://strategis.ic.gc.ca/SSG/pi00011e.html.*

4

The Comprehensive Intellectual Capital Management (CICM) Approach

THE STAGES OF BUSINESS MANAGEMENT AND THE CICM APPROACH

To develop ICM as a business management approach for the IC-intensive organization, it is important to understand the business cycle of IC and to tie it to the elementary stages (or functions) of business management. These include:

- Managing resources
- Managing the production process
- Maximizing value to stakeholders (be it defined in terms of bottom line, meeting a mission, or simply success)

These stages (or functions) are the basis of business management in every organization. The first stage ensures having the raw resources for operation or production, while the second stage converts these resources through various processes into valuable assets, and the last stage leverages this value to maximize return to stakeholders. In an economy where 80 percent of business value is made of IC, ICM should be engrained at each of these stages. That is the gist of the CICM approach.

The business cycle of IC follows the same stages as those enumerated above. Under this business cycle, IC progresses from being a resource with a potential value to an asset with a perceived value, to becoming a product with a market value. As a resource, the value of IC is latent; hence, the task of management at this stage is to create value from intellectual resources. Once value is realized, it then can be extracted through business processes where the intellectual resource is transformed into an intellectual asset with perceived value that can be estimated. The intellectual asset is ready at this stage to be packaged as a product[1] and launched into the market. At this last stage of development, the value of IC is maximized through legal protection, allowing the further commercialization and promotion of the underlying IC to related markets. This expands the definition of IC to comprise raw knowledge resources that are processed into innovation resources, the basis of a marketable product, and then to a legally identifiable and protectable bundle of rights—intellectual property (IP).

To demonstrate, brainpower, expertise, and the body of knowledge in a certain area represent the raw resources required for production. The value of these resources is in the potential of their development through business processes into a certain application; for example, applying knowledge resources and people's skills and brainpower to develop a software program. Once a specific application is developed, a product concept is formed, or a prototype made, the value of IC crystallizes to a degree that it can be perceived and measured. The NPV method is often used at this stage to measure the revenue stream that such IC may generate in the future after being transformed to a marketable product. At this stage the software program is developed further into its marketable form by being passed through the various business and innovation processes. That, however, still does not ensure that the extracted value has been fully exploited. The latter happens only when the organization acquires all forms of intellectual property possible to protect the IC in question, and thus enhances its competitive power. In the software program example, the organization at this stage should protect the program with a trademark/brand, copyright and trade secrets, and possibly a patent. Later, the various intellectual property rights can be exploited independently of the program through various licenses and transactions maximizing the realized value of the IC. The progress of IC from a knowledge resource, to an innovation (or intellectual) asset, and finally to intellectual property represents the IC business cycle.

To incorporate the IC business cycle and stages into business management, the CICM model adopts a functional classification of intellectual capital as the underlying IC model. Under the functional classification, the generic forms of IC (human, customer, and structural) are grouped in relation to their function in the business cycle, into three groups:

1. Knowledge resources
2. Innovation resources and processes
3. Intellectual property

These groups are then managed, each according to its stage of development under three stages as follows. It is noted that though all forms of IC are managed under each of the management stages, as illustrated in Exhibit 4.1, each stage by its nature is predominantly focused on managing one particular form of IC.

INTELLECTUAL CAPITAL/ STAGE OF DEVELOPMENT	HUMAN CAPITAL	CUSTOMER CAPITAL	STRUCTURAL CAPITAL
Knowledge management stage	Tacit knowledge, experience, brainpower, vision	Experience, knowledge, relations, networks	IT databases, knowledge base, best practices, culture
Innovation management stage	Ideas, product concepts, skills	Ideas, product concepts, feedback, relationships	Work systems, business processes
Intellectual property management stage	Know-how, know-why	Brand identity, reputation, strategic alliances	Patents, trademarks, copyrights, trade secrets

EXHIBIT 4.1   The Types and Stages of IC under the CICM Model

The First Stage: Managing IC as Raw Knowledge Resources

At this stage, IC—whether human, customer, or structural capital—is still in its raw form and hence is used as a resource for production and operation. The best way to describe IC at this stage is to use the term *knowledge resources.* These knowledge resources comprise employees' brainpower—human capital, customers' experience and insight—customer capital, and the organization's information databases and knowledge stored in its routines and business practices—structural capital. Managing IC at this stage of its business cycle is the management of the organization's knowledge resources in every form they come in, hence the stage of *knowledge management.* This stage is predominantly focused on the management of human capital since employees are the main carriers and processors of knowledge.

The Second Stage: Managing IC as Innovation Resources

At this stage the IC uncovered in the first stage is transformed through the organization's various business/production processes into *applied knowledge,* that is, a product, process, or solution that can be commercialized. Hence, the value of IC in the first stage is extracted and materialized at this stage. The best way to describe IC at this stage is as *innovation resources.* These innovation resources comprise ideas and product concepts generated and developed by employees—human capital; ideas and concepts generated through networking and contact with customers—customer capital; and business processes, work systems, and methods used to transform ideas into marketable products—structural capital. Management of IC at this stage of its business cycle is the management of the innovation processes through the whole organization, hence the stage of *innovation management.* This stage is predominantly focused on the management of customer capital since innovation in the knowledge economy is increasingly reliant on network-based innovation, as further explained in Chapter 7.

The Third Stage: Managing IC as Intellectual Property

At this stage, IC has reached its optimal level of materialized value. IC can then be defined in very precise terms, separated into identifiable items of intellectual material, and used as competitive and marketing tools. The best way to describe IC at this stage is intellectual property or intellectual assets. Intellectual property comprises know-how and information of defined commercial value, that is, trade secrets—human capital[2]; brand identity, personality, reputation, and emotional value[3]—customer value; and defined technologies, patents, software programs,[4] copyrighted works and trademarks, trade dress, and logos that the organization owns—structural capital. Management of IC at this stage of its business cycle is the management of intellectual property (for business, not legal, purposes), hence the stage of *intellectual property management.* This stage is predominantly focused on the management of structural capital given that IP is owned by the organization.

The CICM model purports to manage all forms of IC at each stage of their business development, where each stage supports the next in the cycle by feeding back to where it started. As illustrated in Exhibit 4.2, knowledge management supports the innovation and IP management stages by supplying the raw knowledge resources, and is thus the platform of the CICM model. Both innovation and IP management stages produce more knowledge resources that are recycled back into the knowledge management stage, where they get circulated and reformulated as the basis of new knowledge that in turn proceeds to the other two stages and so on, as shown in Exhibit 4.2. The comprehensiveness of the CICM model lies in managing IC from A to Z at

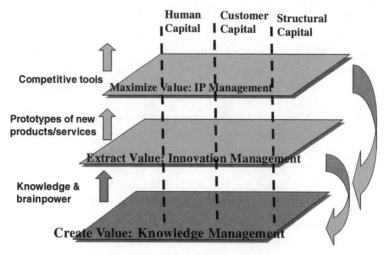

EXHIBIT 4.2   CICM Model

every stage of its development to ensure that value is created, extracted, and maximized in a systematic way.

Though these stages overlap and closely interact with each other, it is important that they be separated for management purposes. This is because the nature of IC at each stage is intrinsically different from the IC at the other stages, which requires a different management system, and should be managed to meet different objectives. Exhibit 4.3 shows the various management objectives and purposes for managing IC at each stage.

Each stage commands different management objectives, which in turn command the use of different rules, systems, practices, and tools. The different management objectives at each stage

CICM STAGE	IC GROUP	PURPOSE	MANAGEMENT OBJECTIVES
Knowledge management	Raw knowledge resources	Value creation	Recognize and leverage the knowledge resources required to sustain the organization's processes
Innovation management	Innovation processes and resources	Value extraction	Unleash and reconfigure innovation resources to create new ways of doing business and new products faster
Intellectual property management	Intellectual property	Value maximization	Enable the use of intellectual property to enhance the organization's competitive positioning and revenue generation

EXHIBIT 4.3   Management Objectives and Purposes for CICM

provide a guide for the performance measures that can be used. At the first stage of knowledge management, the main purpose is the maintenance of a good flow of information and knowledge resources, to facilitate organizational learning and sustain everything that the organization does (i.e., value creation). This main purpose is translated into a set of management objectives, namely, determining the main knowledge resources required for the organization to meet its goals and facilitating knowledge sharing to leverage the organization's existing knowledge. Unlike investment at the other two stages, investment at this stage is long term with no direct financial outcomes. Nonetheless, performance measures can be developed to monitor the effect of knowledge management on learning, productivity, and turnover rates.

The stage of innovation management has the main purpose of extracting value from all the knowledge resources available to the organization by the use of innovation processes. The challenge of managing IC at this stage, however, is how to manage the innovation resources, dispersed in networks inside and outside the organization, to enable their effective reconfiguration to get to the market faster. Return on investment at this stage can be measured with more certainty as improvements relate to definite production processes, unlike knowledge management wherein the benefit permeates to everything that the organization does. When it comes to performance measures, both qualitative and quantitative metrics can be used (e.g., time to market, product success rate, and percentage of revenue from new products).

The purpose of the IP management stage is to maximize value to stakeholders by using the legally defined properties as competitive and marketing tools. This translates to management objectives that include the use of IP as a competitive weapon to block competition from entering or gaining a stronghold in a certain market segment, as a protective shield to secure the organization's own competitive positioning efforts, and as a marketing tool to generate revenue. Performance measures here are easier to form as royalty streams provide ample evidence as to the effectiveness of managing IP. Other measures need to be developed as well to measure IP management program effectiveness in enhancing the competitive positioning of the different business units by monitoring growth rates, for example.

But the CICM model does not only bring different practices, objectives, programs, and tools together in an understandable framework. It also presents a methodology that harmonizes and synchronizes between the different programs needed under the various stages to liberate and leverage the value of IC, and hence enhance business performance. Above all, it develops a new management approach. Here's how.

THE CICM MODEL—NOT ANOTHER SET OF CIRCLES

The projects focused on various goals and approaches: team management, destaffing, organizational learning, empowerment, delayering, . . . The problem? Managers attacked the issues piecemeal. Investing incrementally in new models of management, they tried to bolt them onto their old structures and integrate them into their old management doctrines.

—Christopher Bartlett[5]

The aim of the CICM model is far from being a melting pot in which the various programs and initiatives are simply brought together. It is designed to assist management in strategic planning related to the development of their IC for achieving and sustaining a competitive advantage and generating revenue from their largest asset base. In particular, it enables management to:

- Develop a new management approach that is better accustomed to business management at a time when IC represents critical business resources, processes, and assets.
- Make sense of the different approaches offered to discern how and when any of these approaches fits in the CICM model.
- Synchronize the various programs implemented to manage a group or more of IC to prevent waste of resources and achieve better results.
- Generate the maximum value from an ICM program by addressing the three functions that IC plays in the business cycle of an organization, namely, creation, extraction, and maximization of value.
- Set clear objectives for their ICM activities and thus provide a platform for a suitable measurement system.
- Set priorities to enable effective resource allocation decisions.
- Customize the generic CICM model to the strategic goals and the industry/business of the organization.

The last two points will be discussed in Chapter 14, but for now let's have a closer look at how the CICM model purports to do that.

New Management Approach

The CICM model does not construct a model from scratch. Instead, it builds on the rich body of knowledge that developed in the subdisciplines of knowledge management, innovation management, and IP management. It builds on the experience of companies in the United States and elsewhere that, for around a decade—some even longer—have been experimenting—some with great success—with new business models for managing their IC. The novelty of the CICM model lies first in the classification of IC according to its function in the business cycle, and in streamlining the so-called subdisciplines into a synchronized model for the management of IC throughout the whole organization, at every stage of its development. The CICM approach brings all this into a comprehensive model that advances a new approach to business management.

Though new in its framework and pragmatic application, the CICM approach builds on the disciplines of knowledge, innovation, and IP management. The concepts, methods, practices, and tools that have been developed under these disciplines are presented through the lens of the CICM approach, where they are presented as stages in a comprehensive approach. The CICM model starts with the knowledge management stage in which an organization lays the foundation for ICM, without which any ICM program will suffer from a serious dysfunction as a result of undermanagement of resources. A business that has deficient resources suffers serious impediments to all its operations, threatening its very existence. With increased reliance on learning, and hence the generation of knowledge resources, organizations lacking a program that identifies, develops, and sustains their knowledge base will lag behind, if they manage to survive.

The knowledge management stage is one in which most attention is paid to developing the human capital and that part of the structural capital that enables knowledge and information sharing for two main purposes. The first is creating value through invigorating the natural function of the human brain and heart, which is to divulge knowledge, create, and communicate ideas. The second is to create a learning organization. To become a learning organization represents the optimal stage of organizational evolution in the knowledge economy, wherein the organization knows what it knows, knows how to find who knows internally, can apply and reuse its knowledge, and can advance on its evolutionary journey of acquiring higher intelligence (discussed in Chapter 5).

But business management is more than cultivating resources—in this case, intelligence. It is mainly about production, development, and growth—hence processes. Business processes and methods are what enable people to apply knowledge to new products and to package knowledge into new services. This is where innovation management, the second stage, kicks in. New ideas have to be collected and new product concepts generated. Then these concepts have to be assessed and filtered down to a number of new product development projects, which may eventually develop into separate businesses. The various business processes and systems used to generate ideas and turn them into marketable products, services, and new businesses form the crux of the business production process. But what does this have to do with ICM? As far as business management is concerned, innovation management as a discipline emerged as early as the 1890s with Edison's practice of innovation and was perfected as a process around the 1970s (discussed further in Chapter 7).

Despite this, a closer look reveals that business innovation has been transformed in the knowledge economy by the appreciation of the value of IC to business—what I will refer to hereinafter as the IC concept. This happened in two ways. First, the IC concept liberated the innovative power of the organization out of the confines of one department, namely, research and development (R&D) or new product development, into the fabric of the whole organization. Second, the IC concept (particularly appreciation of customer capital) expanded the innovation process to include networks and alliances with customers and sometimes even competitors so that they can combine mutual strengths to get to the market faster. Overall, innovation management became closely linked to the management of relationships and networks.

The CICM model recognizes and highlights the move of the innovation process to becoming network based. To that effect, it addresses how business management should be transformed to enable the management of the organization's innovation portfolio across the dispersed internal and external networks. To do this, business managers need to know the competencies and skills of their people (human capital), as well as those of their existing or potential partners (customer capital), and bring the right team together to develop new products and to grow the business.

Once a new product or service is successfully introduced in the market, the options available for expansion are numerous. Being mainly made and composed of IC, marketing of new products assumes a new dimension. That dimension relates to the potential of marketing the IP (whether a patent, a trademark, or a copyright) independent of the original product (or process) with which it was associated. This is managed under the IP management stage of the CICM model.

Though IP management as a discipline was developed well before the 1970s with very successful franchises and technological licenses, the changes introduced by the IC concept go beyond an increase in the volume of IP transactions or the appreciation of its commercial value. The IC concept, like what it did to innovation management, made IP management the job of everyone. Only when IP management infiltrates business management is a business enabled to effectively use IP as both a competitive weapon and a business asset. That is what the CICM incorporates in the IP management stage by liberating IP from the confines of the legal department to the function of business management (discussed in Chapter 8).

As a result, the CICM model brings the three disciplines (or subdisciplines) of knowledge, innovation, and IP management together to form a synchronized approach of business management based on the IC concept. The model's main proposition that it is effective strategic management of IC that enables an organization to sustain a competitive advantage. Under CICM, managing knowledge or innovation or any form of IC is not merely about implementing a program or creating a licensing unit or a new information technology (IT) system. It is more of a philosophy that has to permeate everything that the organization does and be embedded in its culture. It has to be part of its vision and strategy (discussed further in Chapter 10).

The CICM model enables management to make sense of the myriad of solutions and approaches offered under the banner of ICM and knowledge management.

Making Sense—Overcoming Business Skepticism

A number of management approaches and solutions started to appear in the 1960s or earlier. All are offered with the promise of value maximization and results that impact the bottom line favorably. Business process engineering, total quality management, R&D management, technology management, time-based competition, lean production/enterprise, customer-focused organization, knowledge management, and employee empowerment—the common thread among these approaches is that all of them aim to manage one form or another of IC as the means for acquiring and sustaining a competitive edge. Those concerned with reengineering and quality management focus on process capital. Customer-focused and network-based approaches focus on customer capital, while the rest aim to manage human capital in the innovation process.

The fact that these approaches do in some cases improve an organization's competitive position proves that the management of any form of IC and to any degree of depth will result in some benefits. Nonetheless, the more prevalent fact is that organizations usually move in dissatisfaction from one approach to another in their struggle to make sense of a messy and rich landscape of business solutions.

Business executives are faced with many questions. Would a knowledge management solution facilitate ICM? Which approach should management implement? Which approach is needed to solve the immediate problems without limiting the organization's ability to implement other approaches in the future at a later stage of development? Does an organization have to start all over again and in some cases reinvent the wheel every time a solution seems to offer more than its predecessors? How different is innovation from IP management? Is it sufficient to establish a licensing unit to manage IC?

This messy landscape where no practical guide exists to explain the basis of these solutions (other than some consulting firms[6]) and how to make an informed decision between them cultivates two problems. The first is business skepticism, and the second is what has been called the "knowing–doing" gap.[7] The messy landscape and rate of failure[8] generated a lot of skepticism in business managers and leaders. This is more than expected given the speed with which different management approaches or solutions appear and disappear. Who would know whether a new approach is a management fad that is yet another attempt by the consulting profession to create opportunities?

That skepticism is very serious and widespread beyond the leadership and senior executive level. It filtered down to middle management and frontline levels. Even when management is convinced of the efficacy of a certain approach, the skepticism of employees who have seen one approach come and another go is not resolved. The skepticism of employees is more serious as it results in both apathy and indifference, and hence jeopardizes the success of any approach regardless of its merit. This is more serious in organizations where employees are not empowered and hence are not part of the decision-making process. Many employees in such organizations do not feel that they own the new approach and may even believe that an approach does not deal with what they see as the more serious problems.

This widespread skepticism also accentuates the knowing–doing gap identified by Pfeffer and Sutton. The authors conducted extensive research and found that though in most cases leadership *knows* what needs to be done and launches the appropriate initiatives, there are certain factors that impede, and sometimes result in the failure of, effective implementation—hence the knowing–doing gap. The authors give varied reasons for this gap, the most important being the divorce of complex solutions from the business core processes, the excessive focus of knowledge management programs on IT while ignoring the human side, and the failure of remuneration systems to foster teamwork rather than internal competition. The most prevalent reason for this gap, however, is that organizations implement programs that are contradictory to their culture and the business/knowledge needs of employees, and are thus doomed to failure from day one.

What seems to be lacking is a perspective that clarifies where everything fits in the big picture as well as explains the conditions that should be present for successful implementation of a certain approach as opposed to another. In general, an organization should not implement any solution until it is confident that the right culture (i.e., one that conforms with underlying values of any ICM program) exists. Implementing the best program when organizational culture is not ready for it jeopardizes the chance of a successful implementation at some other time in the future. If that happens, the practice will be made taboo forever, except after a strong change in perspective or leadership.

Assessing the culture and the specific situation of the organization is of particular importance, as it reveals the starting point of the organization, and hence determines its ICM needs. What is suitable for one organization may not be so for the other. The CICM model deals with this by incorporating tools for identifying and changing an organization's culture and values, as well as formulating the right vision to make it ready for the stage of evolution suitable for ICM.

In addition, the CICM model provides management with a framework on which it can determine which management approach or practice may be used, if it should be used, and how it should be used to conform to the strategic goals and objectives of the organization, business unit, or department. By defining the management objectives and goals under each stage, the CICM model guides management as to where each practice fits in the big picture, expected returns, and requisites for its implementation. This enables management not only to implement the right practice or program but to synchronize these practices with other practices across the organization as well.

Synchronization and the Role of IC Strategy

Accentuating the problems outlined above is that programs that purport to manage IC are usually scattered throughout the organization, and managed by different departments and divisions. Departments usually apply their own approaches or solutions to manage often different but overlapping forms of IC. For example, the human resources department is usually entrusted with programs to develop the human capital, the legal department develops programs for IP management, while marketing implements programs for managing customer capital, and R&D or the engineering department manages innovation resources for new product development. In some cases, the licensing of IP is managed by both the legal and the marketing (or special licensing) departments. Of course, this advances the focused development of the various forms of IC, each by those who understand it most. But without an underlying unifying IC strategy, this will eventually lead to the development of isolated and eventually conflicting approaches.

Furthermore, the conflicting purposes and interests of the various departments often will create conflict, rivalry, and misunderstanding. Allowed to grow, this tension will block effective communication among the various departments and business units, promoting the wrong culture and defeating knowledge sharing. Any initiative that attempts to implement isolated and separate programs without the collaboration of key people in the various departments and business units will result in more harm than good. In addition to resulting in disorientation and isolationism on the departmental level, it will waste management resources.

Boeing learned this the hard way in 1997 when they tried to implement two separate programs, one for knowledge management and the other for IP management.[9] Each program was implemented in isolation with separate departmental ownership despite the fact that the programs were developed by the same consulting team. On completion, the consulting team found irreconcilable differences between the approaches of the two major groups that they called knowledge managers and IP managers. These differences revolved around definitions, choice of practices, and conflicting goals and approaches. Lacking a unified IC strategy, departmental differences created departmental rivalry and misunderstanding, undermining the benefit of the whole program.

Without a shift in the way the organization sees itself (vision) it is impossible to implement an effective ICM program. Strategy emanates from the vision, whereby it taints everything the organization does as it defines its mode of operation. A well-formulated strategy that is based on the vision represents the mind of the organization and directs operations, decisions, and actions performed by every business unit, department and individual. As such it brings various disciplines, perspectives and objectives under one end goal. Pursuing the common goal enables all those involved to overcome differences and create a comprehensive plan to address the collective and respective needs. The CICM promotes this through the formulation of the IC strategy at the organizational, business-unit, and departmental levels. A shared vision and well-formulated IC strategy fosters the right culture and enables the synchronization of the missions of the various businesses. This leads to creating an environment where all the pieces not only fit together but also reinforce each other, and enables the maximization of value at every stage of IC development.

Unlocking the Mystery of Value Creation and Maximization

All the IC models discussed in Chapter 2 stressed that value creation is not dependent on the strength of a particular form of IC but on the relationship between the various forms. Edvinsson goes as far as proposing that if one form is not strong enough, then that will impact the value creation process and render the other forms, even if strong, less effective.[10] Despite this insight, it is not clear exactly how the mismanagement of one form impacts the other, at which stage of value creation, and how this can be remedied. This vagueness further mystifies ICM to management, as it does not clarify what value is expected to be gleaned from IC management in the first place.

The CICM model explains exactly not only how value is created, but also how it is extracted and maximized through the various stages of CICM. It is important to see the stages of creation, extraction, and maximization of value as distinct rather than one and the same. The metaphor of a plant illustrates this distinction. Planting a seed and watering it until it blossoms to the first leaves is creating value. Through natural development the seed grew into a plant, because that is what it naturally does. Intervention was necessary only to provide the needed nutrition to facilitate the growth of the plant, but it didn't make it happen. The role of intervention is merely to provide the right environment.

That is exactly how intellectual resources, whether individual or organizational knowledge, should be managed, to create value from them. Providing the right environment and culture for employees to facilitate knowledge sharing, will eventually activate the natural process of knowledge and value creation. Nurturing knowledge workers with the required information and knowledge (how things were done in the past and how other people in the organization think it should be done) will only spur more leaves—or ideas. But having the most dynamic group of people with the most brilliant ideas is not sufficient.

The next level in the business cycle is value extraction. Now that you have the plant, how about taking these leaves out, processing them, and producing an ointment? The main enablers here are your imagination, creativity, research, intelligence, experimentation, development skills, and understanding of market needs.

What enables extraction of value from the leaves once they have sprung into life is the modus operandi of the business—the various processes that make things happen. The effectiveness of these processes in extracting value and creating something new for which there is considerable demand in the market will determine the success of the project. It was noted that it usually takes 3,000 ideas to come up with four development projects and one winning product. This means the processes used to collect the leaves, the eyes used to pick the right ones for further development, and the means by which these few will be tested are the processes that shape the end product. At this stage consideration should be given to the tastes and needs of the end user who will use the processed leaves and hence understanding customers' needs. This per se should be designed as one of the value extraction processes. But, again, it doesn't stop here. There is another step, maybe the most profitable: value maximization.

What if the same leaves can be developed further by the owner or someone else for veterinary applications? What if the same ointment can be sold through new distribution channels or by a partner to other market segments? A multitude of ifs can maximize the value I have extracted from the leaves. That's where another set of IC comes into play. First, I have some rights in the leaves, which I can offer for assignment or under license. Even if I have no legal right in the leaves, for some reason or another, I still have the lead in the market for discovering and extracting their value first. My process may be secret, limiting the competition's ability to catch up. That in itself is a privilege that I can use to maximize value. Then there are strategic alliances with distributors, partners, and even competitors that I can negotiate to maximize my revenue generation opportunity. That's where IP (as business tools, not as legal rights) and relational/customer capital (as networks, supply-distributor chains, strategic alliances) come into play.

Thus, different forms of IC come together to perform three main functions in the business cycle of any enterprise: creation, extraction, and maximization of value. Understanding that cycle and how each group fits in clarifies how each group should be developed, what to expect from such development, and hence how to set management objectives and measure results. This also enables spotting weaknesses and finding out the weakest link in the chain of the value maximization process. If the immediate problem is in the raw knowledge resources, management should focus on knowledge management; if it is rather in getting to market, the focus should be directed to innovation management; and so on. Distinguishing among the three stages of the value maximization chain also enables management to take ICM to the operational level.

Setting Objectives—Taking ICM to the Operational Level

The IC model provides very general guidelines regarding the objectives that management should aim for in managing IC, namely, the cyclic conversion of human to customer and then to structural capital. At best, this presents an end goal, that which should be achieved after an ICM program has been in place. But "how" is the challenge, which management is not given any strategy to confront. What is needed first of all is a framework that presents a skeleton of the changes that are required—a framework that can be used by management to formulate the strategies needed to tackle the challenge of "how," and to operationalize such strategies.

The CICM's framework leads organizational change by starting from the top at the strategic level, where leadership gets itself and the whole organization in the right mindset for managing IC. This is facilitated mainly by the reformulation of IC strategies that inspire and lead the CICM model. Strategy is the mastermind of organizational change. Without it, organizational change does not go beyond an inspirational leadership speech, the momentum of which withers away shortly after the applause. The CICM guides leadership and senior management on the various IC strategies that can be used at each stage of CICM to effect the necessary changes and lead the organization.

The CICM then moves on by outlining the structural and cultural changes that should be effected, as well as the enabling systems and tools that should be provided, to take ICM to the operational level. Structural changes relate to the departments, teams, and support positions that are needed to effect changes at each of the stages.

When it comes to culture, the CICM outlines changes that are needed to create the right culture and the appropriate work environment at each stage. Though changing the organizational culture is something that relates to the whole organization and is not a change that is peculiar to one stage, there are steps that should be taken at each stage to engrain the right values in the way of doing business. For example, an innovation management program that does not allow time for employees to experiment with their ideas and make that part of their job will not promote cultural change no matter how many vision and mission statements are written about the importance of employee innovation. Culture being engrained in an organization's routines and practices can be changed only by consistent practices aimed at fostering the desired behavior. Hence, each of the stages includes the practices and steps required to change culture in a way that provides the optimal environment for the success of management objectives under the particular stage.

Finally, the CICM framework provides guidance as to the systems and tools that are required to enable the main processes under each of the stages. The most important of the systems is the knowledge base and the IT architecture discussed under the knowledge management stage. That is not to undermine the significance of valuation tools for IP management or idea banks for innovation management, for example.

Presented in this framework, management is provided guidance as to what exactly needs to be done to create, extract, and maximize value at both the strategic and operational levels. It also enables management to spot weaknesses in their ICM program as lacking structural changes for example the program will not be effective, or lacking the right culture it will simply not work. One of the most pragmatic applications of the CICM framework is that despite its comprehensiveness, it presents the required changes under each stage separately. This provides management with the flexibility to design a phased-out (short- to long-term) implementation plan. The only condition is that management knows where a certain program or practice fits in the big picture, and how it affects the other parts, and hence to align it with the business strategy.

Part Two presents each of the three stages separately by first introducing each of the underlying disciplines (knowledge, innovation, and IP management), exploring how they were transformed by the IC concept, then outlining the changes that should occur at the strategic and operational levels under each stage. Part Two includes three case studies, the Navy model of knowledge management, and the CICM models of two pioneers—Skandia and Dow Chemical. This would then introduce the reader to Part Three, where the implementation of the CICM model is outlined step by step.

NOTES

[1] The term *product* is used throughout this book to include a manufactured good, a solution, a process, or a service.

[2] One of the major issues that trade secret law deals with is where to draw the line between the experience and know-how that an individual owns, as it represents acquired knowledge, even if gained while at the employ of a particular organization, and where that know-how is divorced from the knower (i.e., the employee) and is owned by the organization. It seems that once

codified and identified, know-how becomes the property of the organization. There is a level of knowledge that is still considered to be owned by the employee, particularly that which affects the employee's livelihood and ability to earn a living.

[3] A brand is here divided into two components—the trademark, which is owned by the organization, and the emotional value of the brand as perceived by the customer, which, though controlled by the organization, cannot be owned by it.

[4] Software programs are mentioned separately from copyright works, as patents and trade secrets as well can be used to protect them. Patents can be used to protect these software programs that incorporate a new business method. Trade secrets protection is used by keeping most of the source code secret.

[5] Bartlett, C., "The Knowledge Based Organization," in Ruggles and Holthouse (editors), *The Knowledge Advantage* (Oxford, U.K: Capstone, 1999), p. 111.

[6] Fast Company reported that in 1996 alone $43 billion was spent on management consulting in the United States. See "Blurb Buddies," *Fast Company,* December 1998, p. 54.

[7] J. Pfeffer and R. Sutton, *The Knowing–Doing Gap* (Boston: Harvard Business School Press, 1999).

[8] Pfeffer and Sutton, op. cit., report that there is a 70 percent failure rate for reengineering approaches and that only one of five companies implementing total quality management succeed. They also reported failure of a number of knowledge management initiatives, particularly those limited to IT.

[9] See Sproule, R., and Sullivan, P., "Case History: Integrated IP Management," *Les Nouvelles,* June 1999, p. 70.

[10] Edvinsson, L., and Malone, M., *Intellectual Capital* (New York: Harper Business, 1997), pp. 145–146.

Part Two

The Three Stages of Intellectual Capital Management

Part Two presents the new discipline of knowledge management as the first stage of comprehensive intellectual capital management, where the knowledge resources are obtained, sustained, and managed for value creation. Part Two then proceeds with presenting the disciplines of innovation and IP management as the subsequent stages for value extraction and maximization, respectively. Each of the management stages is presented in a way that outlines the changes that are required at both the strategic and operational levels to put in place the necessary strategic objectives, structure, culture, practices, systems, and tools for the management of IC at that stage.

In addition to the real-life examples used throughout the book, Part Two also includes three case studies to illustrate as we go along how ICM can be effectively implemented at the various stages. Chapter 6 presents the U.S. Navy's model of knowledge management and examines the changes the Navy went through, based on the framework outlined in Chapter 5, to implement knowledge management successfully. Chapter 9 also uses the frameworks outlined in Chapters 5, 7, and 8 to illustrate the comprehensive systems that both Skandia AFS and Dow Chemical Company have developed to manage their IC across the whole organization and through the various management stages.

5

The Knowledge Management Stage and Organizational IQ

Albert Einstein's hypothesis that an average person uses only 10 percent of his or her brainpower is still faced with great amazement. Pondering on what an extra 1 to 5 percent of brainpower will produce, scientists starting with Einstein tried to unlock the mystery of how the brain works, with very little luck. Knowledge management (KM) practitioners, however, seem to have more luck when it comes to the organizational brain. Observing that organizations use only 20 percent of the knowledge available to them,[1] KM practitioners set out to find ways for organizations to recognize and leverage their knowledge. This is the quest of knowledge management. KM is the art of managing the knowledge accumulated in an organization's databases, practices, and routines (explicit knowledge) and that contained in the heads of its employees (tacit knowledge) to create value. To some, KM is one and the same thing as intellectual capital management (ICM), where innovation processes and intellectual property (IP) are seen as knowledge resources. This, however, is not the view taken in this book. Although, theoretically speaking, the management of any intellectually based asset or resource is a management of the knowledge underlying that asset, from the practical perspective, managing innovation and IP (though knowledge based) is very different from managing the raw knowledge resources. To classify and manage innovation and IP as knowledge resources under the same stage of KM runs the risk of confusing the objectives that management should aim for in managing each of these stages.

Knowledge management is presented in this book as the stage at which the knowledge resources of an organization are deployed and reconfigured to create value, to form the platform for achieving the organization's mission through action, innovation, or commercialization. Above all, KM is the stage at which the organization knows itself by knowing what it knows, where it recognizes the value of the tacit knowledge, as the basis for decision making and hence the real source of value creation. Only when that happens will the organization use more of the knowledge available to it, learn from its mistakes, and not reinvent the wheel. Before outlining the main concepts of the discipline of KM, it is important to elaborate on the main problems facing business management and that KM promises to solve.

The most obvious problem is dissipation of an organization's knowledge resources, which directly affects performance and hence the bottom line. In particular, two main problems will be highlighted: organizational memory loss and brain drain. At the heart of organizational memory loss and brain drain is an organization that does not know what it knows and lacks the capability of leveraging the tacit knowledge of its employees. To that we now turn.

ORGANIZATIONAL MEMORY LOSS AND BRAIN DRAIN

The brain never seems to lose a memory. What really happens is that the memory gets lost somewhere in the brain (except, of course, if the brain cells are dead). That's exactly what happens with organizational memory loss. Parts of the organizational brain do not know the experience or have access to the knowledge of other parts, and the knowledge is lost. No matter how advanced the knowledge in one part, if not communicated, transferred, and transformed to organizational learning, then it is apt to be lost.

Organizational memory loss occurs when one part of the organizational brain is oblivious to the knowledge that other parts possess. Memory loss is also noted when the same department or division forgets the knowledge it gained from previous experiences or projects. As a result, organizations tend to reinvent the wheel every time a new, yet in many respects similar, project is undertaken. This also means the organization will repeat the same mistakes, given that it has not learned from previous experiences. Many organizations that are skeptical of the business value of KM can hardly deny the losses they sustain as a result of losing valuable knowledge resources. Memory lost is knowledge lost, which requires investment to be recreated, jeopardizing the efficiency and quality of the value creation process, and the productivity of the organizational operations. Indeed, the Gartner Group forecasted that in 2001 organizations that lack KM programs will lag by 30 to 40 percent in speed of deployment of new products and services.[2]

The main reason behind this is that organizations do not know what they know. Not knowing what you know as an organization would result in serious underutilization of knowledge resources, as strategic decisions get made without full appreciation of the actual ability of the organization to compete in a certain area of knowledge. It cuts both ways. In some situations, there is an overestimation of the depth or breadth of organizational knowledge that an organization possesses compared to the desired competitive position, resulting in impaired ability to attain that position. Discovering this at a time when things can still be saved is not enough since the cost of acquiring the requisite knowledge resources will undermine profits. On the other end of the spectrum are organizations that underestimate their knowledge and as a result lose many opportunities to capitalize on these resources. What makes this more eminent is that knowledge as a resource has a short life cycle and can be rendered obsolete in a short time if not grown and developed.

Examples abound. Look at your own organization. How many times has your division or department spent thousands of dollars to acquire the required information or knowledge, only to find out that another department has done most of the work before? How many times has a team adopted a solution that another team in the organization has tried and, finding that it does not work, perfected another? Repeating the same errors, looking for resources externally that are available somewhere else in the organization, and not being able to repeat your success are all manifestations of organizational memory loss.

Take Ford, for example. Deciding to replicate its unprecedented success with Taurus, Ford looked for the practices behind Taurus success. Though the procedures and processes were codified, that did not provide the reason why and how Taurus was so successful. There were other secrets that only those who worked on the project possessed. Ford found that the team who worked closely with the Taurus model, and thus had the requisite tacit knowledge, had left the company without passing this knowledge to any other employee. The knowledge behind Taurus's success was lost forever. The only way Ford could regain it was to invest again in creating that knowledge from scratch.[3] Not wanting the Taurus experience to recur, Ford created the Best Practice Replication (BPR) program, with the main goal of collecting, verifying, and transferring best practices between the 53 plants of the organization with exponential profits. Ford's BPR program generated more than 2,800 best practices by 2000, with an actual added value of $886 million and a projected added value of $1.26 billion.[4]

In fact, the phenomenon of memory loss is very prevalent, particularly in big organizations. Departmental and divisional isolationism, as well as knowledge hoarding, have been behind many financial losses and poor performance. In a food processor company with 42 plants, it was found that although all the plants used essentially the same manufacturing processes and tech-nologies, their practices differed greatly. Not only had each plant developed its own practices, but performance levels were so varied that there was a 300 percent difference in performance between the worst and the best performing plants.[5] The different plants, and the organization as a whole, were learning from neither their mistakes nor their successes. No plant knew what the other plants knew.

The memory loss problem is compounded by another deficiency in the organizational brain—the brain drain, wherein valuable knowledge resources are lost with employees leaving the organ-ization. It happens when management fails to capture the tacit knowledge of its employees by transferring it to explicit knowledge.

Only 10 to 30 percent of an organization's codified (explicit) knowledge in databases and man-uals is the knowledge needed for them to operate the enterprise.[6] The rest are tacit knowledge resources. This means that employees' brainpower, tacit knowledge, or human capital is the most important resource in the organization's value creation process. If employees remained with organizations forever, then there would be no real need to instill the critical knowledge of employ-ees into the organizational knowledge base or transfer it to other employees. However, high turnover makes it inevitable that some knowledge workers will walk out with valuable knowledge resources that the organization will lose forever and have to reinvent again. An estimated 30 per-cent of the workforce in the U.S. private sector leaves in the first couple of years of employment. The figures are more alarming for government agencies, with an estimated 50 percent of the work-force retiring every year.[7]

Confusing knowledge with information, many organizations thought implementing robust infor-mation technology (IT) programs would enable them to capture the tacit knowledge of their employees. Information databases were kept sometimes of e-mail communications, and tools were provided to facilitate information flow across the whole organization. The result was a great disap-pointment. Information management and technology, though important enablers of KM, will not do the trick. People will not share their knowledge simply because they have e-mail, nor will they update the information resources in databases if not related and relevant to their jobs. The brain drain problem cannot be solved without understanding that knowledge creation is also a social process. That is what KM offers by explaining what knowledge is in the organizational context.

Defining organizational knowledge is one of the main contributions of KM. KM practitioners repeatedly stress the distinction between knowledge and information resources. By doing so, the relationship between knowledge and information, tacit and explicit knowledge, and hence KM and IT/information management is clarified. This is very important since there are still many organizations that mistakenly believe that to implement an IT infrastructure to connect people together, and to build a database, is to manage knowledge. This confusion stems from a mis-understanding of what knowledge is. So what is knowledge, anyway?

WHAT IS KNOWLEDGE? KNOWLEDGE IS TO KNOW!

"What is knowledge?" is a 5,000-year-old question, which is still the subject of much philosophi-cal, psychological, and epistemological research. It is defined as the act of knowing where a per-son analyzes information, evaluates the situation, and then creates knowledge! Luckily, the discipline of KM found a way to avoid joining this 5,000-year-old debate by adopting two work-ing definitions of knowledge. The first is that knowledge is not information, and the second is that the knowledge of an organization is more than the aggregate knowledge of its individual members. Understanding these two definitions lays the basis for KM.

The Information/Knowledge Interface—Two Sides of a Coin or Two Levels of Consciousness

If information and knowledge are one and the same, then an organization with the best information databases and technology should be the most knowledgeable. Information cannot substitute for knowledge despite the fact that to know is partly to have all the information you can get about something. This is because knowledge, unlike information, cannot stand alone from the knower—the human being. Knowledge is the outcome of the human cognitive abilities to understand, perceive, sense, and evaluate a situation. The human element is what distinguishes knowledge from information. This means the best information databases and technology systems cannot result in knowledge unless and until processed by the human mind. It is the human mind that transforms data and information into applicable knowledge expressed in action or stored in the mind as experience.

The link between information and knowledge is so close that some define knowledge as the next level of abstraction that information is taken to when applied to more specific situations by the human mind.[8] Others define knowledge as "information that has been understood, interpreted, and validated in the context of application."[9] The relationship between information and knowledge has been studied thoroughly, because if the process by which information is converted into knowledge can be rationally analyzed, then it can be computed. Interestingly, this is the quest of Artificial Intelligence, wherein the goal is to have a computer replicate human thinking. In fact, many attempts have been made to replicate the brain's neurological transfer of information in computing programs without success so far, other than in providing what is called intelligent decision support programs.[10]

However, it seems that until they can install a heart into a computer, no computer will be able to replicate the human brain's ability to know. This is because, as neurological research has shown, information bits transferred by the neurons of the brain are loaded with parcels of emotional charges that trigger memories. When the memory is triggered, the brain accesses reservoirs of past experiences, sometimes unrelated experiences, to judge a certain situation, producing knowledge. Added to that is the human intuitive or psychic ability, which intensifies the depth of human knowledge. The external input of information into one's brain alone is not what produces knowledge, but those combined with internal inputs as well. The relevance of this to KM is that no matter how robust your computational and technological systems are, unless the human aspect of knowledge generation is understood and accommodated, a KM program will not be effective.

While IT is a crucial enabler of communication, and hence sharing and transfer of information and knowledge, it alone cannot capture the depth of tacit human knowledge. Though IT tools facilitate change of behavior, they will not necessarily enable or enhance the knowledge creation process. Trillions of dollars are spent every year on IT with very few returns, and studies of computers in the workplace have shown no increase in efficiency or effectiveness.[11] In fact, overreliance on IT by organizations implementing KM programs was found to be the main reason behind the failure of these programs.[12] IT supremacy should not be confused with knowledge, and value, creation. Many organizations declare "We operate at Internet speed, and we have an internal response time of 10 minutes" without realizing that it is not the number of e-mails or user hits that are critical for knowledge creation. A survey by Ernst and Young of 431 U.S. companies in 1997 showed that almost all of the companies restricted their KM initiatives to creating an intranet (47%), creating knowledge repositories (33%), or implementing decision support tools (33%). Only 24% created networks of knowledge workers (a structural/cultural change), and 18% mapped sources of internal expertise (to locate tacit knowledge).[13]

To enable knowledge creation, the IT system should enable the conversion of tacit into explicit knowledge resources on a continuous basis, in order to retain as many resources as possible when employees leave. To do that, the IT system should accommodate the human/social aspect of knowledge creation. This human/social aspect of KM stems from the nature of organizational learning itself. While individual learning is a cognitive venture, group learning is more of a social activity in which the members interact, share, and challenge each other's interpretation, then act. Through this interaction, new knowledge is created and individual tacit knowledge is transformed into explicit organizational knowledge. The IT system/infrastructure should not only provide the necessary communication tools, but should also be designed to support the knowledge creation cycle of the core business processes of the organization. The IT system should also be based on a clear understanding of how individual knowledge is converged into organizational knowledge and vice versa.

The Individual/Organizational Knowledge Interface—
One for All and All for One

The definition of knowledge as the understanding gained from experience, and applied to new situations, ties knowledge closely to the individual. This implies that the term *organizational knowledge* is a mere metaphor to denote the aggregate knowledge of an organization's employees. After all, an organization cannot have a brain or a memory to have knowledge. But if an organization's knowledge is merely the aggregate knowledge and brainpower of its employees, then how do we classify organizational behavioral patterns reflected in databases, records, and hundreds of practices and operations? What about the wisdom gleaned from the organization's past experiences and transactions, and the insight gained from contact (relationships and networks) with customers, suppliers, and possibly competitors? Though all these resources have been created and are still maintained by individual employees, a considerable part of them remains with the organization after employees leave at the end of the day.

There is no doubt that the knowledge of a newly established organization with few members is that of its employees. But as organizations grow in size and life span, organizational knowledge takes other forms as well. As the organization grows, its knowledge base surpasses the knowledge of its individual members, to include past experiences and behavioral routines that develop as a result of the application of knowledge to an insurmountable number of settings. These behavioral patterns and routines have stored in them past experiences, and hence knowledge or wisdom, that affect the organization's modus operandi and the way it responds to the changing environment.

In addition to these routines and practices, an organization has a wealth of information resources that it collected and codified through the years. This represents the informational platform, which the employees process to produce more knowledge, and hence is part of the organizational knowledge base. The value of information databases lies in their potential to facilitate the generation of new knowledge by employees and thus should be based on their learning needs and the competencies that the organization plans to develop. That is why knowledge managers refer it to as the knowledge base, since it provides the basic knowledge resources that an employee needs to advance on the learning curve. The interaction between the individual knowledge and the various forms of organizational knowledge, and the conversion from one form to the other, is what creates value in an organization.

But, like the information/knowledge interface, it is hard to determine with any precision when individual knowledge ends and organizational knowledge begins. This is because of the complex nature of knowledge, human and organizational behavior. To clarify the matter, KM practitioners

	Tacit	Explicit
Tacit	Tacit to Tacit **Socialization**	Explicit to Tacit **Internalization**
Explicit	Tacit to Explicit **Externalization**	Explicit to Explicit

EXHIBIT 5.1   Tacit/Explicit Knowledge Conversions

created the concept of tacit/explicit knowledge, which incorporates both dichotomies (information/knowledge and individual/organizational knowledge) in a manner that enables an organization to understand the knowledge and value creation process.

Under the tacit/explicit distinction, explicit knowledge includes all that can be codified or expressed in documents, manuals, and databases. Tacit knowledge, on the other hand, encompasses all that cannot be clearly articulated but is the real source of knowledge and the basis of decision making. In addition to experience, skills, and competence, tacit knowledge includes intuition and things that the employee "just knows." The most efficient and effective way to pass this knowledge is through personal contact. To enable effective decision making, KM practitioners search for ways by which an organization can locate, externalize, and capture the tacit knowledge of its employees. Once captured, the tacit knowledge is converted into explicit knowledge, by being codified, and later shared. But there are other individual/organizational or tacit/explicit knowledge conversions that take place as well.

Nonaka and Takeuchi[14] explain that there are four modes of knowledge conversions based on the tacit/explicit concept, as illustrated in Exhibit 5.1. First, knowledge can be converted from tacit to tacit through mentoring and apprenticeship and other forms of personal contact (i.e. socialization). Second, knowledge can be converted from tacit to explicit when the individual articulates the basis of her or his decision and thus conveys knowledge (i.e., externalization). Then there is the internalization of knowledge wherein explicit is transferred to tacit knowledge when the employee learns from the organization's codified knowledge (reports, manuals, etc). Finally, explicit is transferred to other explicit knowledge where documents or information are shared and added to the organizational information database.

These four modes of knowledge conversions on the individual/organizational interface and the information/knowledge conversion in the human brain are what KM tries to boost to maximize value creation. Misunderstanding of these knowledge relations and conversions lies at the heart of so many failed KM initiatives. It is important to note that KM is not only about implementing a number of solutions to minimize organizational memory loss, prevent the brain drain, and supplement IT tools, though many organizations use it just for this purpose. Using it restrictively limits the potential of KM in advancing the whole organization on its journey to become a learning organization. British Petroleum proved that by implementing a robust KM program whereby the whole organization was transformed to a "big brain," boosting its overall performance extensively, and pulling it from the brink of bankruptcy.[15]

KNOWLEDGE MANAGEMENT—A MEANS TO AN END

> The ability of an organization to learn, accumulate knowledge from its experiences, and reapply this knowledge is itself a skill or a competence that, beyond the core competencies directly related to delivering its product or service, may provide strategic advantage.
> —Michael Zack, Northeastern University Professor[16]

The competence to generate knowledge resources, being deeply embedded in the organization's practices, routines, and brainpower of its people, can hardly be imitated by competition, and hence can be the source of sustainable competitive performance. Consequently, the ability to manage knowledge effectively becomes a critical organizational competence for achieving the organizational mission. It is the ability to recognize the availability of knowledge resources within the whole organization, develop them through transfer, and deploy and redeploy them to meet strategic objectives.

To develop KM as a core competence, a number of changes are needed at both the strategic and operational levels. On the strategic level, a shift in the organizational vision is necessary if the organization is to get on the road to becoming a knowledge/learning organization. For leadership to steer the organization in that direction, the organization should envision itself as a knowledge machine or a big brain. To manage knowledge effectively, however, leadership's commitment alone is not sufficient. Two things are needed at the strategic level to implement KM— (1) applying a gap analysis, also known as a knowledge audit, to the organizational knowledge resources to ascertain what the organization knows and needs to know; and (2) adopting the knowledge strategies that will enable the organization to meet its goals or mission, taking into account the strengths and weaknesses of its knowledge resources.

On the operational level, many changes need to be implemented that affect the structure of the organization, including the IT infrastructure, its culture, the use of practices and tools, and the job design. These changes will be discussed next.

STRATEGIZING KNOWLEDGE MANAGEMENT: VISION AND THE ROLE OF LEADERSHIP

> Problems cannot be solved at the same level of consciousness that created them.
> —Albert Einstein

Einstein's statement cannot be truer when applied to organizational behavior. To motivate employees to collaborate in sharing and creating knowledge, a shift in the way the organization sees itself is crucial. An organization needs to have a strategic shift of vision where it recognizes itself as a knowledge organization. Neglecting this step will replicate the experience of many organizations in which leadership's commitment to KM boils down to changing the IT architecture. This is why a strategic shift in the vision of the organization to one in which it sees itself as a knowledge organization should be championed by leadership and communicated down to all levels of the organization from the start. To do that, an organization may also need to undergo an audit of its culture and values to ensure that the new knowledge-oriented vision is not stifled by an adverse culture. Though effecting a cultural change is among the first steps in implementing KM, it is a change needed at the operational level and will be discussed later in the chapter.

To cultivate a vision for the knowledge organization, leadership and top management need to acknowledge the role that knowledge and learning play in attaining the mission of their organizations. One of the most successful applications of KM is by British Petroleum (BP), where leadership reformulated the vision of the company as a knowledge machine by calling themselves the "big brain." And what happens in a brain? You guessed it—dynamic transfer of neural charges carrying bits of information and experience from the memory. The message communicated is that "Our work is to communicate and learn." Another example is Chevron Corporation. After recently decentralizing its operations, Chevron found that valuable knowledge would be lost if the corporation did not learn how to share knowledge. Chevron leadership articulated and promoted "The Chevron Way" as the strategic vision dedicated to build Chevron as a "first-rate learning organization." That was the first and most important step that fueled and directed its KM program.

Knowledge Audit and Gap Analysis

Following setting the right vision and the right mindset, leadership needs to take KM to the next step at the strategic level where it decides on the knowledge strategies that will enable it to achieve its goals. This step cannot be effectively undertaken without first carrying out a knowledge audit and a gap analysis to discover the knowledge resources that the organization has and lacks. To discover gaps, an organization should be able to assess weaknesses in both its explicit and tacit knowledge resources that will hinder it from attaining the desired competitive position. These gaps may also be identified by reference to the products that an organization aspires to introduce into the market in comparison with the products of the competition as a benchmark.

A number of approaches have evolved for knowledge audits and gap analysis: stock/inventory taking, mapping internal and external knowledge flows, and mapping knowledge resources. Under the first approach of inventory taking, the organization looks at the available knowledge resources (e.g., databases, information, experts, and best practices) and then assesses these by reference to their identified knowledge needs. Sometimes the knowledge audit is performed by reference to competencies and knowledge areas in which the organization competes or plans to compete.

The second approach focuses on mapping knowledge flows internally (within the organization) and externally (with customers and other partners). Maps are created by collecting information on who consults what (database), and who consults who (experts), to detect how knowledge is both applied and generated. The results are then depicted in a graph that shows how knowledge flows between individuals, departments, and from and to the organization. Gaps under this approach are defined as blocks in the knowledge flow or weak knowledge flows that adversely affect the knowledge creation process.

The third approach relates to depicting the state of knowledge resources at a given time by reference to the business processes they support. Though similar in concept to the stock-taking approach, it differs in that the focus is on the knowledge resources available to support the specific tasks and actions of the key business processes. They are designed to enable the organization to eliminate redundancies where the same action is supported by too many resources, and shift attention to those processes that are not adequately supported.

Each of these approaches is designed to uncover a certain aspect of the state of knowledge creation and transfer in view of the business needs at a specific point in time. It is advisable to use a combination of these approaches to uncover both the state and flows of knowledge resources in an organization. Once the organization knows what it knows and needs to know, the critical knowledge networks and flows, and how knowledge resources are being and should be used to support critical business processes, it is time to strategize. The audit enables top management to assess the strengths and weaknesses of their knowledge resources, by reference to the competitive position they want to attain, as well as assess the opportunities and threats that their resources present. Before leadership implements any of the knowledge auditors' recommendations, it is essential that they consider the knowledge strategy that would best fit their business needs and future vision.

Knowledge Strategies

Strategy is the mind of an organization; without it, the organization's actions will lack direction, consistency, and hence impact. It is highly probable that leadership's failure to adopt knowledge strategies suited to their business needs is the cause of the setback of many KM initiatives. Sporadic writings in the literature address the issue of knowledge strategies in the knowledge economy. Most KM literature focuses on building a knowledge base and remodeling the IT architecture after stressing the need for leadership's commitment. Without a knowledge strategy, leadership runs the risk of reducing the KM initiative to another IT program, maybe this time with a stronger human flavor. Before moving any further, leadership needs to choose the suitable knowledge strategies for their respective industry. Deciding on the knowledge strategy is the most important step of KM as it guides leadership's decision making as to how to acquire the knowledge resources required to attain a certain competitive position. In this respect, the knowledge strategy is part of the competitive strategy as it relates to the acquisition of the knowledge resources necessary to support the organization's mission, future product, and market positions. This part of the knowledge strategy (i.e., relating to competitive performance) should be aligned with the innovation and IP strategies, as together they form the organization's intellectual capital (IC) strategies.

Knowledge strategies play an additional role in the management of the organization by defining how KM will be used to sustain the organization's competitive performance by creating new knowledge. This is because the knowledge strategy shapes the design of the knowledge base and the IT infrastructure in a way that supports business processes. Major costs are involved in building a knowledge base and an IT infrastructure. To embark on implementing a KM program, therefore, without first determining the appropriate knowledge strategy may jeopardize the success of the whole program.

A number of generic knowledge strategies are outlined here to guide the KM initiative. Joseph Daniele, Xerox's Corporate Manager of Intellectual Property,[17] mentions two knowledge strategies. He explains that a company can choose between a follower or acquisition strategy to fill gaps in its knowledge resources, identified by reference to a particular competitive position. Xerox started by listing its core competencies in 28 knowledge areas and assessing the strength of these competencies, whether comprised of "general" (organizational or explicit) or "specific" (individual/tacit) knowledge,[18] by reference to desired competitive positions. To fill the identified gaps, Daniele explains, Xerox had to choose between the two strategies.

The acquisition strategy entails acquiring state-of-art general knowledge in a certain area, which, though costly, is available from public and private sources. The fact that the acquired general knowledge does not compensate for the lack of specific knowledge makes the case for a follower strategy stronger as it enables the internal development of the required competencies. The follower strategy, adopted by the Japanese in the 1970s to compete with U.S. companies, entails reverse engineering of the products of the competition for insight. The follower strategy, Daniele explains, though not very effective in bridging specific knowledge gaps, will reduce the cost of entry to a certain field of knowledge, and provide the organization with the minimum knowledge required.

It cannot be an overstatement to say that the knowledge strategy would affect the overall competitive strategy and strategic decisions of an organization. The acquisition strategy, for example, may direct the organization to seek a strategic alliance or a merger to get both the tacit and explicit knowledge resources required from the market. No doubt this has been to a great extent fueling the merger mania of the knowledge economy. At the same time, the organization would need to invest in training, mentoring, and maybe retaining experts to convert as much of the acquired explicit knowledge resources as possible into tacit knowledge, and vice versa. However, adopting a follower strategy will direct an organization to augment the competitive intelligence function and place more emphasis on internal learning and experimentation, as well as develop its reverse engineering capability.

When it comes to knowledge strategies for defining how internal knowledge will be created and leveraged, rather than acquired, four generic strategies are identified: personalization, codification, best practices-oriented, and communities of practice (CoPs)-oriented knowledge strategies. The personalization and codification strategies were identified by Hansen et al.[19] Though the authors studied and reported on the use of these strategies in service industries, they are relevant to all industries. The personalization strategy entails reliance on individual experts and their tacit knowledge where a high level of creativity is needed to address unique problems. The great need for tacit knowledge entails the development of individual expertise and the implementation of systems to connect experts.[20] The authors note this strategy is highly desirable for service companies that offer customized, highly specialized, and high-priced services like McKinsey in the consulting industry and Memorial Sloan-Kettering Cancer Center in the health care industry.

The codification strategy is adopted by organizations in the same industries that provide solutions to common problems, which recur with considerably limited variations. As a result, the codification of past experiences (explicit knowledge) to create a knowledge base of common problems and solutions is very useful. In this case, the authors found the services offered to be moderately priced, requiring a moderate level of creativity. Examples of this are the big accounting firms' consulting services like PricewaterhouseCoopers and KPMG, and Access Health, a call-in medical center. Adopting either of these strategies affects the design of the knowledge base, the IT system, and the recruitment policy in different ways.[21] While the personalization strategy stresses the need for a KM system with a focus on connecting individual experts, the codification strategy focuses on building comprehensive databases dealing with the various but identifiable client needs. The authors explain that though businesses usually use both strategies for different purposes, they should adopt one as the predominant strategy (80 percent to 20 percent) for their KM program.

The best practices knowledge strategy entails capitalizing on what the organization knows but does not know that it knows—the knowledge that the best performing divisions have of a certain business practice. A best practice is one that "has been shown to produce superior results, selected by a systematic process and judged as exemplary, good or successfully demonstrated."[22] The concept of best practice is based on the value of experience gained from repeating a certain activity a great number of times. Repetition means long use and experimentation that with time may result in the perfection of a certain practice. This strategy may entail benchmarking an organization's best practices with those of the competition, or leaders in other industries. The choice of the benchmarked competitor will depend on the competitive position that an organization aspires to attain. Transferring such best practices perfected in one division to other divisions and business units results in renewing and leveraging the organization's knowledge resources in a certain area.

Nothing explains the best practice strategy like British Petroleum CEO John Brown's statement: "As a big company we have more experiences than smaller companies . . . So the question is what do we do with that experience? How do we find it? How do we interpret it? How do we apply it?"[23] The gist of this strategy is to leverage existing knowledge and experience by identifying the best practices that develop over time, and disseminating them for use. The success of this strategy inspired and shaped the KM initiatives of many organizations. Chevron, for example, built its knowledge base around this strategy. Chevron started with mapping and storing best practices organization-wide in the knowledge base to make them easily accessible by all departments. Chevron identified different levels of best practices, including industry and local best practices. A few years later, Chevron estimates this effort saved them $130 million annually, and reduced operating expenses by $1.6 billion in 1992 alone.[24]

Many organizations combine a best practice and a CoPs strategy wherein communities of practice are formed for the main purpose of identifying and disseminating best practices across the organization. Ford adopted both strategies for their KM program by creating the BPR program in which the proven valued practices, called gems, are captured, verified, replicated, and monitored. A CoP is responsible for each of the practices, with 1,800 CoPs representing between 60 to 70 percent of Ford's 350,000 employees, replicating more than 2,800 best practices, resulting in $866 million of actual value added to the company in 2001.[25] The BPR was first introduced in 1995 with a pilot to replicate the best practices of four plants. Upon success, the program was launched across Vehicle Operations in the 53 plants in less than a year. In 1999, Ford adapted the same model and applied it to Health and Safety concerns, to environmental application in 2000, and six sigma project replication in 2001. Again, Ford's knowledge base was designed around this strategy, installing an intranet and content management application system for sharing, replicating and leveraging proven best practices among multiple units across the world.

Other organizations use a predominantly CoP strategy by allowing the free formation of CoPs by employees in strategic areas of knowledge, provided the CoP's value proposition is aligned with business needs. An example is Siemens, where any employee may suggest the formation of a CoP. Once the value proposition of the CoP is approved, the CoP members are taken through the formation steps and provided with requisite support. Siemens uses the CoP strategy to enable the transfer of knowledge among its 100,000 employees worldwide. Another is Shell International, which started with small communities of 20 to 200 members, growing to over a hundred CoPs in 1998. The communities evolved and consolidated into three global communities with thousands of members each addressing a common problem. Shell estimates that through questions and answers on the three technical global communities it saved $35 million in 1999 and contributed $200 million in value in 2000.[26] The CoP strategy shapes the design of the knowledge base into a centrally managed intranet with decentralized content centers managed by CoPs, where CoPs create new content and monitor content as subject matter experts. Under this strategy a strong expert directory is required to facilitate building more CoPs of people who have common knowledge needs.

The role of knowledge strategies in the organizational strategic planning phase is what prompted some organizations to appoint a chief knowledge officer (CKO). The CKO's role is distinct form that of the CIO in that the former is concerned with capturing and leveraging knowledge resources dispersed in various divisions, and orchestrating its use through the use of IT and other tools. Despite some overlaps, the CKO's role would also involve identifying the areas where change needs to be effected and facilitating that change, hence, the CKO's role involves change management and organizational development. In contrast, some organizations created the position of chief learning officer (CLO). The CLO's responsibilities are similar to those of the CKO with more direct focus on the development of human resources through training and mentoring. At Coca-Cola, for example, the CLO job is described as "creating and supporting an environment in which learning and applying what you learn is a daily priority."[27]

The CK/LOs have the unenviable responsibility of deciding on the appropriate knowledge strategies and leading the implementation of practices and systems that are apt to operationalize them. The challenges that the CKO faces stem from having to decide on the combination of knowledge strategies, rather than choosing between strategy A or B, that are best suited to address the organization's needs to leverage existing knowledge and create new knowledge, as evident from the examples of Ford and Siemens. The CKO needs to explore the generic knowledge strategies and how to combine them in a way that responds to the organization's KM needs and line of business. Regardless of the strategies adopted, certain changes to the structure, culture, and IT and knowledge base architecture need to be implemented at the operational level, to which we now turn.

OPERATIONALIZING KNOWLEDGE MANAGEMENT

> Structure is just the skeleton. Organizations also have a physiology—the flow of information and knowledge is their life blood—and a psychology, representing people's values and how they think and act.
>
> —Christopher Bartlett, Harvard Business School[28]

Taking KM to the operational level involves a number of steps aimed at emancipating the knowledge creation process from the rigid organizational structure, ensuring that the right culture is in place, and supporting knowledge creation processes with requisite knowledge resources (knowledge base) and IT tools. On the structural level, the need of employees to associate freely around their areas of knowledge, by reference to practice or interest, unfettered by governance hierarchies or departmental boundaries, should be accommodated. Mapping knowledge flows and undertaking the knowledge audit can provide guidance as to how COPs and the supporting structure can be created. The CoP structure should be kept informal, as the most flexible of structures become stagnant and their purpose is defeated when formalized. To be effective, structural changes should incorporate the creation of new knowledge-related positions entrusted with supporting the knowledge creation process by focusing on KM-related functions (e.g., retrieval of knowledge resources and connecting members).

Structural changes address the skeleton or physical aspects of the organization, while culture addresses its psychology. Without a value system that encourages knowledge sharing, the structural changes related to KM will remain dormant. Cultural values act as the motivational force that activates the new structure to produce change. For knowledge sharing to reach its optimal level, certain cultural values should infiltrate to the level of the individual employee. This is achieved partly by incorporating these values in the job design so that knowledge sharing becomes part of the employee's job and career development.

This leads us to the last step at the operational level—building the knowledge base and the IT infrastructure. In Bartlett's metaphor, this is the part where channels are put in place to permit the lifeblood of the organization to flow. To be effective, the architecture of the knowledge base and the IT system in general should enable and support the knowledge creation process. This process is different for every organization depending on its core or critical business processes. Regardless of the business process, however, the IT infrastructure should support KM in two major ways. The first is through building a knowledge base that enables employees to jump the learning curve and stay on the cutting edge in their area of knowledge. The second is providing technological and nontechnological tools that facilitate knowledge sharing and connect those who know with those who need to know, as elaborated further next. Following is a discussion of the changes needed to take KM to the operational level.

Augmenting the Organizational Structure— Communities of Practice and the Freedom to Associate

Tunnel vision, departmental rivalry, and bureaucratic boundaries are problems that any organizational structure suffers from, regardless of form (functional, market oriented, or matrix) or flexibility. These problems are incapacitating to any KM program in which collaboration, and cross-pollination of knowledge from different departments and perspectives are essential. Organizational learning and knowledge creation occur through social networks that are not related to the organizational chart or departmental boundaries. These social networks evolve around those who know, and are maintained by the interest of their members, who see the value of sharing knowledge for job performance. To create and generate knowledge and to fill gaps identified in an organization's knowledge resources, it is important to allow employees to form knowledge networks around their areas of practice and interest, hence CoPs.

Employees form informal communities or networks all the time, where they refer to certain people for their knowledge, expertise, and trustworthiness. Even before the spread of the concept of CoPs, savvy organizations ventured to discover such networks in their quest for better performance and increased productivity. For example, in the early 1990s, Xerox sent an anthropologist from the Palo Alto Research Center (PARC) to observe how technical reps do their job. The anthropologist noted that reps meet at the corridors and tearoom to discuss the challenges they encountered during the day and share their solutions and experiences. Traditionally, this would be viewed as a waste of time and more controls would be imposed to ensure efficient time management and less talk in the workplace. Instead, the anthropologist recommended a supply of headphones to open "knowledge channels" for reps while on the job. The result was an improved rate of problems solved, in less time, and improved employee morale and customer satisfaction.[29]

This led KM practitioners to champion the concept of CoPs and communities of interest (CoIs) to allow such free associations between employees based on their knowledge needs. A CoP is a group of employees who come together voluntarily to share and develop knowledge in a common area of practice or interest. CoIs are similar in concept but have a looser structure compared to CoPs. In some organizations, like BP and Siemens, management allows the free formation of CoIs that are later encouraged to become CoPs if the need for them persists, and demonstrable value is added. At Siemens, any group may propose the formation of a community, which is then guided through the community development process and provided with the supporting tools on the corporate intranet.

One of the main attractions of the CoPs is their independence from the formal structure of the organization. CoPs form and dissolve based on the value they provide to their members, and the organization as a whole, in solving problems and generating strategic knowledge. This independence ensures that CoPs are formed whenever the need arises for new knowledge creation in identified strategic areas. The voluntary participation also means that the continuing existence of CoPs will depend on the value (learning) they deliver to their members through mutual exchange and continuous learning. Being member driven and egalitarian is important for the success of CoPs. An interesting incident is the insistence of a Xerox's CoP on being self-ruled, rejecting close supervision by management. The CoP demanded to be "self-managed, only be accountable for results."[30]

CoPs have been used with great success by many organizations based on a common area of interest (Cap Gemini Ernst & Young), a common best practice (Ford), a common technological area (DaimlerChrysler and Siemens), common technological and strategic questions (BP Peer and Federal Groups), and common problems with a common pursuit of solutions (Xerox). In all of these cases, the CoPs are not incorporated into the formal structure, to stay free from bureaucracy and professional tunnel vision. CoPs, regardless of the reason behind their formation, focus on a domain of interest and expertise that is strategically aligned with the objectives of the organization. An American Productivity and Quality Center (APQC) benchmarking study in 2001 found that, despite the absence of explicit/formal selection or strategic alignment criteria, CoPs are formed in the best organizations to respond to an important business opportunity.[31] The APQC found certain types of CoPs are common: best practices, innovation, helping, and knowledge-stewarding CoPs.

Innovation CoPs are cross-functional in nature and form to create new solutions and applications for the knowledge they have. Helping CoPs focus on problem solving to support certain processes or teams. Best practices CoPs identify, validate, and disseminate best practices, while knowledge-stewarding CoPs focus on connecting people who need to know with the knowledge resources, and with those who know, across the organization. The types of CoP that an organization adopts depends on its knowledge strategy and the purpose and desired outcomes for its use. More than one type may exist in an organization in which the business units have different knowledge strategies or business needs. Ford, for example, uses mainly one type—best practices CoPs—while Siemens uses more than one type, but mainly innovation CoPs for problem solving and generation of new ideas. One of the robust uses of CoPs, however, is that employed by DaimlerChrysler, based on its CoP/codification knowledge strategy. DaimlerChrysler CoPs, the "Tech Clubs," are focused on technological areas and cut across business units. Each one of these CoPs is responsible for content creation and management of a part of DaimlerChrysler's Engineering Book of Knowledge (EBOK), hence the codification component of the strategy. The success of Chrysler's CoPs, prior to its merger with Daimler in 1998, drove the creation of more CoPs, this time focusing on solving problems facing the postmerger integration and called Issue Resolution Teams (IRTs). Each IRT was headed by executives from both companies focusing on various business processes and cutting across functional departments and the various layers of the new giant. Most importantly, the IRTs were concerned with enabling knowledge transfer and sharing among the engineers of the two companies, and integrating their knowledge systems.[32]

Another major component of structural change involves the creation of new positions to support the KM program and strategy. In adopting new techniques, practices, and structures, many organizations found the need to revamp their recruitment design to create new jobs and career paths with the sole focus on managing knowledge and other IC. For example, Ford created a number of new positions to support its BPR program. These included a BPR deployment manager, and BPR specialists and managers. The U.S. Navy designed one of the most extensive career paths, creating a great number of positions with various responsibilities relating to information and knowledge, including knowledge engineers and specialists, as will be further explored in Chapter 6. Skandia has created the position of "Navigator Ambassadors," who facilitate the use of the Navigator in the various subsidiaries and act as consultants for employees who wish to use the Navigator on the individual level. All these positions fall under the ambit of the knowledge intermediation concept. This concept contends that with the knowledge intensity of business and work processes, the function of finding knowledge, facilitating its transfer, and enabling its replication or application to new situations, new positions should be created to perform knowledge intermediation. Knowledge intermediation comprises retrieving the knowledge from various sources in the organization, both explicit and tacit, as well as codifying that knowledge in a way that it can be replicated and transferred across the organization.

Structural changes, no matter how insightful and robust, will enable KM only if the culture is right. Chapter 10 covers the range of values that an organization's culture should foster, through formulating a shared vision based on the organizational identity. Effecting cultural changes, however, involves much more than identifying and promoting the right set of values across the organization. It involves implementing certain steps that mesh the right values into the way business is done. These steps are different for each of the ICM stages, and are over and above general cultural changes discussed in Chapter 9. These steps are outlined below for KM, and in Chapters 7 and 8 for innovation management and IP management respectively.

Culture, Job Design, and Recruitment Policy

> It is essential that we accept the challenge of figuring out how to make the necessary investments so that Shared Learning will secure a place at the core of Amoco culture.
> —William Lowrie, President, Amoco Corporation[33]

KM requires a culture in which knowledge sharing, shared learning, and collaboration are entrenched. The organizational psychology reflected in its culture is what motivates the employees to adopt such values in their daily work. Taking knowledge sharing values to the level of the individual employee involves a number of steps, starting with making it part of the job to engraining it in the organizational recruitment and professional development policies. The focus of the recruitment and professional development policies should be the investment in human capital to increase employee learning, satisfaction, and hence loyalty. In the knowledge economy, employee satisfaction does not depend on financial compensation as much as on being intellectually challenged, given a chance to develop, and getting recognition. To reinforce a KM-oriented culture, employee compensation, reward, and professional development policies should be aligned.

Job Design and Awards—It's All Part of the Job.   If employees do not see that knowledge sharing and generation is part of their jobs, for which they will receive recognition, they will not do it even if top management encourages it. Even when knowledge workers demand a higher financial compensation, it is because they see it as a proxy for recognition of their contribution. Research has shown that in organizations in which the culture is right for knowledge sharing and the enabling IT tools are in place, the main hurdle is that there is no time to share knowledge because it is not connected to the job and therefore is not perceived as work.[34] A number of changes in the organizational job design should occur to make knowledge sharing and collaboration part of everyone's job.

First, it should be incorporated into job descriptions. At 3M, time for sharing knowledge and collaboration is accepted as part of the job, where employees may devote up to 20 percent of their time to pursue their own projects. Once Dr. Spence Silver invented the coiling adhesive, it was part of his job to go around the organization to brainstorm about possible applications of his invention. If that was not perceived by him, and promoted by 3M as such, he would not have kept doing it for five years. BP, however, realized that moving competent personnel between business units would not be in the short-term interest of any business unit, though beneficial to the whole organization in the long term. Therefore, BP implemented a formal personnel transfer system that ensures geographic mobility of engineers wherein knowledge sharing becomes part of the business unit work system, and part of the duties of every employee.

Second, appreciation of knowledge sharing should be reflected in employees' performance review and compensation and reward system. In the mid-1990s, PricewaterhouseCoopers added knowledge sharing to the criteria of its performance appraisal. Employees must show evidence of actual knowledge sharing (e.g., "development of methodology, publishing and presenting on topics, coaching and mentoring") to be promoted.[35] In addition to incorporating knowledge sharing as one of the criteria for promotion, many organizations have an annual knowledge-sharing day, at which time business units display their best practices. Awards are then given for those business units that display outstanding cases of knowledge sharing, with booths where best practices are displayed and offered.

Culture and Recruitment Policy.   The same vigor required to incorporate knowledge sharing in the job design is required to develop the recruitment and professional development plan. All organizational dealings with employees should communicate the same consistent values to create a reinforcing effect. An organization that stresses knowledge sharing as a skill and character that current employees should possess, then recruits new employees, particularly in executive positions, whose values are patently contrary to those promoted by the organization, is never taken seriously. In such a case, leadership's commitment to knowledge-sharing values will be seriously questioned and then ignored, jeopardizing the positive cultural transformation of the organization. This is why most successful organizations focus on prospective employees' attitudes, values (not moral but work related), and interpersonal skills as prerequisites to employment. For example, recruiting the right people who fit the culture of Saturn was the main factor behind its success in the automobile industry. Saturn had a careful recruitment process followed by two days of orientation and a substantial investment in training. As a result, Saturn had the lowest turnover in its industry.[36]

Closely related to the recruitment policy is the professional development policy and the organization's view on employee retention. Different organizations view employee retention differently. The majority of organizations prefer to retain their employees as long as possible, given the high costs of recruiting and training. Other organizations promote a lower retention rate as the flow of recruits may enhance innovativeness. This is why it is important that top management thoroughly consider their retention policy to inform decision making as to the kind of employees that will be recruited, trained, and developed as well as outplaced. McKinsey, for example, adopts an "up or out" retention policy wherein young graduates are recruited and trained. Depending on their performance and development they have a number of years and identified stages that they go through, after which they are made partners or outplaced. Once an employee is at the partner position, the company aims to retain the employee as long as possible.

The retention policy or idea should be carefully considered given its grave impact on culture and knowledge sharing. An employee who feels threatened will not collaborate or share knowledge, since the element of trust necessary for knowledge sharing is missing from the work relationship. At the same time, the organization needs to address what Sveiby calls the life cycle of employee competence. Sveiby explains that the length of this life cycle depends on the level of creativity required from the employee, which will eventually come to a plateau.[37] Most organizations in this situation do nothing, incur future losses, or fire their employees, saving losses yet affecting morale and turnover rates. The solution may lie in training to keep the knowledge worker's knowledge current and fueling creativity in new areas or, alternatively, in retraining to "find an alternative use for the capacity, that is, create an alternative professional carrier as a mentor, teacher, [or] networker,"[38] hence knowledge stewards. An example is the personnel plan of USAA, a global *Fortune* 500 financial services company, which provides that displaced employees should be retrained, not fired. Turnover is less than 6 percent for the whole organization, and morale is high.

Investments in human capital through training that raises the employee's educational level by 10 percent have resulted in an 8.6 percent increase in productivity, compared to a 3.4 percent increase due to investments that raised the value of equipment by 10 percent.[39] Return from train-ing produced two and half times the return accrued from investing in equipment. Training and retraining employees should be part of the overall personnel plan, to create as secure a working environment as possible in which trust is fostered. One way of doing that is by shifting the responsibility of keeping current and getting retrained to the employee him- or herself. The APQC found that best-performing companies use a "pull" philosophy when it comes to human capital development. According to this philosophy, it is the responsibility of employees to make themselves continuously employable by pulling the knowledge resources they need from within or outside the organization.[40] Other organizations, like Skandia,[41] provide placement services to their outplaced employees to help them explore career opportunities somewhere else.

The Knowledge Base and IT Infrastructure

The IT architecture of an organization should serve two major functions: (1) creation and man-agement of content, and (2) provision of technological enablers.

Content Management and the Knowledge Base.   Content management[42] involves creating con-tent, maintaining it, and using consistent taxonomy so that content created by a CoP or a subject matter expert can be properly stored and later retrieved by anyone in the organization. Content creation by various departments, business units, and CoPs results in divergent use of taxonomies and idiosyncratic approaches to content management. Many organizations find they have the information but cannot effectively retrieve it or, once retrieved, it is not understandable due to the divergent models used for their creation, defying assimilation of content with other departments. Add to that content received from external resources (e.g., subscriptions and customers' and sup-pliers' feedback). But streamlining content to make it comprehensible and accessible to those who need it is only part of the problem. The more critical challenge is weeding out old obsolete content, updating it and creating new content. Although central IT departments maintain the sys-tem and own the process for the whole organization, only subject matter experts can create new content relevant to local and business unit needs.

The practice of content creation and management was launched decades ago with the use of the first servers and increased digitalization. The KM concept, however, revolutionized content management by centralizing content management and decentralizing content creation to CoPs and subject matter experts. KM also transformed the substance of content creation and the archi-tecture of the IT system through the idea of the knowledge base. The knowledge base has the distinct goal and function of supporting business processes, and hence decision making, by pro-viding knowledge and not just information or data. A knowledge base is different from an infor-mation or database in two ways. First, it enables access to both explicit and tacit resources, with the goal of maximizing learning of users. To perform this, the explicit resources needed to carry out critical business processes are organized in the knowledge base in knowledge/content cen-ters by reference to the key decisions in the business process. The knowledge/content centers should have all the knowledge an employee needs to make a critical decision, plus learning tools and materials. Second, the knowledge base enables access to sources of tacit knowledge required to make key decisions, through expert directories. In that respect the knowledge base refers to CoPs, their areas of knowledge, how to contact them, and how to gain access to their content centers.

To create a knowledge base the taxonomies used should coincide with the critical knowledge creation processes it is designed to support. Taxonomies and classification systems should reflect the way users work, and thus follow the knowledge creation process. For the knowledge base to enable effective KM, the knowledge base's content should be classified in a way that resonates with the various stages in the critical business processes. Because critical business processes are specific to organizations, the design of the knowledge base should take into account how work is done. Therefore, the input of the end users, whose decisions and learning needs are being supported by the knowledge base, is of absolute importance.[43]

That being said, general classifications include grouping knowledge resources by reference to process, practice, topic area, or by reference to the decisions that need to be made. In some cases, organizations classify knowledge in terms of problems commonly faced and lessons learned. In all cases and regardless of the taxonomy and classification methodology used, the knowledge base should be developed with a clear vision of the common business problems or processes it is meant to support.

Once the knowledge base design is clear, then and only then can the organization examine the design of its IT infrastructure. All software programs have underlying models that control the progress and sequence of electronic applications and flow of information. If that model conflicts with the knowledge creation process underlying a certain business process or decision-making loop, it will both confuse and counteract the KM effort. In general, the IT infrastructure should at least enable the following applications for effective KM.

IT and Other Enablers.   Enablers of KM comprise technological and nontechnological tools designed to facilitate knowledge transfer, sharing, and conversion of knowledge from explicit to tacit and vice versa, with the main goal of promoting organizational learning.

Technological tools should enable the following applications:

- Retrieval of information through search tools.
- Digestion and making sense of information through visualization and other tools that detect information patterns. Many tools have emerged in the past few years that enable the presentation of a vast volume of information and data in a comprehensible way through topographical maps and citation trees. The user is instantly able to detect concentration of information in certain areas, as well as the referencing relationships between them.[44]
- Location of experts through expert directories. Consultation companies first championed expert systems in which the need for tacit knowledge is greater, especially in companies that accept clients with unique needs and problems. Examples are Pricewaterhouse Coopers' Knowledge View software; Booz, Allen & Hamilton's Knowledge On-Line; and McKinsey's Knowledge Resource Directory.
- Communication tools, including document transfer capability. A multitude of tools are available mainly by e-mail through intranets, videoconferencing, and virtual centers. Many organizations have created virtual workplaces where employees can "meet" and share knowledge. Other organizations instead provide videoconferencing. In one case, videoconferencing was used to help solve a drilling problem in one of BP's remote sites, with reported savings of $270,000 that day alone.

Nontechnological Enablers.   Enabling KM also involves the use of nontechnological tools and methods that accommodate the human/social aspect of tacit knowledge creation and transfer. Of course, CoPs, if looked at as a tool, are the best enablers for tacit knowledge transfer, particularly when face-to-face meetings are used. In addition, other tools are required (e.g., storytelling).

STORYTELLING OR ANECDOTE MANAGEMENT—
AN ANCIENT ART REVIVED

> Stories are powerful because they show us rather than tell us, dramatically enacting a truth that can move us and influence the way we see things.
>
> —S. Denning, The World Bank[45]

Technological tools, though effective in facilitating communication, do not convey the rich context of knowledge. This rich context can be conveyed only through human social interaction, which has led KM practitioners to create tools that adapt social activities to the business environment. Storytelling and discussing and reflecting on past actions have become KM tools.

David Snowden, Director of Europe IBM Institute of Knowledge Management,[46] shows that in a case study of how pilots use their tacit knowledge to solve problems and make decisions, the pilots usually make decisions based on their gut feeling, and then rationalize them after the facts. The rational explanation is hardly as valuable as the "real" one, which is the source of wisdom and thus effective decision making. Snowden explains that the rational explanation for the decision is usually not the real reason for or the basis of the decision and thus does not effectively transfer the pilot's tacit knowledge or make it explicit. Rationalization of the decision afterwards to fit the norm or the organizational protocol (which is part of the explicit knowledge) has a restrictive effect. Snowden therefore concludes in his presentation that transfer of tacit knowledge can occur only through direct human interaction in a community of trust, hence communities of practice, using social tools like storytelling.

The storytelling approach to KM was originally introduced by Thomas Davenport and Laurence Prusak and popularized by Stephen Denning, formerly of the World Bank. This approach asserts that the use of stories to communicate knowledge is very powerful in conveying the rich context of knowledge. Stories do not convey just content but the meaning of experience from one person to another in a way that the recipient can easily recall. Stories are narratives about past experience that show how a certain department, group, or even organization solved a certain problem. Their contextual richness makes them very effective in communicating layers of meaning that the mind can later access.

Take, for example, KM's assertion that knowledge is not contained in a particular practice but in the why of it. No story communicates this better than the lamb roast recipe. A 5-year-old girl asked her mother why she cuts the end part of the lamb loaf before she roasts it. Her mother replied that she had watched her mother do it this way, and since the grandmother cooked the best roast, the mother used the same method. So the little girl went to her grandmother and asked about it, the grandmother replied that she had watched her own mother, who used to make the best roasts, do it this way. Eventually, the girl got to visit her great-grandmother, who was on her deathbed. Luckily, the great-grandmother had an explanation for cutting the end part of the lamb loaf before roasting it—the pot she had was not big enough!

As an approach, storytelling comes in many forms (e.g., Lessons Learned and After Action Reviews [AARs]). Lessons Learned are similar to success stories but are more about delivering a certain message about what works and what does not as knowledge gleaned from experience. AARs, originally developed by the U.S. Army in the 1970s, involve meetings to review past operations and explore ways in which these operations could have been performed differently for better results. The recommendations from an AAR session are then tested in future operations, and hence learning is facilitated through doing. At the U.S. Army, AAR sessions are conducted so that soldiers meet with their superiors, who sit in the back rows of a round setting to encourage soldiers' contributions and overcome the constraints of military ranks. The first replication of AAR in the corporate setting is BP's "learn after doing" program, which aims to answer "What can we learn from the difference between what happened and what should have happened?"[47]

CONCLUSION

The goal of KM is to advance the organization in its journey to becoming a learning organization, where knowledge sharing, creation, and application is a way of doing business. The optimal beneift of KM is to prevent organizational memory loss and brain drain—in short, dissipation of knowledge resources—and hence enhance the efficiency of knowledge work and the innovative capability of the whole organization. To get there KM should be systematically implemented at the strategic and operational levels. However, an organization first needs to transform the way it sees itself and adopt the identity of a knowledge organization. This involves formulating a strong vision that drives the long process of becoming a learning organization. This chapter outlined the main KM concepts and practices, including undertaking an audit of the knowledge resources, adopting the appropriate knowledge strategies, effecting necessary structural and cultural changes, and adjusting the IT infrastructure to support KM processes. Though the organizational context is important in the design of any program, Chapter 11 will guide the reader further step by step to implement the KM stage of the Comprehensive Intellectual Capital Management (CICM) model. To highlight and demonstrate some of the complex issues of KM, however, the next chapter outlines the Navy's KM system.

NOTES

[1] B. Brinker, "Intellectual Capital: Tomorrow's Asset, Today's Challenge," CPA vision, available online at *www.cpavision.org/vision/wpaprer05b.cfm.*

[2] Havens, C., and Kapp, E., "Easing Into Knowledge Management," available from Pricewater-houseCoopers at *www.pwcglobal.com/extweb.*

[3] R. Margulis, "Memory Loss Can Lead to Disaster," Washington CEO Inc., 1998, *www.waceo.com/archive/nov98/1198-knowmgt.html.*

[4] Presentation by Henry Fradkin, Ford Global Technologies VP of Licensing, January 2001.

[5] J. Pfeffer & R. Sutton, *The Knowing–Doing Gap* (Boston: Harvard Business School Press, 1999), p. 8.

[6] Results reported in a survey conducted by D. Skyrme & Co., in Skyrme Insights, available online at *www.skyrme.com/insights/10knet.htm.*

[7] A Murray's Knowledge Management Workshop, E-Gov Conference, Washington, DC, April 22, 2002.

[8] Roger Mizumori, "Knowledge Management—5 Ws and 1 H," CRC Press LLC, *www.brint.com/members/20120418/whatiskm/whatiskm_1.html.* Knowledge management practitioners use the pyramid depiction to represent stages of abstraction where data at the bottom of the pyramid is transformed into information where patterns are detected, then to knowledge where information is applied in a specific context, then to the final stage of wisdom where experience plays a major role.

[9] H. St. Onge, "How Knowledge Management Adds Critical Value to Distribution Channel Management," *Journal of Systematic Knowledge Management,* January 1998.

[10] See R. Ruggles (ed.), *Knowledge Management Tools* (Stoneham, MA: Butterworth-Heinemann, 1997).

[11] M. Zack (ed.), *Knowledge and Strategy* (Stoneham, MA: Butterworth Heinemann 1999), p. 3.

[12] See R. Ruggles, "The State of the Notion: Knowledge Management in Practice," *California Management Review* 40, Summer 1998, p. 83.

[13] *Id.*

[14] I. Nonaka & H. Takeuchi, *The Knowledge Creating Company: How Japanese Companies Create the Dynamics of Innovation* (Oxford: Oxford University Press, 1995).

[15] See Chapter 1 for BP's experience.

[16] Supra note 11, p. xi.

[17] J. Daniele, "Understanding and Managing Knowledge Assets for Competitive Advantage in Innovation and Product Development," in P. Sullivan (ed.), *Profiting from Intellectual Capital* (New York: John Wiley & Sons, 1998), pp. 305–318.

[18] Daniele uses the terms *general* and *specific* knowledge, which are close equivalents of explicit and tacit knowledge, respectively.

[19] M. Hansen, N. Nohria, and T. Tierney, "What's Your Strategy for Managing Knowledge?", *Harvard Business Review,* March–April 1999, p. 106.

[20] *Id.*

[21] *Id.,* p. 109.

[22] American Product and Quality Center (ACPQ), APCQ Benchmarking Terms, 2000, *www.acpq.org/free/terms.*

[23] Supra note 5, p. 216.

[24] J. Roos, G. Roos, L. Edvinsson, and N. Dragonetti, *Intellectual Capital: Navigating in the New Business Landscape* (New York: New York University Press, 1998), p. 49.

[25] Supra note 4.

[26] D. Skyrme, "I3 Update," No. 56, December 2001, available online at *www.skyrme.com.*

[27] L. B. Ward, "In the Executive Alphabet, You Call Them CLOs," *New York Times,* February 4, 1996.

[28] C. Bartlett, "The Knowledge Based Organization," in R. Ruggles and D. Holtshouse (eds.), *The Knowledge Advantage* (Oxford, U.K.: Capstone, 1999), p. 119.

[29] J. Brown and E. Gray, "The People Are the Company," *www.fastcompany.com/online/01/people.html.*

[30] APQC, "Building and Sustaining Communities of Practice: Continuing Success in Knowledge Management Report" (APQC, 2001), p. 10.

[31] Id., pp. 8–10.

[32] For more information on the merger of Daimler and Chrysler and the integration of their KM systems, refer to M. Rukstad and P. Goughlan, "DaimlerChrysler Strategy," Harvard Business School case 9702412, 2001.

[33] Carla O'Dell and C. Jackson Grayson, Jr., with Nilly Essaides, *If Only We Knew What We Know: The Transfer of Internal Knowledge and Best Practice* (New York: Free Press, 1998), p. 77.

[34] Supra note 30.

[35] *Id.,* p. 83.

[36] *Id.,* pp. 85–86.

[37] K. E. Sveiby, "Measuring Intangibles and Intellectual Capital," in Morey, Maybury, and Rhuraisingham (eds.), *Knowledge Management: Classic and Contemporary Works* (Cambridge: MIT Press, 2000). Available online at *www.sveiby.com/articles/KOS9.html.*

[38] *Id.*

[39] Results reported in a 1995 study by the National Center on the Educational Quality of the workforce, mentioned in note 2.

[40] Supra note 30, pp. 80–81.

[41] See Chapter 9.

[42] On the relationship between content and knowledge management in a number of U.S. companies, see the APQC report "Managing Content and Knowledge" (APQC, 2001).

[43] Despite the fact that the critical business processes are organization specific, the basic knowledge creation process that underlies most business processes is the same. This basic knowledge creation process is outlined in Chapter 10 to guide management as to the design of the knowledge base.

[44] See, for example, StarTree at *www.inxight.com,* Themescape at *www.cartia.com,* The Brain at *www.natrificial.com,* and Ebizinsights at *www.visualinsights.com.*

[45] See S. Denning, *The Springboard: How Storytelling Ignites Action in Knowledge-Era Organizations* (Stoneham, MA: Butterworth-Heinemann, 2000).

[46] Presentation by David Snowden at the Intellectual Capital Congress, McMaster University, Canada, January 18, 2001.

[47] D. Skyrme, "I3 Update," No. 25, November 1998. Available online at *www.skyrme.com/updates/u25.htm.*

6

The U.S. Navy Knowledge Management System: A Case in Point*

If you ask Alex Bennet, former Deputy CIO for Enterprise Integration, about knowledge management, be prepared for a captivating answer. A pioneer in the area of knowledge management (KM) and one of its main champions in the Navy, Bennet believes KM is powerful enough to transform a whole organization, maybe even society as a whole. Advocating the need to cultivate oneself as an agent of change in one's environment, Bennet became one herself. As an agent for change, she worked on transforming the concepts of KM into comprehensible practices of relevant operational applications. How she accomplished this with the help of her team and other KM champions, in the Navy and other public agencies, is a case in point.

Bennet saw in KM the answer the Navy needed. The Navy has over 700,000 employees, including civilian and military personnel on active duty and reserve, some deployed all over the world. To be more accurate, the Navy is even bigger than that, with its diverse support networks including contractor organizations and other governmental, private, and academic organizations. Managing the knowledge of these diverse groups to support the Navy's mission of national defense seemed impossible initially—but not to Bennet, who met the challenge head on, realizing the need to integrate knowledge from the far corners of the Navy. A few years after the concept of KM was introduced, the Navy emerged as a global leader in the area of KM.

BACKGROUND

Knowledge management is of particular importance to the Navy, unlike the stages of innovation and intellectual property (IP) management. This is because the Navy does not offer products or services, making the innovation management stage, in its definition as the new product development stage, irrelevant. Innovation in the Navy is related instead to the creation of new processes and work systems that enable effective decision making. In addition, the Navy as a government agency cannot own patents or copyrights on technologies and works they develop; hence, IP management as well is not relevant. Though government labs are concerned with defining their rights when entering into research and development (R&D) collaborations with universities and industry, they do not use their IP for commercial gain. This makes KM by its definition—the stage at which intellectual resources of an organization are managed to enable the organization to meet its mission effectively—the most critical stage of intellectual capital management (ICM) for the Navy.

*Thanks are due to Alex Bennet, former Deputy CIO of the Navy, and the Co-Chair of the Knowledge Management Working Group, for her gratuitous assistance with resources and review of this chapter.

The Navy realized the value in cultivating KM as one of its core competencies. After all, the wisdom of war entails that knowledge, intelligence, and wisdom, properly applied, lead to success.[1] Thus, KM to the Navy was not merely an addition to its information technology (IT) systems but a means to becoming what Bennet calls a knowledge-centric organization. For that to happen, the Navy adopted KM as a way of doing business by implementing it at both the strategic and operational levels.

The first step was to introduce the concept of KM in a methodical way to facilitate its introduction within the structured system of the Navy. To do so, the CIO Office developed the "KCO Toolkit" CD-Rom (the Toolkit) and distributed over 15,000 copies within the Navy. The Toolkit introduced the concepts of KM, defined its stages, and provided various tools and best practices to guide the various Navy organizations in their KM initiatives. The CIO Office did not stop there. Instead, they demonstrated the value of KM by acting as the central organization in the Navy with prime ownership of the KM process by recognizing its strategic importance for the Navy's mission and vision. In addition, the CIO acted as an agent of change by continuously and consistently defining the parameters and practices of KM. In addition to the widely distributed Toolkit, the CIO targeted leaders to cultivate KM champions, and advance implementation of KM at the strategic level. That's when the ship was ready to sail.

THE STRATEGIC LEVEL: HOW THE NAVY'S CIO CONVINCED COMMANDERS THAT KM IS A WAR STRATEGY

> Knowledge superiority accelerates commanders' decision-making processes, enabling them to effectively lock out a foe's intended actions and overcome his defenses.
>
> —Alex Bennet[2]

Meaningful change always starts with a vision that inspires and motivates. That's why the CIO embarked on defining its vision with KM as a core component. The 2000 Information Management/Information Technology (IM/IT) strategic plan issued by the Secretary of the Navy, the Chief of Naval Operations, and the Commandant of the Marine Corps articulated the Navy's future vision as one in which the Navy would not only provide invisible technology but would also create a "knowledge-centric culture where trust and respect facilitate information sharing and organizational learning."[3]

This vision informed the knowledge strategy of the Navy in which "knowledge superiority" was adopted as a core strategy along with the Navy's longtime maritime strategy of "forward presence."[4] According to the Navy's knowledge superiority strategy, KM enables the Navy to maintain a competitive advantage over adversaries by enhancing the Navy's knowledge of the battlefield. The transfer and sharing of explicit and tacit knowledge in real time enables effective strategic and tactical decisions to be made. Even after decisions have been made, sharing knowledge about them creates an appreciation of past decisions and enables future success through Lessons Learned.

To promote the vision of a knowledge-centric organization and get key players to buy in to the knowledge superiority strategy, the Naval Academy started the "knowledge superiority" dialogue. This facilitated the emergence of KM champions among the commanders. Soon, KM champions appeared at the commander level in a number of Navy organizations. Commanders started communicating their success stories, leading to the establishment of the KM leadership network. This in turn fostered leadership commitment at the various organizational units of the Navy for KM. But leadership commitment did not stop here. In addition, the Navy created and defined the duties of the position of chief knowledge officer (CKO).

The CKO's position was elevated to the highest level by reporting directly to the Navy's CIO. The Navy CIO, with the KM Working Group sponsored by the Federal Chief Information Officers Council,[5] defined the responsibilities and credentials of CKOs, creating the first comprehensive guide on this new position.[6] The guide makes clear that the CKO's role in the public sector is markedly different from that of the CIO in that the former focuses on changing organizational behaviors, processes, and technologies rather than focus on computers and IT networks. The strategic role of the CKO involves leading the organization to becoming knowledge-centric by forging knowledge strategies, defining best practices, fostering a knowledge-sharing culture, and developing knowledge bases and resources.

With KM objectives appearing on the strategic agenda of the Navy's organizations, the Navy was ready to take KM to the operational level. But first, the Navy needed to know if it had what it takes.

Gap Analysis: Knowing What We Know and What We Need to Know

The Navy's model uses gap analysis not only to take stock of the existing and required knowledge resources but to discover whether they have what it takes to attain the "knowledge superiority" strategic vision. Under this approach, gap analysis is applied "to identify the forces and factors in place that support or work against the implementation of the knowledge management system."[7] The CIO performed gap analysis both on the enterprise and individual levels, while leaving it to knowledge managers at the command levels to conduct their own gap analysis for their respective units. The CIO still guided gap analysis on the command level by defining its purpose as identifying "the gaps between the current knowledge management strategy, mission, and profile as compared to what will be necessary to realize the desired state with regards to knowledge management in your Command."[8]

On the individual level, the Navy set out to determine the individual competencies required to survive in the information age, mainly, to create and share knowledge. The Navy decided that to be able to generate knowledge and make effective decisions, an employee needed to be "information literate," a concept developed by Alex Bennet. Bennet explained that information literacy is not only an important skill but one required for survival in the information age. Information literacy is the ability to:

- Determine the nature and extent of the information needed.
- Access needed information effectively and efficiently.
- Evaluate information and its sources critically.
- Use information effectively to accomplish a specific purpose.
- Understand the economic, legal, social, and ethical issues surrounding the use of information in a virtual world.[9]

The definition of information literacy further clarifies the relationship between information and knowledge and spells out the basic knowledge creation process. The explosion of information makes an individual's cognitive abilities alone insufficient to produce knowledge. To enable knowledge creation, the individual worker needs to develop a set of skills for finding and analyzing the right information. Thus, "information literacy" should be recognized and developed as a general competency of knowledge workers to increase the effectiveness and efficiency of their knowledge work. This point is crucial, yet seldom stressed. Defining the requisite individual competencies, however, is not enough for implementing a robust KM system; hence, gap analysis should be applied to the competencies of the whole workforce. This moves gap analysis to the enterprise level.

On the enterprise-wide level, the CIO assessed the gaps in the competencies needed to operationalize the Navy's "knowledge superiority" strategy. In general, to attain knowledge superiority, the Navy needed to cultivate KM as a core competency, thereby building individual competencies and tacit knowledge. Several gaps in both the explicit and tacit resources were discovered. One explicit knowledge gap is related to knowledge about KM as a practice in its own right. As a start, the Navy produced a number of CDs that contained extensive training and learning materials about KM. This was the easy part, as the case always is with generation of explicit knowledge. The challenge was to fill gaps in the tacit knowledge resources.

To do so, the Navy organized a number of knowledge fairs, where experiments in KM at different divisions and commands were shared and assessed. Participation in the knowledge fairs was high, reaching around 3,000 participants, including people from academia and industry. These knowledge fairs later became a venue for sharing knowledge and actively exchanging views on strategizing and operationalizing KM. Subsequently, the Knowledge Management Community of Practice (CoP) was formed, in which the knowledge about KM was further developed and tested.

Though this was a great achievement in filling the various knowledge gaps, the CIO realized that more was required to develop KM as a core competency. The integral milestones to reach that goal are building the knowledge base, capturing and transferring best practices for solving problems, and facilitating quick and easy access to knowledge to shorten learning curves and move the organization forward to becoming a learning organization. None of these milestones can be achieved without building KM-related competencies. The only way, the CIO found, is to create new job positions to cultivate the required new competencies. To that end, the CIO created the most comprehensive new career paths in KM, covering managerial and frontline positions.

Interestingly, the KM career paths and positions are distinct from those related to IT. In addition to the CKO's position, the new positions included knowledge managers, knowledge systems engineers, knowledge process engineers, knowledge community leaders, performance measurement engineers, knowledge assurance managers, and knowledge assistants. This major change made it clear that those who work on KM are not simply "futurists" beating their heads against the walls, but are "champions," enabling the Navy to attain its "knowledge superiority" vision.

The new positions fall under three main categories: "knowledge brokerage," "knowledge research," and "knowledge stewardship." They apply the concept of knowledge intermediation wherein certain individuals are entrusted with the responsibility of locating information and expertise efficiently and disseminating knowledge to those who need it, saving time and shortening the learning curve. While knowledge brokers assist in locating tacit knowledge resources (i.e., experts), across the enterprise, knowledge researchers retrieve and transmit explicit knowledge resources to seekers. The responsibilities of knowledge brokers revolve around relationships and networks while those of knowledge researchers focus on data and information management. Both positions are in contrast to the positions of knowledge stewards, whose primary responsibility is to act on senior management's mandates to capture and codify tacit knowledge in a certain area of knowledge.

Addressing knowledge gaps at the strategic level and devising ways to fill them equipped the Navy with the capability to move KM to the operational level. To take the "knowledge superiority" strategy to the operational level, Bennet explained that the Navy had to address the issue by looking at the infrastructure, the processes, the organization (structure), and the culture of the Navy. So far, the Navy has reached the "Community of Practice" stage of their Strategic Approach for Implementation, illustrated in Exhibit 6.1. The journey is long and is far from simple, so a rough plan was needed, and that's what the CIO provided in the Toolkit.

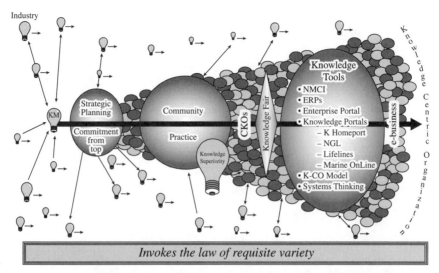

EXHIBIT 6.1   Strategic Approach to Implementation

OPERATIONALIZING KNOWLEDGE MANAGEMENT: THE ROUGH PLAN

According to the Navy's model, the journey to becoming a knowledge-centric organization is divided into seven stages. They include:

1. *Stage One: Building awareness of the concept.* At this stage, the organization is made aware of the concepts and terminology of KM. It also involves articulating in relevant ways the value of KM in attaining the strategic goals of the organization. This stage is particularly important for KM as the theoretical frameworks, which are very rudimentary in this new field, are developed.

2. *Stage Two: Exploring issues affecting knowledge sharing.* This is the stage at which knowledge audits and gap analysis are undertaken to assess the status quo of the organization's culture, leadership commitment, processes, resources, and practices. The goal of Stage Two is to determine the starting point, formulate a vision of the ideal KM situation, and identify milestones, targets, issues, and objectives.

3. *Stage Three: Identifying KM strategic goals and processes including measurement.* At this stage, KM is taken to the operational level through a number of programs and initiatives with defined objectives. Monitoring and measuring performance by reference to the objectives developed under Stage Two are essential to guide management as to evaluating the progress of the program and determining the required adjustments.

4. *Stage Four: Developing knowledge-sharing processes.* Once management obtains results from Stage Three, they will be in a better position to determine what works for the organization and to develop the best practices into defined KM processes. At this stage, management has a clear idea of how the KM program will be designed.

5. *Stage Five: Refining knowledge-brokering concepts.* In addition to the processes and practices implemented at Stage Four, the organization creates at this stage positions for owning and overseeing the various processes of KM.

6. *Stage Six: Building CoPs.* At this stage, the structure of the organization is augmented with informal communities that work on creating and sharing new knowledge in areas of strategic importance to the organization.

7. *Stage Seven: Reviewing the journey.* At this stage, ways to review and continuously monitor the KM initiatives are implemented, with the focus on promoting learning.

The rough plan offered a general guideline for organizations in the Navy on how to implement KM in their work routines and daily operation. In addition, the Navy as a whole has undergone a number of changes to operationalize KM. These changes are presented following the framework presented in Chapter 5, starting with changes to the structure, culture, and IT architecture of the whole enterprise.

Structural Changes—CoPs

An important feature of the Navy's KM is stressing that the development of CoPs is an integral step in operationalizing KM as illustrated in Exhibit 6.1. The Navy's CIO provided very detailed guidelines to individuals and organizations on how to develop CoPs. The Navy adopted the CoPs' informal structure as a shade structure along with its rigid hierarchical one. A number of CoPs have emerged to date. The first formal CoP in the Navy is the Knowledge Management Community of Practice (KMCP), which was formed after the 1998 and 1999 knowledge fairs. Another community of interest (CoI) with the same domain of focus evolved with 600 members. The two communities are focused on one area of knowledge: KM. The Navy is also part of a government-wide CoP, the KM Working Group mentioned previously. The KMCP has played a major role in operationalizing KM by providing learning materials, training, and guidance. In addition, the KMCP facilitated exchange of best practices through the Navy via knowledge fairs, where more than 75 best practices of KM were displayed and explained.

A number of CoPs, reaching around 23 CoPs of variable types and sizes, also emerged. With the CoPs' leaders being mainly of senior ranks, the CoPs are given leadership's sponsorship as well as the administrative and financial support they need. CoPs are spread throughout the Navy, hosted by various organizations, each with a defined domain, value proposition, and defined method to transfer its knowledge both to the members and to the organization as a whole. The 23 CoPs comprise best practices, innovation, and helping and knowledge-stewarding communities, with the last type being the most common.

It seems that the CoP structure is not foreign to the Navy. The Navy Seals have always operated as mission-based groups with a flat structure similar to a CoP. The knowledge of each group is maintained and passed through the commanders and Lessons Learned to the rest of the organization. Like the CoPs, the Navy Seals have a focused domain of knowledge, enabling quick and responsive decision making. Indeed, the ability to deploy and redeploy armed forces in small operational groups has been recognized as the competency that the U.S. military needs to develop to respond to the opportunities and threats of a knowledge-intensive world.

The CoP guidelines provided by the CIO were the major starting point to operationalize KM and enable knowledge sharing. However, it is change of the Navy's culture that made knowledge sharing a reality.

Culture—Not a Question of Sharing But of Security

Before knowledge sharing was at all possible at the Navy, a cultural shift was imperative. Generally speaking, the Navy's culture, and that of other government agencies to varying degrees, is to withhold information and hoard knowledge as much as possible for counterintelligence and security purposes. The main hurdle is how to balance knowledge sharing for enhanced decision making with the critical need for information security. The dilemma is similar to that faced by private organizations in which the need to share knowledge internally and externally should be balanced with the need to protect competitively harmful information. The dilemma, of course, is of greater magnitude and more serious ramifications when it comes to the Navy. On one hand, the Navy needs to ensure that the information available to the public cannot be interpreted to result in knowledge or intelligence about classified operations. On the other hand, withholding information and knowledge can hinder and undermine learning and effective decision making. The Navy's culture of secrecy, characterized by limiting information and knowledge sharing on a need-to-know basis, intrinsically conflicts with an open knowledge-sharing approach required to attain the "knowledge superiority" vision of the Navy.

The conflict between the two sides and the need to transform the Navy's culture were appreciated from the start. In 2000, a pilot study of 250 people in one department identified change in the Navy's culture as the most important factor for successful KM.[10] Thus, KM must be developed hand in hand with information/cyber security, counterintelligence, and encryption technology. Indeed, the CIO portrayed the need for this balanced approach in the 2000 IT/IM strategic plan by recognizing both security and KM as twin strategic objectives. The CIO sent a strong message across the Navy that a balance should be struck between the two, while having the unenviable role of guiding the balancing effort.

To do so, the CIO approached the issue methodically by showing that information decays with time and that only by sharing it in the critical time does it produce knowledge, where both time and knowledge are of the essence in the art of war. Though withholding information may seem more appropriate for the Navy's need for security, only by sharing information could successful decisions be made in the critical time. The CIO used the "knowledge life cycle model" shown in Exhibit 6.2, to communicate the idea that information gets obsolete with time. Only circulated, shared, and brainstormed information results in knowledge that can be leveraged to the benefit of everyone in the organization at the critical time. Simultaneously, advances in technology should be developed to ensure cyber security. Only when a culture of trust is cultivated, coupled with technological supremacy, will the Navy be able to strike the sensitive balance between knowledge sharing and security.

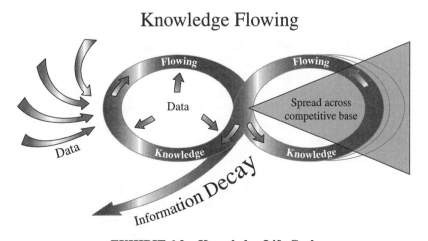

EXHIBIT 6.2   Knowledge Life Cycle

For the CIO, changing the culture of an organization is difficult, particularly for the Navy, in which an adverse culture has existed for a long time. The CIO stressed that the key to success is "consistency in approach" by aligning performance measures, accountability, incentives, and rewards with the value of knowledge sharing.[11] As noted in Chapter 4, cultural change requires much more than speeches from leadership on the value of knowledge sharing to the success of the organization and statements of strategic objectives. It requires integral changes to the job design and reward and compensation systems to reflect knowledge sharing as part of the job, and not just a value to be revered. And that is what the Navy did.

The Navy rewarded departments that implemented KM, which sent a strong message that knowledge sharing is not only acceptable but appreciated by leadership. In the annual knowledge fair, the Navy presented a number of KM awards. Past awards included the "Outstanding Knowledge Expert System," "Outstanding Collaborative Knowledge Sharing Approach," and "Operationalizing KM Concepts." The increasing number of projects and programs recommended for these awards indicates the success of the Navy in effecting the required cultural shift. Moreover, the progressive step of creating new career paths in KM made it clear that sharing knowledge is not part of the value system but part of the job.

Moving forward with enabling KM in the Navy, the CIO needed to address another very important role in operationalizing KM—the role of IT and the knowledge base.

Infrastructure, IT, and the Knowledge Base: The Interrelationship

One reason KM initiatives fail is that organizations lack theoretical frameworks to explain the relationship between KM and IT. Without such an understanding, the structure of the two systems may counteract each other. Installing new IT tools and systems without identifying the role they will play in KM is a futile exercise. As explained in Chapter 5, the design of the IT infrastructure and choice of tools should be tailored to enable the knowledge creation processes that are specific to each business. The Navy's model addressed this both on the theoretical and practical levels.

On the theoretical level, Bennet's insightful analysis of how information management (IM), IT, KM, and infrastructure interact and support each other provided the basis.[12] As shown in Exhibit 6.3, Bennet explained that "knowledge management cannot be effective without both information management and IT, where all are supported by the organizational infrastructure." Additionally, all of the various layers have intellectual capital components, which Bennet classifies as human, social, and corporate capital. The effective management of each of these components should be aligned through the layers of KM, IM, and IT. The structure and tools of IT and IM should be designed to enable effective KM by accommodating the social, human, and corporate aspects of knowledge creation and transfer.

On the practical level, the IT and IM architecture and tools should be designed in a way that activates both explicit and tacit knowledge transfer, across the Navy as a whole, and within the various departments and organizations. The first step was to build an enterprise-wide portal to replace the Navy's shore-based networks—the Navy Marine Corps Intranet (NMCI). The NMCI gives civilians, sailors, and Marines on the front lines direct access to the network of people and information available in government, industry, and academia. In addition, NMCI enables each organizational unit to support local information, of suppliers for example, through a common framework. The main purpose of the NMCI is to provide enterprise content integration (centralized) while at the same time allowing local user focus and content contribution (decentralized).

Though the enterprise-wide portal allows for enterprise content integration, there are knowledge content areas that are unique for certain organizations or departments and thus need to be both created and maintained at the organizational level. As mentioned in Chapter 5, a knowledge

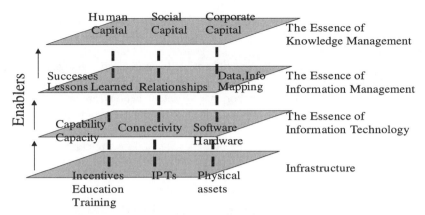

EXHIBIT 6.3   Interaction between KM, IM, and IT

base has two main functions: (1) creating and managing content in a way that makes knowledge accessible when needed, and (2) locating experts in defined knowledge areas. The choice of the taxonomy and method in which knowledge and information resources are stored in the knowledge base is of critical importance since it directly impacts its effectiveness in supporting knowledge/business needs. For the second function, the adoption of appropriate tools that facilitate communication and exchange of information are essential. In addition to providing guidelines on how to develop taxonomies, the Navy's CIO identified two main ways in which knowledge resources can be grouped for future reference—*clustering* and *clumping*.

The Toolkit explains that, traditionally, knowledge and information resources have been *clustered* by reference to topic areas. Another approach called *clumping* can also be used, in which knowledge and information resources are grouped by reference to the decisions that they support. Each of these approaches can be used for their respective advantages. While clumping enables effective decision making, clustering is useful for comparing and contrasting sources in one area to determine best practices, for example. Despite this, it seems that for the Navy's purposes the use of clumping as the main approach for building the knowledge base is the preferred approach, for its support of the decision-making process. Bennet notes that "[I]f the Knowledge-Centric Organization is able to help the human process of 'clumping' by organizing information and knowledge around key decision points, decisions can be made more efficiently and effectively."[13]

By following the order in which decisions are made in an organization, clumping facilitates the classification of knowledge and information resources according to the knowledge creation cycle. To aid the various organizations across the Navy in designing their own knowledge bases, the CIO provided a guideline on the steps involved[14]:

1. *Identify the core strategic process.* The strategic process is defined as the core process that each command follows to accomplish its mission. The core process is mapped to identify the actions taken, decisions to be made, flows, and documents used.
2. *Identify critical actions.* In this step the actions (or tasks) that are critical to the success of the mission of the given process are identified.
3. *Identify critical action personnel.* Those are the people that make the decisions or perform the critical actions involved in the process. This helps identify the expertise (tacit knowledge) and the explicit knowledge resources that are needed to support the various actions, leading to Step 4.

4. *Identify knowledge, skills, and information requirements.* This step goes deeper into identifying the types of knowledge, skills, and information required to enable choosing the appropriate taxonomy.
5. *Aggregate knowledge needs into content centers.* Resources are aggregated in various centers based on clustering (i.e., around topic areas). It is suggested that the resources be prioritized in hierarchies of importance. Content centers are formed by listing resources under their different types (e.g., documents, databases, and personnel).
6. *Design a communication strategy.* The final stage involves examining the existing IT architecture and tools and determining how these should be augmented or changed to support the information flow and social interaction between those who know with those who need to know.

This leads us to the next step as to the choice of tools to facilitate KM. On the enterprise level, the portal and the intranet provided the necessary IT tools. But more important than IT tools are "social" and analytical tools that enable the creation of an effective KM system.

Knowledge Management Tools

The Navy's model emphasizes the use of two major types of tools for KM: *social tools* to facilitate transfer of tacit knowledge and *analytical tools* to facilitate implementation of KM initiatives. For social tools, the Navy uses storytelling to transfer such of the tacit knowledge that cannot be made explicit. Storytelling has been facilitated by the creation of databases of Lessons Learned and success stories. For analytical tools, the Navy advances two main approaches—systems thinking and KM performance measures. Systems thinking is advanced as a tool that enables management to go beyond the surface into discovering the mental modes and behavioral patterns of an organization that preclude change. Once discovered, they can be dealt with, and hence the KM initiative can be effectively implemented. Performance measurement, the Navy way, is presented as a tool to monitor the progress of the KM initiative and to adjust it along the way. Below is a presentation of these tools.

SYSTEMS THINKING: THE PSYCHOLOGY OF ORGANIZATIONAL ACTION AND INACTION

As a new approach, KM requires highly complex changes in organizations. Added to the complexity is the fact that KM requires changes in the way the individuals and groups relate to, and interact with, each other in the organizational context. The action of one group, or individuals in a group, affects the activity of another in many ways, impacting the ability of the whole organization to change. Change is thus a complex process that needs a systemic approach to be tackled in the most effective way. That is why Bennet saw a promising tool in the "systems thinking" approach that could dramatically enhance the ability of knowledge managers and champions in the Navy in dealing with situations in which change seems impossible.

Systems thinking is identified by Peter Senge, in his book *The Fifth Discipline*,[15] as one of the five major disciplines that a learning organization has to master. Senge defines a learning organization as one that has an expanding capacity to create its future. Among the various disciplines, including personal mastery, shared vision, mental modeling, and team learning, systems thinking is viewed as the most important. Systems thinking provides an approach for managing complexity by helping decision makers understand the cause-and-effect relationships that underlie a problem or a pattern of events.

By studying and exploring the hidden structures, systems thinking takes one beyond noticing and reacting to events to appreciating the structures that give rise to them. Usually, we can connect events to a number of trends and patterns and thus improve our ability to anticipate and plan for these events before they happen. But it is not until we are able to go deeper in our analysis of the problems that we can discover the tangible (e.g., organizational charts) and intangible (culture and mental models) structures that are triggering such events on a continuous basis. By understanding this relationship, an organization is able to create and maintain a systemic approach to change in a complex setting.

Bennet explains that systems thinking is relevant from the perspective of organizational learning, as it provides a "method of collective inquiry that helps us see the whole relative to our aspirations. We also need models about how disparate parts of an organization can better coordinate their strategic choices and actions to achieve desired results." Systems thinking is a tool that involves analyzing a problem by visualizing the loops of relationships and how they reinforce or cancel each other out, resulting in the perceived problems. By seeing how actions of a certain group or department affect the actions in the other, and give rise to certain problems, management is able to close the gap between what is envisioned and the status quo.

PERFORMANCE MEASURES: THE USE OF LIMITS TO FOCUS ATTENTION

Chapter 2 outlined the various measurement systems developed to monitor the performance of an organization's ICM efforts, including the Balanced Scorecard, the Intangible Assets Monitor, and the Skandia Navigator. The common theme that runs through the IC measurement systems in varying degrees is that they are to be used as navigation tools or guiding principles rather than strict measures. In contrast, measures under the Navy's model play the role of "setting limits" by defining a set of objectives that should be met. The theme of "setting limits" is one that runs throughout the Navy's KM model, including its measurement system. As Bennet[16] explains, "Despite the negative connotation of 'limits' in American culture, they have an incredible power because they focus attention on something generating new thoughts and ideas." Though the measuring unit is given the liberty to choose any of the above mentioned measurement systems it has to do so within the limits, or guiding principles, set by the CIO.

It Is Not How You Measure But What—Of Limits and Guiding Principles

The enactment of the Government Performance and Results Act in 1993 in the United States conditioned approval for funding on the proven performance of the federal government agency in question. Though government agencies do not have to produce a profit, they still have a bottom line—to achieve their mission.[17] Achieving the respective mission is the yardstick by which the performance of an agency will be judged. This made performance measures of particular importance in the management of public agencies as they have to show "non-financial" results. To respond to this challenge, a number of government agencies developed a set of guidelines on how to design performance measures, to prove that they are using their financial and human resources effectively in attaining strategic objectives.

The Navy's model accepts measurement systems, outlined in Chapter 2, without limiting their use, as long as the guiding principles are kept in mind. Still, the Navy's Metrics Guide for Knowledge Management Initiatives provides guidance on how the different measurement systems can be adapted to address the Navy's KM needs. The four perspectives under the Balanced Scorecard system, for example, are modified for the Navy's purposes as follows:

1. Business value replaces financial perspective—"How do we look at management?"
2. User orientation replaces customer perspective—"Are we satisfying our user needs?"
3. Internal perspective is focused on "Are we working efficiently?"
4. Future readiness replaces renewal and growth perspective—"What technologies and opportunities/challenges are emerging?"[18]

Interestingly, the Navy's model also encourages the use of what have come to be known as "soft measures." These are success stories or "lessons learned" that communicate financial or other returns (e.g., success of an operation) that have been realized from a KM program.[19]

The differentiating characteristic of the Navy's performance measurement system is its focus on what should be measured rather than how. This is clarified through a number of guiding principles that determine the variables that should measured, the types of KM initiatives, and the various types of measures that can be used.

The First Guiding Principle: What to Measure.   The Navy's CIO clarified from the outset that it is not how you measure, but what you measure that is important. The Toolkit explains that when it comes to knowledge assets or IC, there is a lot of confusion as to whether performance measures should calculate the value of the asset/capital or the effectiveness of the initiatives designed to leverage them.[20] Without delving into theoretical discourse, the Navy's model stresses the latter, that is, effectiveness of the KM initiatives is what should be measured.

But the question remains, what type of KM initiatives should be measured? The Navy classifies initiatives into three groups. The first is program and process initiatives that relate to organization-wide activities. These are usually designed to streamline business practices and transfer the best practices across the organization.[21] The goal of these initiatives is to prevent "reinvention of the wheel" and duplication of error. An example of such initiatives is the management of customer relationships.

The second type of initiatives are those related to program execution and operation, including transferring expertise and getting the right knowledge to support the effective execution of operations. These initiatives should aim at facilitating collaboration and knowledge sharing to increase productivity, effectiveness, and quality. They apply to operations like R&D, manufacturing, and computer and software systems.[22]

The third type of initiatives deals with personnel and training, or the development of the organization's human capital. The goal of this initiative is to foster employee satisfaction through improving the quality of life and enhancing employees' learning experience (e.g., fringe benefits management and distance education). The Navy's model proceeds to identify the measures that can be used.

The Second Guiding Principle: Not All Measures Are the Same.   Like the Intangible Asset Monitor model, the Navy's model provides standards that point to the results that should be targeted in a KM initiative. These standards identify the final outcomes, outputs, and the effectiveness of the initiative as a whole. Again, to measure the effectiveness of any of the three types of KM initiatives (program/process, execution/operation, and personnel/training), a mix of the three types of measures should be used.

Outcome indicators measure the impact of a KM initiative on the effectiveness of the organization as a whole. They attempt to measure things like increased productivity and the ability to meet strategic goals more effectively. Typical indicators include time, money, or personnel saved by implementing a practice, rates of change in operating costs, and improvement in quality.

Output indicators measure the direct process outputs for users, the lessons learned in capturing new business, and doing old business better. These measures attempt to monitor, in quantitative terms, how the initiative contributed to meeting the organization's objectives. Typical indicators include time to solve problems, usefulness survey, time to find experts, and user ratings of value added from the initiative.

System indicators measure whether the individual systems are fully operational and deliver the highest level of service to the users. They monitor the usefulness and responsiveness of identified practices and tools. Typical indicators for an IT system, for example, include number of hits, frequency of use, viability of the posted information, usability survey, and contribution rate over time.

The indicators mentioned are specific to the initiative introduced but mainly aim at monitoring the effectiveness of initiatives in achieving identified goals. What makes the Navy model's measures and indicators outstanding is the assertion that measurement is only a step in a continuous process of a number of steps. These steps include designing, building, and implementing a program; designing performance measures; assessing these measures; then returning to the design phase, as illustrated in Exhibit 6.4.[23] Like the Navigator model, measures under the Navy's model are not seen as indicators that have to be monitored consistently and remain the same over time, but rather as "a valuable means to focus attention on desired behaviors and results."[24] Distinctive to the Navy's model is the use of the life cycle principle in designing the measures.

The Third Guiding Principle: The Life Cycle of an Initiative.   One of the main challenges that the authors of IC measurement systems face is measuring the flow rather than the stock of IC. The Navy's model addressed the problem of flows by allowing for change in the measures depending on the life cycle of the initiative being measured. This practice, according to the Navy's *Guide,* is taken from the American Productivity and Quality Center's (APQC) benchmark study of the best practices in measuring KM initiatives. The APQC report[25] states that a program goes through a number of stages in its life cycle, from preplanning, start-up, and pilot project to growth and expansion. Each stage determines the type of measures required. For example, the pilot project stage measures the success of the initiative to deliver real value to business objectives, such as efficiency rates through the transfer of best practices. By adopting this system as a guiding principle, the Navy model tries to overcome the static nature of measurement by accommodating the dynamic nature of knowledge/value creation.

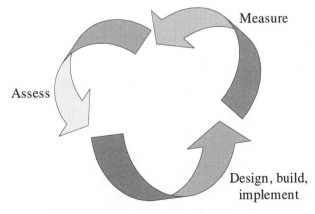

EXHIBIT 6.4   Performance Measures

The Navy model does not attempt to take the measures out for external reporting purposes because one of the goals of measurement is to secure funding across the organization for the KM initiative and programs. As such, measures are used as transient communication tools that change according to the audience and the message intended to be delivered.

CONCLUSION

The Navy implemented KM by effecting a number of changes in the organizational structure, culture, and IT architecture. This chapter outlined the changes that the Navy implemented using the framework outlined in Chapter 5 as a guide. To effectively implement KM, the Navy introduced the CoP structure to loosen what is an otherwise rigid structure. One of the Navy's main means of doing this was to recognize knowledge sharing as one of its strategic objectives, highlighting how liberal—rather than on a need-to-know basis—knowledge sharing will enable the Navy to achieve its mission of mastering the art of war. The emergence of KM champions at the commander level, coupled with the Navy's awards for successful operationalization of KM strategies, gradually transformed the Navy's secretive culture to one amenable to knowledge sharing. The Navy's IT infrastructure also underwent major changes to respond to the knowledge needs of decision makers at all levels, and led to the development of the knowledge base. One of the drivers of the Navy's success in KM is that it considers KM a developing effort, and hence involves academia, industry, and other government agencies to remain on the cutting edge. Equating its final goal as becoming a learning organization, there is no limit to the Navy's success with KM.

NOTES

[1] A. Bennet and Dan Porter, "The Force of Knowledge," in A. Bennet (ed.), *Handbook of Knowledge Management* (New York: Springer-Verlag, to be published).

[2] A. Bennet, "Knowledge Superiority as a Navy Way of Life," *Journal of the Institute for Knowledge Management,* Spring/Summer 2001 (vol. 3 No. 1), pp. 46, 48.

[3] Department of the Navy, Information Management and Information Technology Strategic Plan, 2000/2001.

[4] "Forward presence" is a U.S. maritime strategy assuring that forces are deployed in strategic locations worldwide to enable quick response. Supra note 3, p. 1.

[5] The Knowledge Management Working Group is a U.S. government–wide group, sponsored by the Federal Chief Information Officers Council, formed to address issues relating to knowledge management, and includes experts from industry and academia.

[6] A. Bennet and R. Neilson, "The Leaders of Knowledge Initiatives: Qualifications, Roles and Responsibilities," in A. Bennet (ed.), *Handbook of Knowledge Management* (New York: Springer-Verlag, to be published).

[7] The Toolkit.

[8] *Id.*

[9] A. Bennet, "Information Literacy: A New Basic Competency." Available online at *www.chips. navy.mil/archives/01_fall/information_literacy.htm.*

[10] Pilot study reported in note 1. The study identified success factors for KM as follows: culture 29 percent, processes 21 percent, metrics 19 percent, content 17 percent, leadership 10 percent, and technology 4 percent.

[11] The Toolkit.

[12] Supra note 1.

[13] *Id.*

[14] The Toolkit.

[15] P. Senge, *The Fifth Discipline: The Art and Practice of the Learning Organization* (New York: Currency/Doubleday, 1990). Systems thinking is adapted from systems engineering, first pioneered by Jay Forrester as "Industrial Dynamics" in the 1960s.

[16] Interview on January 10, 2002.

[17] Department of Navy CIO, *Metrics Guide for Knowledge Management Initiatives* (the Guide), August 2001, p. 9.

[18] *Id.,* p. 18.

[19] The approach of managing and measuring knowledge through lessons learned or storytelling is also known as "anecdote management." See Chapter 5 for more details.

[20] Supra note 17, p. 5.

[21] *Id.,* pp. 29–30.

[22] *Id.,* pp. 43–44.

[23] *Id.,* p. 11.

[24] *Id.,* p. 5.

[25] APQC, *Measurement for Knowledge Management,* February 2001. Available at *www.apqc.org/ free/articles/dispArticle.cfm?ProductID=1307&CFID=154242.*

7

The Innovation Management Stage

Thomas Edison created the "innovation factory"[1] in the 1890s, and so laid the foundation for the discipline of innovation management (IM) and the new product development (NPD) process. The NPD process organizations use today has the same stages and steps that Edison perfected over 100 years ago. One may wonder, therefore, if IM in the knowledge economy has changed in any way other than through the use of technological solutions that speed up the process and cut both testing time and complexity. Though the NPD process has remained substantially the same, the crux of IM has been revolutionized by the IC concept. Like knowledge becoming the main raw resource in everything produced today, innovation has become the main organizational process that adds, and hence extracts, value. This is true whether the innovative capacity of the organization is turned inward, in search of excellence and better ways of doing business, or turned outward to make new products.

Innovation management is the stage at which value created at the knowledge management (KM) stage is extracted by transforming knowledge into a product or a work process. Innovation in the knowledge economy is not a mere process for making new products, but is the main production process at a time when organizations innovate or perish. The need to manage innovation as the core production process has overbearing implications on business management as a whole. Under the IC concept, innovation expanded beyond the confines of the research and development (R&D)/NPD department to the whole organization, and beyond the organizational boundaries to external partners. The need for a high turnover of ideas drove top management to solicit ideas from a wider base of people, covering almost everyone in the organization and overflowing to networks of outside partners. Innovation thus progressed from being department based to organization based and eventually to network based, where innovation is managed over a number interorganizational and external networks.

Before proceeding with the concepts and methods of IM under a comprehensive intellectual capital management (CICM) approach, we will first explore Edison's style of IM.

EDISON'S STYLE OF INNOVATION MANAGEMENT

Edison made innovation more of a science than an art by systemizing the innovation process into certain steps. His innovation factory transformed the image of the sole inventor working in his or her lab to a team working together to transform an idea into a product. Edison and his team conducted research, brainstormed new ideas, experimented with new product concepts, and developed them into marketable products, laying the basis of the NPD process as we know it today.

Edison's NPD process included the following stages:

- *Conducting the necessary research.* In Edison's words: "First study the present construction. Second ask for all past experiences . . . study and read everything you can on the subject."[2]

- *Applying imagination to the problem and comparing alternative solutions.* At this stage, brainstorming with various concepts is undertaken. In Edison's words: "Result? Why man, I have gotten a lot of results. I know several thousand things that won't work."[3]
- *Developing new product concepts* where various prototypes are created and tested for technological and design feasibility.
- *Scanning the environment.* This practice is designed to determine the requisite and desirable conditions required for the new product to succeed. It may involve investing in changing the environment in cases in which the change introduced by the innovation is radical.
- *Commercializing the product.* This involves forging a number of alliances to exploit the product across related markets and multiple distribution channels.

Maybe Edison was not the greatest inventor of the time, but he certainly was a great innovator. His invention of the light bulb was not the most superior in technological terms, but he knew how to innovate. First, he bought fields of bamboo, what is called in business terms vertical or backward integration, to ensure a constant supply of raw materials.[4] That was not enough since the existing infrastructure did not support his invention in a society accustomed to gas lamps. To solve this problem, Edison bought a small electrical company and transformed it to provide electricity to domestic outlets. Thus, he adopted another strategy of vertical forward integration—buying the distribution channels. Edison also invested in educating customers as to the utility of the light bulb and created one of the best social innovations of the twentieth century.

Starting in the 1960s, the NPD process has been streamlined across and within industries to a major extent, with divergence detected only between the "best" and the "rest" of organizations.[5] A survey by the Product Development Management Association (PDMA) in 1997 of the NPD stages used by 600 U.S. firms revealed that 60 percent use a formal NPD process consisting of six stages,[6] very similar to Edison's. Even those firms that had no formal NPD process developed their new products through similar stages. These stages consist of "exploration, screening, business analysis, development, testing, and commercialization."[7] While the goods manufacturing industry often uses more than six stages, companies in the service industry tend to use fewer stages, discounting the manufacturing and testing stages.[8] Furthermore, the six stages have also been found to be consistent regardless of the level of innovation (i.e., whether it is incremental/evolutionary or radical/revolutionary). This confirms that the generic NPD stages used today, illustrated in Exhibit 7.1, have been substantially the same since the dawn of the twentieth century.

Though the structure of the NPD process and the main stages remain substantially the same, that does not at all mean that IM has not been transformed by the IC concept. The shift in the knowledge economy to IC as a source and means for value extraction transformed innovation

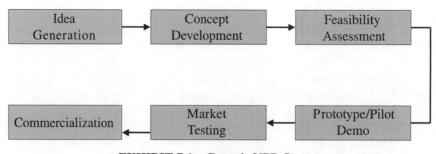

EXHIBIT 7.1   Generic NPD Stages

management in many ways taking it away from the Edison model in substance, if not in form. The most prominent change is the emergence of a new business model for IM that is used by the most innovative organizations regardless of industry—the network-based innovation model.

THE INTELLECTUAL CAPITAL CONCEPT AND NETWORK-BASED INNOVATION

The high demand for new ideas and new product concepts in the knowledge economy posed a major challenge to the organizational innovative ability—a challenge that can be tackled only by liberating innovation from being the function of one department (R&D or NPD) to an activity to which everyone in the organization contributes. Increasingly, IM progressed into managing an innovation portfolio across a set of dispersed internal and external networks. Internally, IM entails knowing the competencies and skills of employees across the whole organization (human capital) to form the right team according to the needs of the innovation project. It also involves knowing the skills of existing or potential partners (customer capital), to forge the alliances that facilitate the innovation process.

In addition to spreading inside, the innovative activity overflowed to encompass networks of suppliers, distributors, customers, and sometimes competitors. In addition to the move from the department-based (Model A in Exhibit 7.2) to network-based (Model B) innovation, the innovative activity spread out through the various levels of the organization as well. Hence, innovation did not only spread sideways and outside the organization but also downward to the frontline levels. With all this activity, organizations found they had to use cross-functional teams to manage what is otherwise a chaotic activity over widely dispersed networks. Cross-functional teams are formed by bringing people together from across the organization with multi-disciplinary skills, experience, and qualifications that best fit the needs of the innovation project at hand. Cross-functional teams

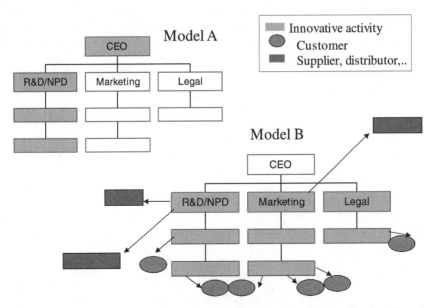

**EXHIBIT 7.2   Innovation from Department-Based to Organization-Based
to Network-Based**

serve the innovation process under the network-based model in two ways. First, by bringing people from all the concerned departments together (R&D, legal, marketing, manufacturing, etc.), time to market is reduced. Second, the cross-pollination of ideas and experiences of people from different business units, and sometimes from outside the organization, increases the market orientation of the product and hence increases market success rates.

Effective IM amidst the prolific innovative activity, and hence intellectual process, is impossible without ICM. The IC concept redefined IM in the knowledge economy by stressing the role of IC in the innovation process. To yield successful results, an IM model should enable the organization to tap into the employee brainpower (human capital) and that of external parties (customer capital), while at the same time effectively utilizing the business processes of the organization (structural capital). Under the Comprehensive Intellectual Capital Management (CICM) approach a number of changes on the strategic and operational levels are needed to make IM the job of everyone.

On the strategic level, it became much more important than ever to decide on innovation strategies to lead the pulsating innovative activity spreading in the whole organization. The role of top management in IM shifted, with idea generation being pushed down to the operational level and out to partners, to deciding on innovation strategies for competitive positioning. In addition, network-based innovation meant that top management needed to manage innovation projects as a portfolio over the dispersed networks and across the whole organization. The innovation portfolio serves two crucial IM needs. First, it enables the management of risks associated with innovation by diversifying the portfolio mix to include projects of varying levels of innovativeness. Second, it facilitates cultivation of the ability to get to market fast by presenting a snapshot of all the innovation projects across the organization, enabling allocation and shifting of human and financial resources to meet strategic priorities.

On the operational level, network-based IM entails effecting a number of changes to the organization's structure, culture, processes and tools. Not only does structure have to be flexible enough to facilitate formation of cross-functional innovation teams from people within and outside the organization but it should also allow the formation of competence centers where competencies are grouped, developed, and later accessed. The structural changes should also address the R&D function, and how it will be organized to operationalize the innovation strategies. Certain changes must also take place to engrain innovation in the culture of the organization, and thus motivate employees to innovate and customers to contribute. A number of methods and tools devised for that purpose will be outlined. We will first examine the changes required at the strategic level.

STRATEGIZING INNOVATION MANAGEMENT

Innovation is a chaotic activity, particularly at the early stages of idea generation, and can be unruly if left without a clear strategy. Innovation strategy defines how top management intends to use the organization's innovative capacity to enhance performance and attain the targeted competitive position. It may seem that the most innovative organizations don't have an innovation strategy, since they give free rein to their employees' innovative flair to take them in any direction. The fact of the matter, however, is that they do have a very defined strategy—an employee-driven innovation strategy, as will be explained in this section. Innovation strategy is crucial, particularly with innovation being pushed as far down as possible to the frontline, emphasizing the need to direct the innovative surge from the top of the organization with defined strategies. Innovation strategies play two roles. First, they form part of the competitive strategy of the organization by defining the areas in which new products will be introduced (i.e., the markets and segments they will compete in). Second, innovation strategies shape the mix of the innovation portfolio and the way innovation is managed across the whole organization at the operational level.

Following is an account of a number of innovation strategies for managing the innovation process.[9] The interaction of these strategies with the organization's overall competitive strategies and the creation and management of the innovation portfolio will be outlined.

Innovation Strategies and Competitive Positioning

> Trade-offs are essential to strategy. They create the need for choice and purposefully limit what a company offers.
>
> —Michael Porter[10]

In 1980, Michael Porter, of Harvard Business School, identified three main generic competitive strategies that organizations use for long-term competitive positioning in the market.[11] According to Porter, the three strategies are cost leadership, differentiation, and focus. In cost leadership, a business strives to supply a more cost-effective product compared to competitors, and compete through price. Differentiation is achieved by supplying products with higher value to the customers, commanding premium prices. Differentiation can be achieved by producing superior product qualities, new features, branding, and customer service. Focus strategies narrow the focus of a business to a certain product market segment, where both cost-leadership and differentiation strategies can be pursued.

Porter explains that usually an organization adopts one of the three as the primary competitive strategy without losing sight of cost control or operational efficiency under a differentiation strategy, and of quality and customer service under a primarily cost-leadership strategy. Porter further explains that while cost-leadership strategies require tight cost control and the need to meet strict targets, differentiation strategies require strong coordination among functions and the ability to attract skilled and creative people.[12]

Despite the insight that Porter's analysis provides, it remains too broad for the strategic management of the innovation process. This is because whether an organization adopts a cost-leadership as opposed to differentiation competitive strategy, innovation will remain the main enabler for operationalizing both strategies. This applies in cases in which innovation is applied inwardly to finding new ways of doing things, making products with less cost, or alternatively making new differentiated products. The challenge is that innovation is a very broad activity that includes any new development under the sun, big and small, accentuating the need for an innovation strategy that sets some parameters to lead the innovation process, and to make the necessary trade-offs.

Though strategic planning is a situation-specific exercise, there are a number of generic innovation strategies that can be used to steer the innovation surge. Four innovation strategies are identified: customer-driven, inward employee-driven, outward employee-driven, and technology-driven innovation strategies. These strategies can be combined with Porter's differentiation and focus strategies, while cost leadership can be combined only with inward employee-driven innovation strategies. Choosing one of the generic innovation strategies guides top management as to steering the innovation surge of the whole organization, as well as selecting the innovation practices and methods that are aligned with the innovation strategy. How to choose the strategy that suits the organizational situation and needs is dealt with in Chapter 11. But for now the four innovation strategies are outlined.

Customer-driven innovation strategies steer the organization's innovation activity to satisfy the perceived needs of the customers, where customers' input into the innovation process is essential. Many service businesses adopt customer-driven strategies, particularly if the majority of their business revolves around one or few primary customers. The use of such strategies, however, is not limited to the service industry, and has been used for breakthrough innovations in other industries. The use of this strategy requires careful definition by each business of who the customer is and what needs are to be focused on. As a result, the role of marketing, sales, and customer service departments in the NPD process is integral, since they have maximum exposure to customers' needs.

Inward employee-driven innovation strategies tap into the organization's employees' innovative capability, and steer it inward to the improvement of the way business is done (i.e., process innovation). Though less studied than the NPD process, process innovation has always been used by organizations to secure competitive positions through cost leadership. PricewaterhouseCoopers "Technological Barometer 2000" reports that 83 percent of organizations direct their resources to the development of new products, while 47 percent direct their resources for cost reductions through process innovation.[13] Though this strategy may seem similar to cost leadership, it should be distinguished from economizing and cost control as it relates to innovating new ways that may or may not reduce costs but always improve job performance and hence productivity. This strategy entails empowerment of employees by allowing them to implement their process innovation ideas within set budgetary limits. Organizations adopting these strategies can compete through cost leadership (e.g., Wal-Mart) or differentiation (e.g., Home Depot).

Outward employee-driven innovation strategies are a new development in the knowledge economy. Organizations that adopt these strategies emancipate the innovative capability of their employees and allow it to flow in any direction, unhampered by strict control but smoothly steered into broad business areas. They practice what can be called organic innovation, wherein the innovative spirit is left to its natural dynamics. This strategy is adopted by organizations that see innovation as what they do and who they are. They usually grow into huge conglomerates by diversifying into a multitude of businesses in which their innovative capability enables them to compete. An example is 3M, which, following this strategy, has grown tenfold, with 100 core technologies and 66,000 products, compared to Norton, which started the same time as 3M in the abrasives business and remained an abrasives company. Many of the organizations adopting this strategy, when not as revolutionary as 3M, have independent skunk works where employees may experiment freely with their own projects. It must be noted, however, that those organizations that built such skunk works without adopting an employee-driven strategy failed to attain the same degree of success.

Technology-driven strategies[14] steer the organization's innovative activity to join and win the technology race. Most of their NPD process is directed to developing the more technologically superior product or service, or the next generation of technology. Being a race, organizations operating under such strategies compete to invent the next new thing, and to establish their technology as a market standard. Organizations adopting this strategy use patenting heavily, given that patents can be the strongest competitive weapons in the fierce technological race. This made patenting strategies among the most important of technology-driven strategies.[15]

Alignment of the innovation strategy with the organizational values, culture, purpose, people, and practices is essential to extract maximum value from the innovation process. It should be noted, however, that, like the competitive strategies, adopting one innovation strategy should not blind management as to the main enablers under the other strategies (i.e., customer involvement, employee empowerment, and technological advancement). For example, adopting employee-driven innovation strategies should not cause management to lose sight of customer needs even though it is not adopting a customer-driven innovation strategy. That being said, it is important for top management to decide on one innovation strategy as the primary one, to provide the focus required for strategic purposes.[16] At all times, however, the organization cannot lose sight of the competitive landscape at the strategic planning phase, as will be further explained in Chapter 10.

Innovation management at the strategic level also involves the choice of the innovation portfolio mix. Top management needs to decide whether they will compete by pursuing incremental (or evolutionary) or radical (or revolutionary) innovation projects. More accurately, they need to answer the question of "What is the mix of incremental and radical innovation projects that would best enable the organization to attain its targeted competitive position?" Managing innovation as a portfolio is critical both for allocating resources according to strategy and for managing innovation-related risks. To that we now turn.

Innovation Portfolio Mix and Risk Management

One of the major challenges of IM is dealing with the uncertainty and unpredictability of market success of new products. Highly innovative projects have the highest projected return, as well as the highest risk of failure. An innovation portfolio that is diversified among projects of varying levels of innovativeness enables the effective management of innovation-related risks. Innovation is relative and includes, in ascending level of innovativeness: cost reduction, incremental improvements to existing products, major revisions, line or brand extensions, next generation or platform projects, new-to-the-firm products, and new-to-the-world products.

There is a trend in the knowledge economy to have a portfolio with fewer less-innovative projects and more medium- to high-innovative projects.[17] Regardless, the innovation portfolio mix should be diversified according to a number of parameters (e.g., long term versus short term, high risk versus low risk, and low projected versus high projected return). The use of these parameters with the innovation strategy serves to maintain a balanced innovation portfolio with planned sequential market launches, varying levels of innovativeness and projected returns, and risks. A balanced portfolio should include considerable incremental innovations to leverage existing product platforms with low costs and certain returns, as well as radical innovation projects to discover new breakthroughs. How do you strike this balance? Follow the guidance of the organization's innovation strategy.

Traditionally, organizations used financial methods (e.g., the net present value [NPV][18]) as the criterion to select projects in the portfolio, preferring those projects that have the highest net present value. Recent research,[19] however, shows a decline in the use of the financial method in favor of strategic methods, which evaluate a prospective project according to its strategic fit. This is particularly important in cases of breakthrough innovation projects, in which future financial performance is very uncertain to provide an accurate NPV. The survey found that 36 percent of the best and 56 percent of the worst use financial methods as compared to 39 percent of the best and 10 percent of the worst using the strategic approach.[20] Similarly, the Product Development Management Association (PDMA) reported an increasing reliance on strategic planning as a step of innovation management, where 75.9 percent of the best adopt specific strategies to set the innovation portfolio of the entire organization. In addition, the best firms also include a strategic alignment step as one of the screens in their NPD process.[21]

Hewlett-Packard (HP), one of the most innovative companies, with two-thirds of its $40 billion revenue coming from products introduced in the past two years, uses the strategic bucketing method for NPD strategic planning and portfolio management. HP classifies projects into "evolutionary or derivative—sustaining, incremental, enhancing; platform—next generation, highly leveraged, and revolutionary; or breakthrough—new core product, process or business."[22] To manage the NPD/innovation portfolio across the enterprise, HP created cross-functional councils consisting of upper management. The Councils start by setting the strategic directions in which the innovation activity will be directed. The Council then creates strategic buckets accordingly and allocates both financial and human resources between the buckets and between projects within each bucket. Once the Council finalizes portfolio selection, the portfolio is handed to selection committees who oversee project management at the operational level. In this way, top management works together with project managers to articulate the innovation/NPD strategies for the whole organization.[23]

Balancing between incremental/evolutionary and radical/revolutionary innovation projects is essential for IM as it allows the leveraging of existing product platforms with low cost and certain return while investing in the discovery of new breakthroughs to develop and grow business, hence keeping a balance between short- and long-term goals, and keeping a healthy bottom line while not exhausting the ability to move forward. In addition to deciding on innovation strategies and the innovation portfolio, top management should lead the changes required at the operational level to the structure, culture, and processes of the organization.

OPERATIONALIZING INNOVATION MANAGEMENT

Taking IM to the operational level involves effecting a number of changes to the structure, culture, and innovation practices. When it comes to structural changes, the hard borderlines between divisions, departments, and business units have to be relaxed to allow flexible allocation of human resources across the whole organization in cross-functional and cross-divisional teams. This means that instead of task-based divisions and arrangements, experts need to be grouped by reference to skill in competence centers where their skills can be brought together depending on the need of the innovation project. This structure has to be flexible enough to include the networks of alliances that the organization builds to support its innovation process. Managing the innovation portfolio should be entrusted to a central department that coordinates between the various competence centers, manages alliances as a portfolio, and oversees the NPD process.

The organizational culture as well needs to change to accommodate innovation as a way of doing business. For that to happen, the culture should be one that accepts failure as a part of the learning process and motivates employees to innovate. A number of practices designed for this purpose will be outlined. This overlaps with systems and methods that emerged to enable the organization to better tap into its IC by seeking employees' ideas (human capital), and customer feedback and contribution in innovation projects (customer capital).

Structural Changes—Loosen It Up or, in Jack Welch's Words: "Shake It, Shake It, Break It"

Under the network-based innovation model, organizations need to arrange their innovation resources into two networks—internal and external. Internally, expertise and competence should be arranged in competence centers (R&D labs, departments, or business units), to enable bringing the right team together from talent across the whole organization. Externally, overcoming the NIH (not invented here) syndrome, organizations should outsource more and form more strategic alliances to address their IM needs. Managed effectively as a portfolio of alliances, the external networks should be open enough for the organization to access talent and innovation resources whenever needed. A network-based innovation model requires the organization to undergo a number of structural changes, including the following:

- Arranging organizational skills in competence centers or R&D facilities across the whole organization that can be tapped for flexible team formation
- Arranging external skills in a portfolio of alliances to facilitate access when needed
- Managing innovation projects centrally to reduce time to market and ensure that low-performing projects are weeded out to minimize investment losses.

Cross-Functional Teams and Competence Centers. One of the most prominent phenomena in IM in the knowledge economy is the increasing use of cross-functional teams for innovation projects. Though seemingly a minor change, its implications transformed the management of the whole organization. The use of cross-functional teams is not a new phenomenon, particularly for the best organizations. It has been used in the NPD process since the 1970s. The PDMA's survey reports that projects with high and medium levels of innovativeness are always entrusted to cross-functional teams, while such teams are used for least-innovative projects only by the best,[24] regardless of industry. However, since the 1990s, not only has the use of cross-functional teams increased, but the mix of the team has become more diversified as well.

To add to the complexity, these teams are increasingly becoming cross-divisional as well, where team members are also chosen from different business units. Take, for example, Dow Chemical. In 1994, Dow's Polyplefyn Research Lab identified elastomeric foam as a material that may be used in athletic shoes. To tap into their entire intellectual resources, Dow formed a team made up of researchers from four other labs and business units. The team consisted of researchers from the Ohio foams business group; technical service and marketing personnel from the Hong Kong operation, where most of the sales will be made; and researchers from Michigan Central R&D lab involved in fundamental foam research. Finally, the team was led by a material scientist from the Texas lab.[25]

The use of cross-functional teams has increased the challenge of allocating human resources. To enable the development and reconfiguration of innovation resources for IM, innovative organizations arranged and allowed the free development of skill, knowledge, and experience of employees into competence centers. This clustering of competencies happened naturally in some organizations where a certain unit or department developed a competency based on the skills and talents of its people and the focus on a certain area of knowledge or business process. Other organizations appreciating the effectiveness of the model systematized this arrangement, which multiplied their ability to bring the right people together and hence manage innovation projects more effectively. For example, on discovering that quality and time to market suffered as a result of inconsistent resource allocation, disorganized project schedules, and too many projects, IBM's AS/400 Division moved 40 people to key skill areas, where their expertise can be tapped depending on the needs of the various projects.[26] A central unit was formed to allocate teams to the various projects in the innovation portfolio, with demonstrable reduction in time to market and waste of resources.

Systemizing and arranging skills across the organization in competence centers dramatically transformed the role and sometimes the structure of the R&D/NPD department. Most large organizations moved to partial decentralization, where R&D departments are kept on both the central (corporate) and the business unit levels, where the central department functions as an independent contractor. Usually, the central department/lab conducts basic research while the business unit labs focus on NPD projects. The central lab is also used as an independent lab to which business unit labs may outsource certain projects. In such cases, the business unit concerned funds the research. In 2000 75 percent of the funding of the central R&D department has shifted to business units.[27] In many organizations where this model is used, the central R&D lab has been transformed into an incubator for new businesses.[28] It has become more of an intellectual reservoir, which both internal units and external parties may tap. 3M, GE, Dow, and DuPont use this model.[29]

Even in organizations where the centralized R&D structure was kept,[30] competence centers are represented by skill-based groupings in the R&D department itself, where again cross-functional teams get formed by accessing these groupings as well as other functional departments. For example, at Rohm & Haas Pharma, senior management hands down the innovation portfolio agreed to in the strategic planning phase to the NPD committee. The committee then allocates the various projects to cross-functional teams that are formed on the basis of the skills needed for each project. The team usually includes representatives from the legal department (patent attorney); the R&D department, based on their skills (scientists); and the manufacturing and sales departments.

Competence centers also facilitate the building of external innovation networks and alliances. It is more feasible for a competence center to forge relationships with outside experts and parties practicing in the same area of knowledge. With the focus on networks, another change to the structure of IM is needed to incorporate these networks and alliances in the organization's base of innovation resources.

Alliances Portfolio—Who's Who.   As R&D departments became more open to incoming and outgoing contract-based research, central R&D departments increasingly accept projects from outside the organization as well as outsource their own projects. PricewaterhouseCoopers reports that in 2000 the number of companies that outsource parts of their R&D to university labs and other R&D organizations had grown to 41 percent, spending 16.9 percent of their annual R&D expenditure.[31] In the chemical industry, this figure reached 50 percent in 1997.[32] The systemization of organizational skills into competence centers facilitated further the building of alliances and external networks. This is because employees in a competence center are usually aware of experts in their area, whether these experts work for suppliers, distributors, customers, consulting firms, university labs, government agencies, or even the competition. To enhance their performance, competence centers usually forge a number of relations with these experts either in the form of an informal network with the experts themselves or a formal alliance with their organization.[33]

The main driver of these alliances and networks is to reduce time to market, augment mutual expertise and share knowledge.[34] In many cases, alliances are forged with competitors wherever sharing knowledge will be in the interest of both parties. However, while collaboration with noncompetitors is usually carried out through contractual arrangements, those with competitors are usually forged as joint ventures, for the obvious reason of keeping things under close control. Regardless of who the alliance is with, one strategy seems always to be employed. This strategy revolves around developing key technologies, or solutions in the case of service organizations, in house while co-developing or outsourcing supporting and complementary technologies. Overall, this multiplied the number of alliances and networks that an organization's various departments and units forge with external parties. This made it necessary for organizations to keep track of the various networks, hence the alliance portfolio.[35]

The alliance portfolio enables the organization to keep track of whom the organization has an alliance with at a particular point in time with reference to the project, value added, length of the alliance, and potential further collaboration. The portfolio should be managed by a central unit that keeps track of the alliances at any one time to avoid duplication of effort and the risk of having more than one business unit competing for the same alliance. This brings us to the last structural change.

The Central Unit—To Set the Rules.   Decentralization of any organizational function always brings into play a myriad of approaches, giving rise sometimes to conflicting criteria and priorities.

This is multiplied in the IM stage by the establishment of competence centers and the formation of external networks. Though this decentralization enhances the organization's innovative capability and the quality of its innovation resources, it may jeopardize the innovation process as a whole. Lacking a central management function will result in innovation projects being managed according to various criteria, introducing chaos and competition over resources. The structure of the organization should therefore incorporate a central unit responsible for systematizing and managing the innovation process through the various stages of the NPD process and across the whole organization. The central unit has the significant task of defining the criteria upon which innovation projects will be prioritized, evaluated at the various NPD stages, and terminated if need be. Adopting formalized systematic criteria to carry out this task is integral for developing the ability to get to market fast. HP, for example, reported a reduction in half of its time to market time following the systemization and supervision of the NPD process by a central unit.[36]

Given the fact that only one out of 6.6 projects makes it to market success,[37] the central unit is faced with the main challenge of weeding out less-performing projects as soon as possible to reduce investment losses. This should be done within each of the strategic buckets. Many central units, therefore, adopted the role of the gatekeeper. Under the gatekeeping concept, an innovation project has to satisfy a set of defined criteria before it can pass the gate to the next stage of the NPD process. Common gates include strategic fit for the idea generation stage, and establishing market feasibility of product concepts before they are passed to the development stage. It is important that the evaluation criteria be applied uniformly across divisions and throughout the NPD process to create consistency and to ensure that projects that fail to satisfy the set criteria are weeded out as early as possible. To be effective, gatekeeping should incorporate "defined gatekeepers per gate, clear gate outputs, and rules of management for the gatekeeping or leadership team."[38] Gatekeeping has been reported to reduce time to market and cost, and enable prioritization of projects more effectively.[39]

Ineffective gatekeeping may result in maintaining mediocre projects to the detriment of more worthy ones; or worse, it may result in launching a defective product. It is thus important not to skip any gate as the project may be terminated at any of these gates, with reduction of cost and loss. In one case, UniLever skipped the testing gate and launched the product to beat Procter & Gamble (P&G) to the laundry detergent market. When used domestically, the detergent shredded clothes and had to be withdrawn from the market. Meanwhile, P&G perfected its detergent and launched it into the market using the shredded clothes comparison in its advertising campaign. Overall, UniLever sustained $300 million in losses.

In addition to weeding out low-performing projects, gatekeeping guards against a "do it all" approach. Baxter IV Systems Division, for example, found in 1996 that its 95-project portfolio, in which new platform projects received a third of the resources, was both imbalanced and slow. The "do everything" approach proved to be fatal, affecting time to market and overall performance. To solve this problem, Baxter IV adopted a clear stage-gate process, with clear criteria for each gate. A central team was also appointed, with four full-time facilitators as the gatekeepers of all the projects across the division.[40]

No structural changes will be fully effective without having innovative values engrained in the organizational culture. Like the knowledge-sharing culture, the innovation-enabling culture is one that fosters teamwork and collaboration. However, a number of other cultural values are crucial for IM, particularly the empowerment of employees.

A Culture for Innovation—Liberate the Innovative Spirit

Despite many claims that organizations are empowering their employees and encouraging their innovation by opening the idea generation stage to employee input, very few organizations have actually implemented such systems, and, of these few, even fewer did it effectively. The PDMA survey reports that idea generation is still concentrated or mainly managed by the engineering function in goods manufacturing industries and the marketing function in service industries. This is usually performed at senior and middle management levels, with attention directed to lower management or frontline levels only in limited cases. At a time when 3,000 ideas are needed to come up with a good one for commercialization, the input of every employee in the innovation process is essential. Many organizations therefore implemented systems to solicit ideas from employees and encourage their input with no real success, mainly because these systems had no culture to give them life. When it comes to IM, culture provides the motivation, the passion to innovate, and the recognition that innovators need to carry themselves through the frustrations of the innovation process.

The most important value to cultivate in the organizational culture to unleash the innovative power is acceptance of failure as part of the learning and experimentation process. To engrain these values in the organizational culture, the same methods used under KM of rewarding employee innovative activity and including the values in the appraisal criteria apply. Awards and incentives can be provided, for example, for idea submissions exceeding a certain number and recognition for ideas that make it to market (e.g., 3M's Hall of Fame to honor the most innovative employees).

The most important consideration, however, is to make innovation part of everyone's job, which can be done only by providing time and resources for employees to experiment and pursue their ideas. 3M, for example, allows all employees 15–20 percent free time to work on projects of their own. Depending on the level of success, the project may be spun off into a new business in which the employee who submitted the idea is given an equity share. Another example is IBM, where bureaucracy stops at the doors of the labs, allowing researchers time to experiment and even to play. The story of inventing the application of laser for eye surgery is indicative of how this functions. A group of IBM scientists, while experimenting with laser for improvements to IBM's existing products, started to play. One scientist wanted to see *what* the effect of laser would be on his finger cut. Getting more intrigued, the scientists started experimenting on cows' eyes and eventually developed its application to human eyes. IBM decided to develop the technology and later licensed it all out, making millions in profit.

It must be noted that both 3M and IBM regard innovation in its own right as their core business and thus are willing to pursue any idea of their employees even if outside the core business areas in which they specialize. IBM in particular encourages the development of any new product or technology, as it perceives licensing of the technology afterwards as a business, hence the development of the laser for eye surgery. Other organizations, however, do not share the same ideology and rather focus their innovative capability on defined core business areas. As a result, employees' ideas that are outside the strategic and growth plans of the enterprise are suffocated. This not only hampers innovation, but it may cost the organization millions in lost opportunities and business. Far from being a remote possibility, innovators leave their organizations in many instances and successfully pursue their ideas on their own. Bill Gates and his departure from IBM, Steve Jobs and his borrowing from Xerox, and the former Lucent employee who established Intel are all striking examples that are continuously repeated. To avoid such a risk and to maintain a culture where innovation—even if outside core areas—is fostered, many organizations incorporated in their business model venues for the unruly innovator—hence the emergence of skunk works labs and venture capital units.

Skunk works labs are separate labs or parts of labs either in central or business unit labs, where entrepreneurial employees have access to state-of-the-art equipment to experiment with their own ideas. Such units are not controlled by the central or business unit–level lab, and thus impose no research agenda or a certain area of focus. Once the project gains momentum, the researcher can approach the business development or venture capital unit for funding and support. Venture capital units are either independent profit centers or part of the business development department. These venture capital units invest in employee ideas by spinning off start-ups in which the organization owns an equity share. For example, Lucent's venture capital unit looks for opportunities within Bell Labs, where 30,000 scientists apply for four patents every day. The venture capital unit invested and spun off around 12 companies by 1999,[41] most of them successful. PricewaterhouseCoopers reports that 27 percent of surveyed companies in their "Technological Barometer 2000" study had such units.[42] These companies had grown by 30.6 percent in 1999, 31 percent higher than other companies of similar R&D investment that lacked such units.

Skunk works units seem to be used by scientists or researchers only and are not open to everyone in the organization, again limiting the innovative potential of the organization. To effectively maximize the organization's innovative ability and extract maximum value from human capital, it is important that organizations *empower their employees.*

Many organizations limit IM to the NPD process and thus undercapitalize their human capital. By limiting innovation to the NPD process, only ideas for new products will be encouraged and promoted, excluding improvements to business process. Therefore, the key to empowering employees, and hence extracting maximum value from the IM stage, is to foster process innovation. Of course, for organizations that offer no products or services, process innovation is of utmost importance. In addition to cost reduction and enhanced performance, employee-driven process innovation can yield great results in increased employee morale and productivity. One of the most successful models where the promise of empowering employees is taken seriously is that of Dana Corporation, a manufacturer of automobile parts.

The brilliance of Dana's employee-empowered innovation lies in the utilization of its human capital to grow in a mature traditional industry. Dana was serious about its appreciation of the value of its employees' intellectual capital and set out to encourage its transfer into intellectual assets. Dana started with implementing its model at the Parish Light Vehicles Structures Division, based in Pennsylvania, with 36,000 employees.[43] Idea submission was made mandatory, where each person, starting with the CEO to the newest hire in the plant, was expected to submit two ideas per month. New ideas could be submitted in relation to "*combining* operations, functions, and processes. On *improving* accuracy, quality, customer service, system techniques, storage, shipping, production control, machine performance, material handling, house-keeping, working conditions, paperwork, plant and office efficiency, and security. . . . on *reducing* rework, scrap, tool breakage, personal or property hazards, waste maintenance, repairs, downtime, person-hours, cost. On *saving* time, space, material, and manpower. On *simplifying* design, procedures, and forms."[44]

Dana encourages employee implementation whenever it involves expenses within certain budgetary limits. Once exceeded, the employee must obtain the approval of the supervisor; a first-line supervisor can approve up to $10,000 in capital expenditure.[45] Dana not only set an implementation target of 80 percent of ideas submitted, but incorporated rewards in its compensation system for people who submit more ideas than mandated. The Division achieved a 77 percent implementation rate in 1995, with considerable financial gains and enhancements to its culture and employee loyalty. Dana reported a 40 percent increase in profitability and a 13 percent increase in productivity.[46] In one example, record-high customer demand prompted top management to spend millions of dollars to expand the assembly line facility. Just before the decision was made, an idea was submitted by employee on the frontline to add workstations to the assembly line in a certain way. Dana instead implemented the idea for a $70,000 investment and was able to "eliminate a third shift, go from a seven- to a five-day workweek, and at the same time boost line rate productivity by 23 percent."[47]

The fact that IM in the knowledge economy is increasingly reliant on networks and the ability of the organization to tap into IC, gave rise to a number of methods designed to mine human and customer capital for ideas and product concepts. In addition, a number of tools emerged to enable management to mine business and technological data for insights to steer the innovation process. A number of these methods and tools are outlined next by reference to the IC they aim to tap.

ENABLING SYSTEMS, PRACTICES, AND TOOLS: THE ART OF INNOVATING

The choice of practices and tools should always be informed by the organization's strategy and business needs. Overall, however, there are a number of methods that are important enablers of IM under the IC concept. These are presented next in three groups by reference to the IC they are designed to tap.

Human Capital—Idea Banks

Intellectual capitalism resulted in the multiplication of the number of ideas needed for successful projects. Research has shown it takes 3,000 ideas to come up with a good one for commercialization.[48] It is not the quantity alone but also the quality that is directly affected by the source of ideas. Research has shown that 89 percent of successful new products are market driven as opposed to 11 percent that are technologically driven. Thus, an idea that may seem great in the lab or the boardroom with considerable technological (or social) push in its favor is no guarantee of market success. In contrast, ideas have more potential in achieving market success when generated by employees who have more contact and thus knowledge about market needs. That emphasizes human capital as the richest source for ideas for new products as well as new ways of doing business.

To tap into human capital *idea banks* emerged in many organizations to collect ideas from everyone in the organization, filter these ideas for viability, and then transfer them to a business unit that can commercialize them. In cases in which the ideas generated are noncore and don't relate to any existing business, the idea bank can form a project team, and later maybe a new business, to commercialize the idea or transfer it to the venture capital unit if one exists. An example is General Motors' (GM) idea bank, which GM calls "New Ideas Database."[49] Ideas for new products and new features are solicited from everywhere in the organization as well as suppliers. The ideas are entered electronically into an idea database, which a group of people from all functions and brands can access. This group evaluates the submitted ideas and then, if approved, transfers them to the appropriate engineering group for further development. More focus is introduced by providing that any new ideas that relate to the design of existing vehicles are transferred to a newly established department called Design and Technology Fusion where a number of "Creative Engineers" work on prototype development.[50]

Though attractive, idea banks suffer from a number of shortcomings. Being removed from the NPD process with no transparent selection criteria, it seems to be on the fringe like the venture capital unit rather than a system engrained in daily business. Being a voluntary system, idea banks as described create the impression that employees' ideas are not really required, though welcomed. Thus, idea submission becomes more of a luxury activity of secondary importance to getting the job done. As such, it merely provides an outlet for employees who feel the urge to share their ideas, while shedding doubt on the seriousness that the organization accords to employee-initiated innovation.

To be more effective, idea banks should proactively encourage idea submission, by setting submission quotas or allowing employees free time to experiment with implementing their ideas. Otherwise, idea banks may undermine the empowerment promise and "we value your ideas" statements that top management make now, if seen as a charade. To avoid appearing apathetic to employee' ideas, Motorola uses an interesting method. Rejected ideas are placed in a database that later makes the substance of a Minority Report to be evaluated by the "boss's bosses." The importance of this procedure is that it shows that idea banks are not a mere venue for expression but a reservoir of resources that top management takes seriously in planning the innovation portfolio.

Customer Capital—The Malleable Innovation Resource

Increased customer awareness, sophistication, and knowledge make customers a valuable resource not only for ideas but, more importantly, for new product concepts[51] and solutions. At the concept development stage, product concepts are evaluated on technical, financial, and marketing criteria. Involving customers at this stage has proven to help the NPD team to form better new product concepts and reduce time to market. Another indirect result is increasing customer loyalty by forging working relationships and supporting networks. This is of particular importance for service organizations and has always been one of their strategies to gain customer loyalty. Customer loyalty, however, is not the main motivator behind involving customers at the concept development stage. Developing a new successful or breakthrough product is. Two methods are discussed here, *value-chain management* and the *lead user* methods. The value-chain management concept, while not new, has gained added popularity in the knowledge economy. In contrast, the lead user method emerged to enable organizations to tap into customer capital to develop platform technologies and breakthrough products. Both can be combined to manage an innovation portfolio with projects of varying levels of innovativeness, particularly for businesses that adopt a customer-driven innovation strategy.

Value-Chain Management—Where to Fit Customer Feedback. Value-chain management is not a new method, but one which experienced resurgence under the IC concept for its focus on customer capital. It is based on streamlining among the design phase, product development, and manufacturing and marketing/sales phases by co-coordinating input from suppliers, distributors, and customers into the NPD process. Feedback from distributors (distribution agents in service industries or distribution channels in goods manufacturing industries), being more aware of customer complaints and needs, has been found integral in raising customer satisfaction rate, and creating a trust relationship.[52] Most organizations in the software industry open up their concept development stage as a general rule for all innovation projects, regardless of the level of innovativeness. Ideas are always sought from software users, developers, techies, and prospective customers. This increases market success rate as the product gets developed with users' needs in mind. Even in goods manufacturing and traditional industries, value-chain management has proven very beneficial both in introducing a more superior new product and increasing customer loyalty. For example, involving customers in the design of Motorola's i1000 phone favorably impacted bottom line. Thirty-five percent of sales in 1999 were attributed to the design aspect, and Motorola received the equivalent of $2 million in free advertising.[53]

But the benefit goes beyond the introduction of one product, particularly when the ideas of parties closer in the value chain are sought. Take, for example, Patagonia, which works with 60 partners, suppliers, and distributors around the world. To tap their customer capital, Patagonia holds an annual conference where 260 suppliers from 175 countries are brought together. The attendees are allocated to various workshops where they are asked for their "input on specific challenges."[54]

The value of involving suppliers and distributors has been repeatedly affirmed and proven. The question, however, remains about the value of involving customers in the NPD process. This is demonstrated by 3M's experience with Post-It Notes. Prelaunch market research showed that consumers would not be willing to pay for the Notes when they could use free pieces of paper to mark pages. Two of 3M's product managers, not convinced by the research, still launched the product with huge success. There is considerable data that involving customers undermines market launch or success. How much you should be tuned to potential and current customers, and how responsive you should be to their expressed needs has been the subject of many publications. Most publications are heading toward incorporating within the concept development and other stages in the product development process ways to detect and respond to these needs. But other publications warn about being swayed by the divergent and sometimes conflicting needs that customers express or the needs of different customer segments.[55] A balance should be maintained between keeping a strategic focus—that is, not being swayed by conflicting customer needs and expectations—and remaining aware of market conditions and trends.

Other studies suggest that, when it comes to customers' involvement in the NPD process, it is not a question of whether to seek customer input, but rather how to define the customers that you really want to listen to. This is what the lead user method, introduced by Eric Von Hippel in 1986,[56] aims to achieve by defining the customers as those users who are at the leading edge of their market segments, and who have innovated ways to address their most important needs. The lead user method has proved very effective in generating successful breakthrough products.

The Lead User Method—The Quest for Breakthrough Innovation.   The lead user method for new product concept development, though introduced in 1986, did not gain wide popularity until applied by 3M in the mid-1990s. The method is similar to all customer-focused approaches. It targets prospective and current customers to assess their needs and to seek their contribution. What is different about it is the choice of these customers and the sort of information sought from them. Under the lead user method, information is sought from lead users, who are defined as those on the leading edge of a number of related markets, who face similar problems. Those customers are different from ordinary customers in that they are able to articulate their needs and usually develop their own solutions to deal with such needs ahead of everyone in the market. The main challenge is to find the lead users.

Once the NPD team finds the lead users they work together to develop new product concepts. The importance of tapping into the experience of the lead users lies in the depth of their understanding of the problems faced in their respective markets. To detect such problems and needs after ordinary customers experience them is too late for the development of breakthrough products or new markets. As John Pournoor of 3M Biomaterial Technology Centers explains, "by the time a trend shows up in a traditional market study, it's too late to create products that can change the basis of competition."[57]

Applied by 3M, the lead user method was proven to be very beneficial, particularly in producing breakthrough innovations and creating new businesses. 3M reported that its sales projections for lead user projects are eight times higher than those for traditional projects.[58] They are expected to generate $146 million after five years, with a 68 percent market share, as compared to 33 percent of market share for traditional projects. Another benefit is reducing the concept development time by half. Mary Sonnack, champion of 3M's lead user method, reports that the method is best for new-to-the-world products and breakthrough innovations that create new markets under 3M's long-term growth strategy.[59]

Sonnack explains how 3M's Lead User Center, of the Strategic Business Development Department (central department) provides training to 3M businesses on the use of the method and provides support throughout the process. The project team that leads the search for lead users is composed of four to six people devoting a third of their time over a period of four to six months. Project teams "network their way up pyramids of expertise" to find lead users in a target market and other related markets.[60] The lead user team usually brings together experts from various fields with their experiences and insights about problems that have a common solution. As a result, the team can demonstrably widen the scope and number of new product concepts.

3M's Medical-Surgical Division lead user team wanted to generate new product concepts for dealing with the global challenge of increasingly antibiotic-resistant bacteria. 3M wanted to be a world leader in the infection-control field. The project team traveled widely to meet users who faced the challenge of fighting resistant bacteria on a daily basis and had formulated ways to deal with it. First, the team met with medical practitioners of a Mobile Army Surgical Hospital (MASH) in Bosnia. MASH expressed a need for products that have a focus on speed, and rely less on antibiotics for their lifesaving mission. The team heard next from a leading veterinary surgeon expressing the challenges he faces dealing with "furry" patients. Finally, the team met with a Broadway makeup artist, who shared what he learned from attaching masks to skin. The team used the knowledge they gained from those and other experts to develop concepts for products that ranged from draping products to ways to reduce surgical site infections. The Infection Prevention Development Unit explained how this helped them to move from adding line extensions to developing a new strategic platform with many new products in the horizon, in just three years.[61]

The variety of perspectives and depth and breadth of experiences that are presented by lead users enable the project team to generate many product concepts from one idea. A revealing example is Nortel Networks' lead user team, formed to develop product concepts for wireless communication. The lead user team comprised a broadcast engineer, an aviation specialist, a meteorological researcher, a storm chaser, an animal tracker, a mobile telemedicine researcher, and next-generation law enforcement researchers. The lead users in the group not only faced the same problem but each of them had used methods of dealing with its limitations. Exploring these methods and working with the lead users, the project team was able to decide on the technology they needed to use and the roadmap they should follow to develop their new products.[62]

If anything, the lead user method reveals the complex layers that an idea goes through before it can be the basis of one or more new product concepts. Besides the use of the knowledge of lead users, or customers on the cutting edge of their field, organizations in technological areas need to find ways to introduce their products in heavily patented technological areas.

Structural Capital.   One of the most important functions and tools of IM is competitive intelligence. Though competitive intelligence is relevant to all the stages of an ICM model, its significance for IM lies in the fact that innovation involves both responding to change and anticipating change. In both cases, the organization's success relies on the speed and insight with which it is able to detect the competition's moves, market trends, and customer needs. Competitive intelligence for the purpose of IM is needed at both the strategic and operational levels. It is discussed in this section to highlight its use as an enabling tool in managing the innovation process. New technology management tools will also be discussed.

Competitive Intelligence

> . . . [B]y the 1980s, many business managers were wondering why it [strategy] worked so poorly. Part of the answer may be that strategy without intelligence had become a contradiction in terms.
>
> —William Sammon, Mark Kurland, and Robert Spitalnic[63]

For any effective IM model, a competitive intelligence system should be incorporated in the organization's work systems (i.e., be cultivated as part of the structural capital). Competitive intelligence is relevant to all levels whenever decisions that affect the organization's competitive position need to be made. At the strategic level, it is important for leadership to comprehend the organization's competitive position relevant to its competitors, before making any competitive moves or deciding on strategies. At the senior management level, competitive intelligence enables the formation of the innovation portfolio while keeping competitors' strengths and weaknesses in mind. Other forms of competitive intelligence (e.g., technical/patent intelligence) are important at all levels for technology-driven industries.

By definition, competitive intelligence (CI) is "the refined intelligence product that meets a decision-maker's unique needs for understanding a competitive aspect of the internal and/or external environment."[64] It involves the use of "public resources to locate and develop data that are then transformed into information about competitors, their capabilities, current activities, plans and intentions."[65] It includes more than one form, ranging from competitors' profiles, project-based or scouting, market and technical intelligence. All types, however, follow the same process, which involves collecting data from public resources, analyzing the data, then disseminating it to the strategists and decision makers.

The most effective CI is that aimed at critical intelligence needs. In general, however, intelligence efforts should focus on discovering through lawful means "future goals that drive the competitor," "what the competitor does and can do," "assumptions held about itself and the industry," and its strengths and weaknesses.[66] More specifically, on the strategic level, CI should provide a systematic review of the organization's competitiveness and relative position (product positions, market shares, alliances, etc.). This should be augmented with competitors' profiles, which assess competitors' positions and predict future moves. The focus of these profiles will depend to a great extent on the innovation strategy. A customer-driven strategy, for example, requires finding out the major customers of the competitor, market segments, customer involvement methods, marketing campaigns, and pricing policies.

Competitive intelligence as a system may be centrally managed, wherein periodic reports are produced on competitors' moves and teams are allocated on a project/need basis. The CI operation may also be decentralized to various units across the organization. The best model, however, is one in which every employee is trained to be a detector of competitive moves in their respective areas, and tools are provided according to the type of intelligence that each group needs to perform. Interestingly, many organizations are incorporating CI in the work of the innovation team itself. We have seen that to a high degree with the use of the lead user methods. In addition, many organizations require that their researchers spend more time with customers. Researchers are encouraged to leave their ivory tower for the ivory basement, where they can have access to the insights of frontline employees from marketing, sales, and other departments; they are encouraged to move to the ivory street to have access to customers as well. IBM, for example, increased the time that researchers should spend with customers from 5 percent to 25 percent at the beginning of the 1990s.[67] When it comes to technology management, however, the stress is increasingly shifting to the use of technology/patent intelligence.

Technology Management and Patent Intelligence

The rise in the number of patents owned by major players in the market facilitated the emergence of a number of tools and methods that can be used to aid in obtaining patent and technology intelligence, and hence aid in directing the innovation process. These methods can help in providing directions for the innovation portfolio and perfecting the design of the product under development.

Patent documents can be used as reservoirs of information that can be analyzed to assess the competitive position and expected competitive moves. The patenting history of a competitor reveals the technology road map they are following and provides insight as to future moves. Patent data analysis can also be used to reveal the strengths and weaknesses of the competition's technological position. An examination of the file wrapper, for example, will reveal areas that the patentee agreed to limit and thus can provide guidance as to getting around a competitor's blocking patents. The most valuable intelligence that can be gained from patent data analysis is how the competition is reacting to the organization's own patenting activity. How does the competition get around the organization's patents? How often are they cited in the competition's patent applications? And what types of patents are the competition filing for that are built on the organization's patents?

For the innovation portfolio, this aids in revealing past patenting activities of the competition to decide areas where the organization can only design around existing patents (i.e., introduce incremental changes) and areas where they would have less competition. Patent citation trees can help management to find the parties who are applying for patents on improvements related to their own products, and thus incorporate in the portfolio projects for doing the same in relation to the competition's products. This will enhance the organization's bargaining power in negotiating cross-licenses if seeking a license is strategically required. In addition, patent visualization tools, which present a bird's-eye view of the patenting activity in a certain technological area, should be used in determining the areas where the organization will aim to develop next-generation and breakthrough products.

When it comes to perfecting the design of the product under development, it is important to thoroughly assess the design, which will be able to withstand competitive forces longer. Even though the organization can protect all possible product designs with IP, it should focus on the design that will be harder to replicate regardless. For example, when designing Gillette's Sensor shaver, the engineers came up with seven designs relating to how the twin blades can be mounted on the cartridge. To enable the choice of the best design, Gillette undertook a full patent analysis of all seven versions of the design, comparing them to the existing patents of the competition. Gillette chose the design that it believed competitors would have the most difficulty in getting around.[68]

CONCLUSION

The goal of IM is to develop the organizational ability to manage a growing number of ideas, product concepts, and ultimately innovation projects, with one main focus—to get a successful product to market as fast as possible. The optimal benefit of IM is to prevent the undercapitalization of IC often caused by limited contribution from employees and customers into the innovation process. To effectively tap into its human and customer capital, an organization needs to create and manage internal and external networks by incorporating IM in the way business is done. Effective implementation of IM involves effecting certain changes at the strategic and operational levels, to create a balanced innovation portfolio, adopt the appropriate innovation strategies, manage and allocate financial and human resources across innovation networks and projects, and effecting a number of structural and cultural changes.

Chapter 12 provides a step-by-step guide on how to implement IM. Chapter 8 outlines the intellectual property management stage.

NOTES

[1] The authors use this term in their article. A. Hargadon and R. Sutton, "Building an Innovation Factory," *Harvard Business Review,* May–June 2000, p. 158.

[2] *Id.*

[3] S. Martin, "Strategic Research Partnerships: Evidence and Analysis," National Science Foundation Workshop, 2001.

[4] In Edison's light bulb the filament was made of bamboo to withstand the high levels of heat.

[5] Definition of "best" and "rest" is based on a variety of criteria, depending on the surveying body. A common thread between the mentioned surveys is that they all selected criteria that apply across and within industries. Criteria included the top 30 percent in each industry by reference to revenue and time to market.

[6] Abbie Griffin, "PDMA Research on New Product Development Practices: Updating Trends and Benchmarking Best Practices," *Journal of Product Innovation Management,* Vol. 14, 1997, pp. 429–458.

[7] *Id.,* p. 431.

[8] *Id.,* p. 441.

[9] For a discussion of innovation strategies, see Donna Prestwood and Paul Schumann, "Innovation Strategies: Having the Right Innovation Strategy Determines the Ability of the Enterprise to Create Wealth." Available online at *www.glocalvantage.com/InnovationStrategies.htm.*

[10] M. Porter, "What Is Strategy?", *Harvard Business Review,* November–December 1996, pp. 61, 69.

[11] See M. Porter, *Competitive Strategy: Techniques for Analyzing Industries and Competitors* (New York: Free Press, 1980).

[12] *Id.,* pp. 40–41.

[13] PricewaterhouseCoopers, "Technological Barometer 2000." Available online at *www.pwcglobal. com.*

[14] These strategies can also be called competitor-driven innovation strategies as the focus is on following or beating the competition in a certain technological field, with the aim of creating a new technological standard in the market.

[15] Patenting strategies are discussed in Chapters 8 and 13.

[16] On how choices and trade-offs are made in the context of strategic planning, see supra note 11.

[17] Supra note 6, p. 443.

[18] The NPV is the sum of the present value of project's future earnings discounted to date (discounted also by probability of technical and commercial success) minus the commercialization (or launch) and development costs.

[19] Product Development Institute (PDI), "Portfolio Management for New Product Development: Results of an Industry Practices Study" (PDI, 2001), pp. 10–16. The Product Development Institute defines the best companies as the top 30 percent in their industry while the worst represent the bottom 30 percent. The criteria applied include revenue from new products, R&D expenditure, and market value.

[20] R. Cooper and S. Edgett, *Portfolio Management for New Products,* Working paper No. 11 (PDI, 2001), p. 4.

[21] Supra note 6, p. 441.

[22] R. Englund and R. Graham, "From Experience: Linking Projects to Strategy," *Journal of Product Innovation Management,* Vol. 16, 1999, pp. 52–64.

[23] *Id.,* p. 53.

[24] Supra note 6, p. 442.

[25] *Id.*

[26] *Id.*

[27] C. Larson, "R&D In Industry," in American Association for the Advancement of Science Report XXIV, 1999, p. 36.

[28] See J. Deschamps, "Half of Your R&D is Wasted," *Prism,* First Quarter 1999, pp. 61–71.

[29] *Id.*

[30] For organizations in heavily regulated industries (e.g., the pharmaceutical industry), the centralized R&D model seems more suitable. It is still attractive to a number of big R&D investors, like Microsoft, for the benefits it has in cost control and coordination of technological development.

[31] Supra note 9.

[32] Supra note 9.

[33] The trend of outsourcing and networking with external partners indicates that R&D-intensive or patent-intensive industries are moving to a network-based innovation business model, which has always been used by organizations in the service industry. Service organizations have always been open to collaborating with outside parties in their R&D/NPD process, whether suppliers or distributors. In that respect, patent-intensive organizations are getting closer to the service organizations' model, or to the knowledge organization model.

[34] See A. Thayer, "Outsourcing R&D To Gain An Edge," *The American Chemical Society Chemical & Engineering News,* February 10, 1997.

[35] This need is also addressed under KM in mapping knowledge resources and creating expert directories.

[36] Supra note 22.

[37] Supra note 6, p. 431.

[38] Supra note 6, p. 5.

[39] See reference supra notes 6 and 20.

[40] A. Page, "Pipeline Management," *PDMA Visions,* April 1996.

[41] "Innovation In Industry," U.S. Patent Law, February 20, 1999, p. 13.

[42] Supra note 13.

[43] Southwood Morcott, "Igniting a Firestorm of Creativity," in *Straight from the CEO,* G. Dauphinais and C. Price (eds.) (Riverside, NJ: Simon & Schuster, 1999), p. 238.

[44] *Id.,* p. 239.

[45] *Id.*

[46] *Id.,* p. 240.

[47] *Id.,* p. 245.

[48] The PDMA survey reports other numbers that are substantially less, like 4 out of 100 ideas. The discrepancies can be caused by not distinguishing between ideas and product concepts and the level of innovativeness introduced by the idea (i.e., incremental as compared to radical).

[49] Supra note 43.

[50] *Id.*

[51] Product concept is a written prototype statement of a new product and the customer needs it satisfies. Traditionally either the leading NPD department or the project team has performed concept development as a step. The team will take the idea and brainstorm the product concepts that this idea can create and explore the various market segments that the different concepts can serve.

[52] See, for example, H. St. Onge, "How Knowledge Management Adds Critical Value to Distribution Channel Management," *Journal of Systematic Knowledge Management,* January 1998.

[53] APQC, "NPD: Gaining and Using Market Insight," APQC, 2001.

[54] S. Bonner, "Patagonia: A Green Endeavor," *Apparel Industry Magazine,* February 1997.

[55] See, for example, J. Blau, "Shorter Time-to-Money Drives Philips R&D," *Research Technology Management,* March–April 1994, where the author explains how customer input is used to correct the direction of research when it is far removed from the product markets.

[56] Eric Von Hippel, "Lead Users: A Source of Novel Product Concepts," *Management Science,* Vol. 32, no. 7 July 1986, pp. 791–805.

[57] "The Innovation Engine: Lead User," *3M Stemwinder,* March 20–April 9, 2001, p. 3.

[58] Newswise, "Products Created through Lead User Process Generate Higher Sales," Penn State Smeal College of Business, March 18, 2001.

[59] *Id.*

[60] Supra note 57.

[61] *Id.*

[62] Pierce, "The Art of Creating a Flexible R&D Organization," *CHEMTECH 1998,* Vol. 28, no. 2, pp. 6–11.

[63] W. Sammon, M. Kurland, and R. Spitalnic, *Business Competitor Intelligence* (New York: John Wiley & Sons, 1984).

[64] C. Fleisher, "An Introduction to the Management and Practice of Competitive Intelligence," in C. Fleisher and D. Blenkhorn (eds.), *Managing Frontiers in Competitive Intelligence* (Westport, CT: Quorum Books, 2001), p. 7.

[65] J. McGonagle and C. Vella, *The Internet Age of Competitive Intelligence* (Westport, CT: Quorum Books 1999), p. 4.

[66] M. Porter, *Competitive Strategy: Techniques for Analyzing Industries and Competitors* (New York: Free Press, 1980), p. 49.

[67] C. Larson, "Industrial R&D in 2008," Industrial Research Institute, 2002. Available online at *www.iriinc.org/publications/cfl-industrial 2008.cfm.*

[68] K. Rivette and D. Kline, "Discovering New Value in Intellectual Property," 78 *Harvard Business Review* 54, p. 58.

8

The Intellectual Property
Management Stage

AN IP ECONOMY

I am tempted to call it the *IP*[1] *Economy*. At first, this may seem frivolous, given that IP is a knowledge-based asset and hence the term *knowledge economy* should suffice. But that is inaccurate for two reasons. First, IP, though knowledge based, draws its power not from the knowledge it protects (despite its critical importance) but from its capacity as a competitive and marketing tool. Repeatedly, whether it is a patent, a trademark, or a copyright, IP is enabling organizations to enter and create new markets, and to block competition from gaining a strong hold in certain markets. Indeed, IP is at the core of competitive performance in any industry.[2] Second, the value of IP can be measured with greater certainty than any other intellectual capital (IC), given that IP is the most tangible of the intangibles. As a business asset, the value of IP to a business (a patent, a brand, or a copyrighted work) can reach hundreds of millions.[3]

On the macroeconomic level, the effectiveness of a country's IP system is a determining factor in its economic performance.[4] In the United States, patenting activity rose dramatically a few years after the establishment of the Federal Circuit in 1986 as the court of final review for cases involving patents and copyrights, which made a murky area of law more predictable. The same is true for copyrights, where copyright industries have been growing at rates exceeding the national gross domestic product (GDP).[5] Furthermore, reform in trademark law with stronger protection of famous trademarks and measures against cyber squatting[6] encouraged huge investments in brands, making American brands the largest U.S. export.[7] Globally, the technological prowess of countries is increasingly being measured by their patenting activity, research and development (R&D) investments, and the strength of their software industry and brands.

Surprisingly, despite the strong impact that IP has on the performance of an economy and on the success of an organization, IP is generally viewed as a legal instrument that protects a technology, an expression, and a mark or proprietary information. It is true that IP is a legal creature, but behind all its legal charm IP is a powerful competitive tool and a valuable business asset. Independent of its legal identity, and from the product or process it was originally acquired to protect, IP can be commercialized as the "product." Appreciating this is the key to viewing intellectual property management (IPM) as the stage at which the value created at the knowledge management (KM) stage, then extracted at the innovation management (IM) stage, is maximized to the optimal level. That is the goal and function of IPM under the Comprehensive Intellectual Capital Management (CICM) model.

Though IPM is not new, the IC concept transformed it from being a legal affair to becoming engrained in the management of business as a whole. Before exploring how, we will first briefly outline how IPM programs developed.

THE BIRTH OF IPM AND ITS MANY SHADES

Viewing IP merely as a legal instrument, the first IPM programs merely focused on managing two main legal processes. The first is the acquisition of IP rights to secure for an organization the use of a certain intellectual material (a technology, a term, or an artistic expression), what is generally known as the "freedom to operate" (FTO). The second is the enforcement of IP rights by ensuring that others do not capitalize on such intellectual material without the owner's authorization. As a result, IPM was seen merely as a legal affair in which effective management revolved around prosecution of patent applications, registration of trademarks and copyrights, protection of trade secrets, detection of infringement, litigation, and, in limited cases, negotiation of licensing agreements. This comprises the legal approach to IPM.

Only when organizations started looking at IP not merely as a legal right but as a business opportunity did IPM slowly move from being a concern of the legal department to becoming part of the strategic management function of an organization, hence the business approach to IPM. The business approach to IPM gained more following starting in the late 1980s, with the focus moving to capitalizing on the value of IP to enter new markets and enhance business performance. The gist of the business approach, or what is generally referred to as *intellectual asset management*,[8] is recognizing IP as a business asset. Once recognized as such IP can be used to create more formidable entry barriers for the competition, set a standard in some markets, expand into new markets, create a variety of networks through strategic alliances, and generate revenue through licensing. More and more organizations are shifting from the legal to the business approach with growing appreciation of the value of IP. But not all IPM programs were born equal!

Using the term *IP* in a general way may be deceiving. Though all forms of IP are created by the effect of law, they are different animals indeed. Patents and trade secrets are more technological, and, with the exception of some software programs, copyrighted works tend to be artistic, while trademarks are market-oriented emotional tools. As a result, and regardless of the similarity in legal processes pertaining to the various IP forms, IPM programs that developed in various industries were different. When for patent-intensive industries IPM meant managing patents and trade secrets, it meant managing trademarks and brands for consumer products industries, and managing copyrights for entertainment and software industries. This distinction is important for two reasons: (1) to avoid the common mistake of limiting the term *IPM* to patent (and trade secret) management, and (2) to be able to examine the different characteristics of IPM programs that developed in different industries.

In patent-intensive industries, patent departments emerged as early as the 1960s in major organizations, with the focus on patents and trade secrets. Trademark and very limited copyright concerns were left to the general legal department. Patent departments grew in number and size with the rising patenting activity. In addition to the legal processes outlined under the legal approach, patent departments coordinated between patenting plans and projects of the various business units across the organization. Early on, patent departments worked closely with R&D departments to ensure FTO, and to solicit invention disclosures from inventors. Another major role that patent departments played, and still play, is supporting decision making as to the most appropriate type of protection for the technological invention (i.e., patent and trade secret protection). Starting in the late 1980s, the business approach gained more following, expanding the patent department's role to exploiting IP value through licensing. The number of licensing personnel started to grow in patent departments, and in some organizations developed into separate licensing units.

In copyright-intensive industries, the matter was not much different. In the software industry, the legal and R&D departments worked together in supplementing the automatically vesting copyrights with other forms of IP protection (e.g., trade secret and patent protection). Software licensing is closely linked to offering the software as a product with either a shrink-wrap license or a software development agreement and thus was not pursued as a separate strategic business. Similarly, the legal department's main role in the entertainment industry was to ensure FTO through copyright clearances, and to acquire copyright licenses of the works they decide to produce. Licensing is used heavily in the entertainment industry to enable the commercialization of the copyrighted work in various media and through varied channels of distribution. The business approach of IPM seems to have been engrained in copyright management all along, particularly that the copyright is seen as the product.

The IPM program that developed in the consumer product industry had one prime focus—brand management. Brands being a combination of IP (trademarks, logos, advertising slogans, right to publicity, and trade dress), and IC (the brand promise, value propositions, organizational character, and marketing campaigns), the IPM program that developed was by nature business oriented. Brand management goes back to very early origins. In his review of the history of brand management, Dartmouth College Professor Kevin Keller notes that as early as 1890s branding was largely driven by the organization's leadership.[9] The first brand management program was developed by Procter & Gamble (P&G) in the 1940s,[10] and by 1985 most organizations had implemented a brand management program marrying branding and business strategies together, and investing heavily in building brands.[11] The American Productivity and Quality Center (APQC) reports that brands have not only gained prominence in the knowledge economy, but manufacturing industries have turned to branding strategies more than ever in the last 20 years to gain a competitive advantage.[12] Despite that, the APQC notes that only 66 percent of the surveyed group (across all industries) have implemented a methodology to manage their brands.

One common development, regardless of the form of IP managed or the industry in which the organization competes, is the increasing involvement of departments other than the legal and R&D departments in managing IP. With appreciation of IP as a business asset, it started to appear on the radar of the sales, marketing, customer service, human resources, and information technology (IT) departments. Customer service departments assisted in detecting infringements of IP in the course of handling customer complaints, especially trademark and copyright infringements. Sales personnel also detected patent infringements in their comparison of other products in the market. Personnel and human resources departments also had to understand IP to educate employees as to the organization's ownership rights and trade secret protection (exit and entry interviews). Increasing awareness of the risk of leaking proprietary information, trade secret protection became the concern of every department. The risks of cyber attacks on the organization's databases and copyright piracy of its Web content brought the IT department into the picture as well.

From the foregoing, it is clear that IPM programs, in their varying shades, have developed in a haphazard way in which a number of departments are involved with little or no synchronization. Overall, IPM programs represent a messy landscape of practices that developed as organizations reacted to business pressures and needs, rather than on the basis of a well-thought-out methodology. This started to change with the emergence of the IC concept.

IPM AND THE IC CONCEPT—THE JOB OF EVERYONE AGAIN

> With the increasing role of intellectual capital, and the further emergence of what we can call intellectual capitalism, it is conceivable that IC management will develop engulfing IP management.
>
> —Ove Granstrand[13]

The IC concept brought to the forefront the challenge of managing IP as a business asset throughout the whole organization to ensure that the potential value of IP is capitalized upon to the maximum. Many books have been published in the past few years[14] to provide guidance on the ideal ways to manage IP as a business asset, to "mine the IP portfolio," to create "intellectual asset management" teams, to present success stories, and "how they did it" studies, and to provide insight on how to use the emergent search and management tools. These books all stress that IPM has to shift from a defensive and legal-oriented to an integrative approach wherein it is engrained in the management of business as a whole.[15] The focus of most such books is on the management of patents and the ancillary use of trade secrets to protect know-how, with a very modest treatment of trademarks and copyrights. As a result, despite the great insight they provide, these books neglect issues faced by a number of industries where trademarks and copyrights, rather than patents, are the primary value drivers. The IP wealth of the fastest-growing service, consumer products, entertainment, and software industries is primarily made of trademarks and copyrights.

The emphasis on the value of IP to business pushed IP into the attention zone of chief financial officers (CFOs) and CEOs in their quest to maximize value for stakeholders.[16] IP strategies started to emerge as part of the overall business strategy, where it is used both for competitive positioning and generation of revenue. The emergence of licensing units in some organizations, the rise of brand managers to senior executive levels, and integration of copyrights in investment plans[17] are all indicative of the push to perceive and manage IP as a business asset. The IC concept thus liberated IP from the reign of the legal department into the world of strategic business management. As a result, the most successful organizations recognized IP as the most important business asset, a source of regenerative value, which under proper management can be the core source of business growth in every industry.

A brief digression is warranted here. Under the CICM, managing IP does not mean that an organization should manage all forms of IP as a business. That would place great strain on resources and result in confusion of strategic focus. Instead the IPM program should focus on what we can call the "primary" form of IP in the industry of the organization. Not every form of IP is of strategic importance to every industry. For example, when patents are of strategic importance in the chemical industry, they are only of secondary importance, if any, for the entertainment industry.

The primary form of IP[18] for an industry is the one that has a crucial impact on competitive positioning and business performance. For most industries,[19] one form of IP is of prime importance while the others are of secondary importance. As such, organizations competing in a particular industry need to develop the competency of managing the primary form of IP to create and sustain a competitive advantage. Regardless of industry, organizations should incorporate in their IPM programs working knowledge of patents, trademarks (brands), copyrights, and trade secrets to create synergy between the management of the various forms of IP, and to use the secondary forms as supporting tools, as will be discussed under the value transference strategies. This is of utmost importance because the primary form of IP affects in particular the substance of the IP strategy employed by an organization for the management of its business.

Engraining the management of the primary form of IP in the strategic management of the whole organization is what enables maximization of value at the IPM stage. Let's look at examples where the various primary IP are managed as a business. IBM, an organization with a very strong patent portfolio, decided to unlock its value, and thus embarked on an aggressive investment plan. The plan was carried out in cooperation among all the business units and departments across the organization. A unit was established to reverse engineer the products of the competition to detect infringements of IBM patents. Researchers were given the green light to pursue projects even if outside the core business areas to build the patent portfolio. A strong organizational culture was implemented in which increased patenting and licensing were encouraged. Every business unit, and every sales personnel, was a prospective licensing agent. After a few years of investment, IBM's $800 million royalty stream grew to around $1.5 billion annually.

In industries where trademarks and copyrights are the primary IP forms, the same results can be achieved. For example, Coca-Cola in the consumer products industry treats its $40 billion trademark as the most strategic business asset. The company invests heavily in reinforcing the brand identity and promise with a myriad of marketing and advertising campaigns, well-thought-out strategies that take the brand promise and make it relevant to local markets over the globe, and an aggressive merchandising strategy that alone brings around $1 billion annually in royalties. Similarly, Disney focuses its strategy on leveraging the creative content of each of its copyrighted works internally across the business divisions, and externally through a number of licenses generating billions in merchandise royalties alone.

Managing IP as a business involves much more than establishing a licensing unit or marrying IP and business strategies. It involves engraining IPM in the management of the business as a whole by using IP both for competitive positioning and business growth. To that effect, the IPM stage under the CICM approach engrains appreciation and management of IP as a business throughout the whole organization. This involves effecting a number of changes at the strategic and operational levels.

At the strategic level, top management needs first to know the IP they have across the whole organization with reference to its value to various businesses and market segments. That facilitates creating the IP portfolio, which is the platform for managing IP as a competitive tool and a business asset. Following the creation of the IP portfolio, top management should decide on the appropriate strategies for utilizing IP both for competitive positioning and commercialization purposes. The responsibility of capitalizing on IP should then be handed down to the various business units, to operationalize the IP strategies forged by top management. Each business unit is entrusted with managing the part of the IP portfolio that is relevant to its strategic focus. That is when IPM can be effectively taken to the operational level.

To activate IPM at the operational level, certain changes are required. First, structural changes are required to create teams at the business unit level and cross-functional teams at the organizational level that focus on the use of IP for competitive positioning and commercialization purposes respectively. Second, cultural changes are required to create an IP-aware culture to promote the proper use of IP and protect against practices that may jeopardize the strength of the IP portfolio or result in loss of IP rights. At the operational level, businesses should also be provided with tools and methods (enablers) that aid decision making in the IPM processes.

STRATEGIZING IPM

Managing IP at the strategic level involves undertaking an audit of the primary form of IP to create an IP portfolio, based on an assessment of the individual strength of the audited IP. Creating a portfolio aims at making sense of the IP wealth of the whole organization by presenting it in a snapshot showing the relationship between the IP and its use by various businesses and in various market segments. Following that, top management should decide on the IP strategies to lead the organization's efforts in maximizing the value derived from IP by using it as both a competitive tool and a business asset.

The IP Audit and Portfolio Creation—Not a Legal IP Audit

IP legal audits have been used for decades by organizations for a multitude of reasons, for example, due diligence, to check legal compliance, to discard unused IP, and as a form of stock taking for mergers and acquisitions. The difference of an IP audit performed for business, rather than legal, purposes is that the audit (or stock taking) is performed to assess the commercial value and competitive use of the IP by respective businesses. Another difference is that while an IP audit for legal purposes lists all forms of IP owned by an organization, a business-oriented IP audit collects information about the primary form of IP and is therefore patent, trademark, or copyright specific. A legal audit lists all forms of IP and considers their legal status (e.g., expiration, licensed or not, registration and maintenance dates and fees, etc.). A business-oriented audit focuses on how the primary IP form is being used in relation to products, services, market segments, its connection to sales, whether used in a strategic alliance, and its expected (business) life cycle. We deal here with the business IP audit only.

The audit is the preparatory step to creating the IP portfolio. It should reveal the potential uses of the IP for strategic purposes, whether to generate revenue or to strengthen a competitive position. To do that, information should be gathered from the various businesses regarding the use of IP in business, its current and planned use, and possible commercialization opportunities as well as threats from IP owned by others that may undermine its value. This data should then be used by the auditing group to create a portfolio that presents a bird's-eye view of the strengths, weaknesses, opportunities, and threats associated with the primary form of IP. In cases in which the organization competes through using more than one form of IP (e.g., some software and consumer products organization that focus on both patents and copyrights), a shadow portfolio should be created for the other primary IP forms, again with reference to their use in business. Chapter 13 provides guidance as to undertaking the audit and creating a patent, trademark (brand), or copyright portfolio. It should be mentioned here, however, that every portfolio, regardless of the primary form of IP, should include reference to trade secrets, that is, know-how related to the various IP in the portfolio.

An IP portfolio provides insight in two major ways that are crucial for any IPM program under the CICM approach. First, they reveal the strengths and weaknesses of the current IP base of an organization, and hence provide a sketch of the organization's competitive prowess. Second, they provide a preliminary assessment of the opportunities and threats that the IP portfolio poses for business management and growth. These two purposes should be kept in mind in creating the IP portfolio, and well before that, in designing the audit exercise. To that effect, the audit questions should uncover the current and expected uses that IP is being put to by the various businesses. This provides a preliminary assessment of its value for business and guides future plans. Dow Chemical followed this methodology in its audit of its 29,000 patents. The auditing team required every business to classify the patents they have under three groups: most valuable patents related to high growth business, patents that had no current or planned use but are still of value to others, and patents that are unlikely to be used. The first group was left for the business unit competitive purposes, the second group offered for licensing, and the last either donated or abandoned.

The purpose of these and similar classifications is to facilitate IP portfolio management. In general, there are a number of guiding rules for portfolio management:

- Leveraging strong IP
- Combining weak IP with strong ones
- Divesting low-performing IP, or donating it for nonprofit organizations to claim tax deductions[20]

The same rules apply to managing any IP portfolio regardless of the form of the primary IP. Procter & Gamble's (P&G) trademark/brand portfolio can be used for illustration. Following an audit of its brands, P&G leveraged strong brands like Crest and Tide by introducing a number of brand extensions, combined weak brands with strong ones (e.g., White Cloud and Charmin), and sold low-performing brands (e.g., Lava Soap).

In addition to the general rules of portfolio management, there are a number of IP strategies that an organization can devise to utilize IP for competitive positioning and commercialization purposes.

IP Strategies Defining the Focus of IPM

Armed with the knowledge gleaned from the IP portfolio, top management should then formulate the IP strategies to strengthen the organization's IP portfolio in a way that enhances its competitive position and revenue-generation ability. Though there is some literature on the use of patent and branding strategies, there is no work that discusses the use of IP strategies for the distinct purposes of competitive positioning and commercialization. Most of the literature on patent strategies focuses on whether to patent or trade secret and the countries in which to patent. Despite a number of recent books on the use of IP (meaning patents) strategies[21] for competitive purposes, only slight mention was made of trademark strategies and none of copyright strategies. It is important for IP strategies to distinguish between the uses of IP for competitive as opposed to commercialization purposes, since the two are based on conflicting contentions. For competitive purposes, IP is used to gain entry into a market and prevent competition from securing a stronghold in a particular market segment, where exclusivity of use is the main enabler. Managing IP for commercialization purposes, however, aims at offering it for use by others as widely as possible to generate revenue, hence the importance of providing guidance from the top on when and how to use IP for the conflicting purposes, and which purpose should be the strategic focus of the business unit and why.

The CICM model incorporates the two types of IP strategies, referred to as competitive and commercialization IP strategies. The main goal of IP competitive strategies is to block competition from undermining the organization's competitive position, and from gaining a strong competitive position themselves, as well as to deactivate the competition's IP-related competitive tactics. They are also used to carve new competitive positions where the organization can set new market standards, and thus mark out the rules of the game. While competitive strategies look at IP as a competitive weapon, commercialization strategies look at it as a business asset, and hence aim at investing in it to use it for revenue generation. How to cultivate and exploit IP as a business asset is the concern of IP commercialization strategies. It should be mentioned that although licensing is used as a tactical tool under competitive strategies (i.e., to create a specific effect), it is used more as a strategic tool under commercialization strategies, as will be explained below.

IP strategies, whether competitive or commercialization, mean different things to different organizations, depending on the primary form of IP and the respective industry. Patenting strategies are intrinsically different from trademark/branding strategies, and both are different from copyright strategies. While patent strategies focus on technological wars, brand strategies focus on winning consumers through making promises, and copyright strategies focus on capitalizing on popularity of authored works. The same goes for commercialization strategies. Though all commercialization strategies are based on level of resource invested in pursing deals and opportunities, they are operationalized differently, depending on the primary form of IP. That being said, I developed two blueprints that are used as the basis for competitive and commercialization strategies related to the primary IP form—be it patent, trademark, or copyright.

A BLUEPRINT FOR COMPETITIVE IP STRATEGIES—OF WAR

Competitive strategies comprise the following:

- *"Design around"* strategies create a number of IP rights around a major IP of the competition, in order to weaken the competition's ability to use the IP as a competitive weapon. Also used to strengthen the organization's bargaining power in cross-licensing or other IP-based transactions.
- *"Build a fortress"* strategies acquire a number of IP rights around one's own IP to create a strong competitive position and build a fortress that is hard for the competition to penetrate, hence preempting the competition's use of "design around" strategies. These strategies always involve the aggressive use of litigation to deter competition from coming close to the "fortress."
- *"Mapping"* strategies map all IP activity in a certain market segment or field to map a road for developing new IP in a new area to secure market leadership. These strategies involve heavy reliance on competitive intelligence and overlap to a certain extent with the organization's innovation strategies.

As shown in Exhibit 8.1, while "design around" and "build a fortress" strategies are used in heavily protected areas and market segments, "mapping" strategies are used to find undiscovered territories where market leadership can be established. Below is a detailed account of how this blueprint can be used with patenting, branding, and copyright strategies. In addition, there is a competitive strategy that applies to all forms of IP:

- "Value Transference" strategies are used to augment the competitive position or market share of the primary form of IP through the use of secondary forms of IP. This strategy

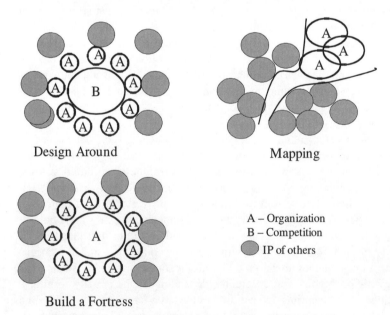

Design Around

Mapping

A – Organization
B – Competition
IP of others

Build a Fortress

EXHIBIT 8.1   Blueprint of IP Competitive Strategies

leverages the competitive power of the various forms where value of the primary form is transferred to another secondary form to lengthen the business life cycle of the product.

Patent Strategies—Of Technological Wars

> If patents are the "smart bombs" of tomorrow's business wars, then companies that fail to develop offensive and defensive strategies for their use will do so only at their peril.
> —Kevin Rivette and David Kline[22]

Technological wars turned organizational patenting into a frenzy, with the most successful filing up to 5,000 patent applications[23] and receiving over 3,000 a year.[24] In 2001, the U.S. Patent and Trademark Office (USPTO) received a record 344,717 patent applications, a 21.4 percent increase over applications filed in 2000.[25] A war it is, where patents are the most powerful competitive weapons. "What to patent" forms the core of the organization's competitive strategy since it determines not only the areas in which the organization competes, but "how." In the "how" lies the key to using patenting as a war strategy by deciding whether to design around, to build a fortress, or to map a technological road.

Under "design around" strategies, patents are used to barricade the technological field covered by another. The key to these strategies is to spot the competition's domineering patents and file for patents on improvements to it. The competition will soon discover that though it owns the domineering patent it cannot introduce desired improvements that are already patented by another. The competitive force of this strategy is that the owner of the improvement patents enhances its bargaining power and can force its entry into the market by forging an IP-based transaction with the market leader for a cross-license or a joint venture. Japanese companies used "design around" strategies in the 1970s to catch up with U.S. companies in certain technological areas, with demonstrable success.[26]

"Build a fortress" strategies can be used defensively to disarm the competition's design around strategy by feverishly patenting around one's own domineering patents. Offensively, these strategies are used to force competition out of the area by keeping ahead of the competition in patenting improvement to one's own domineering patents. Under this strategy an organization should patent very heavily in the targeted technological area, making it nearly impossible for the competition to infiltrate the fortress. This not only secures its competitive position but also opens gates of opportunity where the IP can be leveraged to enhance a competitive position even further. An example is Dell Company, which obtained 42 patents to cover its business method of providing custom-built computers while keeping its inventory at a minimum. Dell leveraged this strong position in cross-licenses with IBM, giving IBM access to its method, while freeing itself from paying tens of millions in royalties for using IBM's components[27]—a move that would have been impossible if Dell did not own every patent that can be owned to cover the business method.

"Mapping" strategies are used in searching for the "largest" patent territory in an existing or new technological field away from all the patent empires and territories. This strategy is used when the organization wants to create another battleground (platform innovations) where it sets the rules of the game and defines standards. The use of patent intelligence tools are essential here as well as future scenario planning to enable the organization to anticipate future needs and trends. But beware of vanity—any technological position no matter how superior can be defeated if the owner does not succeed in making it a market standard. While ahead, the organization should license the technology widely to establish it as a market standard. Indeed, licensing to a network of suppliers and distributors should be part of the investment plan, under this strategy. An example is Sun Micro Systems' offer of Java script for free, despite the hefty development cost, to establish a network of users. A lucid demonstration of this also is the case of VHS and Betamax. While Betamax had a more superior technology for videotapes, it had a strict policy against broad licensing. VHS licensed its technology widely to manufacturers and had a wider market presence, which later facilitated the market's adoption of VHS technology as the market standard.[28]

Savvy IP organizations use the three mentioned strategies in various combinations to create a set of defensive and offensive competitive tools. An outstanding example are the patent strategies developed by Ronald Myrick, General Electric Chief IP Counsel, as a guide for the patent departments and attorneys at GE to strategize the use of patents both defensively and offensively. Myrick defined four patenting strategies[29] for GE where patenting strategies are utilized as business strategies for patent-intensive businesses. These four strategies are

1. Benign neglect
2. Live and Let Live
3. Freedom of action
4. Exclusion

Benign neglect strategies are based on an assumption that the technology can be licensed in, if and when needed. They are used in cases where the prospective invention is of no strategic importance for the concerned business. Under these strategies, however, patents may be filed for such inventions to avoid a turn of luck, lest unexpected market changes give the invention added significance. *Live and let live* are largely defensive strategies where patents are "secured to be placed on the shelf" just in case they are needed. They can be used defensively whenever the competition poses a threat to the business's competitive position, by threatening one of its patents or products.

Freedom of action strategies, in contrast, involve broad patenting activity in many technological areas, in order to license them out or use them to leverage the position of the business in cross-licensing or joint venture transactions. As such these strategies use patents as competitive tools to force entry into new markets. The use of these strategies requires strong competitive intelligence to assess the direction of the competition. *Exclusion* strategies are purely offensive and are used to secure strong competitive positions in defined market segments. Under these strategies, licensing the technology out is discouraged, at least until a strong competitive position is established in the market. The main motivation for this strict exclusion is to provide price support to the products of the business, or at least add cost to competitors.

Myrick explains that patents should be managed as a business, and hence the patent strategy chosen should both support and be aligned with the competitive strategy of each business unit. Thus, variations and combinations of the four and other strategies are to be used in devising the competitive strategy according to business needs.

Now let's see how the competitive IP strategies blueprint translates into branding strategies.

Trademark/Branding[30] Strategies—Of Wars Over Consumers' Hearts

> Fighting brands can be meant as warnings or deterrents or as shock troops to absorb the brunt of a competitive attack. They are also often introduced with little push or support before any serious attack occurs, thereby serving as a warning.
>
> —Michael Porter[31]

Equally effective in competitive wars are branding strategies, but the war is of a completely different nature. It is not about technological supremacy and patent "lands," but about promises and winning consumers' hearts. Brand loyalty commands higher market share and enables the brand owner to maintain strong entry barriers for the competition, to have higher immunity to market changes, to protect against price erosion and hence to sustain a competitive advantage. The basis of competition here is not the tangible features of the product nor its technological superiority, but rather the promise and emotional value of the brand, which influences first and repeat purchase decisions. This is of particular importance in the knowledge economy, where the erosion of product superiority—now that most products are very close in terms of functionality, quality, and price—intensified the effect of brands on purchasing decisions, and hence became recognized as an important source of competitive advantage. The emotional value conveyed by the brand's identity became the final focal point to win the customer. As a result, branding strategies gained more prominence in the knowledge economy even for industries that don't deal directly with the consumers, as seen in the increasing use of ingredient branding.[32]

Using the IP strategies blueprint identified above, branding strategies for competitive positioning include "design around," "build a fortress," and "value mapping." "Design around" branding strategies involve the introduction of brands to counteract the competitive moves by producing a duplicate in terms of the value proposition (not the trademark, of course). To avoid creating confusion in the minds of consumers as to the origin of the product—which is the gist of trademark infringement—the house mark can be used in conjunction with the new brand. An example is Maxwell House's introduction of Horizon, in similar packaging to that of Folgers in markets where Folgers started to gain a stronger position.[33] This strategy is also used by Cadbury, Mars, and Nestlé to compete in the confectionary market where they match each other brand for brand.[34]

"Building a fortress" brand strategies involve investing heavily in building a brand by extending the line of products horizontally across product categories. In addition the brand is augmented by other supporting brands to extend it vertically along different market segments on the value hierarchy, as shown in Exhibit 8.2. This strategy also entails reinforcing the main brand with a number of slogans, aggressive marketing campaigns, trade dress, and licensing widely to a network of partners (customers, suppliers, and distributors) to maximize the penetration of the consumer attention zone. An example of the use of this strategy is Coca-Cola's defense of the

EXHIBIT 8.2   Use of "Build a Fortress" Branding Strategy

fortress it built around the Coca-Cola brand. First, the brand is supported by a close web of slogans, designs, color schemes, and advertising campaigns. Second, litigation is used as a tool to aggressively deter the slightest competitive maneuvers as shown by its major suit to stop Pepsi Cola's subsidiaries from offering Pepsi Cola under the term "Coke"!

"Value mapping" strategies are used to build a new strong brand or to revitalize an old brand, by mapping the competitive landscape to uncover brand personalities and value propositions available in the market, in search of the brand promise with the strongest emotional impact. Research has shown that the most valuable brands are those that are rich in the emotional package they deliver and invoke in the receiver and have a defined personality that is conveyed consistently. With the saturation of the market with brands, and the multiplication of common communication channels, the brands that have the most "loved" personality are the ones that command larger market shares. Branding specialists argue that the most successful brands are those that are loved rather than respected, because the consumers identify with the brands at a personal level.

Value mapping is aimed at discovering a unique brand promise that will enable the organization to set itself ahead of the rest, one that builds on the organizational history, identity, and core values, and hence can hardly be imitated by the competition. Mapping strategies involve searching for and devising the brand promise and value that set the organization ahead of the rest by building on its core ideologies and avoiding those projected by others if not rooted in the organization's culture. Value mapping is essential in revitalizing old brands as well. For example, to overcome its brand personality as being "cold and aloof," IBM undertook extensive consumer surveys, consulted its history and culture, and mapped advertising promises in the market to revitalize its brand's image. These efforts resulted in new advertising campaigns portraying IBM's international reputation with the "Solutions for a Small Planet" campaign showing people in different parts of the world discussing IBM computers in their own language.

Copyright Strategies—Of Soft Wars and the Next Hit

In copyright industries, the war is over creative content—the organization with the most creative people and content has the biggest chances of introducing a hit. The creativity of the development team (whether working on a software program or a motion picture) is the key determinant of success. It's a war over talent and over taking a good idea and expressing it in the most creative way. The key to using copyrights as competitive weapons lies in the fact that copyrights protect expressions and not ideas. Using the blueprint of IP strategies, copyright strategies for competitive positioning include "design around," "build a fortress," and "creativity mapping" strategies.

"Design around" copyright strategies involve creating works similar to those of the competition, based on the same idea but expressed differently to prevent the competition from securing a stronghold in the market. It is based on using the unprotectable elements of the competition's popular work. This strategy is based on appreciating that copyrights protect only expressions and not the underlying ideas. To use this strategy, therefore, the ideas (plots, functions, themes, etc.) should be distilled from the competition's work and then used to create new works around the competition's successful work. This strategy is used by the most successful organizations in both the entertainment and software industries. In the software industry, for example, Borland International Inc. copied the Lotus program commands menu and provided it as part of its software program. Ruling that the commands menu is a functional feature, the court denied it copyright protection.[35] The strategy is of equal force in the entertainment industry as well, where it is repeatedly used. Once a work hits the jackpot, many works are produced based on a similar thematic plot to the successful work (e.g., the range of vampire movies).

"Build a fortress" copyright strategies are based on leveraging existing creative content of a copyrighted work by surrounding it with multiple reproductions in varied media, strong brands, and adding more creative content to it by producing a number of versions and hence making it as immune as possible to competition's imitation. That is achieved by rendering the competition's imitation works useless through augmenting the core idea(s) with very highly expressive content, and forging a web of networks around the work—hence creating a fortress. As a result, competition will be disabled from reproducing a similar work as the risk of infringing becomes higher, and the cost of replicating the supporting networks prohibitive. Microsoft uses this strategy vehemently. A number of networks with PC manufacturers, a number of versions, adaptations for personal devices, Internet updates, and strong customer service support the sale of its Windows programs. Again, litigation is used as an aggressive tool to deter competition from coming close to the fortress.

"Creativity mapping" strategies depend on the way that the organization develops its creative content, that is, whether it is developed in-house or licensed in from outside sources. In the former case, the use of this strategy entails mapping the talent base to assess the level of creativity, compared to successful works in the market, and adopting the creative practices necessary to activate the talent base. Disney and Microsoft use this strategy for the development of new copyrighted works where the focus is on the creativity of their in-house talent. In the latter case, organizations need to map talent agencies, and keep close watch of the market to spot any rising talent. In both instances, the use of this strategy entails the mapping of talent, popularity trends, creative content quality, and the reasons for success of popular works. Distilling reasons for success and tying that to consumers' tastes would enable the organization to create a work that can set a new standard in the respective industry. An example of this is Disney's *Lion King,* which created a new standard for animated films in adult entertainment, to the extent of being called the "*Lion King* mini-industry," which alone generated around $1 billion in merchandise.[36]

VALUE TRANSFERENCE STRATEGIES

Value transference strategies can be used in conjunction with "build a fortress" strategies to lengthen the business life cycle of a primary form of IP, and hence preserve as long as possible the competitive position. It involves investment in secondary forms of IP near the end of the business life cycle of the primary form, as shown in Exhibit 8.3. The detailed use of this strategy is outlined in Chapter 13, but for now two illustrations are used. For pharmaceutical companies, the expiry of a patent is followed by a major drop in the sales of the patented product, sometimes

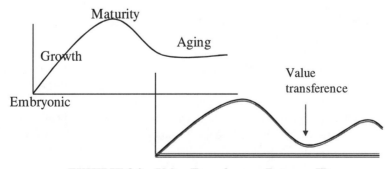

EXHIBIT 8.3   Value Transference Between IPs

reaching 80 percent. Investing heavily in a trademark/brand, however, near the end of the patent life cycle (whether legal or business) can save a considerable market share (e.g., in the case of Zantac). Another example for brands is the use of the right of publicity (IP) to revitalize a brand's popularity by seeking celebrity endorsement (e.g., Nike's Michael Jordan campaigns).

BLUEPRINT FOR COMMERCIALIZATION STRATEGIES—OF PEACE

> One should be vigilant not to let the best intentioned licensing program generate royalty revenue at the expense of suffering a diminished market strategic position.
> —James O'Shaughnessy (Chief IP Counsel Rockwell International Corp.)
> and P. Germeraad[37]

Commercialization strategies relate to using the IP portfolio to generate revenue by offering IP for licensing, using it to gain equity in joint ventures, or trade it for other strategic IPs (cross-license). IP commercialization strategies are either passive, reactive, or proactive, referring to the level of activity that the organization will expend in seeking and pursuing opportunities to commercialize IP beyond its use in support of products and processes. The various strategies may be used by the same organization for different classes of IP in the IP portfolio as follows:

- Passive commercialization strategies can be used with IP for which competitive value cannot be ascertained, particularly at the early stage of the business IP life cycle. Such IP is kept and developed on a wait-and-see basis to see how it will venture in the market. Under this strategy, it still may be commercialized following offers from noncompetitors or under a joint venture for their further development with a competitor.
- Reactive commercialization strategies can be used with IP that is of more ascertainable value as a competitive weapon. Opportunities for commercialization of these IPs should be pursued only after the organization has secured the targeted competitive position, where commercialization poses no competitive harm. Ford Global Technologies, for example, calls this strategy "Ford First," which means that Ford should establish its position in the market before the IP can be offered for commercialization, a period estimated to be three years on average.[38] Reactive strategies are also used to commercialize IP to partners (customers, suppliers, and distributors) to create synergy and reduce costs. An example is Toyota's offering of its patents to its original equipment manufacturer (OEM) manufacturers to increase their productivity, and hence improve Toyota's overall competitive ability. These strategies enable the use of IP to augment the competitive impact of a chain or a network of partners, and in that case should not be offered to competitors.
- Proactive commercialization strategies are used when it is clear that the IP concerned is of no competitive or strategic use for the organization but is of value to others. Proactive commercialization entails the active pursuit of opportunities through industry liaisons, contacts, agents, and any channel possible to generate revenue from the IP portfolio. These IP can be freely offered to competitors. Organizations like IBM that have a liberal patenting philosophy, encouraging innovation in noncore areas, multiply their chances of building an IP portfolio that can be offered in the great part for commercialization. Under this strategy all forms of IP, not only the primary forms, are used to create the best deal. Exhibit 8.4 shows the various forms of IP used for different types of licensing.

TYPE OF LICENSING	TRADEMARKS	PATENTS	COPYRIGHTS	TRADE SECRETS
Technology transfer		X		X
Franchising	X		X	X
Software licensing		X possible	X	
Merchandising	X		X	
Patent licensing		X		
Publishing, digital rights, music, motion picture			X	

EXHIBIT 8.4   IP Forms Used for Different Types of Licensing

The choice of one commercialization strategy over the other depends on striking a balance between the use of IP as a competitive weapon and as a business asset. A proactive commercialization strategy can be used only when the IP can be used dominantly as a business asset. Caution always must be used not to undermine the competitive position by commercializing particular IPs (e.g., by diluting a brand in a franchise, or producing an overkill by overmerchandising). Striking that balance in brand licensing can be achieved by maintaining close control of the use of the brand by the licensees. Striking such balance, however, when it comes to commercializing patents, can be achieved by limiting the transfer of trade secrets (know-how), that is, focusing on the licensing of the patent without the technological know-how. Achieving that balance is more challenging when it comes to patents compared to trademarks and copyrights.

Business based on brand developments always views trademarks as commercial tools that convey the brand promise to the consuming public. Commercialization of the trademark, therefore, is realized as the main object at the preliminary stages of brand development and investment, provided close control is kept on the use of the trademark. A similar trend can be seen when it comes to copyrights as commercialization of the work is actively pursued, being a (if not the only) motivating force behind investing in creativity. At an early time, organizations in all industries capitalized on their strong trademarks and copyrights, exploiting them through multiple commercial transactions and distribution channels. Once established as a strong IP right, the market will be flooded with consumer products and merchandise that revolve around these rights. This, however, was not the case with the commercialization of patents. Patents were traditionally viewed as a way to secure the right to use certain inventions or compositions in production and/or to obstruct competition's activity in a certain field. Many patents were left on the shelves to collect dust. A survey of U.S. companies found that "more than 35 percent of patented technologies are orphans that fell by the wayside after a merger because they were not part of the combined entity's core business."[39] Such orphan patents were estimated to have commercial value in excess of $115 billion.[40] To date, most organizations exploit only the tip of the iceberg of their patent portfolio. Some estimates report that corporate America, not to mention universities' labs, lose trillions annually for keeping patents on the shelves.[41]

It was not until recently that organizations in this area, being alerted to the value of patents as commercial business tools, started to change their patents' commercialization strategy to more proactive ones. Thus, while proactive commercialization strategies have been used in connection with trademarks and copyrights, they are still in the experimentation phase when it comes to patents. Chapter 13 provides more guidance on the situations under which each of the commercialization strategies can be used. Shifting to proactive commercialization strategies, however, is not sufficient to deal with the IP portfolio as a business asset. Without IPM infiltrating into the business management function and becoming the job of everyone in the organization it is hard to see how every business unit, department, and team can be tuned to pursue commercialization opportunities. That involves, besides the adoption of commercialization strategies, effecting the necessary structural and cultural changes to take IPM to the operational level. To that we now turn.

OPERATIONALIZING IPM—WITH ALL DUE RESPECT TO THE LEGAL DEPARTMENT

Under the CICM, IPM is the stage where the value of an organization's intellectual capital (IC) is leveraged and maximized to the full by realizing that the intellectual property underlying a certain product or a process can now be used on its own as a competitive weapon and a business asset. This understanding has to be infiltrated at all levels of the organization. Just like the innovation process being liberated from the confines of the R&D department, IPM too needs to be liberated from the confines of the legal department. The legal department may act as the process owner, but without a shift in how IP lawyers see themselves, it is hard to see how they can facilitate infiltrating IPM in the whole organization. That being said, IP lawyers whether in patent-, trademark- or copyright-intensive industries are the best equipped as IP managers given their knowledge about the complex anatomy of the various IP animals. Indeed, IP lawyers in the best-performing organizations join top management in forging and aligning IP strategies with the overall business strategies and needs.

To effectively take IPM to the operational level, a number of changes are required to the structure, culture, and systems of the organization. When it comes to structure, two major changes are required: (1) forming units at the business unit level, reporting to a central strategic planning or business development department, to define which IPs will be used as the basis of the business unit's (or SBU) core competence or competitive advantage. These units, called IP Strategy Units, oversee operationalizing the competitive IP strategies; and (2) forming cross-functional/divisional teams responsible for leveraging various IP inside and outside the organization, called IP Synergy Teams.

It is essential as with any of the other stages of CICM to have a culture that supports the management and leveraging of the IC in question. For the IPM stage, the organizational culture has to incorporate values that discourage infringing the IP of others, and promote the preservation of the organization's IP. The definition of the culture for IPM is one of the main tasks of the legal department as cultural change needs to be effected by developing the systems and procedures that engrain an IP-oriented culture in the daily operations of the organization.

Finally, the organization should provide a number of tools and methods to enable effective decision making pertaining to IPM, particularly valuation and assessment tools.

Structural Changes—Of Strategic Focus and Synergy Teams

Structural changes mainly relate to the formation of IP strategy units and the business unit level, and IP synergy cross-functional teams. The two groups will be directly responsible for leveraging IP across the whole organization, for competitive and commercialization purposes.

The IP Strategy Unit—IP and the Business Plan. IP strategy units (IPSUs) participate in the formulation of IP strategies and oversee their operationalization by aligning IP strategies with the overall business plan. The focus of IPSUs is to take strategy from the top to the frontline levels as shown in Exhibit 8.5 below. They are responsible for operationalizing competitive IP strategies by focusing on the part of the IP portfolio that is the basis of the business unit's core competency or competitive advantage. Though the same group of IP may be of strategic relevance to more than one business unit, an SBU or a division, the primary responsibility for developing this group of IP should be entrusted to one business unit as the focal point. In other words, every business unit should build a fortress around the part of the IP portfolio that is the basis of its core competitive advantage. IPSUs should report to a central strategic planning or business development and growth department to ensure coordination between the various business units and overall alignment with the organizational vision and overall strategy.

IP Synergy Teams or Licensing Units. IP synergy teams (IPSTs) are cross-functional teams, as shown in Exhibit 8.5, with the primary responsibility of operationalizing the commercialization IP strategies of the organization. The main task of IPSTs is to explore and pursue commercialization and leveraging opportunities for IPs internally by offering it to business units other than the one where the IP first originated. For patents, this means the business units other than the one where the technology developed and the patents were acquired and initially used. For brands and copyrights, this means product divisions or market segments other than the one where the brand of the copyright was first developed and launched. Exhausting internal opportunities, IPSTs should explore opportunities for commercializing the IP to partners, then to any other interested party over the globe.

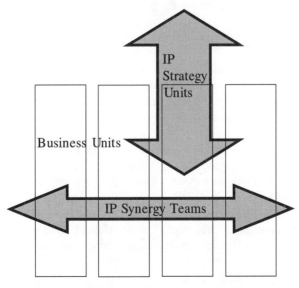

EXHIBIT 8.5 IP Strategy Units and IP Synergy Teams

The task of IPSTs may also be carried by:

- Small focus groups like Dow Chemical's Intellectual Asset Management teams[42]
- An independent business unit like DuPont's Intellectual Asset Management Business
- An independent company like Bell South's, AT&T's Intellectual Property Company, and Ford Global Technologies

Regardless of the organizational form used, IPSTs should be treated as profit and not cost centers. In all cases, their focus should be cross-functional and multidivisional, market oriented and network based.

In addition to the structural changes, the culture of the organization needs to change as discussed next.

Cultural Changes

To effect cultural changes, the legal department should design an IP guide for use by everyone in the organization. The IP guide should have the following sections, each designed to incorporate a certain set of values in the organization's culture as follows:

- IP Literacy Guide—To raise awareness about what IP is and prevent the loss of the organization's IP through leakages and unfair competitive practices
- Detection program—To promote a culture protective of IP rights by being alert to the infringing activities of third parties
- Clearance procedures—To create a culture that is preventive of infringing the IP of others

The IP Literacy Guide. IP cannot be used to maximize value without a minimum level of knowledge about what it is, what makes it stronger, and what dissipates it. Specialized knowledge can always be gained on a needs basis, but a level of IP literacy should be maintained at all times. The IP literacy level required for each organization depends on the organization's industry, hence the primary IP and its IP business strategy. In all cases, however, the IP Literacy Guide should contain guidelines for the various departments, business units, and individual employees on the proper use of IP and the risks that need to be managed in relation to its use. In particular, the Guide should address the following (outlined in detail in Chapter 13):

- Security and confidentiality measures to prevent leakages and misappropriation of trade secrets. Loss of trade secrets cost corporate America $45 billion in 1999 alone.[43] The problem of trade secret misappropriation posed an economic threat that moved the U.S. government to enact the Economic Espionage Act in 1996 criminalizing trade secret misappropriation.
- Proper advertising and marketing procedures to avoid the loss of trademarks through the overuse of the trademark as a generic term. An example is DuPont's loss of the mark Cellophane, and Xerox's coming very close to losing its trademark through the "Don't Copy It, Xerox It" ad campaign.
- Merchandizing and franchising relations to ensure that there is actual supervision of the licensee to avoid loss of trademarks through what is known as naked licensing.
- Clean procedures for development of copyright works to defend against infringement claims by proving that there was no access. This, of course, is not observed where the developing team is trying to design around the work of the competition, but should be kept as a general rule.

- Digital rights management and cyber security systems to protect against copyright piracy and hackers having access to the organization's databases.
- Proper marketing and sales procedures to avoid tying the sales of unpatented to patented products and hence constitute patent misuse. Patent misuse may subject the organization to antitrust proceedings and disable it from claiming damages for patent infringement until the misuse is purged.
- Reporting suspected infringement of any form of IP to the legal department as soon as possible to prevent the loss of the IP right concerned through lack of policing or acquiescence and mitigate losses. This constitutes passive monitoring of the infringing activity, which is pursued more actively under the Detection Program.

Detection Program—Of Competitive Intelligence and Reverse Engineering.   IPs are negative rights that entitle the owner to exclude others from using and commercially benefiting from the use of IP in any manner. The onus is therefore on the owner to protect the exclusive territory conferred by the IP right, detect unlawful violations of this right, and take appropriate enforcement action. This forms an integral part of the ability to preserve the right and enhance its effectiveness. Though the organization should entrust the task of monitoring infringing activities either to an internal unit or to a specialized outside third party, some organizations do neither and instead rely on their customers' feedback to detect infringement of their IP rights. The latter approach is risky as it usually results in delayed detection of infringement, if any.

Overall, the detection program should be entrusted to a unit in the legal department in cooperation with the R&D department[44] for patents and copyrights, and marketing and sales departments for brands. The detection unit should cooperate with the licensing department in recommending the most appropriate enforcement action. The level of aggressiveness of the response depends on whether the infringed IP is predominantly used for competitive or commercialization purposes. In the former case, the IP should be protected fiercely through litigation, while in the latter an offer of a license should be the first resort. If the IP is used merely for FTO purposes, however, then the decision to litigate should be based on a cost–benefit analysis. In all cases, a letter should be sent to the infringing party informing it of the violation and requesting that the situation be remedied. In many cases, the threat of litigation suffices to keep the competition away or at least safely far from the organization's competitive territory.

In making litigation decisions, the organization needs to balance between sending a strong message to the market that infringement of its IP will not be taken lightly, and not committing extensive resources to a suit where costs far exceed expected awards. The organization should take into consideration other factors like the breaking of the business relation and the infringing party's possible retaliatory action. For example, in 1989, Motorola sued Hitachi for infringing a number of its patents, moving Hitachi to countersue Motorola. As a result, the court stopped the sales of the corresponding suspected products of both companies subject to resolution. Both companies, particularly Motorola, suffered losses exceeding the damages awarded.[45] It seems that this case was a perfect one for cross-licenses if both Motorola and Hitachi had sought a more conciliatory approach.

Recently, the use of insurance to transfer litigation risks has grown. Historically, some of these risks were arguably covered under the comprehensive or commercial general liability policies, but only to the extent that they relate to advertising injury relating to trademark and copyright infringements.[46] Now there are policies that specifically deal with both infringement and enforcement risks and the associated legal expenses, covering patents, copyrights, and trademarks.[47] To date, there is no insurance policy that covers the risk of misappropriation of trade secrets, which may result in very high losses. But as the business service sector's (insurance, banking, and investment) ability to treat IP rights as business assets develops, things may change.[48]

As important as detecting infringement and taking appropriate action is avoiding infringing the IP rights of others. This is what the clearance procedures aim to prevent or minimize.

Clearance Procedures—Treading Around Dangerous Waters.   Clearance procedures are more than IP searches. In addition to searching registries, they include procedures for the assessment of the scope and strength of the IP of others. Following that assessment, the clearance procedures assist the department concerned in making decisions on whether to proceed with product development plans (patents and copyrights), with marketing and advertising campaigns (trademarks), and with using a particular process developed by a former employee of the competition (trade secrets). In cases in which the IP owned by another is very strong and wide in scope, to the effect of blocking the business plan, a license should be actively pursued. Failing that, management, in conjunction with the legal department, need to assess the risks involved in designing around the blocking IP, and whether the business plan should be changed. Using the clearance procedures at an early stage of the business plan avoids the possibility of having to divest later and lose the related investment, as well as instill a culture that is preventive of infringing the IP of others.

Enabling Tools and Practices—IP Valuation

> As real estate title may cover a square inch of Arctic tundra or a square mile of Manhattan, intellectual property protection may be broad or narrow, cover various kinds of products or processes, and have widely varying value.
> —Thomas Field, Franklin Pierce Law Center Professor of Law[49]

Not all IPs are born equal; some are much more valuable than others. A domineering patent, a highly distinctive trademark with growing brand equity, and a strong rather than a thin copyright are all terms used to distinguish between the value of various IPs. There are two facets to the value of IP—legal and commercial. Legally, the value of IP lies in its scope of coverage, and the strength of the right (i.e., whether it will be afforded strong protection by the courts). Commercially, the value of IP depends on how customers will react to it. In particular, it depends on whether customers will embrace a new technology (patents), relate to a brand and be loyal to it, and receive the copyrighted work with enthusiasm. The fact that the value of IP depends on commercial and legal considerations makes valuation of IP a very complex exercise. This is particularly true at the early development stages of the life of IP wherein customer reaction and hence commercial value cannot be accurately ascertained.

There are a number of methods for the valuation of IP based on accounting methods, including cost, income and market based. While cost methods look at historical values relating to the IP development costs (past-oriented), income methods estimate the expected royalty streams that an IP may generate in the future and discount the cash flow to the present. Market-based methods rely on data on IP royalties in various industries and make a valuation based on what IP will generate in an arm's-length transaction.[50] Valuation of IP is used widely in cases of mergers and acquisitions, litigation for estimation of losses and awards, major licensing transactions, patent donations, and whenever an IP is used as a collateral security. However, the fact that valuation of any single IP may cost between $25 and $50,000 makes its use for IP portfolio management purposes prohibitive, particularly where the organization owns tens of thousands of IPs.

It is crucial that an organization develop a methodology that includes qualitative and quantitative methods to roughly estimate the value of IP, for IPM to be engrained in business management. A study by the Danish Patent and Trademark Office (DPTO)[51] found that the lack of valuation tools that an organization may use in relation to IPM is one of the main problems hampering management of IP as business assets. The DPTO discovered that though most Danish companies develop IP strategies, they fail to link it to business strategy, mainly because they lack systematic tools and methods to assess the value of their IP portfolios. To promote economic development by unlocking the value of IP portfolios, the DPTO developed the IPScore™ tool for businesses to systematically assess the value of their IP. The IPScore uses mainly qualitative measures and criteria to assess the significance of individual IPs. The IPScore measures represent a guide to the minimum criteria that an organization should apply to value an IP for IPM purposes. They include:

- Technical status of the IP (relates to patents and software)
- Market-related utilization potential
- The company's mission and resources relating to the utilization of the right

CONCLUSION

The goal of IPM is to cultivate the organization's ability to use IC both for competitive positioning and revenue generation, by unleashing the power of IP. The optimal benefit of IPM is capitalizing on what may otherwise remain a dormant IP portfolio, and hence maximize the organization's competitive performance and profit-making ability. For that to happen, IPM should be transformed from being a function of the legal department to becoming a part of the business management function of the whole organization. This involves effecting a number of changes on the strategic and operational levels, including undertaking an IP audit of the primary form of IP, creating IP portfolios, adopting the appropriate competitive and commercialization IP strategies to mine the portfolios, and effecting necessary structural and cultural changes. This is further enabled by the development of systematic tools for the valuation and assessment of IP value. Chapter 13 outlines the implementation of the IPM stage step by step.

But before we proceed to that, it is important to see how the CICM approach exists in real business life, by exploring the comprehensive ICM systems of two pioneers—Skandia and Dow Chemical.

NOTES

[1] Intellectual property consists of patents, trademarks, copyrights, trade secrets, and other rights. Patents protect a novel nonobvious idea that is useful and reduced to practice (applied) pursuant to a patent issued by a government agency, the United States Patent and Trademark Office (USPTO), following a lengthy and complex process of examination. Trademarks consist of a term, a logo, a slogan, or any device (including trade dress) used to identify the origin of a product or a service to consumers. Trademarks that are registered with the USPTO provide an incontestable right of exclusive use upon satisfying a number of conditions. Copyrights vest automatically in the author upon expression of an idea in a fixed medium, and protect the artistic, as opposed to the functional, features of the work against copying and derivative reproductions. Trade secrets protect any secret information originated by an entity from being misappropriated, provided that it is of commercial value, not generally known, and subject to reasonable security measures. For more information please refer to the "Mini Masters in Intellectual Property (MIP)" in Appendix B.

[2] It is hard to imagine an industry in which there is not at least one form of IP that is the source of competitive performance. It is a common belief that professional service businesses (e.g.,

consulting, financial services) are an exception. A closer look, however, reveals that competitive performance in service businesses predominantly depends on know-how, and work systems, which are protected by trade secrets and copyrights, and possibly patents for business methods.

[3] In 1996, *Financial Times* valued the brands of Marlboro, Coca-Cola, McDonalds, IBM, and Disney at $44.6, $43.4, $18.9, $18.5 and $15.4 billion, respectively. When it comes to patents, trade secrets, and copyrights, their value to a business can be ascertained form damages awarded in infringement cases. Since the 1990s, damages awarded in litigation of patent and copyright cases range from tens to hundreds of millions of dollars. It is estimated that U.S. organizations spend around 25 percent of R&D costs on litigation (J. Lernor, "Patenting in the Shadow of Competitors," *Journal of Law and Economics,* Vol. 38, October 1995, pp. 466–473.

[4] Sherwood, R., "Intellectual Property Systems and Investment Stimulation," *IDEA: The Journal of Law & Technology* 37, no. 2, (1997), pp. 261–370.

[5] Siwek, S., "Copyright Industries in the U.S. Economy: The 2002 Report" (Economists Incorporated: Washington DC, 2002).

[6] Anti-Dilution and Anti-Cyber Squatting Acts.

[7] McCarthy, J., "Intellectual Property: America's Overlooked Export," 20 U. Dayton L. Rev. 809, p. 809.

[8] *Intellectual asset management* emerged as a term to overcome the legal connotations of the word *property* and replace it with the more business-oriented word *asset.* I prefer to stick with the term *intellectual property* mainly because the word *asset* can mean other forms of intellectual capital as well. For a thorough treatment of the terms used, refer to Chapter 2.

[9] K. Keller, *Strategic Brand Management: Building, Measuring and Managing Brand Equity* (Upper Saddle River, NJ: Prentice Hall, 1998), p. 28.

[10] *Id.,* pp. 29–30.

[11] *Id.* Two main approaches were used. The first is appointing brand managers responsible for the management of a certain brand across the various product categories, and the second is appointing brand managers that manage a portfolio of brands under a certain product category. Under the first approach, P&G appointed brand managers for each of its brands, wherein the manager was responsible for the financial success of the brand and exploring new business opportunities. The second approach was developed by P&G in 1987 following the major drop in its annual earnings in 1985. P&G found that the first approach fostered internal competition, while the second fostered brand synergies.

[12] APQC, "Brand Building and Communication," APQC, 2001. Available online at *www.apqc.com.*

[13] O. Granstrand, *The Economics and Management of Intellectual Property* (Northampton, MA: Edward Elgar, 1999), p. 257.

[14] See, for example, K. Rivette and D. Kline, *Rembrandts in the Attic: Unlocking the Hidden Value of Patents* (Boston: Harvard Business School Press, 2000); and P. Sullivan, *Value-Driven Intellectual Capital: How to Convert Intellectual Assets into Market Value* (New York: John Wiley & Sons, 2000).

[15] See J. Davis and S. Harrison, *Edison in the Boardroom* (New York: John Wiley & Sons, 2001); and Granstrand supra note 13.

[16] See, for example, Rivette and Kline, op. cit., noting Xerox CEO, Richard Thoman, on maximizing value through managing IP.

[17] For example, the use of copyrights in the issuance of guaranteed bonds. An example is David Bowie, who successfully issued $55 million in bonds, guaranteed by his publisher EMI in 1997, based on his albums. Other examples include Disney, Nestlé, and Calvin Klein, who issued bonds up to $1 billion approximately securitized by copyright, trademark, and film-related licenses. For more information, see J. Hughes and K. Birenbaum, "Insuring Intellectual Property Risks: Creative Solutions on the Cutting Edge," 568 PLI/Pat 203, 233.

[18] The terms *primary* and *secondary* forms of IP are used to refer to either patents, copyrights, or trademarks. Trade secrets are excluded as they are rights that provide a blanket protection to any information of commercial value (know-how), the nondisclosure of which provides a competitive advantage, and hence is an ancillary form of protection that should be used regardless of the primary form of IP in a particular industry.

[19] There are, however, hybrid industries where more than one form of IP is strategically important. An example is the software industry, where patents, trade secrets, and copyrights shoulder together to secure a competitive position. In addition, conglomerates that traverse a number of industries find that certain IP forms are more critical for some businesses than others. R&D-intensive and consumer products companies, like General Electric and P&G, for example, need to proactively manage almost all forms of IP.

[20] The U.S. IRS Code includes IP in the definition of property to which tax deductions will accrue if donated to nonprofit organizations. When it comes to patents, this has been used as a strategy by many organizations (e.g., DuPont, Dow, Ford, and GE), resulting in millions in tax savings. Though theoretically speaking the IRS code definition covers trademarks and copyrights, it is hard to see how trademarks can be donated to nonprofit organizations. The matter may be different for copyrighted works, and it is yet to be seen how business can benefit from it.

[21] Supra notes 15 and 16.

[22] K. Rivette and D. Kline, "Discovering New Value in IP: The Unconventional Strategy of Xerox's CEO," *Harvard Business Review*, January 2001, Vol. 78, no. 1, p. 54.

[23] It is reported that HP, following the introduction of an employee incentive program to boost patent applications in December 1999, increased its patent applications by 30 percent in 2000, and 67 percent in 2001—reaching 5,000 applications. See P. Buxbaum, "IP: Maximizing Return on Intangible Assets," *Fortune*, April 2002.

[24] In 2001, IBM received 3,454 patents, around 10 a day.

[25] E. Jonietz, "Economic Bust, Patent Boom," *Technology Review*, May 2002, p. 71.

[26] For more details, see Granstrand, supra note 13, p. 227.

[27] Supra note 12, p. 57.

[28] For detailed treatment of Betamax and VHS, see P. Lardner, *Fast Forward* (Franklin Pierce Law Center, Concord, NH, 2002).

[29] Based on R. Myrick, "Managing IP in a Large Multinational Corporation," presentation to the Intellectual Property Owners (IPO) Association, conference (June 6, 2001), and an interview with Myrick on August 28, 2002.

[30] It is important to note here that trademarks and brands are not synonymous. Though a brand is made predominantly of trademarks (marks, slogans, trade dress, color design), they also comprise IC. The IC of the brand includes values communicated by employees through customer service (human capital), brand promise and value propositions as perceived and valued by the customers (customer capital) and the marketing relations and networks, and corporate identity

and reputation associated with the brand (structural capital). Therefore, trademark strategies will be referred to as branding strategies.

[31] M. Porter, *Competitive Strategy* (New York: Free Press 1980), p. 84.

[32] An example is DuPont, which requires the use of its brand where its products are used in manufacturing end products. Another example is Intel with its "Intel Inside" mark used on PCs that include its chip. In 1996, *Financial Times* estimated that Intel's brand was worth $10.4 billion.

[33] Supra note 26.

[34] Supra note 9, p. 429.

[35] *Lotus Development Corp. v. Borland International Inc.,* 49 F.3d 807 (1st Cir., 1995). The Court of Appeals affirmed the decision in 1996.

[36] H. Berkowitz and V. Gay, "Mega Mouse," *Newsday,* June 30, 1996.

[37] J. O'Shaughnessy and P. Germeraad, "Tools of Trade for Analyzing IP Opportunities," *Les Nouvelles,* March 2000, p. 32.

[38] H. Fradkin, "Technology Mining at Ford Motor Company," *Les Nouvelles,* December 2000, p. 160.

[39] R. Lee, "Leveraging Relationships for Growth through a Value Network," Deloitte & Touche online publications, *www.us.deloitte.com/vc/0,1639,sid%253D2007%2526cid%253D3272,00. html.*

[40] *Id.*

[41] Supra note 12, p. 65.

[42] Refer to Chapter 9 for more details.

[43] N. Akerman and A. Lachow, "Trade Secrets—Preventing a Leak," *National Law Journal,* September 2000, B5.

[44] R&D departments usually reverse engineer the competition's suspected products, to discover infringing activities.

[45] Granstrand, op. cit., p. 148.

[46] M. Simensky and E. Osterberg, "The Insurance and Management of Intellectual Property Risks," 17 *Cardozo Arts & Ent. L. J.* 321, 329–330.

[47] *Id.,* pp. 325–338.

[48] *Id.*

[49] T. Field, "Seeking Cost Effective Patents." Available online at *www.piercelaw.edu/ TFIELD/seeking.htm.*

[50] For more details, see Gordon Smith and Russell Parr, *Valuation of Intellectual Property and Intangible Assets,* 3rd ed. (New York: John Wiley & Sons, 2000). Also see Gordon Smith, *Trademark Valuation* (New York: John Wiley & Sons, 1997).

[51] Available online at *www.dkpto.dk.*

9

The Pioneers of Intellectual Capital Management—Skandia and Dow Chemical

> It's certainly not to say that Dow or any other corporation has not managed its intellectual assets; in fact, I believe there is a direct correlation between how well the intellectual assets of a corporation have been managed and its financial success. The opportunity is in being able to visualize, better measure and manage them.
> —Gordon Petrash, formerly of Dow Chemical Company and the leader of the Intellectual Asset Management initiative and currently chief strategy officer at Delphion[1]

Petrash continues to explain that though many corporations now know how to manage their intellectual assets, particularly when it comes to innovation and intellectual property (IP), the real challenge lies in two areas—knowing the "how" of managing knowledge, and adopting an appropriate model of intellectual capital management (ICM) as a whole wherein all forms of IC are visualized and managed.[2] Devising a methodology, a system, or a model to deal with these two challenges, as well as tying this with the better management of the organization's intellectual assets (innovation resources and IP) and business as a whole are the main characteristics of the pioneers' ICM models.

In particular, the pioneers' models have the following characteristics in common regardless of industry, strategy, or size:

- A clear vision that recognizes the importance of ICM in the success of the organization and its attainment of strategic goals.
- Commitment of leadership and top management to the success of the ICM reflected in resource allocation and strategic planning. This commitment is encapsulated in a detailed IC strategy for the organization, which each business unit can customize for its own purposes.
- A comprehensive model that translates the IC strategy by creating processes to manage IC throughout the three stages of knowledge, innovation, and intellectual property management (IPM).
- A business model that enables the implementation of the necessary structural and cultural changes, as well as the provision of supporting functions and tools.
- A performance measurement system that tracks and monitors progress and outcomes to aid management decision making as to resource allocation and implementation of appropriate programs.

In this chapter, the experience and models of two pioneers will be outlined and examined using the above criteria and looking through the Comprehensive Intellectual Capital Management (CICM) lens. The two companies, Skandia AFS and Dow Chemical, have been chosen not only for their success in managing their IC comprehensively, but also for their vast contribution to the field. This contribution has been the result of their brave experimentation with the IC concept, and successful application of the concept to business reality amidst all the skepticism surrounding its business efficacy. To that we now turn, starting with Skandia.

SKANDIA: THE LEADER OF THE IC REVOLUTION

> Yes, we care about the money, but intellectual capital management is much more than that to us, it's who we are.
>
> —Jan Hoffmeister, Skandia Group VP of ICM[3]

Renowned for its Navigator, Skandia's[4] name symbolizes the intellectual capital revolution of the time. One that attracts a lot of interest not only for its uniqueness but also because of the vigor with which it is embraced at Skandia. I had the fortune of having a glimpse of this revolution by meeting Jan Hoffmeister, Skandia Group VP for Intellectual Capital Management. It is a revolution indeed because ICM and the Navigator are not seen merely as useful business practices that enable value creation and extraction, but rather as the way of doing business. At Skandia, ICM is a belief system that is so well entrenched in the way the whole organization works that it is hard to discern it as an isolated business process for study. It is a belief so strong in the hearts of business executives that they see themselves not only as agents of change in Skandia, but the whole business environment around Skandia, the whole economy when they can.

Intellectual capital management at Skandia is far from being a system implemented on a faith basis. It is one that Skandia has proven is of immense value. It was started with the inception of Skandia AFS division in 1986/87. Ten years after its inception the division accounted for 60 percent of the profit of Skandia, growing at the rate of 48 percent annually, and eventually comprising most of Skandia. In a traditional mature industry like the insurance industry, such growth rates defy conventional wisdom.[5] This great success is attributed to the unique alliance-based business model that Jan Carendi (the CEO of Skandia AFS division and deputy CEO of Skandia Group at the time) established and to the ICM system—the heart and brains of Skandia's business model.

Being a real revolution, Skandia started at home. Skandia's model of ICM was inducted across the whole enterprise of Skandia Group. In 1991, following the success of the Navigator in Skandia AFS, Lars-Eric Petersson, the president and CEO of Skandia Group, rolled out the use of the Navigator across the whole Group, making its use mandatory in 1999. Petersson's commitment to ICM was so strong that he reformulated Skandia Group's vision to "IC the Future." Skandia Group embraced the revolution, which started in Skandia full-heartedly to the extent that it was the first company in the world to publish a formal IC report as a supplement to its financial annual reports from 1994 to 1998.

This case study will survey the evolvement of ICM at Skandia AFS division, the bedrock of the IC revolution, and how it expanded to the rest of Skandia. It will go beyond an examination of the Navigator, as most case studies on Skandia do, to explore how Skandia manages IC at the knowledge, innovation, and IP management stages.

THE BUSINESS MODEL AND THE IC REVOLUTION—
CARENDI AND THE FIRST TORCH

Carendi introduced a new business model for Skandia based on alliances and relationship management, or as he calls it, "specialists in cooperation." Instead of selling its own savings products or managing its funds, Skandia outsources fund management and product distribution, while focusing on product development and sales support, as illustrated in Exhibit 9.1. Skandia collects and assesses extensive information about fund managers' investment history in the process of approving them as partners. This information, along with Skandia's knowledge of the fund market, is then passed on to financial advisors to aid them in advising their own clients. Skandia thus manages two networks by acting as the link between them instead of managing its own funds or distributing its own products. This enables Skandia to focus on product development.

Skandia's products include two major categories: investment products for end users, and support services and products for financial advisors. Under the first category, Skandia provides solutions (products) for every investment need, each with a platform of investment options. For financial advisors, Skandia provides packaged knowledge on the market as well as training packages. All those specialists, including Skandia, are tied together through a common value chain, but operate autonomously in providing their products.

Skandia's business model is based on the ability to manage relationships over two major networks of fund managers and financial advisors, and hence on its competence to manage IC internally across the various divisions and externally across the portfolio of alliances. A few years into its life, Skandia had around 60 employees at the headquarters in Stockholm, 1,200 key executives at the operating units in the United States and another 20 countries, managed alliances with over 70,000 fund managers and brokers and serviced over a million end users. For every full-time employee and partner Skandia maintained almost 20 end users. This model saves billions in operational costs compared to a traditional insurance company model where agents' networks or distribution sales force are employed.

Analyzing the business model with the CICM lens, the model revolves around three main processes:

1. Managing knowledge resources of Skandia and those obtained from fund managers to share them with financial advisors, and generate knowledge about customer needs and market trends to enable product development
2. Managing innovation or new product development across Skandia's alliances and operating units to provide new solutions that differentiate Skandia from competitors
3. Managing Skandia's primary IPs comprising work systems, business methods, software programs, and trade secrets to enhance competitive performance

Skandia's ICM model is not a program to boost value creation per se but the core process of the new business model. This is why Carendi was not content with appreciation of the value of IC at the top and senior management levels. He wanted this appreciation to penetrate all levels and permeate the way business is done in Skandia as a whole. For this to happen, it was essential to represent ICM in a systematic way and to tie it to everyday business reality. What is needed is a

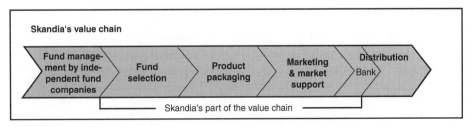

EXHIBIT 9.1   Skandia's Business Model

methodology to define what IC is, how it drives value creation, and how it can be captured and then leveraged. Faced with the challenge of allocating this task to an existing position or department, Carendi found no position that could cover this new revolutionary concept, so he created a new one. In 1991, Carendi appointed Leif Edvinsson as the world's first Director of Intellectual Capital, and entrusted him with making business sense of the IC concept.

PASSING THE TORCH TO EDVINSSON AND HIS TEAM

Edvinsson's job was to create ways that enable both management and employees to visualize and develop IC. The first step was to define what is IC. Edvinsson designed the Intellectual Capital Value Hierarchy, classifying IC into human capital and structural capital, customer and organizational capital, wherein organizational capital includes process and innovation capital.[6]

Combining the IC Value Hierarchy with the Balanced Scorecard concept, Edvinsson developed the Navigator as a tool that translates the IC concept into practical application (see Exhibit 2.2). The core message of the Navigator is that to manage a business focusing on financial results, which reflects past performance, hinders management ability to manage the IC—the core driver of present and future performance. But as portrayed by the IC Value Hierarchy, IC spans practically everything that the organization does and is. Thus, the focuses in the Navigator are provided to enable management focus on certain aspects when managing IC, and hence enable the design of indicators to monitor the development of IC under each focus.

The Navigator forms the crux of Skandia's ICM model. It provides:

- Taxonomy and definitions to see and identify IC
- A method to focus attention at the strategic and operational levels on IC development
- A tool that translates IC strategies into business reality throughout the whole organization including the individual level. By defining key success factors under each of the focuses, each business is motivated to manage and develop its IC.
- A framework that unifies the various approaches that each business unit or department develops for managing its IC, creating overall strategic alignment.

To stress the importance of managing IC, Skandia required the various business units and departments to use the Navigator to report on its IC. The main goal is focusing on capturing and growing IC to sustain and enhance the business unit's future performance. But for everyone to embrace the IC concept and apply it in the daily management of business, more was needed. The revolution needed to be taken to the masses!

ENLIGHTENING THE MASSES—THE NAVIGATOR AND THE NEW VISION

To take ICM to every corner of the organization at Skandia and Skandia Group, it is important to have a vision in which the organization sees itself as a knowledge organization. This was realized across Skandia Group, and in February 2001, Petersson created three groups, with representatives from the various companies in Skandia Group, to create a new vision. The group formulated the vision:

Skandia enables people to provide themselves with a lifetime of a prosperity.

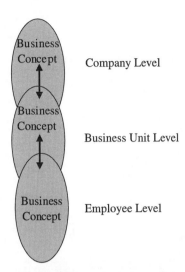

EXHIBIT 9.2 Alignment of Vision, Strategy, and Operations

Stressing that Skandia enables people to help themselves highlighted the partnership focus that Carendi engrained in the new business model. It sees Skandia's role as that of the enabler and hence sets its role as a knowledge broker. In addition, Skandia added "intellectual capital development" to its list of core values, and promoted the use of the Navigator across the whole organization as a tool to focus on IC under its commitment of "IC the future." The use of the Navigator is promoted at multiple levels to align the objectives of business units, departments, and individual employees with Skandia's vision and IC strategy, as shown in Exhibit 9.2.

At the strategic level, the Navigator is used to align the strategy of the various business units with the vision of the whole organization. With a vision and a core ideology that focuses on the development of IC, each business unit has to show how it plans to manage IC under the Navigator's focuses and report on its progress. At the operational level, the Navigator is used by the constituent departments in each business unit to align their programs, objectives, and operations with the business unit's IC strategy, by reporting on how its activities and programs affect the various IC focuses. By 1998, both employees and managers used the Navigator at American Skandia to complete an individual Navigator that charts their performance and growth goals, again in alignment with strategy. In that latter application, the Navigator is used both as a human resources management system and a communication tool. In the first function, it aids setting renewal and growth goals for every employee and hence shape the professional development plan. It provides positive coaching that aligns the individual's goals and the organization's. As a communication tool it facilitates communication between the employee and management by creating a new IC language that everyone is encouraged to experiment with.

Entrusted with creating a framework that guides the implementation of the Navigator across all of Skandia, Edvinsson and his team (Ann-Charlotte Bredahl at the present time) developed the Process model. The Process model breaks the design of the Navigator into a number of planning steps as shown in Exhibit 9.3. The first step defines business objectives and the success factors that enable attaining them. Indicators are then created to monitor performance under each of the success factors. Once the indicators are chosen, they are presented under past performance perspective (financial focus), present performance perspective (customer, human, and process focuses) and future performance perspective (renewal and development focus). The Process model clarified

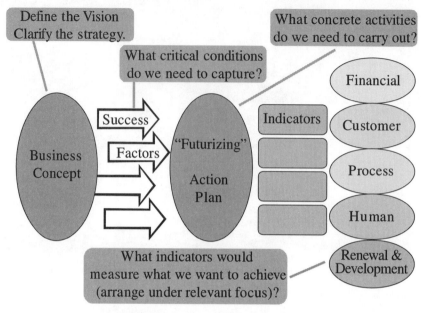

EXHIBIT 9.3   The Process Model

the use of the Navigator to enable its application on the individual level, with the ultimate goal of incorporating ICM into daily business operation. This forms the gist of Skandia's ICM model.

SKANDIA'S ICM MODEL—MORE THAN A NAVIGATOR

Skandia's ICM model can be summarized by one word—the Navigator. The Navigator did not only create an IC language and awareness across Skandia, but it also provided each unit and individual with a tool for the management of IC, each for their own peculiar purposes. Though the Navigator is at the core of Skandia's ICM model, it is much more than that. Using the CICM lens, let's have a closer look how Skandia manages its IC under the various stages.

The Knowledge Management Stage

> What is just as important for the intelligent organization as the accessibility of the growing flow of global information is the development of interpretation instruments which enable the company to identify and learn new patterns from a universal perspective.
> —Intelligent Enterprise 1998 Annual Report Supplement

Knowledge management (KM) is instrumental to organizations in the service industry where the main intellectual value driver is packaged knowledge, or knowledge recipes as Skandia calls it. Developing the stage of KM to an advanced level is therefore essential from the start. Though KM as a concept and a practice has been applied by service organizations for a long time, only advanced and systemized application of KM can enable high business growth and enhanced competitive performance. For Skandia, a well-thought-out KM system is essential for the success of the business model that Carendi designed for Skandia. Skandia's business model cannot be operated without extensive knowledge sharing internally within Skandia and externally across the widespread networks of partners. To manage the flow of knowledge within and to-and-fro Skandia, the right structure, culture, and information technology (IT) enablers were implemented at Skandia from the start.

Structure—Communities of Practice or Knowledge Cafés. Empowering employees and treating them as volunteers is a business reality rather than a promise from Skandia's top management. Employees can volunteer to be on any of the teams that are continuously formed across Skandia to tackle various areas of knowledge, even if outside their expertise in accordance with the concept of communities of practice (CoPs). The process starts with an e-mail sent out about the project, to which employees can assign themselves. Managers then hold an election to determine who will serve the team better, with formalities kept to a minimum.

Meeting face to face for transfer of tacit knowledge and sharing of ideas is facilitated at Skandia in many ways. First, the concept of the "knowledge café" is well accepted and promoted in the culture of Skandia. The main idea behind the knowledge café is that knowledge workers perform better when working in an open environment where dialogue and sharing insights is the norm. The café concept is used by having a set of tables each with a facilitator and an issue posted for discussion wherein groups circulate between the tables bringing their insights to different issues. At American Skandia, the knowledge café method is implemented through the Meet the Cabinet program in which employees meet the management team in an informal, musical chairs–type setting. The sessions are held every six weeks with 4 cabinet members and 25 employees where each cabinet member meets with 5 or 6 employees for four 15-minute segments. After each segment, the cabinet member moves to another table and so on. Employees are encouraged to prepare questions, comments, and suggestions. Due to the success of the program and its positive effect on morale, American Skandia plans to expand the program and increase the duration of the sessions.

Obviously, Skandia is a very social company with a very flexible structure, in which dialogue, knowledge sharing, trust, and collaboration are all part of daily business life. The informality of the structure and the ease with which tacit knowledge is transferred in meetings and knowledge cafés fosters sharing and leveraging of tacit knowledge. This structure is supported by a very strong collaborative culture.

The Right Culture from Day One. From the start Carendi made it clear that the model is alliance-based and hence one that is empowered through relationships and values of mutual trust, collaboration, and partnership both internally and externally. Carendi believed in hiring the right people and then leaving them alone. In Carendi's words: "if you are not going to leave them alone, you don't need to hire the best people."[7] Carendi promoted the concept of volunteers, wherein employees are seen as free agents who give their best only if there is a "high culture of trust."

To reinforce a culture of trust in an industry in which insecurity of employment is "a natural process in today's service companies,"[8] Skandia put in place a system to enable employees to take their professional development into their own hands. First, Skandia established the Leaders College, which provides training for employees and partner financial advisors. Second, with the Navigator's human focus, all business units are pressed to develop their human capital to meet future challenges and reinforce competitive advantage. Third, if employee redundancy is the only resort, Skandia's management cooperates with employees and external consultants to help employees find new opportunities within and outside Skandia.

In addition to trust building, knowledge sharing is stressed through Skandia by the various activities and awards recognizing knowledge sharing at the various units. At American Skandia, for example, knowledge sharing is rewarded through employee nomination of associates who exhibit qualities of open knowledge sharing. The top 30 nominees are narrowed down to three who are awarded an engraved desk clock and $1,000 in reward. The strong knowledge-sharing culture of Skandia makes knowledge sharing part of the job—if not the job.

In addition to the flexible structure and right culture, Skandia's KM stage is enabled by a powerful IT system, which is necessary for its alliance-based business model.

The Knowledge Base and IT Architecture—Navigate with the Dolphins.   The Navigator informs Skandia's design of the knowledge base and the IT architecture. The Navigator provided the bedrock of the knowledge base by facilitating the creation of a unified taxonomy under which all knowledge is codified at Skandia. Automating the Navigator through the Dolphin system enabled every business unit to collect and enter data under a unified IT system regardless of their areas of operation. The Dolphin system stores the Navigators of the various subsidiaries, each with its strategic intent, success factors, and indicators.

Originally based on the Navigator, the Dolphin system was developed as Skandia's knowledge base with knowledge centers, best practices for internal benchmarking, and e-learning centers. The Dolphin system has information on the organization, legal structures, special competencies, staff profiles, and key alliances of every company in Skandia's Group. It also provides competitive intelligence through competitors' profiles and market and customer perspectives. The system is connected to a number of external networks that Skandia employees can access, for example "Savings Bourse," which contains information and knowledge channels for such companies working in the savings product segment.

The central Company Customer Center has documented process descriptions for best-demonstrated practices on two levels. The first level relates to work tasks and business processes while the second relates to tools. Both levels are available and accessible from Skandia's intranet. Skandia adopted a knowledge codification strategy to ensure the streamlining and interoperability of work processes and key tasks. That is a crucial step given the vast array of IT systems and solutions that are continuously being developed and used by the various operating units across Skandia. It ensures that the underlying IT models do not hamper efficient and effective KM. The e-learning center caters to employees' knowledge needs by providing training modules on the various solutions and software packages used by Skandia, accessible by financial advisors as well. In addition to the central IT unit in Stockholm, there are decentralized IT departments in the United States, Germany, Colombia, Spain, and England. Stockholm coordinates among the various IT units and provides the main architecture while the various IT centers create content and manage their knowledge bases in accordance with their local needs.

The Innovation Management Stage

> You have to be able to get in and out of products and services with the competitive energy of a kid playing a video game rather than with the analytical consistency of a grand master trying to hang on in a three day chess match.
>
> —Jan Carendi[9]

The gist of Skandia's business model is outsourcing fund management and distribution of products so that Skandia can focus on what it does best—product development, IT solutions, and sales support—in short, innovation management (IM). Skandia's IM system is characterized by fast new product/service development process with customer-driven strategies. This is based on leveraging information from partners by managing the portfolio of alliances and creating specialized competence centers across the organization. The other major innovation process, which is linked to Skandia's ability to reinvent itself, is future scenario planning used to antic- ipate emerging market trends, and to inform strategic planning. Skandia's Future Centers (SFCs) are places where Skandia employees from all over the world and various subsidiaries can meet to brainstorm and share ideas on the future of their industry and companies.

Structure—Competence Centers, Alliances, and Central Unit.   Skandia's IM system has a flexible structure that allows the formation of project teams from across Skandia and its many networks and alliances. From the start, Carendi managed innovation by recognizing operating units as strategic competence centers whenever they developed a particular capability throughout Skandia. As a result, "Spain became a competence center for design of bank products, the United States for IT, and Colombia for administrative support and back office functions."[10] Project teams from various subsidiaries, countries, and expertise work together on development of systems and software packages that advance Skandia's product packaging and distribution model. In line with the network-based model of innovation, competence centers are sometimes developed in con- junction with a strategic partner where Skandia maintains a considerable degree of control over the competence. An example of this is the system developed by SkandiaLeben in conjunction with one of the largest banks in Germany for online processing of the bank's customers' applica- tions. This competence was leveraged later by Skandia in developing new bank accounts to its distributors called the Cash Management Account.[11]

Managing innovation over the networks of alliances is facilitated by the coordination of a number of units and contact points. The Sales and Marketing Executives staff pay regular visits to customers' back offices two to three times annually to facilitate knowledge sharing and inter- action. In addition, Skandia developed a Customer Asset Management System that can be used by each unit to manage such relations with customers. Similarly, the Key Account Program, developed at American Skandia, is used to share knowledge with brokers, fund managers, and other partners to work on strategies to grow Skandia's business through them. Each Key Account Executive works with a number of partners on opportunities for offering additional services from American Skandia including repackaging of existing products in training programs or support services. The Key Account Program has also helped American Skandia develop and innovate its own work processes and systems.

With the innovation process in Skandia being spread over the various competence centers inside Skandia and multiple external networks, a strong central and leadership direction of inno- vation is required. The Strategic Team, the CEO group, and the Cabinet perform this role on var- ious levels. The Strategic Team is made up of people representing Skandia's various businesses who define "the right questions that lead the company strategically."[12] These questions are then referred to the CEO Group, which is a 13-member group of people including the CEO and other executives from the Strategic Team and the Cabinet, to allocate resources. The Cabinet is made up of 35 executives from the various businesses who then take the identified question to their business units and work on finding the right answers. Involving many departments and personnel from various operating units and companies in Skandia in the innovation process fosters the right culture for innovation.

Innovation Culture and Idea Generation.   The same "ask the right question" culture that is practiced at the strategic planning phase of IM is used at the frontline. This is achieved by empowering employees to ask and own the question, and hence look for the answer. Employees are not only encouraged to submit new ideas, but to take them into their hands and implement them as well. Active delegation of decision making designed to foster individual creativity is instrumental to Skandia's business model. This led to the development of KenNet, an idea bank linked to Skandia's intranet. KenNet classifies ideas into four main categories: proposed innovations, ideas for improvement, knowledge needs (further research), and a bulletin board and dialogue forum (for brainstorming on new product concepts). In addition, the Skandia Opportunity Program manages a global internet to encourage employees to seek and seize entrepreneurial opportunities.

Skandia takes developing its human capital very seriously and in addition to establishing knowledge cafés, it established the Future Center (SFC). SFC is a center located in Sweden in a place removed from the corporate headquarters where employees from all around Skandia can meet to brainstorm on ideas for the future. The SFC is more of an incubator of ideas where the focus is on predicting future trends, and devising ways to deal with future challenges. Employees are encouraged to go to the SFC for its creative environment, where they are away from everyday responsibilities and hence have the time to develop new ideas and experiment with new prototypes. The SFC is equipped with virtual libraries and tools.

The Intellectual Property Management Stage

Skandia's IP Portfolio of Software Programs and Knowledge Recipes.   Skandia refers to IP as "innovation capital."[13] The 1998 report defines innovation capital as "intangible rights, trademarks, patents, knowledge recipes and business secrets." A closer look reveals that copyright and ancillary trade secret protection is Skandia's primary form of IP and hence the source of sustainable competitive advantage. Skandia's copyrights cover a huge number of software systems and applications that Skandia companies develop continuously to improve the way they do business, deliver solutions, and partner with customers. In many cases, these software programs are also offered as products or training packages to financial advisors. The other major copyrighted/trade-secreted product is what Skandia calls "knowledge recipes," which cover a wide range of packaged knowledge products offered to financial advisors to educate them about the market and make their job easier in finding the right solutions for their clients. The genius of Skandia's IPM program is identifying the IP that enabled Skandia to beat the competition to a number of markets (competitive positioning) and create new business opportunities (commercialization) through offering its IP to partners.

IP and Core Competitive Advantage—The Prototype.   One of the main success factors behind Skandia's exponential growth in a mature industry is its use of its main IP, the prototype software, for competitive positioning. The prototype software was developed at the early stages of Skandia AFS establishment and used to spin off new business units and enter new markets. The software captured Skandia's essential administrative and operational processes, including application processing and product pricing, into a business prototype. The prototype is then taken by any business unit and replicated to enter new markets, sometimes in less than half the time, giving years of head start to Skandia over the competition. An example is Skandia's use of the prototype to enter the Swiss, Russian, and Chinese markets. The prototype also saved Skandia millions in establishment costs, sometimes as much as a quarter of the cost, and hence enhancing Skandia's competitive advantage even further.

In addition to the prototype, Skandia's IP portfolio includes a number of computerized work systems that are leveraged both internally across Skandia and externally across the various partnerships.

Leveraging IP Internally—Sharing and the Technology Center. A software system that is developed in one of Skandia's companies or operating units is shared freely across the organization. Skandia's Technological Center (STC) acts as the central unit that provides coordination and streamlining of systems across Skandia and the Skandia Group. The STC conducts research on available technology solutions and makes its findings available to all operating units. At the same time, the STC provides support for units to develop their own new system(s), and to create prototypes that can be leveraged in other business units acting like the IP Synergy Unit (see Chapter 8).

An example of a software that is leveraged across many business units is the Electronic Quotation/Application system (EQA). EQA provides templates for various applications and forms and allows employees to provide quotations on initial customer contact. One of its most important features is the risk filter, which enables the user to determine whether the application needs further risk assessment or can be forwarded to the unit, hence simplifying what is otherwise a complex and lengthy process. The EQA led to reduction in administrative tasks, lower operating expenses, and speedy processing of customer applications. The EQA is used in the Savings Unit at Swedish Skandia Life, SkandiaLink and Foretagsliv.

Other software programs that are leveraged internally include those developed by DIAL for customer service and application processing, namely the Household Expert and the Motor Expert. The first offers claims settlement support and information, and the latter helps decision making as to fault determination, property valuation, and calculation of losses.

Leveraging IP across Partnerships—Commercialization. In many instances, Skandia codevelops and shares its IP with its partners, whether fund managers or financial advisors. One example is SkandiaLeben's development of products for one of its customer banks which later were leveraged as the basis for more banking products. Most prominent is Skandia's offer of packaged knowledge products, which range from training material, market studies, competitive intelligence reports, and the like, to financial advisors. A lot of these products are offered to partner financial advisors for free to solidify the relationship and foster loyalty.

CONCLUSIONS ON SKANDIA

Being a service company in which the main product is packaged knowledge, the KM stage of Skandia's ICM model is the most robust. At the same time and similar to any learning organization in the knowledge economy, the IM stage was developed to a similar degree to enable value extraction from the value created at the KM stage. The IPM stage was developed to the extent that it enabled Skandia to preserve its competitive position and enhance the core competitive advantage of the various business units. It also was developed along the lines of Skandia's business model to leverage Skandia's IP across its various alliances and partnerships. The stress of the ICM model of an organization in a goods manufacturing industry, however, may be different. This is what we will explore by looking at another pioneer in ICM in the chemical industry—the Dow Chemical Company.

DOW CHEMICAL: THE LEAP INTO ICM[14]

The first time I was exposed to the enthusiasm surrounding ICM at Dow Chemical (Dow) was in Atlanta, Georgia, in early 2001.[15] Listening to David Near, the Director of Business Excellence for Dow's polyurethane business talking about ICM at Dow with such belief was an invigorating experience amidst corporate skepticism facing the concept. With his calm disposition, yet deep belief in the topic, Near drives the complex IC concept home with ease and confidence. Two main features impressed me in Near's presentation: the methodological approach that Dow developed to make business sense of a complex concept and the evolution of the IC concept itself inside Dow.

Analyzed under the CICM lens, Dow's journey started early on with IM, progressed to IP (asset) management in the late 1980s and early 1990s, and then to KM in the mid-1990s, altogether forming a synchronized comprehensive model for ICM. Though the various stages were implemented at different times and under varying circumstances at Dow, Dow's senior executives managed and integrated the implementation of the various programs as complementary pieces in a mosaic to form at the end their ICM system. With all the internal and external currents of change that Dow was subject to, Near and other leaders at Dow managed to keep a strategic focus to enable both the evolution and the application of the IC concept to business reality. With its focus on patents as one of its most valuable intellectual assets, Dow's journey started with the Intellectual Asset Management (IAM) initiative.

Petrash's IAM—Paving the Way

Dow's IAM is one of the most advanced models for managing patents and technology and one that gained widespread popularity. It took IPM out from the legal department to over 100 teams spread throughout the organization. Most importantly, it aligned managing intellectual assets, starting with patents, with the strategic management of each of Dow's businesses. Dow's IAM model started with an assignment to one of the R&D managers at the time, Gordon Petrash. With Petrash's demonstrated success in commercializing patents in his own business unit, top management at Dow wanted him to transform his knowledge into a working system that the whole organization could implement. Petrash started with a patent audit of the 29,000 patents that Dow owned at the time. Applying valuation methods, Petrash and the auditing team gathered evidence as to the value of the audited patents. Of course, some patents had demonstrated value reflected in sales of patent-associated products, and thus the growth of the business unit. The largest number of patents, however, did not fall under this category and had to be properly classified.

In addition to the auditing phase, the classification phase went a step further by determining the use of the patent. Each business was required to classify the patents it had into one of three major categories: "use, will use, or will not use."[16] This was followed by the strategy and investment phases wherein the business uses a number of valuation and competitive assessment tools to assess the commercial value of the patent(s) and devise a plan for their exploitation. For valuation purposes, Dow developed with A.D. Little the Tech Factor method in which the value of the patent is estimated as a percentage of the total net present value of the business unit that owns it.[17] Patent citation trees were also used to evaluate the significance of the patent in the market and to gain insight into the competitive and technological landscape.

Patents falling in the second category are then evaluated as to their values to other parties outside Dow. The auditing team took a broad approach, looking at universities and government labs, as well as competitors and noncompetitors in local and global markets. The surprising result was that only 30 percent of Dow's patents at the time were of strategic value to Dow, while the others were expendable either as donations to collect tax deductions or to be sold or abandoned. The result was an instant savings of $50 million over a period of 10 years, drawing support and commendation to the effort. But that is only the tip of the iceberg. This big savings allowed the IAM program of Dow to receive resources beyond the initial $1 million and the handful of personnel that Petrash started with. Dow's IAM model was launched and later integrated as a business process permeating the management of each business at Dow.

The $50 million that Gordon Petrash proved the company can save through effective IAM not only paved the way for a more robust IAM program (what is called *intellectual property management* under the CICM), but it also created the right mindset and culture required to embrace the IC concept—an opportunity that David Near grasped to take Dow into the world of ICM, and in so doing shape that world as well.

NEAR AND THE LEAP INTO ICM

IAM (Intellectual Asset Management) paid off big time and upper management was committed, so we were ready to take the next step in our knowledge capital journey to comprehensive ICM.

—David Near, Dow Director of Business Excellence

Near came on the scene in 1999 well after Dow top management was done celebrating the $50 million savings and the whole culture at Dow was ripe for the next step. Faced with the very challenging job of identifying the elusive nature of IC, Near had to start with setting the basis—definitions. "How is ICM different from IAM?" and "Why should Dow go further into the intangible world?" were questions that Near not only had to answer but to provide a methodology and a model to address. Bombarded with multiple terms flowing around in the business environment—knowledge management, intellectual assets, intangible assets management, intellectual capital, hidden resources—Near had to go to the basics and isolate the object of his attention. Near, along with input from a variety of international experts, laid out the following definitions:

- *Intellectual capital management.* The "process of proactively managing, protecting, leveraging, and reporting all knowledge assets to better enable us to gain and sustain competitive advantage and maximize future value."[18]
- *Knowledge management.* The "process of getting knowledge from the people who have it to the people who need it at the right time to satisfy a business need, while protecting it as a valuable asset."[19]

The importance of Near's work, however, is not limited to determining the IC terminology and frame of reference, but extended to creating a comprehensive methodology to bring the various management approaches developed so far together and incorporate them into the overall business process. Near believed that the "key parameter to making ICM work at Dow is to have it driven by the business decision process at the project level." To that effect, it was important to create synergy between the various processes and approaches by providing a clear IC strategy and a comprehensive approach. Near achieved this in two ways: forming the Business Excellence Group (BEG) and developing the IC strategy.

The BEG identified both ICM and KM as two of the business capabilities and competencies that are essential to succeed in the knowledge economy. As Near explains: "We found out early on that we needed a broader range of partners and capabilities beyond IAM." BEG integrated ICM and KM with project and portfolio management to provide a comprehensive approach for managing IC. The main goal is to marry ICM practices with the way business is done and ensure better management of business assets, resource allocation, general operation, and overall business performance.

All this required the formulation of a clear IC strategy, formulated under the ICM Pilot, which was initiated in 2000 in the polyurethanes business unit. The IC strategy defined Dow's objectives for managing each form of IC, and hence identified what management should focus on for their development:

- *Human capital.* Focus on the Business Management Teams' alignment of human resources with the needs of each project
- *Customer capital.* Focus on the effectiveness of each business in aligning its customer relationships with the project needs
- *Structural capital.* Focus on building work systems, databases, tools, and practices (for example, technology mapping and valuations) that enhance the competitive assessment capability of the business and hence its competitive performance

The IC strategy led and informed the development of various practices, programs, and systems under each of the management stages, as well as an IC measurement system. Dow developed in 1999 a measurement system based both on the Intangible Asset Monitor and Balance Scorecard methods. In addition to the traditional metrics of customer satisfaction and loyalty rates, Near initiated the Human Capital Valuation (HCV) project. The HCV aims at understanding the future value of current employee skills and measuring employee contribution to the success of business projects. While other companies are satisfied with metrics like employee satisfaction, retention rate, and the like, Dow is developing metrics to measure the value added per employee (in line with Sveiby's work), to better allocate and manage human resources. This in turn will improve project management, improve employee development and satisfaction, and enable getting products to the market faster.

Following is an examination of Dow's ICM model presented through the CICM lens.

DOW'S ICM MODEL

When Dow decided to become a pioneer in the area of ICM, it realized it had to undergo a number of changes first. Unlike Skandia AFS, Dow was established in 1897 with a structured business model that to a great extent followed the old economy organizational models. Before implementing any new initiative, Dow had to make sure that its vision, structure, and culture would not defeat change. Fortunately for Dow, the culture was right with its long-term and historical commitment to management of inventions, with the first invention management group being formed as early as 1958, and the first patent department in 1928. Still, Dow lacked a vision to lead the IAM and ICM revolution, and the structure was rigid with too many hierarchical levels. To overcome these hurdles, Dow went through two major changes. First, Dow delayered its structure from 14 to 5 levels, from the frontline operators to the CEO. Second, it adjusted its vision to reflect its newly gained insight into the strategic importance of IC.

Dow's vision now included "creating value from our intellectual assets." This facilitated the perceiving of intellectual assets and capital as enablers of value creation and maximization. Despite the value of this new awareness, more than a progressive vision was needed. Visionary leadership, strategic planning, ICM champions, committed managers and employees, and effective teams and programs were all necessary for the transformation. The vision and the excitement surrounding the potential value of IC inspired Dow's aggressive high-growth strategy—the New

Value-Growth strategy developed in 1998. Under this strategy, Dow aims at increasing earnings per share by 10 percent, and to have 15 percent of revenue from products introduced in the past five years by 2005. Overall, Dow aims to grow revenue by 6 percent annually to reach $60 billion in 2010. To Dow, ICM was not only the new way of doing business, but the vehicle for creating and sustaining future value. Let's closely examine the programs that Dow implemented under each of the ICM stages.

The Knowledge Management Stage

Dow has a matrix organizational structure wherein each business group maintains its autonomy to a considerable extent. As a result, though the KM initiatives are led by the centralized (corporate) top management, the extent of implementation, attention, and resources allocated to this initiative is up to the vice president (VP) of each business group. Dow's KM system is led by the knowledge management director, who reports to the chief information officer (CIO), and supervises a group of senior executives that form the KM Group. The KM Group is an 11-member executive team entrusted to manage knowledge across Dow's 23 businesses, with a budget of $15 million over 5 years. It is responsible for supporting the information stewards, who in turn champion KM initiatives in each of the business groups. The information stewards report to the senior manager of the KM Group and to the VP of each of the business groups. They are supported both by the IT Department KM Program Office and the KM Resource Center, as shown in Exhibit 9.4.

The main criticism made against the use of this model is that leadership's commitment to KM is sometimes diffused by the VP of the business group's decision to limit the role of information stewards.[20] Some information stewards complain that KM is not given priority by certain VPs, resulting in their having two or three roles in addition to KM, spreading themselves too thin to effect the desired changes.[21] Despite this, Dow's Greg Horvath, senior manager of the KM Group, praises Dow's model for the liberty it allows each business to adopt the desired change(s) at their own pace.

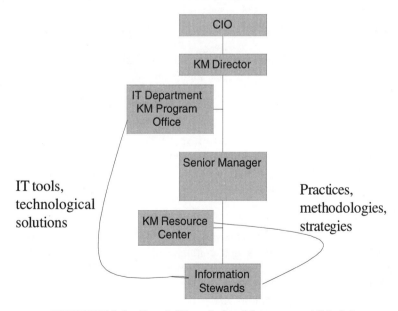

EXHIBIT 9.4   Dow's Knowledge Management Model

Given the extent of cultural and other changes that KM initiatives require, it seems prudent that the decision to adopt KM is left to the business group, according to its state of readiness and business needs. This, however, places greater pressure on information stewards to act both as leaders of the initiative in the business unit and agents of change for the whole organization.

Structure—Communities of Practice and IAM Teams.   Dow's KM system evolved in line with its IAM teams, who operated so much like communities of practice (CoPs). They are formed to satisfy a strategic business need of capitalizing on IC in a defined area of technology from inception through development to commercialization. At the same time, around 80 of the intellectual asset managers are full timers and act as champions for new IAM teams. At Dow, it is not about what you call it but about ensuring that an effective practice is implemented. As Jim Allen, Dow's KM director, explains, the term *knowledge management* may fall out of favor, but the practices and strategies of KM will remain "part of the basic strategy and culture of every successful business."[22] This statement summarizes to a great extent Dow's approach to KM—keep it simple and effective by "get[ting] the knowledge from those who know to those who need to know."

The information stewards have formed a CoP that meets regularly to share experiences and best practices. This community is spread over Dow's 23 business units and global operations, covering services to 50,000 employees. Information stewards form their own committees as well, which meet on a quarterly basis to share knowledge and experience throughout the business group.

A Culture of E-Learning.   Dow's commitment to KM and the value of employees' knowledge is reflected in many programs that are in place for knowledge sharing and professional development. Dow professes that it wants its people to have the "freedom they need to succeed," and hence fosters values of innovation, agility, and individuality. Part of this freedom is to provide employees with the knowledge resources for them to learn and develop. To that effect, Dow created the award winning *learn@dow.now* system which offers online continuing education options to its employees worldwide. In 2001 alone, Dow employees completed over 315,000 courses. The e-learning system proved to be very beneficial in addressing employees' knowledge needs, improving morale, and saving over $45 million in training costs.

The Knowledge Base and IT.   In building the knowledge base, Dow realized that there are three strategic components that their knowledge base should incorporate. These components include[23]:

1. How do we work? (Relates to overall enterprise computing systems including the common workstation and intranet)
2. How do we make decisions? (Relates to KM, building the knowledge base, and connecting employees for knowledge-sharing purposes)
3. How do we connect to our customers? (Relates to e-business solutions and systems and the ability to tap into customer capital)

The most significant change that followed creating the patent database was the creation of the corporate-wide standard workstation. This is the basis of Dow's IT architecture as it incorporates standard hardware, software, IT solutions and communication tools, and database management systems. This formed part of the knowledge base, which was developed to provide information to employees relating to the decisions they make, and based on their knowledge needs. The main focus is on shifting from "reporting to prediction" in the use of information. This is based on Dow's belief that to better mine its knowledge resources, information should be used to predict patterns rather than just provide retrospective data.[24] To that effect a number of information retrieval and visualization tools are provided, including but not limited to patent citation trees and KM tools.

The Innovation Management (IM) Stage

Dr. Herbert Dow, who founded Dow in 1897, managed the innovation process very much in line with Edison's model outlined in Chapter 7. In his career of 40 years, Dr. Dow obtained 107 patents, forming the basis of the first products that Dow made. Today, Dow is a global company with 50,000 employees; manufacturing sites in 32 countries; over 2,400 chemical, plastic, and agricultural products and services; and around $35 billion in revenue. Dow's IM system has evolved immensely from the Edison model to accommodate the network-based nature of innovation in the knowledge economy. Here's how.

Structure—Labs as Competence Centers. Dow arranged the skills and competence of its people across the various business units into competence centers where the skills of every person are known to the lab manager. On determining the critical skills needed for an innovation project, a central department undertakes the responsibility of bringing the right team together. Process ownership is assigned to a central department to maintain consistency and improvement of the process (stage-gate), while team allocation is left to the leadership of every business unit or lab. At Dow Polyplefyn Research Lab, for example, the Tactical Leadership Group is responsible for the management of the innovation portfolio, including team and resource allocation.[25] The Group is made up of senior business managers and scientists. The joint business and scientific leadership is used to ensure a balance between administrative and technical considerations. The Group makes decisions as to selection and prioritization of projects, and then assigns a cross-functional, multiskilled team to each project.

The 42 Plus Alliances Portfolio. Dow manages external alliances as part of its innovation portfolio, with over 42 joint ventures and R&D collaboration agreements with universities, government labs, and independent R&D organizations. When the benefits of collaboration are clear (e.g., increased knowledge and speed to market), Dow does not hesitate to collaborate even with competitors. A prominent example of this happened when a research team discovered a process in 1994 to make ethylene propylene diene monomer (EPDM) elastomers, which were already produced by DuPont and others. The process proved to produce high-performance grades with much lower manufacturing costs. The research team sent the samples developed to DuPont for testing and comparison. On receiving positive feedback from DuPont, Dow decided it could complement its strengths with those of DuPont by working together. Instead of competing in an area where process patents are hard to procure and enforce, Dow formed a joint venture with DuPont to unite their R&D efforts to develop the high-value new process, keeping it secret from other competitors.[26]

Innovation Culture and a Central Idea Bank. Being in a technological race, Dow's innovation strategies seem to be technologically driven. Dow has heavily implemented new innovation practices and tools to perform patent and technical intelligence. Despite their technology-driven strategies, however, Dow incorporates employee-driven methods to empower employees, by fostering a strong culture of collaboration and creativity. To be true to its message that employees' ideas count, Dow established a central idea bank. Though the bank does not actively solicit ideas from employees, it takes those submitted to it from anywhere in the organization very seriously. The ideas are evaluated, filtered, and distributed to the various business units to which they are relevant. If the ideas do not fall within the area of a particular business or are not within the strategic plans, the ideas are then referred to the Business Development and Growth Unit for further consideration. In all cases, the idea originator has to be notified of the action taken within two weeks, and of reasons for rejection if the idea was declined. Near commented that in fact Dow's e-commerce business was a result of a noncore idea around which a whole new business was built.

The Intellectual Property (Asset) Management Stage

Patents and trade secrets constitute Dow's primary form of IP. When it first started with the IAM initiative, Dow owned a patent portfolio of 29,000 patents. The genius of Dow's management of its primary form of IP lies in assigning responsibility for sustaining and leveraging different groups of patents to the business that can and does benefit from them most. In turn, this enabled every business to focus on its core technological competencies and develop new related ones to strengthen its competitive advantage and augment its patent portfolio. At the same time, over 100 IAM teams scattered across Dow function to leverage the patented and other technology both inside and outside Dow.

Structure—IAM Teams and the Tech Center.   During 1992, the Inventions Management Group worked with the business-aligned Patent Task Force to assign primary ownership of each property in the IP portfolio to one of the businesses. Each business unit was required to formulate its patent strategy as part of its business strategy and devise investment plans using the valuation and auditing tools. Consequently, each business unit was required to absorb its respective patents' costs. In 1993, the IAM teams replaced the Patent Task Force. IAM teams are cross-functional teams formed to manage a part of the portfolio according to the investment plan, with over 500 personnel. The teams are comprised of frontline functional managers and key scientists from within the businesses, who meet two to three times a year to review the portfolio and devise strategies for its management.

To support the network of intellectual asset managers, the Global Intellectual Asset Tech Center was formed in 1995. The Center, managed by Sharon O'riel, oversees matters that include maintaining a Web site and communication network, collecting and disseminating best practices, maintaining the patent disclosure and agreements databases, and providing support to both knowledge and intellectual asset managers.

Culture—Patent Talk Equals Patent Friendly.   The IP audit and the identification of the key patents for every business immensely affected the IPM culture at Dow. The exercise of identifying such key patents and determining their value to business promoted debate among R&D, manufacturing, business development, and IA managers, wherein solid understanding and appreciation of the value of patents to business evolved.

Leveraging IP Internally and Externally—A Patent Investment Plan.   The investment plan addresses the business goals of competitive positioning and commercialization. Under the first use, the business unit addresses how the patent(s) can be used for competitive positioning and enhancing its core competitive advantage with the end goal of strengthening its technological capability. In this light, joint ventures and outsourcing agreements are considered.

The second use relates to commercializing the patent through licensing or technology transfer transactions offered to outside parties in cases in which that is not competitively harmful. IAM teams are involved at early stages in negotiations of joint ventures and R&D collaborations. IAM teams initiate negotiations in cases in which they decide that Dow needs to acquire a certain technology or patent to augment its knowledge in a strategic area of business. The IAM teams are also on the lookout for opportunities to license out any of Dow's patents. It is reported that Dow's licensing efforts have resulted in generating an additional $61 million annually.

CONCLUSIONS ON DOW

Dow's interest in patent and technology licensing goes beyond its own boundaries, assisting in creating a secondary market for patents and other forms of IP. Dow was one of the very early participants in online Internet technology exchanges via significant activity with companies like Yev2.com and PLX systems. Near commented that the success in creating a considerable secondary market for IP may open the door for trading in IC—maybe human capital. Near's work to find ways to measure the contribution of human capital to value creation and future performance may be a crucial step in getting closer to this futuristic vision: a vision that is typical of Dow, where shaping the future is part of what Dow does.

NOTES

[1] Gordon Petrash, "Intellectual Asset Management at Dow Chemical," in P. Sullivan (ed.), *Profiting from Intellectual Capital* (New York: John Wiley & Sons, 1998), p. 206.

[2] *Id.*, pp. 214–215.

[3] Special thanks are due to Jan Hoffmeister, Skandia Group Vice President of Intellectual Capital Management, for his gracious support and assistance with information and advice for the completion of this case study. Thanks are also due to Ann-Charlotte Bredahl of Skandia AFS, Stockholm, for her invaluable assistance with materials on the application of the Navigator within Skandia.

[4] Skandia Assurance and Financial Services was originally established as a division of Skandia AB, a leading Swedish insurance group of companies, established in 1855. Skandia AFS has grown exponentially to comprise most of Skandia, with subsidiaries in 25 countries.

[5] From 1991 to 1995, Skandia gross premium incomes rose by 70 percent, again enormously exceeding growth rates of other insurance and financial services companies.

[6] Supra note 4, pp. 34–52.

[7] C. Bartlett, "Skandia AFS: Developing Intellectual Capital Globally," Harvard Business School case #396-412 (March 30, 1998), p. 8.

[8] 1998 Annual Report, p. 11.

[9] Bartlett, supra note 7, p. 5.

[10] *Id.*, p. 6.

[11] See 1994 Annual Report, p. 9.

[12] *Intelligent Enterprise,* Supplement to 1997 Annual Report, p. 12.

[13] A trend that is always found in service industries is avoiding the use of the term *intellectual property*. This is because of the misconception that the term *intellectual property* refers to patents. As a result, many service organizations are under the wrong impression that they do not need an IPM system since in their business patents have no strategic significance. Despite this,

most organizations in the service industry attribute their competitive advantage to a number of strategic IPs, mainly software systems, business prototypes and methods, and a wealth of proprietary information (i.e., copyrights and trade secrets—and patents in very limited situations). Brands also play a strategic role in the service industry given that trustworthiness plays a major part in the purchasing decision given the intangibility of the service product.

[14] Special thanks are due to David Near for his gracious assistance with materials and advice for the completion of Dow's case study, and for sharing his knowledge and experience of ICM with refreshing enthusiasm.

[15] Licensing Executives Society Conference, Atlanta, GA, April 2001, and at Pierce Law on June 6, 2001.

[16] Supra note 1, p. 209.

[17] *Id.,* p. 210.

[18] Supra note 15.

[19] *Id.*

[20] See C. Flash, "Personal Chemistry—Dow Chemical's Information Stewards Are the Catalysts for Sharing across Business Units," *Knowledge Management Magazine,* August 2001.

[21] *Id.*

[22] R. Whiting, "Myths and Realities—What's Behind One of the Most-Misunderstood IT Strategies," *Information Week,* November 1999.

[23] D.E. Kepler (Dow), "Data Mining at Dow," presentation at the CMU Research Corp. "Business Insight Forum," July 12, 2002.

[24] *Id.*

[25] J. Pierce, "The Art of Creating a Flexible R&D Organization," *CHEMTECH* Vol. 28, no. 2, 1998, pp. 6–11.

[26] *Id.*

Part Three

Step-by-Step Guide to the CICM Model

Part Two outlined the changes required to successfully implement the various stages of the CICM model. This part presents a step-by-step guide on how to implement the required changes. However, before implementing any change, it is important to ensure that the organization has first taken some steps that are essential to effect any change. It is essential before implementing any of the programs and practices outlined in Parts Two and Three of this book to formulate a powerful vision that leads change, to adopt a business model with a flexible structure, and to ensure that the culture is the right one. These issues are discussed in Chapter 10. But that is not all.

Every organization is different, not only in terms of size and industry but in terms of goals and objectives. An organization's industry and particular strategic goals may require more focus on one of the stages rather than the others. That is when it is important to customize the CICM model by devising an IC strategy. The IC strategy enables the organization to phase out the required changes over the short and long terms, and hence manage resource allocation. Over the short term, the change initiative should focus on the stage at which there are immediate business needs that affect the organization's performance in its market. Long-term focus should be on the stage that will enable the organization to enhance its future competitiveness and sustain its knowledge resources. Chapter 14 discusses the IC strategy along with the variables that should be taken into account in customizing the CICM model.

10

First Get Your Act Together

The business model, vision, and culture of an organization determine the effectiveness of any new change or initiative that the organization tries to introduce. The business model determines the flexibility of the structure, the command and reporting lines, and affects the way the various departments and units communicate and work with each other. A business model that is too rigid or formal, with prominent boundaries between levels and departments, would defeat any intellectual capital management (ICM) program. Similarly, vision sets the organizational character and the general state of mind of leadership and management. This infiltrates throughout the whole organization and shapes the attitudes of everyone in the organization toward work, coworkers, superiors, subordinates, partners, and customers. A vision that lacks inspirational power and futurism will take the zeal out of the ICM initiative, which is required to champion what is to many organizations a major change. Closely linked to the vision is the culture of the organization, which affects the way business is done and the values that everyone in the organization adopts and functions by. If these values are contrary to those required for ICM then the ICM initiative may die in its cradle. It is therefore essential before embarking on implementing any ICM stage or program to ensure that the organization has the appropriate business model, vision, and culture in place—in short, to ensure that it has its act together.

THE BUSINESS MODEL OF THE KNOWLEDGE ORGANIZATION

Mysteriously, many organizations in the knowledge economy changed their organizational structure and business model in similar patterns. The emerging model has two main characteristics: A flexible structure with few layers and a range of networks that include external partners and customers. The fact that organizations (regardless of size, industry, strategy, and situation) adopted practically the same model—what has been called the knowledge organization model—indicates its significance in enhancing competitive performance in the knowledge economy.

Many writings appeared discussing the need to adopt the knowledge organization model, as opposed to models based on the industrial economy's needs, to effectively compete in the knowledge economy.[1] The knowledge organization model is based on the premise that intellectual capital (IC) is at the core of production, operation, and any critical organizational process. Sveiby explains that the vast growth of business service companies (being close equivalents to knowledge organizations, in his opinion) indicates the preeminence of the knowledge organization model in the knowledge economy.[2] Similarly, Brian Arthur, of the Santa Fe Institute, attributes the success of the knowledge organization model to its agility in dealing with the fast-changing environment by redeploying its knowledge resources to meet new demands or trends.[3] In Arthur's analysis companies in high-tech industries (computer, software, and biotech) are close equivalents of knowledge organizations.

As stressed by Sveiby and Arthur, the knowledge organization model is critical in industries with a high rate of change and hence turbulence (e.g., high tech). Still, the model is of equal importance to organizations in other industries. The knowledge organization model has been adopted by many organizations in traditional industries (e.g., manufacturing, oil), some to save themselves from the brink of bankruptcy, and others to enhance performance in general.[4] The knowledge organization model should be seen as a stage of evolution in organizational development at which the organization develops the ability to leverage the knowledge resources of its employees and systems to respond to change quickly and effectively, with the end goal of becoming a learning organization.[5] Only organizations that are able to cultivate the ability to manage IC are able to successfully benefit from this model to the full, given the high level of interaction it generates within the organization and with external partners across dispersed networks.

Before embarking on implementing ICM throughout the organization, therefore, the following are prerequisite organizational changes:

- A flat structure where the number of layers that knowledge and information have to traverse are much fewer than those of the industrial economy organizational model. The layers in comparison are sometimes less than half of the traditional model. Take for example ABB, a multinational company with 60 businesses and only four layers.
- Active delegation of decision making and innovation to the frontline where alliances and partnerships with suppliers, distributors, and customers are forged and maintained. In contrast, top management would need to maintain a clear focus on strategy.
- Appreciation of the nature of the workforce in the knowledge economy as knowledge workers who need time to experiment, innovate, contemplate, and brainstorm. Hence, the significance of creating the right culture.
- An information technology (IT) infrastructure that facilitates the generation, collection, and sharing of ideas and knowledge across departmental and divisional boundaries.
- A boundaryless structure to enable interaction and cross-pollination of experiences among the different departments and business units. Increased use of cross-functional teams, including communities of practice when needed, to manage innovation and other projects, and maximize knowledge sharing.
- Flexible organizational boundaries between the organization and external partners to tap into the various networks and access them for new ideas for business growth.
- Appreciation of IC as the core of production, the effective management of which will ensure the availability of knowledge resources, the effectiveness of the innovation process, and the leveraging of IP.
- Creation of new positions on the senior and frontline management levels, to deal with the management of knowledge, innovation, and IP. These should include positions at the senior executive level to define the organization's IC strategy, define the ICM objectives, streamline management systems, and coordinate among the various programs.

As evident here, the knowledge-organization business model is flexible, malleable, flat, boundaryless, and based on internal and external networks with knowledge- and innovation-intensive activity. Ultimately management's role under this model is transformed into one of leadership rather than control—hence the need for a well-formulated, inspirational vision.

VISION AND ORGANIZATIONAL SOUL SEARCHING

Vision without action is a daydream. Action without vision is a nightmare.

—Japanese saying

Formulating a vision is an organizational soul-searching exercise wherein the organization defines its identity to itself and the outside world. It sets the mood for leadership and employees alike and thus dictates in a subtle, yet very strong, way the mode of operation. Take for example this part of DuPont's vision: "we deliver the miracle of science." A vision as large as life—or is it? With a vision like this, one wonders if any clear direction is given to leadership for steering the organization into the future, or for employees to understand the organizational overall purpose. But a deeper look at the words reveals the organization that DuPont aspires to be: one that sees itself and is recognized as achieving the impossible. Its vision not only reveals its commitment to do the miraculous, but also reflects the organizational character or personality. The organizational character painted by the words may be considered a little pretentious by other organizations. Another leader in the same chemical industry expresses its vision with equal strength but less flamboyance, providing that "We improve what's essential to human progress." Yet that flamboyance or confidence in their ability to do the miraculous is what sets DuPont's organizational character apart from the rest.

What Is a Vision?

A vision statement should focus on the purpose of the particular organization in a way that defines its character. It should reflect how the organization sees itself now and in the future, and how it wants to be seen by the outside world. The choice of words should aim at provoking a certain mental image in the reader coupled with an emotional charge. Otherwise a vision statement will just be another document that sits in the drawers of some employees (if they can remember where they placed it). Such a vision is more of an idle, and outmoded, tool.

A vision statement can be made of few words or a number of lines. Sometimes it is equated with the mission statement. Opinions differ on what the elements and function of each statement should be but there is a general consensus that a vision statement should reflect the main spirit or purpose of an organization or a business unit. A mission statement, on the other hand, is generally defined as a more detailed description of how the main purpose will be achieved by spelling out the means, the promises to customers, the main enablers (technology, creativity), and the shared values of the employees.

Many vision statements are redundant as they state the purpose of the organization in terms of what it does, and not in terms what it wants to be. An example of this are vision statements that read something like "we want to be the best manufacturer of x in the world." Such vision statements fail to inspire employees or create a distinctive organizational identity, and are thus sterile and ineffective. An organizational vision needs to be so strong as to define the personality, character and identity of an organization or it runs the risk of being counterproductive by creating a fake sense of unity and confusion as to the direction the organization should take.

It is very important to start with formulating or amending the vision of the organization or the business unit before embarking on an ICM. This is because a vision statement, if properly drafted, provides the foundation for an ICM and establishes the business case for it. It grounds the ICM in the everyday business reality by showing how it helps the organization achieve its purpose. This is of particular importance for the KM stage; therefore, it is essential that an organization defines its purpose or vision first. A well-formulated vision serves in several ways.

Find Your People

The other purpose a vision achieves is to broadly define the character of people the organization aspires to attract and will be able to retain. In DuPont's example, the vision reflects that the organization wants to attract and keep employees who do not quit even when their goal seems impossible to achieve.

That is clearly demonstrated by the vision of Disney Company: "We make dreams come true" and "We deliver the magic of Disney." Making dreams come true takes a lot of hard work and commitment, and needs both powerful imagination and advanced means (e.g., the latest in animation technology). This reflects the level of commitment that Disney desires from its employees: imagination, hard work, and commitment until a dream is made true. It also conveys to prospective employees Disney's commitment to provide the environment that fosters and encourages their creativity for them to make magic.

Connect with the Outside World

A vision statement should also define the business of the organization in terms of the real effect the organization has on the outside world. Such effect should be defined in a way that goes beyond the delivery of certain products or services. Coca-Cola is very good at this. It sees itself as being in the business of refreshment and invigoration of people rather than making and selling drinks. Defining its business this way, Coca-Cola creates a distinctive character that impacts its business at both the strategic planning and operational levels. Coca-Cola adopts and implements business plans that reinforce this character by delivering high emotional value with their products and taking an active part in the communities they serve. This translates into consumers who become increasingly loyal to the brand that delivers to them a story—an emotional value—rather than just a drink. That connection with the outside world was a result of Coca-Cola's envisioning itself as refreshing people rather than making a drink.

Taking a look at leaders in other industries, the same trend is detected. Such organizations define their business and purpose in reference to the way they see themselves impacting their society or the whole of humanity. Dow's business is "to improve what is essential to human progress" and not to make chemicals, and Pfizer sees itself as contributing to humanity's quest for a better life. Pfizer is in the business of healing, rather than the business of making and selling drugs. Envisioning its role in this way, Pfizer has created and maintained a distinctive character of being caring of both its employees and its customers—a character that is continuously affirmed by the way Pfizer responds to its community.

Transform the Organization

Visions are usually set by the founding leaders of the organization. Nonetheless, it is common to have an organization change its vision if it is considered restrictive or unsuitable for the times, or if it does not conform to the vision of a new leader who sets out to transform the organization. A vision can transform an organization since it sets the tone, the culture, and the envisioned reality of an organization.

The power of vision to transform a whole organization can be seen in the story of Franklin Pierce Law Center (Pierce Law). Historically, the powerful vision of Pierce Law took it from the farm barn headquarters where it was established in 1973, to become a state-of-the-art school that is renowned globally for its intellectual property (IP) program.[6] Established at a time when the term *intellectual property* (and patent law) was seen as the black sheep in legal education, Pierce Law's vision was to advance IP law to support inventors and promote innovation in business. At times when little academic attention was given to IP, let alone research or law reform activities, Pierce Law's vision was indeed futuristic.

Pierce Law maintained its position as the national leader in this area of law until powerful competitors joined the race,[7] which—though able to join Pierce Law at the U.S. national arena—could not effectively compete with it internationally. The implications of this are crucial from a strategic standpoint. Other competitors, who are supported by powerful financial and administrative infrastructures, now share the once unique competitive advantage of Pierce Law in IP law. Furthermore, IP law courses per se became more of a commodity as these courses were embraced by mainstream legal education. The vision of the founders has brought Pierce Law to where it is, but as it substantially materialized, it can no longer inspire it into the future. Intellectual property law may remain Pierce Law's cash cow,[8] but to maintain its leadership position Pierce Law needs a new vision to take it into the future.

After suffering the loss of two consecutive deans, Pierce Law was deanless for a number of years until the appointment of John Hutson in 2000. Faced with the daunting task of reformulating a vision for the future, Hutson started with organizational soul searching. For months, he focused on consulting key people, feeling the organizational culture, discovering the strengths, testing the depths of the strengths and weaknesses, and dissecting the old vision for insight. Eventually, it became clear to Hutson that connecting business to IP and other areas of law in legal education is the way to the future:

> Our vision is to be business-oriented, . . . our graduates will not hold MBAs but they will certainly have a keen appreciation of business needs and concerns. Augmenting their legal qualifications with appreciation of business we are graduating a generation of lawyers who will facilitate business development.

This vision led change in the school and permeated into the strategies of the various departments from admission—where the vision is offered to prospective students—to faculty committees where new courses are developed and new credentials are recruited. Most importantly, it affected the culture, which should be aligned with the new initiative before any change is introduced, as explained next.

CULTURE—THE MAIN ENABLER

Culture incorporates a set of shared values, mainly implicit, that the members of an organization have. Culture refers to the underlying philosophy, behavioral patterns, and routines or simply: "The way we do business here." The power of culture is that it is well entrenched in the psyche[9] of the whole organization that it can destroy any new initiative that is based on values different from or contradictory to those underlying the existing culture. Nelson and Winter go as far as claiming that culture and organizational routines form the "organizational genetic material."[10] Having the right culture, therefore, has been noted as a major success factor in effecting any organizational change. Conversely, an adverse culture has been found to be the major reason for the failure of many KM and other programs. This is because, when the general consensus of values in an organization are not conducive to sharing knowledge, the employee's willingness to share knowledge is suppressed.

For the success of any ICM initiative (at any of the three stages), it is important that the organization have the right culture. In addition to enabling the changes required for each of the stages outlined in the previous part, the right culture can have a powerful effect on the organization as a whole. First, it emancipates the creativity of employees through recognition of their contribution. Second, it enables employees to make decisions more quickly with less formal control by management, because once the cultural values are explicit, employees are more aware of what is allowed and expected, and what the organization stands for. This leads to the third function of culture, namely, increasing employee loyalty. An employee who feels empowered, part of the organizational community, whose contribution is recognized and appreciated, and who is always challenged to improve and develop displays much stronger loyalty rates. This reduces employee turnover, which in turn reduces the effect of the brain drain, improves customer satisfaction and retention rates,[11] and creates a healthy workplace that attracts more talent. A prominent example of this is Nokia, which keeps on attracting the best talent in the telecommunications market despite offering relatively modest remuneration. Talent is continuously attracted by the popular Nokia culture, which is known to be innovative, challenging workers to higher intellectual realms, making them "happily badly underpaid."[12]

In fact, it has been noted that a strong culture alone can provide a competitive advantage in mature industries (e.g., the airline industry). Southwest's success over the years has been due to its strong culture of unity, teamwork, and collaboration where they work together as one community to beat the competition. This is illustrated by the following excerpt in which CEO Herb Kelleher addresses his people regarding USAirways' entry into the Baltimore market:

> The outcome of the latest attack on Southwest by another of the Big Seven Carriers is just as important to ALL of us . . . Just as against the United Shuttle, the crucial elements for victory are the martial vigor, the dedication, the energy, the unity, the devotion to warm, hospitable, caring and loving Customer Service . . . I am betting on your minds, your hearts, your souls, and your spirits to continue our great pride and our marvelous success.[13]

Pfeffer and Sutton refer to another very interesting role that organizational culture and philosophy can play in changing suppliers' performance. The authors explain how Honda was able to improve its suppliers' performance through alignment between its and the suppliers' cultures.[14] This further highlights the role of cultural alignment in the success of strategic alliances and mergers, where it has been noted that culture alone can threaten to break a merger.[15] So what are the values that an organization's culture should foster for effective ICM implementation? And how does an organization ensure that it has the right culture before it embarks on change initiatives? There are two sets of values that an organization should instill in its culture for successful ICM: knowledge sharing and risk taking, as elaborated next.

Knowledge Sharing or Idle Socialization

Organizational culture should encourage and foster information and knowledge sharing as an activity that is part of the job rather than a form of idle socialization. This requires more than simply incorporating knowledge sharing in the organizational culture. It requires a shift in perceiving knowledge sharing as a professional, rather than a social, activity. A striking example is British Petroleum (BP), showing how the first attempts at KM failed, despite leadership's stress on the value of knowledge sharing. It was not until BP made it part of the job to move personnel to other divisions and departments, where they are encouraged to share their knowledge, that KM succeeded. Incorporating knowledge sharing in the job design resulted in employees changing their behavior, gradually changing the culture to one in which knowledge sharing became one of the most admired professional skills.

The most important organizational cultural value is to encourage the contribution and collaboration of everyone in the organization in order for the organization to meet its strategic objectives. Southwest Airlines[16] is one of the best examples of an organizational culture in which everyone collaborates to succeed. In a fiercely competitive industry, Southwest's competitive advantage was to establish and maintain a reputation of being on time no matter what. From the pilot and crew to its land-based airport personnel, every Southwest employee takes the company's promise seriously and works to maintain it. It is not uncommon for Southwest pilots to help with loading baggage to get airborne on time. The company's outstanding record and award-winning performance are attributed by management to the collaborative culture they have, which the competition has continuously failed to imitate. The second set of values relates to fostering innovation.

Failure or Success—A Matter of Perspective

Innovation, particularly radical innovation and the generation of new knowledge and IC, is a very risky business. A strong brand may be affected by aggressive competition of another or loss of popularity if the organization fails to promote and enhance it. Research capability, no matter how robust, may fail to deliver a breakthrough invention. Intellectual property rights may be rendered less effective by litigation, infringement, or misuse. Still, to be risk averse may not be a choice of business mediocrity versus excellence but to some may be a choice of death over life. Part of encouraging risk taking is not to penalize, even by stigmatizing, failures by employees. A risk-taking culture should at least encourage an attitude of open-mindedness by management—an open-mindedness that may extend for as long as five years as in the following example from 3M.

Research scientist Dr. Spence Silver's attempt to invent a strong adhesive initially failed, and instead he invented adhesive spheres that would not dissolve though still very sticky. For years Silver presented seminars throughout 3M in search for product concepts for his technology. 3M did not kill the invention and allowed it to survive for five years when Mr. Fry, a new product development researcher, attended one of Silver's seminars and came up with what became known as the Post-It Note. Initial market research indicated that the new product, Post-It Notes, would be a commercial failure. But the entrepreneurial spirit and risk-taking cultural values cultivated by 3M prevailed. The two managers responsible for the launching decision visited a number of stationery retailers and were convinced, despite negative market research reports, that the new product had a chance. The result was a $384 million business that continues to grow.[17] But cultural change is not easy. In most cases, it is hard to discern with sufficient clarity the existing values embedded in the culture of an organization. Without such an understanding it is hard to see how such values can be changed.

Cultural Change—Uncovering the Implicit Values

One way to change culture is by effecting changes to the job design wherein knowledge sharing is incorporated as part of everyone's job, as explained in Chapters 5, 7, and 8. Incorporating knowledge sharing, idea submission, and teamwork in the reward and compensation systems of the organization propagates this further. This, however, is not enough; if the implicit values are not made explicit it may be impossible to change them, particularly where the adverse implicit values are those adopted by senior and middle management. In such a case, the organization has to change implicit patterns that are entrenched deeply in its identity. That can only be possible by uncovering these implicit patterns, and comparing the values of management/leadership and the rest of the organization.

To deal with this, Brian Hall of Values Technology suggests going through a value audit. Hall applied his study of the effect of human values on human behavior to organizational cultural values and behavior.[18] He found that although 125 values underpin all human behavior, an individual lives with about 20 and operates on about a third of these on a daily basis. These values change according to the stage of human development, which Hall divides into seven stages. Hall explains that organizational culture is affected by the same set of values reflected in the collective values of employees and the stage of development of the organizational vision and evolution.

For an organization to create and extract value from its IC, Hall explains, an organization must be functioning on values that stem from stages three and four at the least. Stage three values include belonging to a group, communication, workmanship, art, and membership. Operating at this level, an organizational culture will promote collaboration and knowledge sharing by stressing the value of belonging to a group, undermining the role of individual creativity and self-initiation.

The emphasis on creativity, self-assertion, sharing, trust, and collaboration are values stemming from stages five and six of an organization's development. Organizations at these two stages of development are able to create and utilize knowledge not only in their field of operation but other fields as well, depending on the initiative and creativity of their employees. Hall demonstrates how adoption of values at a particular stage affects the leadership, and hence management style and the administration structure as a whole. Conflict and misalignment between leadership and employees' values would result whenever they operate from different stages, particularly when such stages are further apart.[19] Hall explains that a leader with stage-six values will usually expect self-initiated collaboration when entrusting a specific task to an employee. If that employee operates on values of stage three, for example, then he or she will need permission before speaking to others or initiating any decisions. Eventually, this would result in loss of productivity and confusion as to what is the accepted behavioral pattern. Only by making these values explicit, as well as exposing their quality, is it possible to consciously address, change, and align them to the organizational vision. A cultural audit is therefore included as part of the CICM model as well as steps to formulate the organizational vision. To that we now turn.

NOTES

[1] See, for example, C. Bartlett, "The Knowledge Based Organization," in R. Ruggles and D. Holtshouse (eds.), *The Knowledge Advantage* (Oxford, UK: Capstone, 1999). Also see Peter Senge, *The Fifth Discipline: The Art and Practice of the Learning Organization* (New York: Currency Doubleday, 1990).

[2] K. E. Sveiby, *The New Organizational Wealth* (San Francisco: Berrett Koehler, 1997), p. 21. According to Sveiby's analysis, these companies make up 50 percent of the fastest growing companies in the United States. Also note that the Science, Technology, and Economic Development Board reported that in 1999 the service sector accounted for two-thirds of the U.S. GDP.

[3] Brian Arthur, "New Economics for a Knowledge Economy." In R. Ruggles and D. Holtshouse (eds.), *The Knowledge Advantage* (Oxford, UK: Capstone, 1999), p. 195.

[4] An astounding example is British Petroleum, mentioned in Chapter 1, and how it used the knowledge organization model to improve the value of its plummeting stock. Another example is Harley Davidson, which reinvented itself as a knowledge organization, thereby bringing itself back from the near-dead.

[5] See, for example, M. Marquardt and T. Sung, *Building the Learning Organization: Mastering the 5 Elements for Corporate Learning* (Palo Alto, CA: Davies-Black, 2002); and B. Saunders and P. Kline, *Ten Steps to a Learning Organization* (Arlington, VA: Great Ocean, 1998).

[6] Pierce Law has an unmatched IP program that includes over 40 courses in IP law and commercialization taught by 10 permanent IP faculty members and over 35 adjunct faculty. It is the only school that offers a master's degree in IP to nonlawyers (since 1985).

[7] For years, Pierce Law maintained its position as the number one law school in the United States for intellectual property according to the U.S. News classification. By the end of 1999, however,

Pierce Law was pushed into the third position by fierce competition from George Washington University and Berkeley University. Pierce Law still maintains its number one standing when it comes to international students and organizations for IP.

[8] Allusion is made here to Arthur D. Little's classification of businesses as cash cows, dogs, stars, and questions marks, where cash cows are cash-producing businesses, dogs are losing business with low revenue, stars are low or negative revenue-producing businesses with growth potential, and question marks are of questionable growth potential..

[9] It is not new that organizations are referred to in psychological terms. Many theories look at organizations as living entities that not only grow and evolve but also have a personality. Also interesting is W. Bridges, *The Character of Organizations: Using Personality Types in Organization Development* (Palo Alto, CA: Davies Black Publishing, 2000), where the author applies Jung's archetypes of personality to organizations.

[10] Nelson, R. and Winter, S. *An Evolutionary Theory of Economic Change* (Cambridge, MA: Harvard University Press, 1994).

[11] It is common knowledge that higher employee satisfaction rates result in higher customer satisfaction rates, particularly in the service industry. That is why many organizations have started to improve employees' quality of life.

[12] See Roberts, J. and Doornik, K., "Nokia Corp.: Innovation and Efficiency in a High-Growth Global Firm," Harvard Business School case #IB23, 2001.

[13] J. Pfeffer and R. Sutton, *The Knowing–Doing Gap* (Boston: Harvard Business School Press, 1999), pp. 202–204.

[14] *Id.*, pp. 23–24.

[15] *Id.*, p. 79.

[16] Credit for research on Southwest Airlines goes to my students Abdulraheem Mohamed, James Hawkins, and Edward Romano in the Fall 2001 class.

[17] For more details see *www.3m.com/about3m/pioneers/fry.jhtml*.

[18] B. Hall, "Culture and Values Management: Context for the Development and Management of Intellectual Capital," in P. Sullivan (ed.), *Profiting from Intellectual Capital* (New York: John Wiley & Sons, 1998), pp. 43–58.

[19] *Id.*, p. 52.

11

Implementing Knowledge Management under the CICM Model

BACKGROUND

The goal of the knowledge management (KM) stage under the Comprehensive Intellectual Capital Management (CICM) model is to manage the knowledge resources of the organization, whether explicit or tacit, and whether generated by human or customer capital, for value creation. The main goal is to ensure the organization has the requisite resources to enable its production, innovation, or effective decision making. Implementing KM under CICM is based on the definition of KM as the process of managing knowledge raw resources for production.

This achieves the following purposes:

- Recognizes KM as one stage of a comprehensive or total model of ICM where the organization deploys its resources to make new products (manufacturing businesses), new services (for service industries and customer service businesses), and for effective decision making (for public services, e.g., defense).
- Includes KM as part of the management objectives in the overall business plan of an organization, namely preserving, maintaining, and growing the knowledge resources required to sustain the operations of the organization.
- Provides managers with a methodology and a business case for KM that is easy to explain and justify for top management to secure funding. It drives home a familiar understandable message—who would argue with the need to manage tangible raw resources? Similarly, to sustain the main production process of a knowledge organization, the raw knowledge resources should be managed and renewed. Like tangible raw resources, it is important at all times to know the knowledge resources an organization has, maintain an inventory in a way that preserves and improves its value, ensure availability and quality of future supply, and develop strategies that enable the deployment of resources to respond quickly to market needs.

Taking this stage to the practical level, the rest of this chapter will first define management objectives that should be set for a KM program, the main processes to implement at the KM stage, and a step-by-step implementation guide.

MANAGEMENT OBJECTIVES

The management objectives of the KM stage are to:

- Effect a strategic shift in the way the organization envisions itself where the role that learning and knowledge creation can play in the success of the organization is emphasized. This vision should be used to transform the culture to one that fosters knowledge sharing. Though vision setting and creating the right culture are prerequisites to any ICM program, they will be outlined under the KM stage as preparatory steps.

- Know what the organization knows and the expertise it has and use it to maximize value creation.
- Know what the organization needs to know to meet its desired competitive position, by recognizing and analyzing gaps in the organizational knowledge resources, and blocks in knowledge flows.
- Adopt the appropriate knowledge strategies to enable leveraging existing knowledge, creation of new knowledge, and the acquisition of the requisite knowledge for competitive positioning.
- Operationalize the knowledge strategies through creating systems to enable identification and dissemination of best practices, sharing and creating knowledge through communities of practice, supporting knowledge creation processes through the knowledge base and information technology (IT) system.
- Monitor, review, and track results of KM initiative(s) to measure the effect of KM on performance and productivity, hence the development of performance measures.

PROCESSES

The management objectives enumerated above encompass the main processes that the KM stage under the CICM model should incorporate. Exhibit 11.1 represents the framework underlying the implementation steps under this stage. It involves performing a knowledge audit and gap analysis, adopting the appropriate knowledge strategies, and implementing various systems to

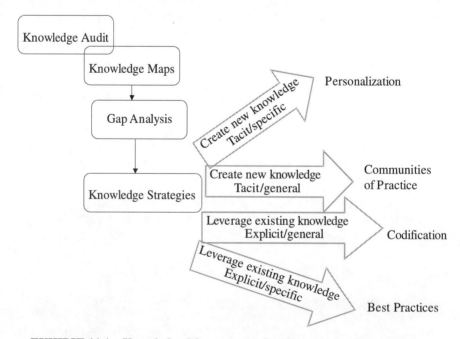

EXHIBIT 11.1   Knowledge Management Implementation Framework

operationalize them. In addition, the model should incorporate a measurement system to monitor results and provide insight for review and adaptation.

For any KM program, or any ICM initiative, to be successful the alignment of the organizational vision and culture are imperative. Therefore, the step-by-step guide in this chapter includes the formulation of vision and transformation of culture as preparatory processes. The guideline then proceeds by outlining the steps to implement the main processes of KM under both the strategic and operational levels.

The main processes include:

- Preparatory Level

  - *Process 1.* To effect a strategic shift in the way the organization envisions itself where it recognizes the value of becoming a knowledge or a learning organization. This will assist in establishing the business case for KM and the whole ICM program.
  - *Process 2.* Carry an audit of the organizational culture and values to ensure that the organizational culture is not adverse, or fatal, to knowledge and IC management.

- Strategic Level

  - *Process 3.* Undertake an audit and gap analysis of knowledge resources to discover gaps in the knowledge base. Discovering gaps in knowledge flows are also covered here to detect dysfunctional knowledge flows and networks. Gaps are defined as those areas where limited or no resources, as well as blocked flows, would affect present and future performance and limit the growth/success rate.
  - *Process 4.* Identify and adopt knowledge strategies to fill the gaps and to sustain the knowledge (value) creation processes.

- Operational Level

  - *Process 5.* Implement a process for the identification and dissemination of best practices either through communities of practice or a central unit.
  - *Process 6.* Provide the guidelines, support system, and structure for the informal formation of communities of practice and interest around strategic knowledge areas, as well as enable free employee movement in the organization for effective knowledge sharing.
  - *Process 7.* Design the knowledge base architecture to support knowledge creation, and key business, processes. Choose the appropriate IT tools to enable tacit and explicit knowledge sharing.

STEP-BY-STEP GUIDE

The following is a detailed step-by-step guide on how to implement such processes with reference to the relevant practices.

Process 1: Formulation of Knowledge-Based (or IC) Vision

Vision formulation should be done for the whole organization. The individual business units and departments can later align their missions with the vision, depending on the size and structure of the organization. There are three main steps to the formulation of the vision. The first step is performed by the leadership where the organizational vision is first formulated. The resulting vision should then be aligned with that of the key people, or the heads of business units. The final step is communicating the vision to everyone in the organization through the necessary changes in culture.

Step 1: Leadership Formulation.   Vision formulation is an inward-looking exercise for the organization where it defines who it really is and who it envisions itself to be. Regardless of the words, a vision statement should contain the following components:

- Purpose of the organization reflecting its character and identity. An organization's purpose is beyond providing a living for its employees, or satisfying a demand in the market. It is also beyond the delivery of a certain product or service. Equating purpose with delivery of a certain product is not only restrictive but irrelevant as well. This is because the activity of delivering a certain product represents what an organization does and will continue to do to sustain its existence. It is like any of the voluntary biological systems of the body (circulation or breathing), which though critical for the continuation of the species doesn't provide personal motivation for advancement and growth.
- The business the organization is in by identifying the difference it wants to make in people's lives.
- The unique value that the organization adds to its customers.
- The role the organization wants to play in the future as it envisions it.
- The cultural values and personal qualities and skills that its people should have.

The vision has to be inspirational and stress the role of IC or knowledge in the future of the organization. There is no magical statement. Actually, the words of the vision are of secondary importance; it is the exercise of formulating, then activating the vision, that has the transformative power. To formulate a vision, leadership of the organization needs to address the following questions:

- *What is the purpose of your organization?* Look beyond what you do to how you do it that distinguishes you from other players, hence your character and identity. Whether you know that purpose on founding the organization or try to extrapolate it in hindsight, it is important to define it. Personality is everything even for organizations; it is no coincidence that organizations with a strong sense of identity and character are the most successful.
- *What is your business?* Business should be defined in terms of the difference you want to make in people's lives; for example, Pfizer's business of caring.
- *What is the unique added value that you deliver or aim to deliver to your customers?* This value should be independent of the products and services that you provide.
- *What is your vision of the future?* Consult the vision of the founding leaders and what they were trying to achieve when they founded the business. Go beyond that vision into your present and envision the future. An existing or past vision that has substantially materialized cannot inspire the organization into the future.
- *How do you want to change or impact your world?* What will success in your envisioned world look like? In defining success and the new environment, you should distinguish between success obtained through increased operational efficiency (i.e., economizing) and innovation (i.e., strategizing).
- *What are the main characteristics and values that your employees should have to enable the organization to attain its vision?* Summarize this in one word by subtracting all the terms that represent the characteristics and competencies that are generally accepted in your industry.

Step 2: Alignment with the Vision of Key People.   Formulating an organizational vision is an interactive exercise where leadership and the key people of an organization go back and forth until they envision a desired future. The role of key people is to assess the competitive landscape and assess future market trends and needs and envision a position in that future. Being more aware of the organizational knowledge resources and those of the competitors can assist leadership in defining the areas in which they choose to excel. Aligning the leadership vision with that of the key people also enables the latter to own the vision and the strategic direction, and hence be better equipped to communicate it to other levels in the organization. Meetings, brainstorming sessions, and retreats are a good idea in performing this step. However, without ownership of the vision by key people little comes from these activities other than socializing. The best way is to assign to a team the alignment of the leadership's vision with that of key people. This team should also be entrusted with communicating the vision to the rest of the organization.

To implement this step:

1. Form a team comprising key people who represent the various functional departments and/or business units.
2. Each representative should perform competitive assessment in their respective area in their envisioning of the future. This is an integral part that is many times ignored, making a vision out of touch with reality and the competitive environment that the organization is part of. Formulating a future vision needs an understanding of self, the competition, and the customer.
3. Assess and align the vision of the leadership with that of the key people through continuous meetings until consensus is reached.
4. Each of the key executives should later act as a champion of the new vision by communicating it to senior and middle management in their respective departments and units as elaborated under Step 3.

Step 3: Communicate to All Levels.   The best way to communicate a knowledge-based vision to all levels of the organization is by periodic (annual) meetings between the key people and their staff to communicate, review and update the vision. These meetings should be aimed at creating a shared vision, team building, and collaboration at all levels. They also facilitate the creation of the desired culture, and may be used for formulation of shared values aligned with the vision. In addition, the following measures should be taken to activate the vision across the whole organization. Specific departments should be assigned to oversee certain components of the vision, where they align their procedures and practices accordingly as follows:

- The marketing and public relations departments should align their advertising, promotions, and branding efforts with the vision components of purpose, organizational identity and character, and description of business.
- The new product (or service) development department should align its screening of new concepts and design of new products with the vision's proposition about the unique or added value to customers.
- The business development or growth and development unit should align its planning for the future with the vision's image of the future.
- The human resources department should align its recruitment and professional development policies with the vision's component describing the organizational values.

Process 2: Cultural Audit and Transformation

Cultural audit and transformation is the process in which the organization tries to find out the implicit values that underlie its behavioral patterns, work routines, leadership style, and decision making models. These values make the organizational culture, which may defeat any ICM or any program that is contrary to the underlying values of the program. Therefore, it is important to undergo an audit of the cultural values, which helps make these values explicit so that they can be effectively changed or maintained. An audit also reveals gaps between the values of management and those of employees, exposing blocks in the way of building the right culture. The right culture for ICM is one that encourages collaboration and knowledge sharing over control and rivalry. In particular, the following values need to be incorporated in the culture of the organization:

- Collaboration, teamwork, and collegiality
- Knowledge sharing and continuous learning
- Creativity, self-initiated decision making, and risk taking
- Acceptance of failure, experimentation, and innovation

Following are the steps required to discover the values underlying an organization's culture and to instill the required cultural values.

Step 1: Audit of Cultural Values. The goal of this step is to discover the organizational culture and gaps between the values of management and those of employees affecting the success of ICM program.

- Undertake an individual profile analysis of leaders, senior managers, and executives to find out the underlying values that define their management style and affect the behavioral patterns, including turnover rates, in their departments.
- Undertake a group values audit in the form of a questionnaire for the employees of each department to assess the need for cultural changes. In many organizations, there is a divergence among the cultures of the various departments, ranging from stress on control/obedience, where following instructions and close supervision characterize how the work is done; to inspiration/innovation, where independence and collaboration are stressed. Research has shown that departments, indeed organizations as a whole, that display the first set of values are poor performers with low employee morale and high turnover. Undertaking the audit on a departmental basis and checking productivity in these departments will reveal the departments where more work in instilling the right cultural values is needed.

Step 2: Effect Cultural Change on Executive and Departmental Levels. Once the results of the audit are available, it is important to implement a number of steps to ensure that the right cultural values are adopted, on both the executive and departmental levels as follows:

1. *On the executive level.* Hold leadership and coaching sessions for executives on a continuous basis to mentor them into adopting the required set of values. Those executives with the right values can act as mentors and suggest ways on how management styles should change. Leadership's values should be monitored constantly and should be taken into account in the process of recruiting new executives. An individual pro-

file analysis is highly recommended before undertaking any recruitment decision, to rule out candidates whose values highly and strongly contradict those of the organization.

2. *On the departmental level.* Hold interdepartmental meetings to brainstorm on what employees see as the desired, compared to the actual, cultural values that would facilitate improved performance and higher morale. The desired cultural values discussed at this level should be aligned with those identified at the top management and executive level. The meetings should proceed by setting milestones on the way to incorporating the desired cultural values in daily operations and business practices. The milestones to be adopted are different depending on each department's progress in fostering the right culture. In general they include: redefining decision-making, teamwork, and project management policies to ensure that they encourage the desired values; recognizing and rewarding practices that advance the adoption of the desired values; and reporting on the progress of the various departments in creating the right culture and how this affects their performance.

Step 3: Cultural Change Across the Whole Organization.   A number of changes are required to promote the right culture. At the least, the following changes should be accommodated:

- Include knowledge sharing as one of the duties in the job design of all positions by linking knowledge sharing to the job in question, and most importantly by providing time for knowledge sharing and creation.
- Include knowledge sharing and collaboration as criteria in the appraisal of employee performance, particularly at managerial levels. Promotion of managers should be based on rewarding those whose teams or departments display the required cultural values and are recognized as the best departments to work at.
- Reward and recognize KM practices of individuals, groups, and organizational units in annual meetings. Though financial rewards are desirable, recognition of contribution is what motivates and drives knowledge workers.
- Recognize and reward departments for transfer of own, and replication of others', best practices (i.e., recognizing all units involved to boost best practices replications).
- Codify and disseminate success stories of how knowledge sharing, innovation, risk taking, and collaboration helped to solve problems, address business challenges, save costs, or improve productivity.

After the first two processes are successfully implemented, the organization can move to KM.

Process 3: Knowledge Audits

Conducting knowledge audits is a key process not only for KM purposes but also for the strategic planning phase, both on the enterprise and business-unit levels, for forging competitive strategies and tactics. For KM, the main goal is to discover the knowledge resources and networks (flows) that the organization has, should have, and hence the critical gaps in the organization's knowledge resources. A critical knowledge gap is defined as lack of knowledge in a strategic area, inefficient use of internal knowledge resources, or a block in knowledge flows that hampers the attainment of strategic goals. More accurately, a critical gap is that between what an organization does and what it can do with its knowledge. Knowledge audits enable the assessment and prevention of organizational memory loss and brain drain, problems that result in undercapitalization and waste of knowledge resources, as discussed in Chapter 4. In particular, this process is designed to discover:

- Available knowledge resources (know what we know):
  - Stores and sinks of explicit knowledge resources
  - Expertise and tacit knowledge resources
- Hidden and undercapitalized resources (we don't know that we know):
  - Key leverage points in the learning process
  - Practices perfected by certain departments (best practices).
- Knowledge resources required to meet strategic objectives (we don't know that we don't know):
  - Blocks in knowledge flows and networks
  - Gaps and unmet needs for knowledge and information

A number of approaches to knowledge audits have been developed: stock or inventory-taking techniques; mapping of knowledge flows and networks; and mapping of knowledge resources. The choice of approach depends on business needs and objectives. Mapping knowledge flows with customers, for example, is of particular importance for service organizations in which strong flows facilitate both customer satisfaction and learning from customers. A comprehensive gap analysis should incorporate the three approaches. The three approaches are presented here as well as a new tool for gap analysis. Once the results of a knowledge audit are gathered and analyzed, a plan should be devised to outline how existing knowledge resources (explicit and tacit) are going to be leveraged through transfer and renewal, and how to put in place the processes for creation of new knowledge. Regardless of the approach used, the audit process can be performed through a mix of interviews and questionnaires sent to all employees of the audited unit or the whole organization. Discussions of results with target groups formed of management and employees should follow to foster ownership of the process for future post-audits. It is important to gain top management's support for the audit, to ensure receipt of maximum response and to ensure that recommendations of the audit report will be considered in planning the KM program. The steps of performing each of the audit approaches are outlined below, including the questions that should be addressed.

Step 1: Stocktaking of Knowledge Resources.   The purpose of this step is to determine the explicit and tacit resources of an organization in terms of what is known, not known, and needs to be known at a point of time. It is important to distinguish between explicit and tacit resources, as filling gaps in these two related resources require different knowledge strategies. Abundance of an explicit resource is not indicative of a strong knowledge base if the tacit resources are in deficit and vice versa. This is because the best databases with state-of-art knowledge (explicit resources) do not provide a strategic strength unless complemented by experienced knowledge workers to apply and develop it (tacit resources). Similarly, the best people with the best knowledge (tacit resources) can be frustrated by lack of explicit resources that provide the information they need to harvest in moving up the learning curve.

Stocktaking cannot be done in a vacuum. The stocktaking step should be performed for defined key business processes. A preliminary step therefore is to define its context, that is, the critical business processes to which the stocktaking audit relates. The questionnaire should aim at discovering the knowledge resources, whether explicit or tacit, that are consulted in performing critical business processes as follows:

- Tacit Resources

  - Who do you consult and for what areas of knowledge? How often? Please refer to both work roles and areas of knowledge. These questions are designed to discover internal knowledge flows.
  - Who do you contact and in which areas of knowledge outside the organization? How often? These questions assess knowledge flows with external sources.
  - Who are the experts inside and outside the organization who you think have the knowledge that you need? This question aims to identify experts through peer assessment.
  - Classify the areas of knowledge in which you are both proficient and willing to share your knowledge. This is designed to locate experts through self-assessments.
  - Who consults you and in what areas of knowledge? This is designed to discover in-flows of knowledge.
  - In what form do you obtain knowledge from these experts and how do you communicate? This is designed to assess types of communicating in order to guide choice of enabling tools later.
  - What are the areas of knowledge that you need but cannot find an expert to refer to? This is designed to discover gaps in the tacit knowledge resources.
  - How much time do you spend to locate experts? This is designed to discover flow bottlenecks and blocks that affect speed and performance.

- Explicit Resources

  - What are the internal and external information and knowledge resources that you have access to? This uncovers the available resources—the ones we have and know that we have.
  - What are the information resources that you need but cannot find? What are the categories of knowledge you need to perform critical business processes? These questions uncover gaps that are easily ascertainable by reference to the required, but unavailable, knowledge resources.
  - Where and how do you gain access to the knowledge you need? Do you have access to all the resources that you need? Are they in abundance, scarce, or obsolete? These questions aim to discover blocks in knowledge and information flows and later guide choice of document and information transfer tools.
  - How is information being obtained or delivered and when? This is designed to assess the effectiveness of retrieval and search functions and tools.
  - How much time do you spend looking for the information and knowledge that you need? This is to assess the efficiency of retrieval and search functions and tools, and provide targets (in terms of information costs and time to find required resources) that management can aim for and monitor.

To know who knows what and whether knowledge resources satisfy knowledge needs is not enough. The knowledge audit should also uncover dysfunctional knowledge and information flows that hinder knowledge transfer and cause loss of knowledge. Therefore, the information about who contacts whom and for what should be mapped to reveal the internal and external knowledge flows related to critical business processes. Compiling answers to these questions will reveal the explicit and tacit resources that are accessed for critical business processes, the efficiency of this access, the required knowledge for increased effectiveness, and to whom others refer as experts and in what areas of knowledge. The auditor should analyze these results and recommend appropriate KM solutions and actions. Before proceeding with mapping knowledge flows, therefore, I present a tool for the analysis of the knowledge audit results.

Step 2: Analyzing Audit Findings.   To judge whether you know or not cannot be expressed in a black or white manner (have and have not), as there are many levels of knowledge or ignorance, many shades of gray. Further, even when various levels of knowledge are identified, the auditor needs a benchmark (market standard, state-of-the-art, or competitions) to base his or her judgment about the state of the organization's knowledge resources. An assessment of the levels of knowledge should equip management to assess the level of investment required to fill the identified gaps. This is why the CICM model distinguishes between the types of knowledge gaps by reference to the Levels of Abundance or Deficiency (LAD) of a certain resource. Gaps are identified as those deficiencies in knowledge resources that may affect the organization's competitive performance adversely or limit its growth potential. Some gaps may demand extensive investment to be filled, and it may be therefore more prudent not to fill it. The LAD classification provides guidance as to the solutions that can be employed to deal with the various levels of abundance and deficiency. These should be mapped for the whole organization and for every business unit or department to show LAD by reference to organizational competencies and those of the various departments and business units. The various levels are represented in colors so that they can be used to produce topographic or graphic maps through visualization software programs to give management a snapshot of the state of their knowledge resources at a specific point in time.

The LAD includes the following four levels:

1. *Green level.* No deficiency. Have abundant knowledge resources that are related to core competencies or strategic knowledge areas (i.e., areas of knowledge that are necessary for meeting the strategic goals). The main question here is to find whether these resources are being disseminated across the organization to those that need them. That is where codification of the knowledge and the development of best practices are the best options. The design of the knowledge base, building knowledge content, and updating the base can be addressed here.

2. *Blue level.* Deficient tacit knowledge but abundant explicit knowledge resources, where the databases and manuals are available, but gaps in tacit knowledge resources detected where there is no expertise in the required area. These gaps should be addressed by the organization's recruitment plan, and training with a focus on development of the required competencies. This strategy is used by Microsoft, who, to build new competencies, assigns new employees to design complex new software systems in teams of three to seven, under the guidance of mentors, moving them up the steepest learning curve in the shortest time possible.[1] Alternatively, communities of practice (CoPs) can be formed around the blue-level areas of knowledge to fill the identified gaps.

3. *Orange level.* Limited deficiencies identified in the knowledge resources of a certain department but the gap can be filled from resources within the organization. This is where blocks in the knowledge flow are detected since such blocks are the main reason the knowledge is not being transferred to those who need it. The use of communities of practice is essential here in transferring the knowledge to those who need it, maintaining a knowledge content center, and creating new knowledge in the area.

4. *Red level.* High deficiencies identified in the explicit and tacit knowledge resources required to meet strategic goals or to effectively compete in a certain area of knowledge. Such gaps can be probably filled from external resources for a cost within budget. Under this, top management needs to consider whether a strategic alliance with a partner who has knowledge in the targeted area is possible. In cases in which such an alliance is not feasible and acquisition of knowledge requires extensive expenditure, top management should consider divestiture, if the area of knowledge is not critical to the organization's growth plans. In other cases, the follower strategy mentioned by Daniele in Chapter 5 is useful. Reverse engineering and closely monitoring how the most successful competitors utilize their resources can provide valuable insight and access to explicit knowledge resources. These resources are available from public free sources (e.g., USPTO patents for technologies, Internet, trade shows); and private sources (e.g. research companies, independent R&D labs, and consultants). That, however, would not be sufficient and management would still need to find ways to develop tacit knowledge in that area.

Looking at the results of the knowledge audit this way enables the auditor to accurately assess the knowledge needs of the organization and which approach will be the most appropriate to address the identified needs. In addition, the level of urgency in filling each of the identified gaps should be assessed to prioritize gap filling. For this to be done the auditor needs to have access to the targeted competitive position of the organization and its business strategy. Cost and time estimations for filling the gaps should also be made. This will better equip top management to plan and unfold the implementation of the knowledge strategies they adopt to fill the identified knowledge gaps within their budgets. It should be noted that knowledge needs are in a state of constant flux. Therefore the organization should periodically assess its knowledge needs to determine whether it has the required knowledge resources to meet certain strategic goals or operationalize a certain competitive strategy.

The stocktaking exercise should also refer to the knowledge needs for carrying on critical business processes. The end goal of KM is to support the knowledge needs of critical business processes to enable effective organizational action. This is done by mapping the knowledge resources in a way that reveals how they are being used to support the key actions and tasks of critical business processes. While the stocktaking exercise shows the availability of knowledge resources, the mapping exercise explained next shows how they are utilized, and the effectiveness of such utilization.

Step 3: Mapping Knowledge Resources.   A knowledge resource map depicts the "as-is" of particular knowledge resources accessed to perform identified tasks in the core business processes. This map reveals how and which knowledge resources are used to support the business process under audit. Mapping knowledge resources also uncovers inefficiencies where critical actions are not supported electronically, and redundancies where such actions are supported by multiple overlapping resources. It also reveals the type of resources that support each of the key actions, (i.e., whether electronic databases, documents, or personnel). By mapping the critical business processes, the knowledge resource map provides important guidance for the design of the knowledge base and IT systems as to which knowledge resources should be grouped in electronic content centers, and which should instead be referred to expert directories and nonelectronic sources.

As shown in Exhibit 11.2, the various actions A–E of a business process are examined to find the type and location of knowledge resources needed to perform the process. For example, action or activity D is supported by database 3 and reports 4, both explicit resources, while process C is

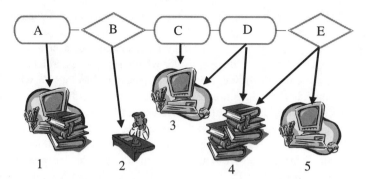

EXHIBIT 11.2   Knowledge Resources Map

supported by resource 2 only. Understanding the relationship among the various resources and actions enables a better assessment of the knowledge creation processes, its strengths and weaknesses. Some knowledge resource maps also refer to external knowledge resources, where external knowledge resources are tapped for intelligence and other purposes.

In performing steps 2 and 3 of stocktaking and mapping knowledge resources, it is important to keep in mind the transient nature of knowledge as a resource. Knowledge is ever changing and ever growing with new technological advances and changing market trends. To remain current and useful, knowledge resources have to be kept in a constant state of flux—hence, knowledge flows are at least as important as knowledge stocks for knowledge creation. Knowledge flows represent the various exchanges that develop over time among people inside and outside the organization, independent of organizational charts, for the sole purpose of getting the job done.

To complete the audit exercise, it is therefore important to map knowledge flows and exchanges in order to detect concentrations of personal knowledge, indicated by a majority of people denoting certain members as experts in a certain area of knowledge, and to detect blocks in knowledge flows where there is less activity or flows between departments or units; hence step 4.

Step 4: Mapping Internal and External Knowledge Flows.   Knowledge networks and flows (also called social networks) are the informal networks that form for sharing and transferring knowledge in a certain area. They are formed in all organizations independent of the formal structure's lines of command (organizational charts) and workflows. Maps of internal knowledge flows show "who contacts whom for their knowledge" and the frequency of this contact. Mapping external knowledge flows reveals flow patterns with external parties in the value chain (e.g., distributors, suppliers, contractors, and customers). Knowledge flow (exchange) maps include maps showing knowledge flows and exchanges inside a particular department or business unit (departmental flows), and those between the various departments in an organization in regard to the performance of a particular business process (interdepartmental flows), and finally flows between departments and outside parties (external flows).

In a knowledge flows map, each person is denoted by a node, and a knowledge flow (both ways) is denoted by a line connecting two nodes. The boldness of a line denotes density of exchange. There are a number of software programs available in which the data can be entered to create knowledge flow maps showing flow activity and blocks. All these maps aim to uncover and depict the following:

- Knowledge exchanges that support a particular business process inside a certain department, as illustrated in Exhibit 11.3, and with other departments, as illustrated in Exhibit 11.4.

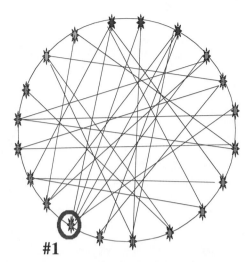

#1

EXHIBIT 11.3   Knowledge Flows and Networks

- Sources of tacit knowledge resources (experts) in a department and across the organization detected by finding nodes (people) where there is intense activity and centrality. Network centrality is represented by the node, which is the center of a knowledge network (e.g., employee 1 in Exhibits 11.3 and 11.4). Those with network centrality can be approached for CoPs leadership in that area of knowledge.
- Places where knowledge sharing is disabled shown by lack of knowledge flows between departments (e.g., departments A and B in Exhibit 11.4). This is alarming, as cross-pollination of ideas and knowledge among various departments is one of the goals of KM. In addition, it shows weak knowledge sharing and collaboration, which may hinder replication of best practices. Weak or missing flows between two or more departments or business units that can benefit from each other's knowledge in performing critical business processes reveal serious knowledge flow bottlenecks.
- How knowledge resources are accessed from outside the organization (external knowledge flows). Exhibit 11.5 is an example of the flow of knowledge between the sales rep-

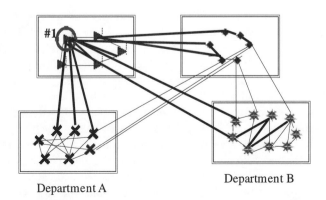

#1

Department B

Department A

EXHIBIT 11.4   Interdepartmental Knowledge Flows

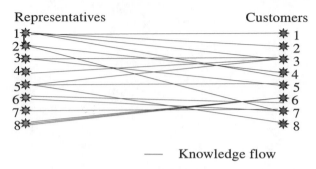

— Knowledge flow

EXHIBIT 11.5   Knowledge Flows with Customers

resentative of a division with its customers. Mapping such flows enables gap analysis of the social or relational capital or, in other words, the interaction between the human and customer capitals in producing knowledge. This enables detection of gaps in the contact points. For example, if customer 1 is a valued customer in terms of knowledge resources then more contact points should be established to build the knowledge base in that area. Another example is representative 8 whose extensive number of contacts shows experience and thus richness in tacit knowledge in a certain area of knowledge. These maps are critical for organizations in the service industry where a lot of learning takes place from contact with major, or what Sveiby calls image-enhancing, customers.

Following the audit exercise, top management should use the audit report to devise the appropriate knowledge strategies to fill the identified gaps and create new knowledge.

Process 4: Strategizing Knowledge Management

As explained under the LAD classification of gaps, the type of the knowledge gap determines the choice of the procedure that is best suited to fill that gap, and hence provides guidance as to the suitable knowledge strategy. In Chapter 5, four knowledge strategies are identified for filling knowledge gaps from internal sources through KM.[2] Under this process, guidance is provided on the use of these strategies. The first step outlines what each of these strategies can be used to achieve, and the way it affects the design of the KM program.

Step 1: Identify Knowledge Strategies to Fill Gaps.   The knowledge strategies referred to here are:
- Best practices strategies for leveraging existing knowledge resources. These resources, though mainly explicit, are usually created through codifying tacit knowledge into forms that can be replicated. Under this strategy, the focus is on identifying and perfecting certain business practices for the purpose of dissemination to other departments, sites and business units that use a similar practice. It is particularly beneficial for mature industries and large organizations where there is a wealth of experience. The strategy is best suited for the transfer of explicit knowledge for specifically defined applications.
- CoP strategies for creating new knowledge through transfer of mainly tacit knowledge, by bringing people concerned with one area of knowledge/practice together. Under this strategy, the focus is on growing the tacit knowledge in a particular area where members' ownership has a great effect on learning and innovation. The strategy is particularly

suited for large organizations where there is a need to find new solutions by tapping into tacit resources.

- Codification strategies for codifying the knowledge, which the organization applies and uses in support of its critical business processes. Under this strategy, the focus is on codifying knowledge and making it available to employees in real time for application and reuse. It is best suited for industries in which solutions in one area can be applied to another with moderate modifications. The strategy deals with codifying existing explicit knowledge of wide application.
- Personalization strategies for locating and connecting experts in specialized areas of knowledge to tap into tacit knowledge where new knowledge is created to respond to unique situations. It is best suited for industries or businesses where unique situations require the application of human intelligence to innovate new solutions. The strategy addresses needs for creating new tacit knowledge for specific applications.

It is further noted that the focus of best practices and codification strategies is operational excellence by leveraging existing knowledge and hence preventing organizational memory loss. The focus of the CoPs and personalization strategies, however, is on innovation and creation of new knowledge to respond to new situations, where tacit knowledge is the main driver and hence preventing organizational brain drain. To decide on the appropriate knowledge strategies, a number of variables should be considered.

Step 2: Understand the Various Variables That Knowledge Strategies Address. To decide on the appropriate knowledge strategies, the following variables should be considered:

- The level to which innovation or creation of new knowledge is required to fill the gap, and hence the mix between personalization and codification strategies.
- The tacit/explicit content of knowledge in the area of knowledge where the gap is detected, and whether the knowledge is expected to have specific (narrow) or general (wide) application.
- The level of replication—whether knowledge in a certain area has narrow or wide application to existing or future situations, and the ease with which it can be replicated (best practices strategy).

Exhibit 11.6 illustrates how these variables affect the choice of strategy. For example, in cases where creation of new knowledge is required in strategic areas, forming CoPs to fill identified gaps is the best strategy. In the converse situation depicted in quadrant four, where the knowledge created is of general application and can be easily replicated for reuse, then the best option is to use a predominantly codification KM strategy.

Step 3: Assess Need for Innovation versus Replication in Critical Business Processes. Every area of knowledge or practice contains both explicit and tacit knowledge components, has features of narrow or wide application, and involves a mix of existing and new knowledge. To decide on the KM strategy, therefore, top management should assess these variables in a matter of degrees. Knowledge strategies should be applied in combinations by reference to the degree of innovation (tacit knowledge) as opposed to replication (explicit knowledge) required for optimal business performance, as shown in Exhibit 11.7. As the tacit knowledge component and the need for new knowledge increases, the strategy should move to more of a personalized and CoP strategy. The nature of variables to which a business is subject depends on the industry/line of business and the organization's vision and competitive strategy.

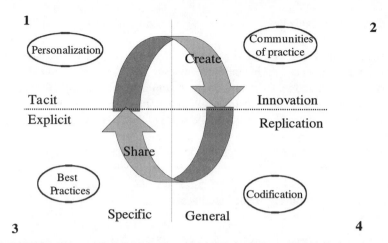

EXHIBIT 11.6   Variables Affecting Choice of Knowledge Strategies

Some organizations compete through operational efficiency or excellence, and hence focus on developing best practices where replication of existing knowledge is core,[3] while others compete mainly through innovation where new knowledge creation via CoP/personalization is core. Needless to say, neither of these two organizations should neglect either operational excellence or innovation completely, even though they should adopt one as the predominant competitive strategy. This step should be aligned with the strategic planning steps under both the IM and IP management stages. Ensuring alignment among knowledge, innovation, and IP strategies is essential to create fit between the various IC strategies and the overall strategy of the business.

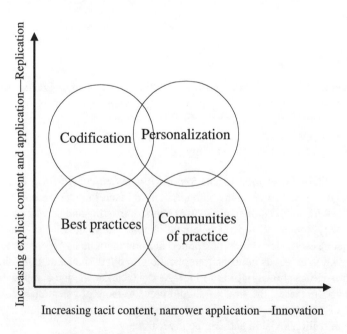

EXHIBIT 11.7   Operationalizing Knowledge Strategies

Strategizing KM is not a question of which strategy to use but rather which one to use in relation to which areas of knowledge, and in relation to which business processes. Under this process, top management should review the audit results, the analysis of the nature of gaps, and then decide the mix of strategies that enable innovation (new knowledge needs) versus replication (sharing knowledge needs) to meet strategic goals. These decisions will affect the role that CoPs will play in the business, the nature of best practices to be collected and codified, and the design and content of the knowledge base, the IT architecture. This will inform implementing KM at the operational level.

Once these broad lines are defined, management can proceed with operationalizing the KM strategies. Though the focus, depending on strategy, will be placed on one approach rather than another, the infrastructure supporting each of the approaches should be considered in the plan for implementing KM. Implementation of the programs mentioned should be phased according to strategic needs, priorities, and budget. Phasing out implementation will also enable monitoring of progress and keeping track of results. Following is a step-by-step guide on the formation and dissolution of CoPs (creating new knowledge strategies), the dissemination of best practices (sharing and reusing knowledge strategies), and the design of the knowledge base and IT architecture (according to the personalization/codification strategy).

Process 5: Communities of Practice

Step 1: Define the CoPs/Knowledge Strategy.   This step involves aligning the CoP structure with the KM strategy. A knowledge strategy focused on replication will favor best practices and helping CoPs, while a focus on innovation favors innovation and knowledge-stewarding CoPs.

1. Define the role that CoPs will play in the KM program by reference to the types of the CoPs that can be formed (i.e. best practices, innovation, helping or knowledge-stewarding communities).
2. Define the general purposes for the formation of a CoP, including jumping learning curves for new employees, pursuing solutions for common problems, preventing reinvention of the wheel, and increasing flow of new ideas.
3. Identify in general terms the strategic areas that CoPs can be formed around by reference to practice or problem. Practice relates to a certain business process wherein membership revolves around users and owners of the process, while a problem focus may bring people from various functions in common pursuit for a solution.

Step 2: Form a CoP Council at the Central or Business Unit Level.   The CoP Council will act as the process owner of CoP formation where training and guidance are provided to the organization or the business unit at large on how to form and manage CoPs. In addition, the Council will provide the following support services:

- Advise on CoP formation and technology needs
- Assist and lobby senior management to recruit executive sponsors or CoP champions as well as procure funding
- Formulate procedures for the starting up of CoPs, including the submission of proposals and the assessment process
- Define the evaluation criteria to determine the continuance or dissolution of existing CoPs, taking into consideration whether the CoP has achieved its purpose and should be dissolved, or whether its purpose should be redefined
- Formulate a policy as to trade secret protection and the sort of information that the CoP should be sensitive in disseminating

- Define the alternative methods available to CoPs to disseminate their knowledge to the respective business units and to the organization at large, including how to create taxonomies and create and maintain content centers
- Keep a portfolio of CoPs that provides a snapshot of the type of CoP, leader and contact person, value proposition, purpose, success criteria and performance metrics, Web site and content centers, domain and areas of knowledge, and size

Step 3: Assess the Case for Forming a Certain CoP. This step can be carried out by the CoP Council or by the management of various business units, where a preliminary assessment is undertaken of the value proposition of the CoP and its fit with business needs and strategies. In addition the following should be assessed:

- Does the CoP have a clear mission and objectives?
- Does the CoP have the people to cover the core roles of leader, facilitator, and administrator? Each of these roles is instrumental for the success of the CoP where the leader's passion motivates members, the facilitator manages communication and knowledge creation process, and the administrator addresses issues of codifying and disseminating knowledge generated by the CoP as well as keeping track of results.
- Does the CoP have the supporting tools, budget, and infrastructure it would need to attain its set goals?
- Has CoP identified performance goals and metrics to monitor performance?

Step 4: Launching the CoP. Following the preliminary assessment done in Step 2, the new CoP is moved to the formation step. Depending on the financial and human resources involved, the CoP may be launched in a pilot phase, after which it may be formally launched. In general, however, the following should be undertaken:

1. Draft a plan for the CoP, which should include the roles (leader, facilitator, and administrator), executive sponsorship, the focal point (practice, problem), value proposition, desired outcomes, list of members, interaction mode, and support needs.
2. Conduct a workshop between the leader and all members of the CoP where the plan is reviewed and finalized, a shared understanding is reached, and a plan of action is forged. The plan of action should outline the knowledge needs of the members, how they will be addressed and in what order.
3. Assign to a number of members the task of developing the taxonomy that the CoP will use for content creation and management, and align with other CoPs and IT departments that are responsible for managing content in the same area(s) of knowledge covered by the CoP.

Process 6: Best Practices

Best practices can be treated as a domain of knowledge for CoPs where CoPs are allowed to form with a certain practice as the focal point, where they own the process of disseminating the practice, tracking its implementation, updating, and validating it across the organization. The CoP council may act as the process owner and the review committee. Alternatively, the process of collection, validation, and dissemination of best practices may be entrusted to a separate review committee that reviews the best practices submitted to it by various divisions or teams. After approval of certain best practices the committee should entrust the implementation, review and update of the best practices to a Best Practice team.

Step 1: Submission of Best Practices to the Review Committee.   Upon receipt of a submission to consider a certain practice as a best practice, the Review Committee should undertake the following:

1. Define the areas where best practices are expected to be identified and circulate this list to heads of concerned departments and divisions for them to motivate their staff in identifying and collecting best practices.
2. Define the criteria upon which a practice will be judged and the data that need to be submitted in the proposal, regarding how the best practice improves productivity and enhances performance.
3. Put in place incentives (e.g., an award system) for such departments that submit their own and implement other's best practices. Hold an annual best practices day wherein departments display and explain their best practices.
4. Create a portfolio of best practices wherein the type of the practice, number of users, success stories, results, originators, and subject matter experts are identified. This portfolio should be supported by a best practices database with a resource map that enables location of best practices.

Step 2: Assessment, Approval, and Dissemination.

1. Perform an internal benchmarking exercise to determine whether the submitted practice is the best (i.e., assess if it is a proven practice).
2. Assess if the practice can be replicated and assign a best practice team to monitor its implementation across the organization and collect data on its performance.
3. Upon approval as a best practice, disseminate the best practice through publishing it in the organization's best practices database and informing the departments and divisions that may be interested.

Step 3: Local Assessment, Application, and Reporting.   Upon receiving a notification of a best practice, local management of a certain department or division should undertake the following:

1. Assess the applicability of the practice to local business needs and strategies.
2. Assess the costs involved in the implementation of the practice against expected gains.
3. Decide on implementation or otherwise, with a justified rejection in the latter case, and submit to the Review Committee.
4. If implemented, report to the Best Practice team with plan of implementation, targeted results, and performance metrics.
5. Monitor and track performance, review and report to the Best Practice team.
6. Any major changes to the best practice should be submitted to the Review Committee for consideration as a new best practice.

Process 7: Knowledge Base and IT Architecture

Step 1: Design the Architecture.   The knowledge base, as explained in Chapter 5, is the database, which provides access to knowledge resources needed to support critical business processes. The knowledge base is built on, and supported by, the IT infrastructure of the organization. Though the content of the knowledge base should be created and maintained by knowledge centers or subject matter experts across the whole organization, the central IT department still plays a crucial role. The central IT department's role includes, but is not limited to, ensuring the interoperability of the various work systems and software programs, and providing technological enablers that facilitate retrieval of information and communication across the organization. The latter will be outlined in step 3.

The architecture of the knowledge base is affected by the functions it serves in KM. The knowledge base should have the following four components, or centers, as depicted in Exhibit 11.8:

1. *Knowledge Centers.* Contain knowledge, not merely information or data, to support critical business processes—building of knowledge centers is outlined in step 2.
2. *E-Learning Centers.* Maximize learning by providing e-learning material responding to identified knowledge and professional development needs.
3. *Best Practices Database.* Provides access to best practices with guidance as to replication and collection of results. This should include Lessons Learned and solutions developed to deal with common problems. Refer to process 6.
4. *Expert Directories.* Provide contact information of knowledge and subject matter experts classified according to areas of practice, knowledge, and experience.

The following steps guide the design of the knowledge centers, taxonomies and choice of technological enablers for KM. Though any IT system should comprise the four abovementioned components to support KM, the knowledge strategy adopted by management directly impacts both the focus of the IT system and the components that will be given prime importance. Exhibit 11.9 shows how different KM strategies, which should be aligned with the business focus of an organization, shift attention to different components in the IT design. For example the IT system for a KM program based on personalization strategies would focus on enabling the creation of CoPs and building communication channels to ensure the extraction and transfer of tacit knowledge.

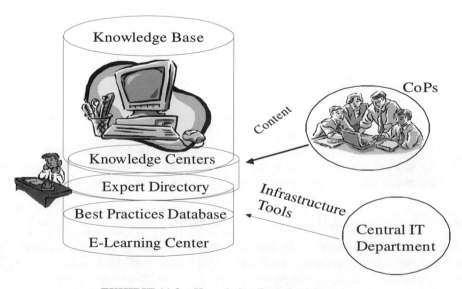

EXHIBIT 11.8   Knowledge Base Architecture

KM ASPECTS	INFORMATION/DATA	HUMAN/SOCIAL	SYSTEM/PROCESS
Business focus	Information management	Knowledge flow & creation management	Information technology & application (automation)
Main business objectives	Mine data & detect informational patterns	Create new knowledge, innovate & solve problems	Support decision making in critical business processes— Operational efficiency
KM Strategies	Codification strategies	Personalization and CoPs strategies	Best practices strategies
Main IT component	Content centers maintained by CoPs or subject-matter experts, e-learning centers	CoPs web-enabled applications, expert directories	Best practices collection & dissemination applications & database, intranet
Enablers	Taxonomies, retrieval & search tools	Communication tools	Decision-making tools, internal benchmarking

EXHIBIT 11.9   The KM Strategy and the IT Design

Step 2: Design the Knowledge Centers.   The purpose of the knowledge centers is to provide the knowledge resources that support critical business processes. Therefore, to start, the knowledge resources supporting critical business processes should be mapped first. Given that business processes are specific to every organization, I will use a generic knowledge creation process here to show how this step can be implemented. The generic process of knowledge creation involves the following steps illustrated in Exhibit 11.10:

1. Collection or gathering of information and data
2. Interpreting and evaluating the information
3. Assessing the situation
4. Taking a decision
5. Verifying the decision
6. Communicating the decision (this is sometimes done before or after action, depending on the nature of decisions)
7. Taking action

After mapping the business process in question, do the following:

1. Examine the knowledge resources that need to be consulted in every step of the business process.
2. Assess the tacit/explicit component of the knowledge resource needed to support the various steps of the business process. Note that the tacit/explicit classification of steps

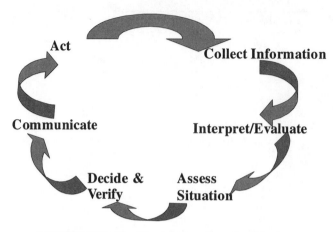

EXHIBIT 11.10   Knowledge Creation Process

is to some extent artificial, since the tacit/explicit interface is blurred most of the time. Exhibit 11.11 shows the tacit/explicit components needed to support the various steps of the generic knowledge creation process. As shown in Exhibit 11.10, there are steps in which tacit knowledge is used predominantly and others that are mainly based on explicit knowledge. Some steps involve both; for example, collecting information, which is explicit knowledge, depends on one's understanding of what needs to be collected (tacit knowledge).

3. Group explicit knowledge resources into knowledge centers and allocate the responsibility of managing the content, and creating new content, to subject matter experts. This responsibility could also be allocated to the CoPs, if any, whose value proposition is to grow organizational knowledge in that area.

4. Group references to personnel (tacit resources), as discovered by the knowledge audit, into expert directories.

Step 3: The Development of Taxonomies for the Knowledge Base.   It is essential for a knowledge base, or any database, to be easily accessible and for the knowledge contained therein to

STEP	TACIT RESOURCES	EXPLICIT RESOURCES
Collect information	X	X
Interpret/evaluate	X	
Assess situation	X	
Decide	X	
Verify decision	X	X
Communicate		X
Act		X

EXHIBIT 11.11   Knowledge Resources Supporting Knowledge Creation Process

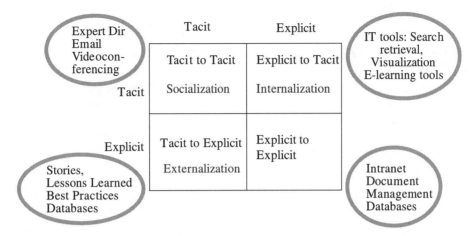

EXHIBIT 11.12   KM Tools

be efficiently retrievable. That is where the role of taxonomy comes in. The choice of taxonomy for the knowledge base is a very critical step that should be managed by subject matter experts (each in his/her areas of expertise), software programmers, and the IT department. This is an effort that requires the contribution and coordination between the central and business unit level IT departments for the knowledge base to become one relevant to the needs of the whole organization, and for the knowledge contained therein to be leveraged across departmental and business unit boundaries. Adopting a taxonomy is not enough, as new terms are added and information becomes obsolete. Therefore, it is important to employ knowledge stewards for retrieving knowledge resources, updating the knowledge base and the taxonomies used, as well as keeping those involved informed. This role is separate and different from that of the IT department in that knowledge stewards address the knowledge needs associated with critical business processes.

Step 4: The Choice of Enabling Technological Tools.   Following Nonaka and Takeuchi's account of the four knowledge conversions involved in KM, as outlined in Chapter 5, Exhibit 11.12 outlines the various technological enablers needed for KM.

CONCLUSION

The KM stage is the platform upon which the innovation and intellectual property management stages are built. Under this stage the IT infrastructure is redesigned to support the knowledge needs of all business processes and operations, and hence KM overlaps at various facets with the two stages discussed in Chapters 12 and 13. Wherever appropriate mention will be made of such overlap.

NOTES

[1] See J. Quinn, P. Anderson, and S. Finkelstein, "Managing Professional Intellect," *HBR* March/April 1996, p. 71.

[2] These are distinguished from the acquisition and follower knowledge strategies, which relate to filling knowledge gaps through external sources. The acquisition and follower strategies are briefly discussed under the LAD Red Level.

[3] For example, Ford combines CoP and best practices strategies to attain its "Process Leadership" vision, by forming CoPs whose area of knowledge is to identify best practices, with around 100 CoPs responsible for finding and disseminating best practices across the 150 plants worldwide across an organization of 345,000 employees. It is noted, however, that Ford CoPs are more structured than others in organizations that use a combination of CoPs and personalization strategies where the focus is on innovation (e.g., Siemens).

Implementing Innovation Management Under the CICM Model

BACKGROUND

The goal of the innovation management (IM) stage under the Comprehensive Intellectual Capital Management (CICM) model is to extract maximum value of knowledge resources through the innovation process, whether directed inwardly to improve performance (process innovation), or outwardly to make new products (new product development (NPD) process). IM is the stage for converting ideas into new or improved products, services, solutions, or processes.

Innovation has become the main means of production and adding value in the knowledge economy. Under the CICM model, IM has to be implemented throughout the whole enterprise and be incorporated in the way business is done. For that to be possible, the value of innovation has to be reflected in the vision and culture of the organization, as a first step, covered in Chapters 10 and 11. Once the cultural and philosophical bases of innovation are laid, the organization can implement the steps mentioned below. The following sections present a step-by-step guide to the implementation of IM at the strategic and operational levels, with detailed practices to operationalize the various innovation strategies. But first, the management objectives for the IM stage are outlined.

MANAGEMENT OBJECTIVES

The management objectives of the IM stage are:

- Effecting a shift in the way the organization sees itself wherein innovation is recognized as the way of doing business
- Deciding on the innovation strategy that best fits the organization's situation, and enables it to attain its vision and strategic goals
- Creating a portfolio of innovation projects to translate competitive strategies and to manage risk across the whole organization
- Defining criteria for the selection and prioritization of projects within the portfolio to weed out less probable projects as soon as possible
- Effecting the necessary structural changes to arrange skills throughout the organization in competence centers, to enable the formation of the right team for the purposes of the innovation project
- Arranging current and potential future alliances in a portfolio that can be tapped when needed, and defining when and how such alliances are to be made (governing conditions)

- Fostering an organziational culture that promotes innovation by allowing employees time to innovate and the implementation of their own ideas for improving job performance
- Developing and implementing methods that enable tapping into the organization's IC

PROCESSES

The management objectives define the main processes that an IM program under the CICM model should include. This involves a number of processes, starting with adopting the appropriate strategy at the strategic level and using it to decide what goes into the innovation portfolio. To proceed to the operational level, certain structural changes are needed to enable network-based innovation through the recognition of competence centers and creation of an alliances portfolio and a central unit to manage the internal and external networks. The operational level also includes effecting the necessary cultural changes and providing the enabling practices for tapping into the organizational IC. Exhibit 12.1 presents a framework for implementation. Though according to Exhibit 12.1 these methods are best suited for specific innovation strategies, they still have a general application depending on changing business needs and objectives.

The main processes are:

- Preparatory level

  - *Process 1.* Gap analysis—before getting started with implementing IM it is important to find the "is" and compare it to the "should" position.

- Strategic level

  - *Process 2.* Deciding on the innovation strategy that best fits the organization's situation and vision.
  - *Process 3.* Creating and managing a balanced portfolio mix of innovation projects across the whole organization. The mix should reflect the innovation strategy, and enable effective resource allocation and risk management.

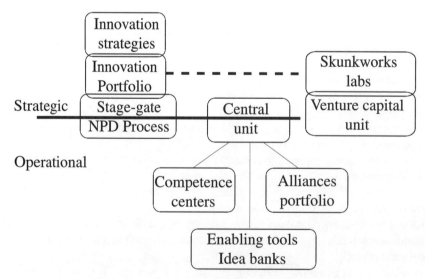

EXHIBIT 12.1   IM Implementation Framework

- Operational level

  - *Process 4.* Effecting the structural changes required to create and manage internal competence centers and the portfolio of external alliances. This includes setting the policies on which teams will be formed and allocated, and alliances sought and formed.
  - *Process 5.* Effecting the required cultural change through a system that fosters employees' implementation of ideas for the improvement of business processes and job performance.
  - *Process 6.* Implementing the appropriate methods to tap into human capital for ideas for new products. This also involves maintaining a database of ideas to form a pool that the organization can access when needed.
  - *Process 7.* Implementing the appropriate methods to tap into customer capital, depending on the level of innovativeness required and the overall approach to customer relations. It is important to determine what the term *customer* refers to, and align methods implemented here with the innovation strategy. In this guide, only the Lead User method will be outlined.
  - *Process 8.* Choosing the right tools to enable effective management of technology and technical/patent intelligence activities.

STEP-BY-STEP GUIDE

The following is a detailed step-by-step guide on how to implement such processes with reference to the relevant practices and tools.

Process 1: Getting Started and Gap Analysis

It is important before starting any change to determine the starting and desired positions. When it comes to implementing IM this involves ascertaining the state of the innovation process and its ability to accommodate business present and future needs. Though undertaking a gap analysis of the innovation process as it stands is peculiar to every organization, the exercise should at least incorporate the following steps.

Step 1: Discovering the Innovation Portfolio.

1. Determine the number of innovation projects being managed across the whole organization.
2. Map these projects in relation to their level of innovativeness, strategic fit, estimated costs, expected returns and calculated risks.
3. Collect information regarding time to market and actual returns of past projects, and desired time to market needed to attain the desired competitive position.
4. Consider the efficiency of allocation and use of financial and other tangible resources.
5. Examine allocation of human resources, whether human resources are overcommitted/underutilized, and the way they are being tapped.
6. Determine how talent, skills, and competence are arranged in the organization and the ease of finding the right people and forming the right team to manage the innovation project.

Step 2: Examining the Idea Generation Process and Culture.

1. Include a number of questions in the survey mentioned under Process 2 in the previous chapter under cultural audits to uncover the cultural values that the organization has promoted, promotes, and needs to change or confirm to foster innovation.
2. Include in the culture modification process steps to incorporate such cultural values designed to make innovation a way of doing business; in particular, values that tolerate failure as part of experimentation, encourage risk taking, and empower employees to pursue challenging projects.
3. Map where new ideas come from in the organization and the processes and criteria used to collect, filter and evaluate them.
4. Record the number of ideas received on a periodic basis, implementation rates and how that affects employee morale and innovative activity.
5. Collect information from the venture capital unit, if any, on the projects pursued based on ideas received from employees.

Step 3: Determine Where to Start.

1. Prepare a clear account of the "is" and "should" positions based on the organization's business objectives (e.g., reduction of time to market, increase of employees' idea submission and implementation, or simply moving toward adopting innovation as a way of doing business). This also can be determined by reference to defined competitive positions.
2. Based on the preceding results determine which is the most strategically important business objective that needs immediate attention. This would enable prioritizing implementation of IM practices to address the immediate business needs.
3. Use Exhibit 12.2 to find the required business focus to satisfy the immediate business needs, identified under number 2, and proceed with implementing the corresponding processes first. Though a comprehensive IM program should cover all the components encapsulated in Exhibit 12.2, it is important for resource allocation purposes to phase out such implementation according to strategic needs.

Process 2: Deciding on Innovation Strategies

Deciding on the appropriate innovation strategy depends on the organization's specific situation, including its purpose, culture, desired competitive position, and its people. Therefore, guidance is provided on choice of strategy, taking all these factors into consideration, as outlined in step 1. For each of these innovation strategies, top management need also to assess certain aspects of the competitor's business, as outlined in Step 2.

Step 1: The Innovation Strategy.   Exhibit 12.3 presents a summary of the innovation strategies and the organization's specifications that they are best suited to.

Step 2: Competitive Intelligence.   An essential part of the strategic planning exercise is competitive intelligence, wherein top management is made aware of the competitive landscape to assess the actions that certain competitors may take. Exhibit 12.4 outlines the aspects of a competitor's business that need be assessed under each of the innovation strategies.

	IDEA GENERATION (NEW PRODUCTS)	CREATING NETWORKS	PROCESS INNOVATION	NEW PRODUCT DEVELOPMENT
Main processes	Collect, filter, select customer/market-oriented ideas	Create internal & external networks to select right team, develop product concepts & tap required skills	Solicit ideas from employees in defined areas, encourage implementation	Create balanced innovation portfolio & allocate resources
Business focus	Mine ideas	Mine networks	Reduce cost, improve decision making & productivity	Risk management
Main goals	Maintain a flow of customer-oriented ideas	Get to market fast— market leadership or favorable competitive positioning	Empower employees to improve job performance & decision making	Weed out less probable project ASAP, flexible allocation & reallocation of resources to respond to competitive needs
Strategic thrust	Employee-driven (outward)	Customer or technology driven	Employee-driven (inward)	All
Enablers	Culture, idea banks, venture capital units	Market research, competitive intelligence, value-chain management, lead user (for breakthrough innovations), technical/patent intelligence	Culture, ideas submission & implementation criteria & reports, reward system, budget allowance	Portfolio management, project management, selection & prioritization criteria—stage-gate

EXHIBIT 12.2   Innovation Management Framework

Process 3: Innovation Portfolio Mix

An innovation portfolio should contain innovation projects of varying levels of innovativeness. It is important to adopt a classification of innovation projects that reflects the different levels of risk involved.

Step 1: Create a Classification.   Under the CICM model, classification of low, medium, and high level of innovativeness is provided as follows:

- *Low.* Incremental improvements to products or processes including changes that result in cost reduction
- *Medium.* Major revisions to existing products or processes, and line/brand extensions (new products)

INNOVATION STRATEGY	COMPETITIVE STRATEGY[a]	VISION	PURPOSE	PEOPLE & CULTURE	VALUES
Customer-driven	Differentiation cost-leadership or focus	Number one choice for customers, a partnership with customers	Customer satisfaction is our prime goal	Open to customer communication	Customer-, user- and market-oriented
Employee-driven inward innovation	Cost leadership	Provide the best price for value	Outsmart competition by being more efficient—working smarter	Cost control oriented, employee implementation of good ideas within certain budgetary limits	Efficiency-oriented—doing things better
Employee-driven outward innovation	Differentiation	Be the most innovative organization in industry	Our employees are our best assets; Unleash innovation power of employees	Employee empowerment; Experimentation, play mixed with work	Creative, relentless, attract best talent and leave them alone
Technology-driven	Differentiation or focus	Win the technology race in a certain field	Technology makes things happen. File as many patents as possible	Aware of competitive moves, patent-oriented	Highly skilled, talented

[a]Reference is made to Porter's generic competitive strategies here.

EXHIBIT 12.3   Innovation Strategies Impact

- *High.* New-to-the-firm products or processes, platform or next-generation products, and breakthrough products

Step 2: Diversify the Portfolio Mix.   The portfolio mix depends on the strategy of the organization, but in all situations it should be balanced between low-, medium-, and high-level innovation projects. The low–high classification also refers to the risks involved and the projected returns. Maintaining a balanced portfolio is essential in managing the risk and resource allocation. Time frames differ for these projects with varying levels of innovativeness, and thus having a balanced portfolio means the organization can have consecutive market launches. One of the methods developed to aid management in that role is strategic bucketing, wherein projects are distributed under identified strategic areas or strategic "buckets."

Step 3: Allocate Resources.   Under strategic bucketing, top management translates the innovation/NPD strategies by creating strategic buckets that relate to development of new products in targeted markets, as illustrated in Exhibit 12.5. Each strategic bucket relates to a level of innovation, and is allocated a set amount of financial resources that reflect their needs and respective strategic

REQUIREMENTS/ INNOVATION STRATEGY	BUSINESS INTELLIGENCE TYPE
Customer-driven innovation	Competitive intelligence, market research (trends, market share, etc.), customer's profile, competitor's customer service
Employee-driven inward innovation	Competitive intelligence, industry analysis, benchmarking, best practices
Employee-driven outward innovation	Competitive intelligence, alliance intelligence, competitor profile (product mix, prices, etc.), project-based
Technology-driven innovation	Technical intelligence, competitor's profile, patent intelligence

EXHIBIT 12.4   Competitive Assessment

importance. Within each strategic bucket, financial resource allocation and reallocation are flexible depending on the performance of the project, changing market conditions, or adjustments to strategic directions. It is important to keep some resources and development capacity uncommitted to deal with unexpected opportunities or threats. An example of resource allocation among strategic buckets: 20 percent product improvements, 30 percent line extensions, 15 percent next generation/platform projects, and 25 percent breakthroughs (adding to 90%), where 10 percent of resources are set aside for unforeseen circumstances. The prioritization and continuous assessment of projects takes place under each of the strategic buckets.

Step 4: Identify the NPD Stages and Gates.   Effective management of the innovation portfolio involves management at two levels: the organizational/business-unit level and the project level. At the former level, a central unit/team should oversee the creation of the innovation portfolio, balancing among its strategic buckets and broadly allocating financial and human resources. The team should also set rules to govern the stage-gate NPD process including project selection, evaluation

STRATEGIC BUCKET	PRODUCT MARKET A PROJECTED COST: $7.9M	PRODUCT MARKET B PROJECTED COST: $11.8M	PRODUCT MARKET C PROJECTED COST: $9.8M	PRODUCT MARKET D PROJECTED COST: $5.9M
Level of innovativeness	Low: Product improvements	Medium: Line extensions	High: Breakthrough products	High: Platform products
	Project 1—0.5M	Project 3	Project 6	Project 8
	Project 2—1.1M	Project 4	Project 10	Project 13
	Project 7—3.2M	Project 5		
	Project 15—2.5M	Project 9		
	Gap—0.6M	Project 11		
		Project 12		
Resource allocation	20%	30%	25%	15%

*Project numbers refer to the order in which the projects are intended to be launched onto the market.

EXHIBIT 12.5   Resource Allocation and Strategic Buckets*

and prioritization criteria. At the project level, the management of each business unit or NPD department should oversee the NPD process, ensure that the projects do not proceed to the next stage before satisfying the set criteria at the respective gate, reallocate resources to respond to strategic or competitive needs, weed out less probable projects, and generally act as the gate keepers. The following steps should be implemented:

1. A central unit made up of senior executives from the various business units and representatives of functional departments should manage the innovation portfolio. The unit should meet to determine the areas of innovation and how resources will be allocated among the strategic buckets. The unit should also define in broad guidelines the selection criteria to be applied by various business units to select and prioritize projects within each of the strategic buckets, as well as the various outcomes expected at various stages of the NPD process, hence define the NPD stages and gates. Though the stage-gate method should be administered at the operational level by the project team, the central unit should operate as a process owner wherein support and training are provided to the various business units and teams.

2. The stages and gates used to manage the NPD process should be identified. They should at least include the following, as illustrated in Exhibit 12.3:

   • Market/customer screens for the idea generation stage
   • Market and technical feasibility gate for concept development stage
   • Go to develop gate after business case stage
   • Go to testing gate after development stage
   • Go to launch gate after testing stage

3. A product development master file should be created to show the stages of progress of all innovation projects at any one time and the team members and financial resources allocated to the various projects. Business plans, feasibility studies, and other studies prepared in relation to the various projects should be kept as part of the knowledge base for further reference and learning.

Process 4: Structural Changes for IM

Effect the structural changes to enable management of innovation projects across an internal network of competence centers and external network of alliances. This involves the arrangement of skills and expertise into competence centers across the organization, so that they can be flexibly allocated to various projects, depending on the needs of the innovation project. The organization should also be able to tap into external resources by managing external alliances and networks in a portfolio, as detailed in the following steps.

Step 1: Developing Competence Centers. As outlined in Chapter 7, in some organizations, competence centers develop naturally as specific business units, labs, departments, and groups develop a specialization in a certain area, so that they become known to management for their expertise. But this is not enough; this development should be systemized in a methodical way under the business model. The design of the business model should also define the criteria on which a new competence center will be developed and when to take advantage of innovation clusters. The following steps provide a guide:

1. The manager of each competence center (lab, department, unit, or group) should know the skills, expertise, and competencies of his or her personnel.[1] The manager should also

keep a record of the projects assigned to each one in the center, time availability and ability to travel.

2. Create a competence center, or recognize it as such, whenever the unit concerned develops a specialty in a certain area where concentration of skill is beneficial to improving resource and team allocation.

3. Organize competence centers around areas of knowledge, applications, or skills and not product, process, or location.

4. Create a flexible structure in which personnel from the various competence centers can be assigned to projects across the organization.

5. Keep a log showing what each center has in terms of equipment, access to local talent, and strategic alliances.

6. Consider the desirable geographic location of any new competence center. In particular, consider the following:

   • Advantages of proximity to an innovation cluster with the most advanced technology in the area of practice
   • Availability and cost of highly skilled labor
   • Access to local talent
   • Advantages of proximity of the center to other related centers in the internal network of competence centers
   • Advantages of proximity to external networks focused on the same area of knowledge or practice

Step 2: Create and Manage an Alliance Portfolio. Alliances as a general rule should be sought to combine complementary strengths, increase learning and knowledge transfer, and get to market faster. In all cases, the following steps should be taken into account before making an alliance decision:

1. Align the purpose of the alliance with business objectives and priorities.
2. Set clear goals for the alliance, including defining metrics for monitoring progress in reference to the set goals.
3. Assess the partner's culture and reputation, market reach, and customers. The depth to which this step needs to be performed depends on the type of the alliance relationship and its duration.
4. Create a portfolio of alliances to be managed by a central department. Exhibit 12.6 provides a guide on the information that needs to be included in such a portfolio.
5. The central department should be the final point of approval on alliances, and a first resort to assess the benefits of the alliance. This is important to avoid situations in which different business units compete for the same alliance.
6. Analyze synergies and overlaps in the portfolio to maximize efficiency and control costs.

Step 3: Tap Internal and External Resources to Form Project Teams. In forming the project teams the central unit should follow these steps:

1. Identify the critical issues that are presented by the innovation project.
2. Determine the critical skills that are required to manage and work on the project, and identify the people within the organization who have the required skills.

ALLIANCE	DETAILS
Type	R&D collaboration, joint venture, partnership, license
Party	Supplier, distributor, customer, university lab, R&D organization
Duration	Project-based, commercialization of technology, set or unlimited
Purpose	Combine strengths, reduce time to market, gain knowledge, economies of scale, access to blocking patent
Competitive advantage (competitive assessment of partner)	Customer base, market reach, proficiency and expertise, performance results
Skills accessed	[List]

EXHIBIT 12.6   Alliance Portfolio Chart

3. Consider the skills outside the organization available in the portfolio of alliances developed under step 3 above, as well as explore other potential partners if needed.
4. Assign a team leader with the responsibility of setting the timeline, milestones, workflow, and measures.

Many methods are available to operationalize the generic innovation strategies outlined under Process 2. The most important consideration in choosing a certain innovation method is aligning it with strategy and culture. Otherwise, the method will not be effective and may create confusion if the method's underlying philosophy conflicts with the cultural values or the strategy of the organization. Hence, as a preparatory step to Processes 5 through 8, the organization needs to choose the methods that enable its innovation strategy, according to Exhibit 12.7. It should be noted, however, that even if an organization has a certain innovation strategy, individual business units may still use a method mentioned under another innovation strategy that is aligned with the business unit's specific strategy, goals, and objectives. For example, a service business unit (e.g., financial services) may adopt a customer-driven innovation strategy, while another consumer products business unit may adopt a technology-driven innovation strategy. Alternatively, the organization may choose to implement some of these methods for a new business or when moving to a new market where another strategy is more appropriate. Processes 5 through 8 provide a guide as to the creation of idea banks, implementation of the lead user, and technology management methods.

Process 5: Employee Implementation of Ideas and the Right Culture

It is essential for the implementation of this process that the organization have a culture that empowers employees and fosters their creativity, and a management team who trusts employees' insight and knowledge about the way business is done. Administer the program as informally as possible. The following steps are involved:[2]

Step 1: Encouraging Idea Submissions and Implementation.

1. Set quotas for mandatory idea submissions covering everyone in the organization.
2. Allow for implementation of ideas by employees who submit the ideas, provided the expenditure needed is within set budgetary limits.

LEVEL OF INNOVATIVENESS/ INNOVATION STRATEGY	LOW	MEDIUM	HIGH
Customer-driven	Customer feedback, complaints, Internet, CRM	Value-chain management, focus groups, CRM	Lead User Partnership
Employee-driven process innovation	Frontline implementation	Middle management implementation	Business development implementation
Employee-driven product innovation	Suggestion box, idea databases	Managed idea banks	Employee-initiated projects, venture capital units, skunk works lab
Technology-driven	Citation maps	Topographical maps	Topographical maps

EXHIBIT 12.7   Methods of Enabling Innovation Strategy

3. Define the areas where ideas are needed very broadly by reference to critical business processes, including administrative processes.
4. Define the criteria in terms of what these ideas should cover (e.g., job performance, cost reduction, process improvement, saving time, improving working conditions).
5. When approval is required, respond to the idea originator within days, with justified reasons if the idea is rejected.
6. Set a target for implementation rates and track results.
7. Publish reports of implementation rates, success stories, improvements in productivity, and savings in a monthly newsletter and on the organization's Web site.
8. Reward employees who exceed their idea submission quotas, and departments or units with the highest implementation rates.

Process 6: Idea Banks and Employee Innovation

To foster employee-driven innovation, the culture should be one that does not penalize failure, but rather sees failure as part of the learning experience—"fail soon to succeed later." As mentioned under Process 5, it is essential that the culture empower employees. With empowerment comes accountability, and that is when the highest level of creativity is cultivated. It is essential that employees be given the chance to take part in the development of their ideas. That has a positive effect on the employees' morale, and hence innovativeness, as well as on the quality of the idea. The idea bank outlined under the CICM model is one that requires active involvement of employees in the development of concepts for new products and not simply in submission of ideas. A central department or decentralized NPD departments can be assigned ownership of the process. If the latter model is adopted, then a coordinator should be assigned to oversee the transfer of ideas that fit better with the strategy of other business units. The following steps are involved.

Step 1: Idea Submission and Building the Database

1. Create an idea bank or database and seek submissions from employees on defined areas by general reference to the strategic buckets of the innovation portfolio.

2. Alternatively, distribute the proposed innovation portfolio (with confidentiality measures in place) with its strategic buckets, with blank projects and resource allocation, to be filled by product and business development managers.
3. Arrange the ideas received under type of business, level of innovativeness, required resources, time, and the strategic bucket.
4. Create a file for ideas that do not fit into the innovation portfolio, and follow Steps 2 and 3 for their assessment.

Step 2: Assessment.   This step deals with ideas that fall beyond the scope of the strategic buckets of the innovation portfolio.

1. Transfer the idea to the business unit with the closest fit for consideration under the business unit growth/development plan.
2. Allow free time and the granting of money to the originating employee for further research to develop product concepts in connection with the business unit.
3. If the business unit rejects the idea on the basis that it is outside the scope of its growth plan, then transfer to the venture capital unit for further consideration and action.
4. Refer ideas rejected for feasibility reasons to the originating employee for further study, and allow him or her time and resources (within defined budgetary limits) to produce a prototype and a presentation to senior management for further assessment.

Step 3: Prepare Idea Reports.

1. Produce monthly idea reports that show rate of submission, rates of projects initiated based on employee ideas, and number of ideas implemented by their originators.
2. Prepare reports of rejected ideas with justifications, for further assessment.
3. Collect such reports from various business units and departments to assess their respective innovative activity.
4. Reward departments and units according to their idea generation and implementation records.

Process 7: Implementing the Lead User Method for Breakthrough Innovation

As with other processes, a process owner, preferably a central department, should be assigned the ownership of the process, where it provides support and training for such departments that wish to implement the process. To implement the Lead User method, the following steps are involved.

Step 1: Project Planning.

1. Form the team and plan the project.
2. Through brainstorming sessions, select a need-related trend in the market to focus on.
3. Develop strategies for data collection from target and analogous markets on need-related trends.
4. Collect all the data available on the subject through focused competitive intelligence.

Step 2: Finding Lead Users.

1. Conduct interviews with industry leaders to identify lead users in the target and analogous markets, who have created solutions to deal with the need-related trends, each in his/her field of expertise.

2. Work your way up "pyramids of experts"[3] to locate lead users by getting referrals from experts in the field and identifying who has created solutions to address the needs they have.
3. Get the widest exposure possible to the need-related trend in target and analogous markets by going to the fieldwork of lead users.

Step 3: Concept Generation and Development.

1. Generate preliminary new product concepts that are along the lines of the solutions developed by the lead users to address their needs.
2. Conduct workshops in collaboration with lead users to examine the preliminary new product concepts and explore new ones.
3. Choose the product concept(s) that has the widest applications to customers in the target and analogous markets.
4. Create a road map for development and launch of new products based on the identified platform.
5. Align identified new product concepts with the business objectives and development/ growth plan.

Process 8: Technology Management Methods

The methods discussed under this process fall under the ambit of competitive intelligence. While Process 2 outlined the various competitive intelligence methods that can be used to support strategic planning, it is outlined under this process in relation to decision making at the operational level. It is noted that this process overlaps with other processes at the intellectual property management stage that purport to manage patents for competitive positioning. A number of methods emerged to mine patent data for insights to guide the innovation activity, as outlined next.

Step 1: Uncover Competition's Past Patenting Trends and Anticipate Future Moves.

1. Draw a technology road map of the competition's patenting activity, using past patenting history as a guide.
2. Use patent citation trees (an example is illustrated in Exhibit 12.8) to assess the competition's activity around your patents.
3. Use information from 1 and 2 above to create technology profiles of the competition's anticipated future moves; future scenario planning can be used here.
4. Devise plans to respond to the competition's current and anticipated moves and reflect those plans in the innovation portfolio's strategic buckets.

Step 2: Assess Strengths and Weaknesses of Competition's Technological Position.

1. Assess the scope of the claims of the competition's patents in the area of technology that you want to practice in. Keep in mind that a patent is only as good as its claims.
2. Examine the file wrapper information to uncover areas where the competition has limited the application of their own patent(s).
3. Use information from 1 and 2 above to devise ways to get around the competition's blocking patents, in designing new products. Also refer to clearance procedures under the IPM stage.
4. Consult the alliances portfolio to find potential partners whose strength may augment your ability to weaken the competition's position.

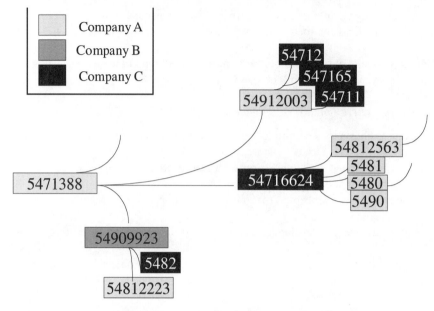

EXHIBIT 12.8   Sample Patent Citation Tree

Step 3: Decide on Projects in the Innovation Portfolio.

1. Include incremental improvements projects designed to obtain improvement patents around the patents of the competition. This is particularly important to respond to similar activity by the competition, as it enhances your bargaining power in cross-licensing transactions.
2. Include incremental improvements projects to obtain improvement patents around your own patents to block the competition from doing the same.
3. Kill innovation projects, seek a license, or enter into a joint venture with the competition in technological areas where the competition is successful in obtaining a domineering patent, following an assessment of the strength of the patent. This is essential to avoid infringing the competition's patents or losing investments.

NOTES

[1] This is related to expert directories developed under the KM stage.

[2] Adapted from Dana Corporation model outlined in Chapter 7.

[3] This step is adapted from "The Innovation Engine: Lead User," *3M Stemwinder,* March 20–April 9, 2001.

13

Implementing Intellectual Property Management under the CICM Model

BACKGROUND

The goal of the intellectual property management (IPM) stage under the CICM model is to maximize the value created and extracted at the previous stages by using the legally defined and protected intellectual capital (IC) (i.e., IP) for two main purposes: securing strong competitive positions and generating revenues. This entails realizing the potential of IP as both a competitive weapon and a business asset. For this to happen, IPM should infiltrate all levels of the organization, be part of business management, and hence be reflected in the management objectives of the organization and individual business units.

MANAGEMENT OBJECTIVES

The management objectives of the IPM stage are to:

- Know and assess the IP wealth of the organization and assess its current and potential uses, particularly in relation to the primary form of IP.
- Build a strong IP portfolio by combining weak with strong IP, reinforcing strong IP through acquiring additional supporting same or different forms of IP, and abandoning low-performing IPs.
- Adopt IP strategies that enable the use of IP as a competitive weapon (lawfully) to hamper competition's efforts in securing a strong competitive position for short- and medium-term purposes.
- Adopt IP strategies to sustain and create new competitive advantage in the long term.
- Adopt IP strategies for the commercialization of IP as a business asset to expand geographically and to enter related/analogous new markets through licensing.
- Take IPM to the operational level by effecting the necessary changes to the structure of the organization, and allocating responsibility to IP teams and units. This would enable every business unit to devise detailed investment plans for leveraging the IP portfolio.
- Instill in the culture of the organization awareness of the proper use of IP by establishing sound management practices, both to preserve the value of IP and to guard against infringing the IP of others.
- Provide tools and systems to enable IPM at the operational levels. In particular, design tools for the valuation and assessment of IP.

PROCESSES

The management objectives enumerated above define the main processes that an IPM program should cover. Exhibit 13.1 represents a framework for the implementation of the IPM stage at both the strategic and operational levels. The IP audit is a preliminary process aimed at creating the IP portfolio, which provides the platform for effective management of the primary IP of the organization both on the strategic and operational levels. At the strategic level, the portfolio is used by top management to forge the appropriate strategies for leveraging IP, for both competitive positioning and commercialization purposes. On the operational level, the portfolio is used by the IP strategy unit and IP synergy teams to operationalize the competitive and commercialization strategies respectively. Three main changes are implemented to operationalize the various IP strategies and to make IPM the job of everyone, and thus develop the competency of managing IP for maximization of value.

The main processes are:

- Strategic Level

  - *Process 1.* Undertake an IP audit and create a portfolio of the primary form of IP to uncover the strengths and weaknesses of the IP portfolio, and enable the spotting of opportunities and risks. This step should aim at creating portfolios that present a snapshot of the organizational IP wealth while at the same time highlighting which of the IPs are of strategic importance. The audit should result in the identification of patents in relation to the businesses of which they are of value.
  - *Process 2.* Decide on IP competitive strategies to enable the use of IP as a competitive weapon to prevent competition from gaining a stronghold in a certain market, protect the organization's competitive positions (short to medium term), and acquire new IP in areas where the organization can develop a market leadership position (long term). Licensing is used here to serve competitive purposes, and to develop new IP for sustaining the business competitive advantage.
  - *Process 3.* Decide on the appropriate IP commercialization strategies to leverage IP as a business asset by seeking commercialization opportunities in related and analogous

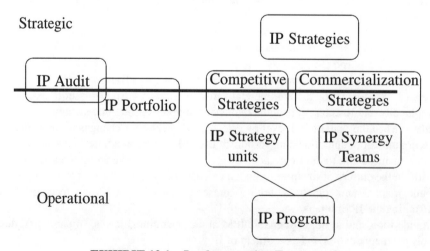

EXHIBIT 13.1   Implementation Framework

markets, and in various geographical locations. The IP should be viewed here as a bundle of rights that may be separated for use in various business transactions.

- Operational Level
  - *Process 4.* Create IP strategy units at the business unit level, or product division level for consumer products organizations, to define and manage the IPs that are the basis of the unit's competitive advantage. This unit should define the areas in which these IPs will be utilized as competitive weapons and is responsible for maintaining them in that regard with the legal department.
  - *Process 5.* Create cross-functional, cross-divisional IP synergy teams responsible for leveraging the IPs that can be used as business assets across the organization as a whole then outside the organization by operationalizing the commercialization strategies. These teams are responsible for developing a commercialization plan in conjunction with the IP strategy unit, concerned business units, and functional departments.
  - *Process 6.* Devise and implement an IP program designed to raise IP awareness and make IPM the job of everyone in the organization. This is done by creating the right culture that is protective of the organization's own IP and preventive of infringing the IP of others.
  - *Process 7.* Provide the tools and methods that enable the use of IP as both a competitive weapon and business asset, hence valuation methods and tools.

STEP-BY-STEP GUIDE

Following is a step-by-step guide on how to implement the main processes.

Process 1: IP Audit and Portfolio Creation

As mentioned in Chapter 8, this is not a legal audit or a simple inventory-taking exercise, but one designed to discover the value of the various IPs to different business purposes and needs. Depending on the structure of the organization, the audit step can be undertaken at the business unit level or across the whole organization.

Step 1: The Audit.   The audit step should be targeted at creating a portfolio of the primary form of IP, the driver of value in a particular industry or line of business. Other forms of IP are included only when they are used in their support. Trade secrets, being a blanket protection over codified know-how, should be covered regardless of the primary form of IP. Examples of trade secrets include: negative information relating to patents, marketing know-how relating to brands and creative methods relating to copyrights (part of the source code for software programs). Trade secrets are the shadow protection of every primary form of IP and hence should be covered in any audit of the primary IP.

The following steps are a guide to the audit exercise and the creation of the portfolio regardless of the form of primary IP:

1. List current and pending (for patents and trademarks) primary IPs and the business unit where they are primarily used. A classification should be used to group the various IP assets by reference to business use for patents, by reference to product categories and market segments for brands, and to market segments and type of media for copyrights.

2. Whenever possible, tie the sales revenues to the various groups of IP and indicate their competitive significance.
3. List any IP assets that do not satisfy the criteria under 2 above but that are believed to be of possible value to other business units across the organization or to strategic partners—suppliers, distributors, and customers.
4. Indicate any IP under 3 above that may be of value to competitors, and indicate how it can be used without jeopardizing the competitive position of the business with which it is associated. Competitive intelligence is required here to reveal other players in the related field of the concerned IP and future implications.
5. List any IP that has been licensed in or out.
6. List any IP that is being used as the basis of business transactions.
7. Estimate the business life cycle of the IP in question as well as the expiration date (not for trademarks). Include maintenance fees and dates for patents and trademarks.
8. List any factors that may affect the strength or the scope of strategic IP assets, particularly issues relating to validity. The scope of the competition's IP should also be considered here to determine its effect on the organization's IP status.

Step 2: Create the IP Portfolio.   Collect the information required under step 1 and present the facts in a portfolio to represent a snapshot of the organization's primary form of IP. Exhibits 13.2 through 13.4 show the portfolios that can be created for each of the primary forms with examples from organizations in the chemical, consumer products, and entertainment industries.

The main areas that an IP portfolio should reveal for IPM purposes are:

- Strategic IP assets that are the basis of a competitive advantage for businesses, which should be used for competitive purposes
- Valuable IP assets, the commercialization of which will not have a harmful competitive effect and thus should be proactively commercialized
- IP assets that are of no considerable value to the business and thus can be sold, donated, or abandoned

The three portfolio types are described as follows:

1. *Patent portfolio.*[1] The patent portfolio should indicate the groups or family of patents that each business unit acquires and uses. The portfolio depicted in Exhibit 13.2 shows the portfolio across the whole organization so that top management can appreciate the strengths and weaknesses of its technological base and hence adopt the appropriate short- and long-term strategies. While the weeding-out process should be performed across the whole organization, plans for strengthening the patent portfolio for competitive and commercialization purposes should be done at the business unit level. The numbers and groups of patents should be indicated under each of the boxes.
2. *Brand portfolio.* A brand portfolio should be created to show the horizontal expansion of a brand across product categories (brand extensions) and the vertical penetration along the value hierarchy (i.e., the brands used in each product category). A number of Nestlé products are taken as an example here (see Exhibit 13.3). Sub-brands are indicated to show the level of branding involved (i.e. use of corporate name, then a product brand, then a sub-brand, etc.). Strong brands should be leveraged competitively by introducing brand extensions along new product categories. They should be leveraged also through merchandising agreements into product categories that the organization

PERFORMANCE PLASTICS SEGMENT/ PATENTS	AUTOMOTIVE	ENGINEERING PLASTICS	POLYURETHANES	WIRE AND CABLE	EPOXY PRODUCTS AND INTERMEDIATES	FABRICATED PRODUCTS
Used currently— Direct application		Use as competitive tools				
No direct planned use —valuable to other			Use as business assets for commercialization purposes			
No direct use or value		Abandon or donate				

EXHIBIT 13.2 Sample Patent Portfolio of a Chemical Company

does not manufacture itself. However, brands created to expand into other market segments across the value hierarchy (i.e., low price entry level to high price/quality luxury brands) are more competitive in nature and, hence are useful for short- and medium-term competitive purposes. Such brands may later be sold if they serve no further competitive purpose. They can also be combined with other brands along the value hierarchy, or combined with the corporate or other product brands to save on marketing and advertising expenses and leverage the brand equity. Of course, to do this, the organization needs to assess how such actions will affect the brand promise.

3. *Copyright portfolio.* A sample portfolio using some of Disney's works is shown in Exhibit 13.4. The portfolio shows the different works and the media/market segment in which they were introduced. The same copyrighted creative content is leveraged across the various businesses. Similar to a brand portfolio, reference must be made to the success of the work and its revenue stream in deciding whether to leverage it across other media, use it as a basis for more reproductions, or commercialize it through merchandising. All the works used in the sample in Exhibit 13.4 have been merchandised in offerings of toys, games, and apparel. Strong works like *The Lion King,* for example, can be further leveraged through sequels.

Process 2: Choosing Competitive IP Strategies

Competitive IP strategies are designed to enable building and strengthening an IP portfolio as well as activate its competitive power by identifying the various competitive uses it can be put to. The blueprint provided in Chapter 8 provides a general guide as to the nature and purpose of these strategies and their variations depending on the primary form of IP. The following steps apply regardless of the form of IP and should be undertaken at the strategic level.

Step 1: Define the Competitive Purpose. The choice of competitive IP strategies depends on a number of factors, including the desired competitive result and the level of resources that need to be committed to operationalize a particular strategy. Each of the strategies also has a different focus: while "design around" strategies focus on the activities of particular competitors, "build a fortress" strategies focus on the competitive landscape in general. The stage of growth, or life cycle, of a particular business area should also be taken into consideration as it indicates to a great extent whether the expected return warrants the use of the needed resources. Exhibit 13.5 lists the various factors that indicate when the use of a certain competitive IP strategy is most appropriate.

Step 2: Combine between Short- and Long-Term Competitive IP Strategies. One of the most important considerations in the choice of competitive IP strategies is to maintain a balance by combining various competitive strategies. Some business units, however, may adopt one strategy as their predominant one, depending on the nature of competition in their line of business and their stage of development. The strategies mentioned require varying levels of resources, and have expected returns that range from short- to long-term benefits, as shown in Exhibit 13.6. The variables shown in Exhibit 13.6 should be used as a guide to combine the strategies in order to maintain a balance between short- and long-term return, as well as small to extensive resource commitment. This should be done in association with the creation of the innovation portfolio under the IM stage.

Step 3: Value Transference Strategies. Using value transference strategies outlined in Chapter 8 involves the following:

- Looking beyond the primary form(s) of IP for such secondary forms of IP (or the primary forms of other business units) that have a strong market value

PRODUCT/ BRAND	MILK	COFFEE	READY DINNERS	SAUCE	PASTA	CHOCOLATE DRINKS	DRIED MILK	CONFECTIONERY
Carnation	X					X X Instant Breakfast	X Coffee Mate	
Tasters Choice		X						
Nescafé		X (Gold, Classic, Decaf)						
MJB Premium		X						
Stouffers			X X Lean Cuisine					
Contadina				X	X			
Bon Bons								X
Drumstick								X
Kit Kat								X
Crunch								X

EXHIBIT 13.3   Sample Brand/Product Portfolio—Nestlé

239

MEDIA/ WORK	FILM	VIDEO DVD	THEATRICAL	BOOKS/ MAGAZINES	THEME PARKS	SEQUELS
Beauty and the Beast	X	X	X	X	X	
The Lion King	X	X	X	X	X	
101 Dalmations	X	X		X		X
Mickey Mouse	X	X		X	X	X
Arial	X	X		X	X	X

EXHIBIT 13.4   Sample Copyrighted Works Portfolio—Disney

240

STRATEGY	PURPOSE	FOCUS	STAGE OF MATURITY OF BUSINESS
Design Around	Block growth plans of the competition. Enhance bargaining power in licensing	Competitor-based	Growth businesses
Build a fortress	Secure a competitive position. Weaken competition's ability to threaten competitive position	Market-based	Embryonic and growth businesses
Mapping	Create new competitive grounds	Organization-based to determine capabilities. Market-based to determine future trends	Mature businesses to develop new areas

EXHIBIT 13.5   The Use of Competitive IP Strategies

- Assessing the business or legal life cycles of the primary IP assets in question
- Introducing the strong secondary form of IP as supporting IP a few years before the end of the expected life cycle, or to revive an old brand in the case of trademarks
- Marrying the two forms of IP in advertising and marketing
- Using this strategy to transfer value of patents to trademarks/brands near the end of the patent legal term or business life cycle, transferring value from technological superiority to brand equity

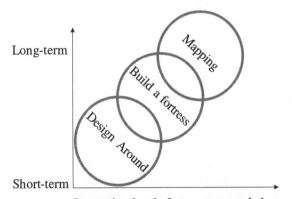

EXHIBIT 13.6   Required Investment and Expected Return for IP Competitive Strategies

- Using this strategy to revitalize a brand and hence preserve brand equity by transferring value from the right of publicity of a celebrity to brand equity, through celebrity endorsements
- Using it with copyrighted works to transfer value from the original copyright to new derivative copyrights based on new versions of the work, to dress the old work with features that respond to new market trends

Process 3: Choosing Commercialization IP Strategies

As explained in Chapter 8, commercialization IP strategies can be either passive, reactive, or proactive. Though proactive commercialization strategies should be encouraged in most cases, a mix should be maintained between passive, reactive, and proactive strategies. This is because in cases in which the use of a certain group of IP assets as competitive weapons is not certain, a passive strategy should be adopted. Exhibit 13.7 provides a guide on when each of these strategies should be used by reference to the primary form of IP. Again, it is noted that trade secreted material should be considered in connection to each of the primary forms of IP.

Generally speaking, passive strategies are used whenever it is competitively harmful to offer the IP for commercialization. When competitive conditions are clearer, reactive strategies can be used to build the business value of the IP, while proactive strategies should be used once the value of the IP is more ascertainable. Proactive strategies should also be used whenever the organization aims to establish the new technology as a market standard. Hence, as the IP identity moves on the continuum, from being a competitive weapon to becoming a business asset, commercialization strategies should get increasingly proactive.

Processes 4 and 5 relate to IP portfolio management where the building of the portfolio in a way that enhances the organization's competitive performance is entrusted to strategic planning units at the business unit level. The emphasis is on the function, which may also be performed by senior management of the business unit or any other strategic planning department. Process 5 relates to leveraging the part of the IP portfolio where IP commercialization doesn't jeopardize the competitive position of any of the business units. IP synergy teams should be formed to leverage such of the IP as are cleared for proactive commercialization. As outlined in Chapter 8, the same function may be performed by a licensing, or business, unit provided its perspective is multifunctional. These teams can also be formed as communities of practice (CoPs) with strategic business focus directed to a technological area or market segment.

Process 4: Building the IP Portfolio: IP Strategy Units

This process involves the creation of IP strategy units at the business unit level, to oversee defining and managing the IP assets that are the basis of the unit's competitive advantage. These units are mainly responsible for operationalizing the competitive IP strategies and applying them to their business needs. Each unit should:

1. Examine the IP portfolio to identify groups of IP that are at the basis of its competitive advantage by reference to scope of use, market share, and business unit growth rate.
2. Devise a plan for the development and augmentation of the IP identified under 1 above through the use of the appropriate competitive strategies.
3. Address in the development plan the use of value transference strategies for sustaining the competitive advantage relating to the identified IP group. This should be a multifunctional exercise.

COMMERCIALIZATION STRATEGY/IP FORM	PASSIVE DO NOT OFFER GENERALLY	REACTIVE OFFER TO PARTNERS	PROACTIVE OFFER TO ANY INTERESTED PARTY
Patents	Strong competitive effect by keeping exclusivity. Technology adoption cycle not clear.	Competitive position strongly established and can be used for cost reduction and expansion in related fields. Offer to competitors only as part of a joint venture or a cross-license	Competitive position strongly established. Need to establish technology as market standard. Offer to competitors and noncompetitors alike in original and analogous markets.
Trademarks	Early brand development. Keep close control over associations, messages, and all brand-related activities to establish brand identity	Growing brand equity —augment with licenses to partners to build brand equity and seek economy of scale. Keep close control and limit licensees	Leverage strong brand equity through non-related product categories (merchandising) and expand geographical coverage (franchising)
Copyrights	Doubtful value, unclear potential	Develop as a service as well as a product for software. Adapt and license work to be included as part of products of others. License to create strong distribution channels	Leverage the same content across every business and market segment. Adapt work in different media

EXHIBIT 13.7   Use of IP Commercialization Strategies

4. Align the various IP plans with the business strategy and objectives of the strategic business unit division, or the whole organization. This can be done with the central business development or growth department.

5. Determine the situations where litigation will be used as a competitive weapon to defend the market position established by the IP. Exhibit 13.8 provides a guide as to when to settle, litigate, or offer a license.

6. In cases of litigation, the following factors should be also considered:[2]

   - The organization's position in the market
   - The effect that enforcement could have on the organizational image or reputation
   - Any legal or other ramifications (e.g., adverse effects on working relations, or retaliatory measures)
   - The effectiveness of the enforcement action
   - The probability of success and expected awards of damages
   - The costs involved

Process 5: Leveraging the IP Portfolio: IP Synergy Teams

This process includes the creation of cross-functional/divisional IP synergy teams to oversee operationalizing the commercialization strategies. IP synergy teams can be organized in permanent units, provided active interaction is maintained (use of CoPs here is an advantage) with various departments and business units throughout and at all levels of the organization. The teams should proactively seek opportunities for leveraging IP across other business units (besides the one it originated in) and external networks, including opportunities around the globe and on the Internet. The following is a guide of the steps that can be taken for seeking opportunities both internally and externally.

- Internal

  1. Provide a profile of groups of IP, cleared for commercialization, for example, groups of patents relating to a certain technology, family of brands relating to a product category for franchising, and copyrights relating to a popular work. The profile should include details on the scope and strength of coverage, strength of protection, projected future uses depending on competitive intelligence, and assessment of present and future market trends.

  2. Post the profile on the organization's intranet with access to business units, subsidiaries, and network of partners.

  3. Oversee transfer and licensing procedures and devise plans for the use of the IP where more than one business unit is interested, to ensure coordination for the further development of the IP in question.

- External

  1. Develop the profile prepared under internal step 1 to include prospective licensees.

  2. Provide information on the IP to Web boards, online IP exchange sites (for patents and trademarks), trade shows, licensing agents, and partners' networks, including global agents.

  3. Create an interactive chat room on the intranet to receive ideas on commercializing IP as well as referrals, leads, and contacts.

  4. Develop relations and contacts with corresponding teams or units in other organizations, including those of the competition.

MAIN USE OF THE INFRINGED IP	WARNING LETTER (CEASE AND DESIST)	OFFER A LICENSE	LITIGATE FORCEFULLY	SETTLE
Sustain competitive position	X		X	
Design around IP of others	X	X		X
Freedom to operate	X	X		X
Commercialization	X	X		X

EXHIBIT 13.8   Litigation Guide

Process 6: Making IPM the Job of Everyone: The IP Program

This process involves three main steps designed to raise IP awareness across the organization and foster a culture that is both protective of the organization's IP and preventive of infringing the IP of others. These steps include preparing an IP Literacy Guide to be distributed to various departments in each business unit. The focus of the Guide should be on the primary form of IP, with general guidelines in relation to branding and trade secret protection in all cases. The second step involves establishing a detection program wherein every department and employee participates in detecting infringement of the organization's IP. Finally, the Clearance program is designed for the various functional departments to prevent against infringing the IP of others, particularly when investing in areas that may be covered by the IP of others. The IP or legal department is the best equipped to design and implement the IP program, which should include at least the following:

Step 1: The IP Literacy Guide. The IP Literacy Guide should provide general information about what IP is and its various forms. Appendix B can be used as a guide. At the same time the Guide should include specific directions to the functional departments, each in regard to their area of practice, to educate them on the proper use of IP. This is essential to protect against jeopardizing IP rights by improperly handling IP in the course of operation or business in general. The following are the precautions that should be taken by the various functional departments:

- To all departments—trade secret protection guidelines

  - Draft a trade secret policy and distribute to all employees to inform what trade secrets are and their importance to business.
  - Restrict public access to sensitive areas where trade-secreted information is kept or handled.
  - Lock gates and cabinets, and use passwords to restrict access to sensitive information in databases.
  - Label trade secret documents, discs, and digital information as such by the use of a "confidential information" stamp or digital notice.
  - Enter into confidentiality agreements with any third party that may come across the trade secrets of the organization.
  - Screen speeches, publications, and presentations by employees to check for any inadvertent disclosure of trade secrets.
  - Undertake any other security measures that are deemed reasonable under the circumstances, based on the value of a certain trade secret to the business.

- Research and development (R&D) departments

  - Alert as to the grace period of one year within which a patent application should be filed following any publication or disclosure of the invention. Such grace period does not exist under patent laws of other countries.
  - Maintain clear and corroborated lab notes to establish the dates of conception and reduction to practice of each invention.
  - Maintain "clean" procedures for copyrights by denying access by the development team to competing software programs, to defend against copyright infringement. This is based on copyright law allowance of independent creation.

- Manufacturing departments

- Control access to products under production to protect ideas and concepts that are not the subject of patent application or protection. Such ideas and concepts are protectable as trade secrets, and hence should be identified and marketed accordingly, as well as protected by reasonable security measures.
- Identify production processes along the same lines and inform the human resources department of key personnel that are in possession of such trade-secreted processes.

- Marketing departments

  - Do not tie the sales of a patented product to unpatented products except if it is a material component of the product. This should be examined in cases in which the business has market power in the relevant market.
  - Do not use any of the trademarks as generic words to describe the product or service in advertising and marketing campaigns, to guard against losing the trademark to the public domain.
  - Do not use the photo or likeness of a celebrity without his or her own permission to endorse a product.
  - Test statements made about competitors' products in comparative advertising to guard against false statements or harmful misrepresentations (see Appendix B for more details).

- Human resources departments

  - Have employees sign confidentiality agreements as part of their employment agreements.
  - Conduct entry interviews with incoming employees to guard against the inadvertent use of trade secrets of competition's former employees, if any.
  - Provide incoming employees with a copy, as well as other details, of the trade secret policy.
  - Conduct exit interviews with departing employees to ensure that they have not taken any trade secrets with them, and prepare statements to be signed by them to that effect.
  - Dispatch a letter to the new prospective employer with notice that the departing employee possesses trade secrets. This is of particular importance when key former employees are joining the competition.

- Licensing units or teams

  - Do not tie the licensing of any patented products to the purchase of nonpatented ones unless the conditions specified under 4 (Marketing) are satisfied.
  - Establish actual supervisory procedures whenever the trademark is licensed as part of a franchise or a merchandise agreement.

- Customer service departments

  - Communicate the brand promise and values to all personnel in customer service. This enables the building of brand equity and hence strengthening of the trademark.
  - Align all contact points with customers with the brand promise. These include, but are not limited to, delivery, maintenance, and customer loyalty programs.
  - Report and document customer complaints to reveal incidents of infringement of the trademark or attempts to pass off other goods as those of the organization.
  - Place customers' complaints on an emergency list until the problem is addressed and resolved, to guard against damage to the brand's reputation. This is particularly

important when the corporate name is used as the predominant brand, in connection with products and services.

- Information technology (IT) departments

  - Ensure that procedures are taken to install firewalls for cyber security purposes.
  - Monitor the Web, or install programs for cyber surveillance, to collect information on the use of the organization's trademarks. This should include spotting the use of the trademark, or confusingly similar marks, as domain names and cyber squatting incidents.
  - Install programs for digital management to indicate infringement of the organization's copyrights, and collect evidence of such infringements.
  - Monitor the Web site records to spot any attempts to deep link or divert Internet traffic from the organization's Web site, which may constitute anticompetitive practices.

Step 2: The Detection Program.   The detection program can be entrusted in large part to the legal department. However, cooperation from all departments—in fact, from all employees—is required for the organization to detect infringements to its IP. The decision to take an enforcement action, and the nature of such action, is something that management must decide later on in accordance with Process 4. The detection program should institute procedures to cover the following practices:

- Create a unit to reverse engineer products of players in the market to spot patent infringements.
- Monitor similar products in the market to spot counterfeit or knock-off products, as well as attempts to pass off goods as those of the organization.
- Monitor the advertisements and marketing campaigns of competition for representations on the organization's products or reveal the use of anticompetitive practices by the competition.
- Analyze works in the market for protectable elements covered by the organization's copyrights.
- Monitor movement of key former employees.

Step 3: The Clearance Program.   The Clearance program is designed to create a culture that is preventive of infringing the IP of others, and keeping the organization aware of the competitor's activity as early as possible. Besides keeping the organization from incurring the high costs of litigation, it also guards against loss of investment funds when a project has to be terminated for infringing on the rights of others. As illustrated in Exhibit 13.9, the Clearance program includes the following procedures (applying to different forms of IP):

1. Undertake a search to get preliminary clearance for the project to proceed.
2. Evaluate the strength, scope, and validity of any blocking IP owned by the competition or another third party.
3. Seek a license to use the blocking IP to proceed with the project. The expected returns of the project should be weighed against the cost of the licensing transaction.
4. If the cost of the transaction is prohibitive or a license is not available, then consider ways to design around the blocking IP. Consult Chapter 8 for the various competitive strategies relating to designing around each form of IP.
5. If designing around the blocking IP is not possible, then terminate the project. Under no circumstances should the project proceed; otherwise, a finding of willful infringement,

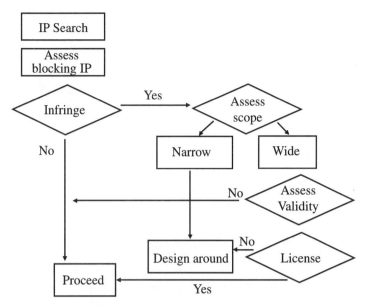

EXHIBIT 13.9   The Clearance Process

where damages can be multiplied by the courts, may be deemed. Exhibit 13.10 provides specific guides as to the clearance procedures involved for each form of IP.

Process 7: Designing Valuation and Assessment Tools

To fully maximize value and leverage IP, tools are required for the business to assess and evaluate the IP assets in question. Valuation of single properties by professional accountants may be essential in cases of litigation, joint ventures, major licensing transactions, acquisitions, and IP donations. The cost of these valuations prohibits their use, however, in the normal course of managing IP. Methods to value and assess IP should be developed by every business to facilitate management of IP in the operation of business in general. The following are suggestions as to how such valuation and assessment methods can be designed.

Assessment and Qualitative Measures.   To create an assessment method, a number of factors should be identified to assess the value of the primary form of IP using qualitative measures (e.g., strength and scope). Each IP is then assessed according to these criteria and given a score from 1 to 5, for example. The various factors are then given different weights according to their importance in determining the value of the IP in the final measure; for example, scope of coverage score can be weighted at 50 percent of the final result. The aggregate of the different scores, according to their respective weights, for each IP indicates its value to the business and thus guides decision making. The following are examples of the factors that should be included:

- Scope of protection under the IP

  - For patents—examine the scope of the claims. A patent is as good as its claims. Compare to other patents covering the same area and classify as domineering or improvement patent.
  - For trademarks—assess brand values and promise and the sub-brands connected to it. Assess the number of market segments and product categories that the brand extends over.

	SEARCH	EVALUATE STRENGTH OF COMPETITION'S IP	LICENSE CANNOT BE OBTAINED
Patent	Prior art searches, USPTO and other	Scope of claims, file wrapper for limitations	Design around
Trademarks	USPTO search, state registers and common law rights	Abandoned, not used, warehoused, naked licenses, acquiescence	Use with house mark to avoid confusion
Copyright	Copyright clearance houses	Assess the unprotectable elements of the work	Distill the idea of the work and regenerate
Trade secret	Entry interview. Ensure competitive intelligence efforts are legal.	Competitive intelligence	Reverse engineer

EXHIBIT 13.10   IP Clearance Procedures

- For copyrights—assess the number of media that the same copyrighted work has been produced in, the market segments it covers, and the various versions in which it has been, or can be, reproduced.

- Strength of the IP

  - The number of patents covering the same technology
  - The level of brand awareness across various market segments, (i.e., level of penetration), and the degree of uniqueness and distinctiveness of the mark
  - The number and quality of protectable versus nonprotectable elements in copyrighted works—assess whether the protectable elements form the core of the work and the degree to which they affect the success of the work

- Other factors

  - The expected business life cycle of the products covered by the IP
  - The potential for licensing the IP and the expected return
  - Protection in other countries
  - Use of the technology in manufacturing and any resultant cost savings

Valuation and Quantitative Measures.   Various corporations have developed methods to value their IP in house, and hence provide guidance as to their management. There are a number of methods to quantitatively measure the value of certain IP assets. The feasibility of each method depends on the accounting system of the organization as well as its industry. Following are methods that can be used to collect comparable data as to the value of the various IP assets to a certain business, and to the organization in general:

- Collect data relating to the sales of patented, copyrighted, or branded products.
- Collect data as to royalty streams from licensing agreements.
- Determine the main IP that is at the basis of each business unit's competitive advantage and how the IP in question affects the profitability of each business unit.

- Compare and assess the growth rates of various business units and connect to the main IP that each business unit owns and manages.

The next chapter presents a guide for customizing the CICM model presented in Chapters 11 through 13, to fit the organization's needs.

NOTES

[1] Adapted from accounts on the patent audit undertaken by Dow Chemical.

[2] Also refer to considerations regarding enforcement issues for each of the various forms of IP in Appendix B.

14

IC Strategy and Customizing the CICM Model

The CICM model is designed to manage all forms of intellectual capital (IC) at three stages, in which management objectives, processes, practices, and tools are different for each stage. The CICM model is multilayered and is presented in a way that is relevant to every type of business and industry. The CICM model presents the general components, essential strategies, processes and practices, and necessary tools for the effective management of IC as part of the strategic management of business as a whole. Therefore, it should be customized to the needs of every business. Not every business needs to implement all the provided components to have an effective ICM system. Rather, the CICM model should be used as the basis for designing the ICM system that fits an organization's, and/or a business unit's, needs and IC strategy. In particular, the CICM should be customized along three variables. These include the organization's industry or line of business, overall business strategy, and situation. These are outlined below.

CUSTOMIZING CICM—THE MAIN THREE VARIABLES

The Industry Variable: Identify the Value Drivers

The industry or line of business in which a certain organization or business unit competes determines the type of IC that drives value. A study by the Financial Accounting Standards Board (FASB) on corporate voluntary disclosures in 2001[1] revealed that different industries, even similar ones like pharmaceutical and chemical industries, have different intellectual (intangible) value drivers. Though a number of value drivers were found common to all industries, like management strategy and brand equity, other value drivers, even when similar, were given different priorities. For example, the main value drivers for the automobile industry included "market share and new products, capacity and cost containment, and workforce" in that order. In contrast, the value drivers of a computer systems company included "revenue streams, efficiency/productivity (of personnel), and new products" in the same order. The interesting observation is that though both included human capital as a value driver, the automobile industry listed cost containment, related to processes (i.e., structural capital) first.

It is further commented that, though intellectual value drivers may be the same in general, the priority given to each, and hence the ones that an ICM system should focus on, are different for each industry. Although every ICM system should include the management of human, customer, and structural capital, their components differ for different industries. When cost containment or operational efficiency may be the first consideration for competitive performance in one industry, it may fall to the second place for another. In addition, the type of the structural capital needed is different, depending on the industry. When service industries depend mainly on codified knowledge and information databases as the source of competitive advantage (to provide advice), chemical industries depend on patents to practice and commercialize technology. Thus, the type of industry affects the strategic importance of different forms and types of IC, wherein those that enable and enhance competitive performance in a certain industry are the most strategic.

The variable of industry is the most important as it is the one that affects the way the CICM model is customized by determining the depth with which any of the management stages should be implemented, and whether its emphasis should be on the management of human, customer, or structural capital. The flexibility of the CICM model lies in distinguishing between the management of each form of IC under the three management stages. This enables its customization by first determining the form of IC that is the main value driver in the industry and then combining it with the management stage that purports to focus on it most. To enable such customization, use Exhibit 14.1 to choose the combination among columns A, B, or C with either of rows D, E, or F. To illustrate, a consulting company whose main value driver is its human capital and how it manages knowledge, where the same knowledge is provided as the main product/service, should choose column A of human capital with row D of knowledge management as a guide to customize the CICM model to its needs. That does not mean that the innovation and IPM stages should be ignored. To the contrary, what it means is that the ICM model of such organizations will be focused on developing a robust knowledge management (KM) program while at the same time implementing the other two stages to a relatively basic level. The IPM stage, though important for the promotion of the brand of the organization, would not need to be as robustly developed as the KM stage. Indeed, examining the ICM model of Ernst and Young[2] reveals that it chose a similar methodology.

In contrast, a chemical business whose main value drivers are patents (i.e., structural capital) should choose the stage that focuses on the management of structural capital (i.e., IPM). The appropriate ICM model will be a combination of column C of structural capital and row F of IPM—that is, a robust IPM program and basic knowledge and innovation management (IM) programs. However, that should also be supplemented by how the organization sees itself. An organization in the chemical industry may choose to develop its KM stage to the robust level as well, if this confirms its organizational identity as a knowledge organization. This brings us to the second variable for the customization of CICM—the strategic thrust.

COLUMN			A	B	C
Row	CICM Management Stage	Main Form of IC Managed	Human Capital	Customer Capital	Structural Capital
D	Knowledge Management	Human capital	Tacit knowledge	Networks, relationships	IT infrastructure, explicit knowledge, and knowledge base
E	Innovation Management	Customer capital	Ideas and product concepts	Manufacturing, co-development agreements, value chain	Work systems, business processes, TQM
F	Intellectual Property Management	Structural capital	Know-how (secret uncodified information)	Brand equity, goodwill, image	Patents, trademarks, copyrights, trade secrets

EXHIBIT 14.1   Customizing the CICM Model

The Strategy Variable: Identify the Source of Competitive Advantage

Strategy is not only unique to every business, but is also time sensitive in the life of that business. There are general strategic thrusts or focuses that are relatively stable (not time sensitive) as they stem from the organization's identification of the source of its competitive advantage. Strategic planning depends increasingly on the organization's ability to create and sustain a competitive advantage. The growth of IC value in the knowledge economy makes IC an inexhaustible source of competitive advantage when properly understood and managed. Each of the ICM management stages is based on managing one form of IC (i.e., knowledge, innovation, or intellectual property) as the main source of competitive advantage. The organization's strategic identification of the main source of its competitive advantage will therefore affect the design of its ICM model, by defining which of the stages will be of strategic importance and which will have the supporting role. For example, an organization that sees itself as a knowledge organization or a big brain, like British Petroleum, recognizes knowledge as the main source of its competitive advantage and thus has its strategic focus set on KM. An organization that sees innovation as the source of its competitive advantage, and not a mere business process, like 3M and Hewlett-Packard, is strategically set on IM. And if it sees itself as a patent factory like IBM, then its IPM stage will be of strategic importance while the other two ICM stages will be supporting programs/systems.

Exhibit 14.2 presents a guide for an organization or business unit to determine which stage of ICM to develop robustly, based on identifying its main source of competitive advantage. Choosing a specific IC (i.e., knowledge, innovation, or IP) as the main source of the competitive advantage affects the unit's strategic focus, strategic objectives, and thus the stage of ICM that should be developed robustly to sustain the source of the competitive advantage. To elaborate, identifying tacit and explicit knowledge resources as the main source of competitive advantage by an organization or a business unit shifts the strategic focus of management to identifying the knowledge resources required to attain the desired competitive position—hence the KM stage. That strategic focus shifts to identifying the level of incremental versus radical innovation required to attain the desired competitive position when innovation is recognized as the main source of competitive advantage. In contrast, if IP is that source, then the strategic focus shifts to identifying ways of using IP to enable competitive positioning in target and analogous markets where the IP assets can be leveraged.

The strategic objectives relating to each of these sources of competitive advantage are different and correspond to the different stages of ICM. Thus an organization or business unit should develop the corresponding ICM stage robustly to sustain its main source of competitive advantage, while at the same time developing the other two stages at least to a basic level. Developing the other two ICM stages is of utmost importance as it supports the main ICM stage (related to the main source of competitive advantage), as well as enabling the organization/business unit to be flexible in responding to change—whenever its strategic focus needs to shift to another type of IC as the main source of competitive advantage.

In addition the character of the organization, its culture, identity, and overall business strategy are significant factors to be considered in the choice of the main source of competitive advantage. Exhibit 14.2 indicates the form of IC that is most suitable as the main source of competitive advantage based on the character of the organization; it also provides examples of such organizations.

In addition to industry and strategy considerations, the organization should also consider its unique situation in customizing the CICM model.

The Organization's Situation Variable: Do Not Start from Scratch

Two major considerations apply under this variable. First, the organization should build on its own successes. Second, it should not implement any stage robustly unless the right culture for that stage is created first.

ICM STAGE	MAIN SOURCE OF COMPETITIVE ADVANTAGE	STRATEGIC FOCUS OR QUESTION	STRATEGIC OBJECTIVES	ORGANIZATIONAL CHARACTER	EXAMPLES
KM	Tacit and explicit knowledge of employees and organization	How are we going to secure the knowledge resources necessary to attain the desired competitive position?	Create the learning organization, enable effective decision-making, be efficient in using existing knowledge and creating new knowledge, provide packaged knowledge	Large with extensive experience and long history/ tradition, government and nonprofit organizations with a certain mission	British Petroleum, Skandia, consulting companies, Siemens, Ford, Daimler/ Chrysler
IM	Innovation: new ideas for product concepts and ways of doing business	How do we choose the level of innovation, incremental versus radical, to attain the desired competitive position or establish our product as the market standard?	Create the innovative organization, reducing time to market, responding & introducing change, achieving market leadership & setting market standards	Daring, young or old but continuously reinventing itself in response to changing technology waves	3M, Hewlett Packard, Xerox, Lucent, Nokia
IPM	Patents (trade secrets), brands and/or copyrights	How do we use IP to enable competitive positioning and leverage our successful or popular IP (technology, brand, or copyright) in target and analogous markets?	Increase competitive prowess by creating stronger entry barriers, leveraging technology, reputation or creative content underlying one product in more than one market, application, or medium	Highly competitive, formidable, aggressive, skill-oriented	IBM, Dow, Disney, Microsoft, General Electric, Coca-Cola, DuPont

EXHIBIT 14.2   The Main Source of Competitive Advantage and the Corresponding ICM Stage

MANAGEMENT STAGE/REQUIRED CHANGE	KNOWLEDGE MANAGEMENT STAGE	INNOVATION MANAGEMENT STAGE	INTELLECTUAL PROPERTY MANAGEMENT STAGE
Strategic level			
Operational level Structural elements			
Cultural values			
Supporting tools			

EXHIBIT 14.3   The CICM Grid

As discussed in previous chapters, every successful organization in the knowledge economy has in some way or another managed part or some forms of its IC. To start from scratch and design a totally new model is not only disruptive of business operations but may also create disorientation problems. The best way to proceed on the journey of implementing the right CICM model for the organization's unique needs is through assessing the organization's present situation by reference to the desired state—an "is" versus "should" analysis. To enable such assessment, use the CICM grid, Exhibit 14.3, to plot in the various work processes, structures, values, and tools that your business unit already has in place. This should reveal the practices or programs implemented under each of the stages, and hence indicate how far the unit is on the road to effecting all the required changes under that stage. Instead of starting from scratch, the unit can build on programs already in place.

To use the CICM grid to guide the change initiative, start with the ICM stage where there are more items (minimal change) required and then proceed to areas where major change will be needed. The CICM grid should be used to devise a phase-out plan, to guide the allocation of limited resources. This plan should be followed unless there is an immediate business need that should be given priority (e.g., a block in the flow of knowledge that warrants starting with the KM stage despite the fact that fewer changes are required under other stages).

The second consideration that should be taken into account under this variable is the "culture imperative." This entails halting implementation until the cultural values required for that stage are put in place. This will avoid the major pitfall wherein an adverse culture defeats the change initiative. As outlined in the CICM model, implementing any of the management stages involves undergoing a number of changes at both the strategic and operational levels. Of the operational changes involved (structural, cultural, supporting tools), structural requires the highest level of expenditure and resource allocation, while cultural changes require the longest time and are the hardest to effect. This is because culture affects the behavioral routines and modes of decision making in a covert way that defies detection. A culture that gives rise to patterns and modes contradictory to those required under any of the ICM stages will disable the effect of any change introduced under that ICM stage. Therefore it is essential, before embarking on full implementation of any of the ICM stages, to ensure that the required culture is in place. Only then would the changes introduced under ICM be activated.

Each of the CICM stages, as explained in the previous chapters, needs a set of cultural values or a certain culture to be successful. In customizing the CICM model, the unit should implement the stage that best fits with its existing culture or start with the required cultural changes before

ICM STAGE	REQUIRED CULTURE
KM	Knowledge sharing, mutual trust, collaboration, collegiality, flexibility, learning and growth
IM	Empowerment of employees, accountability, risk taking, experimentation, encourage submission and implementation of new ideas, experimentation, tolerating (even celebrating) failure
IPM	IP aware, protective of own IP, patent-intensive, or publication-intensive culture, brand awareness

EXHIBIT 14.4   Summary of Required Cultural Values

implementing any stage robustly. Exhibit 14.4 presents a summary of the cultural values required for each of the CICM stages.

NOTES

[1] FASB, "Improving Business Reporting: Insights into Enhancing Voluntary Disclosures," FASB, January 29, 2001, Appendix C. Available online at *www.fasb.org/brrp/brrp2.shtml.*

[2] Information about this model can be found in A. Chard, "Knowledge Management at Ernst & Young," Graduate School of Business 1997, Harvard Business case M291.

Appendix A

Mini Master's of Business Administration (MBA)

This book has proposed and presented intellectual capital management (ICM) as an evolutionary stage of business management for the knowledge organization. A number of business topics have been presented from the perspective of ICM, including vision, culture, organizational behavior, human resources management as management of knowledge resources, business process and operations management as part of managing the innovation process, and strategic management under the formulation of various IC strategies. As such, ICM is closely linked to the art and science of strategic management, where the organization develops the ability to adjust its overall business and competitive strategies in response to change. Of course, it is impossible to tackle all the topics and areas that an MBA covers. This appendix, however, provides the reader with essential minimum knowledge of business management concepts, particularly in relation to strategic management, and touches on marketing strategy and organizational structure.

STRATEGIC MANAGEMENT

The main goal of strategic management is to develop the organization's ability to adapt and respond to change in its environment based on its internal capabilities. It involves managing the organization while having a clear vision of where the organization is and where it wants to be. Strategic management, therefore, is about organizational renewal and growth, wherein nothing is set in stone and practices and processes are constantly monitored, evaluated, benchmarked (internally and externally), and adjusted (either incrementally or radically) to enhance competitive performance. Though the focus of strategic management is on developing a flexible organization that can effectively and quickly respond to change, it also focuses on providing a strong, clear, and continuous course of direction. This makes the role of leadership instrumental not only in leading the organization but also in creating strategic alignment among the vision, strategic objectives, and everything that the organization does at all levels. The role of leadership or top management is essential for defining the organizational identity, philosophy, culture, and overall management system.

McKinsey Consulting notes that not all organizations start with or develop a strategic management system. Strategic management is rather the last phase that an organization's management system evolves to once it passes through three prior phases of simple financial planning, forecast-based planning, and, finally, externally oriented strategic planning. At the third phase, the organization starts to analyze and assess the competitive landscape, devise strategic alternatives to respond to them, and allocate resources accordingly.[1] This evolves in some organizations to strategic management wherein leadership formulates a clear vision of where the organization wants to be and provides systems, practices, and analytical tools to support and monitor performance. Performance in such organizations is not merely assessed on the basis of financial performance but also by other variables, including technological ability, innovation, and social responsibility.

To be effective, managers at all levels should be involved in the process of strategic management according to their respective responsibilities. Strategic planning at each level supports and informs the process at the level below it, where the viability of the strategy and the effectiveness of communicating it is dependent on the level above it. Strategic management involves strategic planning at three levels: top, senior, and frontline management.

- *Top management—the CEO and board of directors.* At this level, top management formulates the vision and the mission of the overall organization and decides on the appropriate organizational structure. Top management is responsible for defining the organizational identity, image, and social standing as well as shaping the culture through policies that define how the organization deals with employees and the outside world. This involves setting the business objectives, creating the reward and compensation system, and formulating management control mechanisms. Strategic decisions at this level involve high risks and affect the future profitability and direction of the whole organization. For multibusiness organizations, this stage also involves deciding on the business portfolio investment strategy, financing options, and growth plans.
- *Senior management—the business unit level.* At this level senior management tailors the overall business strategy to the needs of their respective business units or groups. More specific and multifunctional strategies (e.g., marketing and R&D strategies) are formulated to enable the business unit to meet its set investment goals. The implementation of multifunctional strategies involves significant decision making that affects every aspect of business operation on the medium to long term (e.g., manufacturing, plant location, product mix and innovation). This involves devising action plans and identifying the role that each department will play, with delegation of responsibilities for the attainment of strategic goals to frontline managers whenever appropriate.
- *Middle or frontline management—the functional heads within business units.* At this level, management forges very detailed operational strategies by employing defined tactics and targeting specific goals. These operational strategies are developed into detailed action plans with phased milestones. Decisions at this level are made based on immediate business needs and are in most cases at the departmental level, and limited to the business unit, except in cases in which the same plan is relevant to other business units or correlations exist.

Strategic management and planning involve a number of phases that are summarized as shown in Exhibit A.1. These include phase I of formulating the vision and mission of the organization, phase II of formulating strategic objectives and action plans, and phase III of reevaluating the strategy. To move from phase I to phase II a number of strategic planning tools should be used to assess the external and internal environment of the organization. This is because, as repeatedly stressed, the purpose of strategic management is to enable the organization to respond to the changing needs of its environment, through utilizing its internal resources.

Phase I involves formulating the vision and mission of the whole organization. While the vision defines the purpose of the organization and where it wants to be in the future, the mission statement provides specific details as to the how. The vision statement sets the tone of leadership,

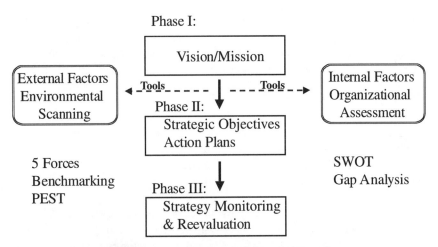

EXHIBIT A.1   Phases of Strategic Planning

the style of management, the culture of the organization, and its overall identity and social character. The mission statement defines the value proposition that the organization intends to deliver to its customers, the distinctive competencies that will enable the organization to deliver such value, and the position the organization aims to attain and sustain in its target market. This mission is translated under Phase II into marketing strategies, distribution and sales strategies, and R&D and human resources strategies. In turn, these functional strategies are implemented through a number of action plans and programs that determine the product mix, market segmentation, innovation portfolio, team formation and allocation, recruitment, training, and professional development. Phase III involves setting the management control mechanisms and performance measures to track and monitor the implementation of strategy and progress in meeting the set goals. This also involves the reevaluation of strategies as changes occur in the organization's environment or internal resources.

Strategic planning involves the use of a number of tools for the assessment of external and internal factors that affect the way the organization intends to respond to changes and thus formulate its strategy. These tools are designed to assess the external factors (competitors, customers, and market) in the organization's environment, and internal factors (competencies, weaknesses) that affect its ability to respond:

- External

  - *Porter's Five Factors.* To assess the attractiveness of an industry for business and the competitive situation, Michael Porter explains that management should consider five forces. These include the risk of new competitors entering the industry—potential entrants, the threat of potential substitutes, the bargaining power of suppliers, the bargaining power of buyers, and the degree of rivalry or nature of competition between existing competitors.[2]
  - *PEST analysis.* To assess environmental factors that are outside the control of the organization, four sources of change should be considered. These include the political, economic, social, and technological (PEST) elements of an industry or a certain market.

- *Benchmarking.* To assess how other organizations respond to change, benchmarking provides insight into how other players are responding. It is a form of competitive intelligence that involves comparing the organization's practices and performance with those of other players in the same industry, and with best performers in other industries.

- Internal

  - *SWOT analysis.* To set the strategic objectives it is important to consider the strengths, weaknesses of the organization, and the opportunities and threats that they pose. SWOT analysis enables management to uncover the organization's capabilities and competencies as well as the weaknesses that affect its performance and the attainment of its goals.
  - *Ansoff's method or gap analysis.* To assess the organization's potential and ability to meet its strategic goals, Igor Ansoff formulated the method of gap analysis.[3] The method involves assessing the difference or gap between the current state of the organization (the "is") and the state envisioned in its objective (the "should"). The organization should then adopt the appropriate strategies and programs to close the gap.

MARKETING STRATEGY

Though part of the strategic plan of the organization, marketing strategies warrant separate mention. Marketing strategies are integral as they constitute the largest embodiment of the organizational overall competitive strategy. Marketing strategy determines the four Ps of the product. These include:

1. *Place.* Distribution channels, market segmentation (where the target market is divided into segments of customers with similar needs, where the marketing mix is adjusted for each segment)
2. *Price.* Cost strategy and structure, sales costs and commission, and pricing strategy
3. *Process.* Delivery mechanism, sales force or agents, and communication channels
4. *Promotion.* Advertising, sales promotion, and communication strategy

They also include an A: *After-sales service,* customer service strategy and plan, repair and maintenance, handling complaints, and technical support.

Marketing strategies are related to branding strategies, globalization strategies, product development, and innovation strategies. In particular they cover five areas:[4]

1. Competitive positioning and market segmentation, which affects the innovation portfolio
2. Product positioning for each segment, which includes pricing and distribution strategies
3. Selection of the marketing mix, which affects the promotion strategy
4. Market entry which determines reentry or exit from a market depending on product life cycle and desirability of business (i.e., competitive strategy)
5. Timing of strategy and implementation

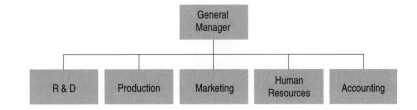

Process-Oriented Funtional Structure

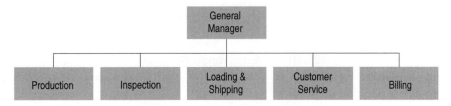

EXHIBIT A.2   Functional Structures

ORGANIZATIONAL STRUCTURE

An organization may assume any structure depending on its strategy, size, and spread of its operations. The following is an illustrative list of structures:

- *Functional and process-oriented structures* as illustrated in Exhibit A.2. The functional structures are usually adopted by single business organizations where activities are organized according to the function. In some organizations, the various functions represent the core processes that the organization performs. The board of executives is usually composed of the heads of the various functions.
- *Strategic business unit (SBU) structure.* Originally developed by General Electric with McKinsey, business units are grouped into SBUs whenever they are strategically connected (e.g., serve the same group of customers). Each SBU contains all the functions to operate independently (see Exhibit A.3).

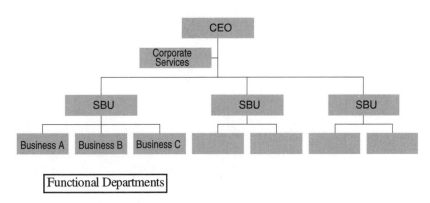

EXHIBIT A.3   SBU Structure

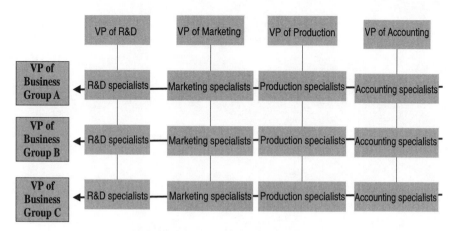

EXHIBIT A.4   Matrix Structure

• *Matrix structure.* Often adopted by multinational and complex organizations where functional managers report to the corporate VP of functional departments and to the VP of their business unit, as shown in Exhibit A.4.

NOTES

[1] See F. Gluck, S. Kaufman, and A. Wallek, "Strategic Management for Competitive Advantage," *The McKinsey Quarterly,* Autumn 1980, pp. 2–16.

[2] See M. Porter, *Competitive Advantage: Creating and Sustaining Superior Performance* (New York: Free Press, 1985).

[3] See Igor Ansoff, *Corporate Strategy* (New York: McGraw Hill, 1965).

[4] Adapted from G. Greenly, "An Understanding of Marketing Strategy," *European Journal of Marketing* 1993, Vol. 23, no. 8, pp. 45–58.

Appendix B

Mini Master's in
Intellectual Property (MIP)[1]

HAVING WORKING IP KNOWLEDGE FOR ICM

Chapter 8 discussed the economic and commercial value and management of IP in the knowledge economy. It is important to note here why a working knowledge of IP is essential for strategic business management.

- First and foremost, protection of knowledge assets through the acquisition of IP rights is an essential step in protecting the business asset base of the enterprise, which amounts in some businesses to 80 percent. Having a working knowledge of IP, therefore, is essential for business managers, accountants, and other personnel entrusted with business asset management in general.
- Failing to understand and thus acquire IP to protect an organization's knowledge assets may seriously jeopardize the competitive advantage of a business unit. A working knowledge of IP is instrumental for a business unit's preservation and enhancement of its competitive power.
- Failure to effectively protect IP may result in extensive losses, particularly at a time when misappropriation of trade secrets, pirating copyrighted works on the Internet and otherwise, producing counterfeit products, and infringing patents are on the increase. A working knowledge of IP is essential to devise protection plans and deter violation of the organization's rights.
- A working knowledge of IP, particularly the primary form, is essential for the design of the appropriate ICM model since IPM is the final stage at which the value derived from the business IC is maximized.

Therefore, this appendix presents a working knowledge of IP for the business manager dealing with acquisition of IP, scope of protection, international treaties and protection in other countries, issues that management should beware of, and, finally, how to deal with issues relating to infringement, enforcement, and litigation. These will be discussed for each of the main forms of IP—patents, trade secrets, trademarks, and copyrights. The table at the end of the appendix presents a snapshot of the main differences between the various forms of IP.

PATENTS

Acquisition and Scope of Protection

Patents are the hardest to acquire with the most stringent legal requirements but provide the strongest protection. They cover "any new and useful process, machine, manufacture, or composition of matter, or any new and useful improvement thereof."[2] A *process* is defined as "a mode of treatment of certain materials to produce a given result."[3] Process patents are also available for new uses of old compounds or products, processes, or machines. The term *machine* includes apparatus, mechanism, device, and engine. *Manufacture* refers to articles of manufacture, whether used as raw or prepared materials, provided they have novel qualities, properties, or combinations.[4] Composition of matter covers compositions made by "chemical union or mechanical mixture,"[5] but excludes naturally occurring compositions except if they were materially changed so that they have characteristics that would not develop naturally. This also applies to genetically engineered life forms, provided they have different new and useful characteristics from those occurring naturally. Since theories, physical formulae, and mathematical algorithms are discoveries of natural laws, they are not patentable, except if incorporated into defined applications.

Patents can also be obtained to protect novel plant varieties, provided they can be reproduced asexually. Those that cannot can be protected through plant varieties certificates, which provide patent-like protection for 20 years, and 25 years for trees.

To apply for a patent, an inventor should file a patent application at the Patent and Trademark Office (PTO). The application is processed and prosecuted through different stages where the PTO examines the patentability of the invention. An average application takes two to three years until a patent issues with prosecution cost of approximately $10,000, depending on the complexity of the invention. An inventor who fails to apply for a patent for a considerable time after reducing the invention to practice may be deemed to have abandoned the invention and lose the right to apply for a patent. A patentee may also be enjoined from enforcing the patent if it was proved that the patent was misused in a way to gain more market power than that enabled by the patent. The courts have recognized certain practices that may constitute patent misuse. The patent may be rendered invalid if it was proven that the inventor misrepresented material facts to the PTO or withheld material information about the patentability of the invention.

To be patentable, the invention should be novel, nonobvious to a person of ordinary skill in the art, and useful. The first requirement of novelty relates to the policy of not awarding patent rights to an idea or an invention that is already in the public domain. The test is very wide, with the effect of excluding from patenting an invention that was in use, known, offered for sale, or mentioned in a printed publication or a previous patent. Though patent protection is limited to the country of the granting body, the public domain scope is universal, including references in other countries and not only the country where the inventor seeks to patent his or her invention. The inventor loses the right to patent a novel invention upon disclosing the invention in almost all countries. In the United States, however, the inventor is given a one-year grace period after first disclosure of the invention to file a patent application.

The invention should also satisfy the requirement of nonobviousness. This entails that the invention should be one that would not occur to someone skilled in the art other than the inventor, when presented with the same problem. In considering this, the PTO considers analogous technologies that are related to the technology field in which the invention falls.[6]

The patent is a grant from the state to the inventor of the exclusive right to exploit and use the invention for 20 years, starting from the date of filing for patent. During that period a patentee may exclude others, including independent inventors, from using, making, selling, offering to sell, or importing into the United States the invented patent or a product that is made by a patented process. More, the patentee can stop any party that manufactures or makes components of the patented invention to be assembled abroad. Nor can another import into the United States a product that was made by a process patented in the United States.

If infringement is found, the courts will award damages that cover the patentee's lost profits attributable to the infringement or reasonable royalties. Damages for patent infringement are considerably high and thus the mere threat of being sued acts as a deterrent to many possible infringers. Contributory infringement of patents, and inducements to infringe patents, are also actionable.

International Treaties and Protection in Other Countries

Patent protection is territorial and depends on the domestic laws of each country. Still, there are a number of international treaties that facilitate patent acquisition in other countries, some of which simplify the process and save costs.

- *Paris Convention for the Protection of Industrialized Property.* The Paris Convention guarantees the priority date of a patent application if within a year of applying in a member country the inventor decides to file in another member country. The Paris Convention does not provide for any cost saving or collective filing procedures.
- *Patent Cooperation Treaty (PCT).* The PCT came into effect in 1978 with over 85 member countries. It provides for an international application to the World Intellectual Property Organization (WIPO) PCT office for a patent, with a listing of the member countries in which the applicant seeks protection. The office conducts prior art searches and issues a response to the applicant. The applicant can request that the same office examine the application for patentability, but the decision will not be binding on the member countries. Pursuant to that the applicant has to apply to each of the countries where protection is sought. This process saves considerable costs, as the prior art searches are performed collectively, and allows around 30 months for the applicant to test the invention in the market before deciding to apply for patents in the designated member countries. Where such countries are members of the European Union, another treaty is of help.
- *European Patent Convention (EPC).* The EPC provides for central filing and examination of the patent application for countries within the European Commission. A successful application will result in the issuance of a European patent that has to be registered in the designated European countries before it can be enforced. The patentee also has to pay separate fees for the registration and maintenance of the patent in each of the designated countries.
- *Trade-Related Aspects of Intellectual Property Rights Agreement under the GATT (TRIPs).* The TRIPs agreement, effective in 1996, harmonizes the IP laws of member countries. When it comes to patents, it introduced patent protection of chemical and pharmaceutical products in developing and least developed countries, and harmonized the protection term to 20 years. In addition, it resulted in the repeal of domestic laws, including those in the United States, that provide for discriminatory treatment based on the place of the invention.

Implications for Legal Management

The most important considerations for management of patents in the United States are the following:

- *To provide adequate resources and databases for inventors to search prior art.* This reduces the costs and avoids investment of R&D time and resources in projects that are already covered by prior art, and are thus in the public domain.
- *To ensure that the organization owns the inventions of its employees.* As a matter of law, the inventor owns the patent except if it has been assigned to the organization. Therefore,

employment agreements should include a provision that the employee assigns any inventions to the employer in the course of employment. Lacking such a provision, the employer may be entitled to a nonexclusive royalty-free license, called *shop right,* if, among other conditions, the invention is in the same area of business of the employer.

- *To provide verifiable evidence in cases in which the first-to-invent status is challenged by keeping clear lab books, records.* Under the U.S. patent law the one who first reduces the invention to practice, and not the one who files for a patent first, is the one entitled to the patent. Lab notes and records help establish when the invention was actually conceived of and reduced to practice.
- *To accurately state the names of the inventors.* Despite the fact that the invention and the patent may be assigned to the employer, stating the wrong inventors, or excluding a rightful inventor, from a patent application may invalidate the patent.

Infringement, Enforcement, and Litigation—What to Do When You Suspect Your Patent Is Being Infringed

1. Determine the occurrence of infringement.

   - Monitor the products of the competitors to find any infringing products.
   - Reverse engineer the products of the competitors to find whether your process is being infringed.

2. Collect the required evidence.

   - Obtain a sample of the infringer's product.
   - Obtain a description of the infringer's process and maintain records of your investigation, as circumstantial evidence may be used in such cases.

3. Determine the type of infringement.

   - *Direct infringement.* The alleged infringer makes, uses, offers to sell, sells, or imports the patented invention.
   - *Contributory infringement.* The alleged infringer contributes to the infringement by knowingly selling or supplying an item for which the only use is in connection with a patented invention.
   - *Inducing infringement.* The alleged infringer actively encourages another to make, use, or sell the invention.

4. Assess the strength of the patent.

   - Assess the validity of the patent by investigating the following:
     - Domestic and foreign patents
     - References in scientific journals and other relevant publications
     - Knowledge of the patentee about the lack of novelty of the invention
   - Assess the scope of the patent.
     - Consider the scope of the claims.
     - Investigate the prosecution history for any amendments.
   - Check any conduct that may amount to patent misuse or may be the subject of antitrust allegations. In particular look for:

- ○ Tie-in provisions in any licensing agreement
- ○ Extension of the term of the patent in licensing agreements by providing for royalty or similar payments after the patent term expires

5. To litigate or not litigate.

- • Examine object of litigation.
  - ○ If it is to stop infringer from free riding on the use of the patent, an offer of a license should be the first step following the cease-and-desist letter.
  - ○ If it is to send a strong message about how you will deal with infringers, then settlement out of court may be an option at a later stage.

- • Determine who will be sued and consider:
  - ○ The number of alleged infringers
  - ○ Relationship of infringers to each other
  - ○ Your relationship with the infringer and whether it will be jeopardized by litigation
  - ○ Any retaliatory measures (e.g., cross-claims that the alleged infringer may take)

- • Estimate the costs of litigation. These include:
  - ○ Attorney's fees and disbursements
  - ○ Your expenses and time
  - ○ Disruption of business and other potential losses

- • Other factors
  - ○ Estimate the maximum possible awards recoverable and compare to the costs involved.
  - ○ Consider when the damages will be paid if you win.
  - ○ Consider the extent and scope of the infringement and whether the infringer can design around your patents.
  - ○ Consider the royalty income that may be obtained if the infringer is granted a license, as well as other benefits (e.g., cross-license).

TRADE SECRETS

Acquisition and Scope of Protection

Trade secrets comprise "any information including a formula pattern, compilation, device, method, technique or process that (i) derives independent economic value, actual or potential, from not being generally known to, and not being readily ascertainable by proper means by, other persons who can obtain economic value from its disclosure or use and (ii) is the subject of efforts that are reasonable under the circumstances to maintain its secrecy."[7] In this respect, trade secret law affords the widest scope of protection, which continues as long as the information is kept secret. Nonetheless, trade secret law protection is weaker than that afforded by patent law. The body of law that developed to protect trade secrets comprises doctrines of federal intellectual property law, state and federal unfair competition law, state trade secret laws, and federal criminal law.[8]

Certain considerations should be taken into account when deciding on limiting the protection of a certain intellectual asset to trade secrets law. First, trade secrets do not guard against reverse engineering or independent invention. Therefore, they are more suited to protection of inventions relating to processes rather than products, except if the product is designed in a way that it cannot be reverse engineered. A good example of such products are food recipes, such as the Coca-Cola recipe, which has been kept a trade secret for over 100 years. Trade secret protection is not suited for intellectual assets whose commercial value depends on publication and dissemination (i.e., works protected by copyrights[9] and trademarks). Once something is recognized as a trade secret, the courts will enjoin competitors from using the trade secret without authorization of the owner, and may award damages up to twice the actual losses of the owner.

Trade secret protection is one of the most critical for the protection of an organization's intellectual assets. When it comes to processes, methods of production or operation, schemes, business plans, market studies and analysis, product and/or services strategies, and the like, the only available protection is that of trade secret. In addition, trade secret protection has been applied by courts to cover negative information. "The definition [of a trade secret] includes information that has commercial value from a negative view point, for example, the results of lengthy and expensive research which proves that a certain process will not work."[10] The importance of trade secret protection lies in the vast number of intellectual assets that can be covered thereby, including all types of know-how, whether business or technology related. Estimates provide that over 90 percent of all new technology is covered by trade secrets. This wealth of knowledge comprises the organization's most valuable intellectual assets, the misappropriation of which may threaten the its vitality.

Implications for Legal Management

Most trade secret infringement occurs through the recruitment and competitive intelligence processes. When it comes to the recruitment process, care should be taken in employing former employees of the competition at the negotiation stage, particularly if the prospective employee is still in the employ of or just left the competition. This is particularly true for key employees whose positions provides them with knowledge of the employer's trade secrets. Similar considerations apply when a key employee is leaving the organization, and both an exit interview and a letter to the new employer should caution against use of the trade secrets in the possession of the departing employee. This is one of the most complex areas of the law since the law has to balance between the employer's proprietary rights to the trade secrets and the employee's ability (and need) to use the experience gained in the previous workplace in career development.

The second consideration relates to competitive intelligence wherein management should ensure that the practices used are lawful and do not amount to improper means of trade secret appropriation. Competitive intelligence and detecting the competitor's moves and strengths is of utmost importance, but care should be exercised that staff are not carried away with the desire to collect more intelligence. Reverse engineering and collection of information from public sources as well as trade fairs are all lawful means of competitive intelligence. Searching the competition's trash, aerial photographing of plant sites, breaking in, and inducing employees to divulge trade secrets are all unlawful means.[11]

A third consideration that has been addressed in Chapter 12 is guarding against cyber espionage by hackers. Appropriate technological measures should be taken and firewalls established to ensure the security of an organization's databases, intranet, and online communications.

Infringement, Enforcement, and Litigation

In general, the steps outlined under Patents should be followed with changes to steps 1, 3, and 4 as follows:

1. Determine the occurrence of infringement:

    *   Track the movement of key employees and examine the circumstances in which they leave the organization;
    *   Track the competitive intelligence activities of the competition to detect the use of unlawful measures.

3. Determine the type of infringement:

    *   *Foreign countries or agents involved.* Criminal liability may arise here. The suspected infringement should be reported to the U.S. Attorney General's Office for appropriate action to be taken.
    *   *Competitor(s) involved.* Willful intention to misappropriate the trade secrets may arise here. Evidence should be collected of the competitor's activities, particularly communications with key employees.
    *   *Employees involved.* Where key employees sell the organization's trade secrets to outside parties or use it to get a better job offer.

4. Assess the strength of the trade secret:

    *   *Assess the validity of the trade secret.* Whether the information acquired trade secret standing by being identified as such and being subject to reasonable security measures under the circumstances.
    *   *Assess the scope of the trade secret.* The extent to which the information protected by trade secret is not part of general knowledge and the time it would take those skilled in the art to uncover such knowledge.
    *   *Assess the value of the trade secret.* The commercial value that the owner gleans from the information remaining secret. Records of sales revenues and profits or cost savings related to the use of the trade secret should be maintained.

TRADEMARKS

Acquisitions and Scope of Protection

Trademark law protects the consumer in that it prohibits the unauthorized use of another's trademark in commerce where such use is likely to create confusion in the mind of consumers concerning the source of the product. From the organization's perspective, trademark law protects the trademark owner's reputation and goodwill that becomes associated with the trademark through advertisement and brand development. In this sense, trademark law is distinguished from both patent and copyright law in that it does not protect specific features of the intellectual product, but rather protects the commercial impression related to the image that the trademark conveys. Thus, trademark law protects the tools that an organization uses to distinguish its products from others in the market by reference to its goodwill.

The right to a trademark vests in the owner through use of the mark in commerce, by being attached to the goods sold or the services offered. Registration with the PTO according to the

Lanham Act provides national protection compared to statewide protection under state law. Trademark law grants the owner the right to perpetually enjoin others in the market from using a similar mark that may confuse consumers as to association between the two similar marks. An application to register a "word, name, symbol, or device" as a trademark should be filed at the PTO for examination. A device has been interpreted to include slogans, colors, product packaging or shape, and trade dress. The Lanham Act also provides for intent-to-use applications which entitle the applicant to reserve a certain mark on the register, provided use is established within two years of the application. In this way the U.S. trademark law comes closer to the laws of most countries where registration, not use, establishes priority rights. A trademark whose validity has not been contested for five years achieves an incontestable status and is presumed valid.

An application is examined to determine whether the mark is protectable under trademark law or not. Those marks that contain a generic name (one that identifies the type of the product), that are not inherently distinctive or have not acquired distinctiveness through use, that are deceptively descriptive (e.g., "Leather Comfort" for vinyl products), or that are confusingly similar to a registered mark, are rejected. Even if registered, such marks may be denied protection later or be afforded only limited protection by the courts.

The Lanham Act also prohibits various practices under the doctrine of unfair competition, which may result in injury to others' business goodwill or trademarks. These include passing off, false advertising, commercial disparagement, trademark dilution, and cyber squatting. Passing off occurs when a false representation is made to directly or indirectly confuse the consumer as to the source or sponsorship of the good (i.e., an attempt to pass one's own goods off as those of the trademark owner).

The false advertising cause of action goes a step further into enjoining activities that are intended or result in injury to the trademark owner by representations made by a third party about the goods. The representation should result in misleading the consumer, and be sufficiently material to affect the purchasing decision. The trademark owner only needs to establish that the false advertising of the defendant resulted to injury to the sales position. Commercial disparagement is similar to the false advertising cause of action but differs in that the misrepresentations relate to the quality of the good or service. In addition, actual monetary loss should be established for the award of damages.

The dilution cause of action provides added protection to famous marks from the use of others where such use is likely to result in the diminution of the mark's uniqueness or distinctiveness, its tarnishing or creation of confusion.[12] The law against dilution protects famous marks against commercial use only and allow for comparative advertising and all forms of news reporting.

The Anticybersquatting Consumer Protection Act was enacted in 1999 to provide protection against the registration and use of domain names (including trafficking) that are identical or confusingly similar to a trademark or dilutive of a famous trademark. The main limitation is that the plaintiff should prove that the domain name was registered in bad faith with an intention to commercially profit from the registration, divert profits from the trademark owner, or dilute/disparage the mark. First Amendment issues may hinder recovery in cases where no commercial gain is proven.

International Treaties and Protection in Other Countries

- *The Paris Convention.* Preserves the priority date for a trademark applicant in one country in the other member countries for six months.
- *The Madrid Agreement and the Madrid Protocol.* Both provide for the centralized registration of marks in member countries. The United States is not a member of either.
- *TRIPs.* Includes provisions on minimum protection of trademarks in member countries.

Implications for Legal Management

The management of trademarks is closely related to brand management. Both legal and marketing issues intertwine together to effectively manage trademarks ensuring the preservation of the rights as well as effective marketing. The following table presents legal considerations for various marketing acts at various stages of the branding plan:

BRANDING	MARKETING ASPECTS	LEGAL ASPECTS
Create brand	Choice of term, concept, value, market segments, market surveys	Legal search, assess level of distinctiveness, apply for registration or ITU
Launch a brand	Advertising, other marketing campaigns	Use of comparative advertising, precautions against genericizing. Caution not to infringe rights of publicity in using likeness or projections of celebrities in promoting the brand
Branding strategies Brand extensions	Strategic and brand fit, customer and market surveys	Registration in other nonrelated classes, search and possible acquisition of prior trademark rights
Licensing	Strategic partnerships, franchising, merchandising, business and marketing plans	Protection against naked licensing where lack of actual supervision may result in loss of trademark rights.
Fortification	Social and community campaigns, management of emotional value, consistency, keep brands current and relevant	Policing of trademarks to avoid a ruling that the owner acquiesced to the unauthorized use or abandoned the mark, protect against tarnishing and dilution. Taking prompt enforcement action on detecting infringement.

Infringement, Enforcement, and Litigation

In general the steps mentioned under Patents should be followed with the following changes to steps 1 through 4:

1. Determine the occurrence of infringement.

   - Determine the likelihood of consumers' confusion caused by the use of a similar mark by another or by introduction of counterfeit products that use identical marks.
   - Determine whether the use may dilute a famous mark.
   - Determine the similarity of the marks by considering similarity of the meaning and sound of the marks, the similarity of the goods, channels of distribution and likelihood of expansion, and the sophistication of consumers.

2. Collect the required evidence.

   • Obtain a sample of the counterfeit product, if any.
   • Obtain evidence of actual consumer confusion.
   • Collect evidence of all losses incurred as a result of the infringing act.

3. Determine the type of infringement.

   • Trademark infringement where confusingly similar marks are used
   • Trademark dilution for famous marks
   • Unfairly competitive practices that result in passing off the infringer's goods as those of the trademark owner or result in commercial disparagement, false advertising, or cyber squatting

4. Assess the strength of the trademark.

   • Assess the validity of the mark.
     ○ Proof of first use in trade
     ○ Incontestable status—registration on the federal register for five years

   • Assess the scope of protection.
     ○ National protection for federally registered marks—geographical limitations apply for trademark rights created under common law or by registration in State Registers
     ○ Strength of the mark—distinctiveness of the mark or the establishment of secondary meaning, particularly for trade dress
     ○ Popularity of the mark—whether it is a famous mark

   • Check any conduct that amounts to genericizing, or abandonment of the mark as well as lack of policing of infringements that may result in a finding of acquiescence to the unauthorized use.

COPYRIGHTS

Acquisition and Scope of Protection

Copyright covers literary and musical works including dramatic, choreographic, pictorial, graphic and sculptural, audiovisual (including motion pictures), sound recordings, and architectural works.[13] Copyright does not protect the idea of the work and thus ideas, facts, functional elements of a copyrighted work, and stock characters and plots are excluded from protection. Copyright is created in a work of authorship at the minute it is "fixed in a tangible medium," through which it can be communicated. Thus, there are no formal requirements that the author should comply with before copyright vests in the work. Registration in the Copyright Office is a mere formality and no examination to assess originality, or to exclude ideas as opposed to expressions, is made. Nonetheless, lack of registration will preclude the plaintiff from seeking statutory damages for the infringement under Section 504(c) of the Copyright Act. Section 405(c) provides that the court may award damages ranging from $750 to $30,000 per infringement and may award up to $150,000 per infringement in cases of willful infringement.

Copyrights are valid for the life of the author plus 70 years, or 95 years from the date of first publication or 120 years after creation of the work for works made for hire. Copyright gives the owner the exclusive right to reproduce, prepare derivative works based upon, distribute, publicly perform and display the copyrighted work. This includes the right of the copyright owner in sound recordings to perform the work publicly by means of digital audio transmission.

Copyrights may be narrowed or completely invalidated when scrutinized by the courts. Litigation may be instituted either by the owner to sue an infringer or by another seeking a declaratory judgment that the copyright is invalid. Under judicial scrutiny the work may be found to contain unprotectable elements that are considered to be in the public domain on the basis that they represent ideas or facts, as opposed to expressions. The matter is far from simple and the tests are different depending on the type of work under scrutiny. Works that are highly creative and expressive enjoy a strong versus a weak protection, or a robust versus a thin copyright, as referred to in this area. A work with a robust copyright enjoys great protection against any form of copying and thus can be used to gain a strong market position. In addition, the Digital Millennium Copyright Act, enacted in 1998, provides protection for copyright owners against circumvention of or tampering with digital rights management systems. The Act also defines the liability of online service providers and enables the copyright owner to demand the takedown of the Web material wherever infringement is suspected.

The scope of protection is further limited by the fair use doctrine, which allows the use of the copyrighted work in certain circumstances, such as those stipulated under Section 107 of the Copyright Act. Section 107 provides that uses for purposes of "criticism, comment, news reporting, teaching (including multiple copies for classroom use), scholarship or research" are fair. To determine if a certain use is fair or not, the court should consider four basic factors under Section 107. These are:

- The purpose and character of the use
- The nature of the copyrighted work
- The amount and substantiality of the use
- The effect on the plaintiff's potential market

International Treaties and Protection in Other Countries

- *The Berne Convention.* Protects the works of nationals of member countries as well as such works that were first published in a member country. The work must be published within 30 days in a member country from the date of the first publication in a nonmember country to be protected. The Berne Convention also provides for minimum requirements of protection including the protection of the moral rights of attribution and integrity. The United States enacted the Visual Artists Right in 1990, limiting moral rights to visual art, on the basis that other provisions of U.S. copyright law afford indirect protection to other works of authorship. The Berne Convention provides in particular that there should be no formalities for the vesting of copyright in a work of authorship.
- *The Universal Copyright Convention (UCC).* The UCC, similar to the Berne Convention, is based on national treatment but has no mention of moral rights.
- *TRIPs Agreement.* Affirms the Berne Convention with the exception of moral rights, and provides that computer programs and compilations are to be treated as literary works.

- *The WIPO Copyright Treaty (WCT).* The WCT is a protocol for the Berne Convention which provides for digital rights. First, the WCT specifically mentions the Internet and the right of copyright holders to distribute their works online. In addition, the WCT prohibits circumvention or tampering with digital management rights, which form the basis of the U.S. Digital Millennium Copyright Act.

Implications for Legal Management

The most important consideration for management purposes is to ensure that the organization has ownership of the copyright in works that it commissions. This area is complicated by the "work for hire" doctrine. Generally speaking, a copyright is owned by the author except if the copyrighted work was made for hire. The Copyright Act provides that if an "employee" creates a work "within the scope of his or her employment," then the employer will be considered the author and will hold the rights of ownership in the copyright. However, if the author is an independent contractor then the work will be deemed for hire (i.e., the hiring party retains ownership) only if the work fits into one of the nine categories enumerated under Section 101 of the Act, and the parties agree in writing that the work will be considered as a work made for hire. It is therefore of utmost importance to make sure that agreements are made in writing and signed whenever the organization commissions a consultant or a contractor to develop its Web site, for example, to ensure ownership of the work.

Infringement, Enforcement, and Litigation

In general, the steps mentioned under Patents should be followed with the following changes to steps 1, 2, and 4:

1. Determine the occurrence of infringement.

   - Determine the protectable elements of the work, keeping in mind that ideas and facts are not protected by copyright.
   - If access to and copying of the protected elements are established, then it is clear that infringement has occurred.
   - If neither access nor copying can be established, then assess the level of similarity between the works. Substantial similarity is required to prove infringement.

2. Collect the required evidence.

   - Proof of access and copying
   - Proof of substantial similarity
   - Proof that the infringing work constitutes a derivative of the protected work through evidence of similarity, and by showing that it limits the ability of the copyright owner to fully exploit the work through reproductions.

4. Assess the strength of the copyright.

   - Assess validity of the copyright—The work has to be the original creation of the author. Independent creation is allowed.
   - Assess the strength of the copyright—The more artistic or expressive the features of the work, the stronger the copyright. This excludes functional features that have to be used for the object to perform the function it was created for, and common plot themes or what is referred to as "scene fairez" as well as the idea of the work, provided it has not merged with the expression.

A Summary

	PATENT	TRADE SECRET	TRADEMARK	COPYRIGHT
Protects	Inventions— an article, composition, machine, process, business method, plant, design, and improvements on any of the above	Business information that is secret and affords the owner a commercial advantage over those who have no access to it	Terms including words, phrases, logos, slogans, packaging, used to identify the source of goods and services	Expressions in works of authorship including literary works, software programs, music, dramatic work, artwork, etc.
Conditions	Novelty, nonobviousness, usefulness	Secrecy, commercial value, reasonable security measures	Use in commerce	Elements are not functional. Ideas and facts are not protectable
Term	20 years from date of application	As long as the information is secret	Unlimited Renewable federal registration every 10 years	Life of author plus 70 years or 95 years for organizations from date of publication, or 120 years from date of creation
Rights provided	Right to exclude others from making, using, selling, offering for sale, and importing goods embodying the invention	Right to prevent divulgence and unauthorized use	Right to exclude others from using confusingly similar marks or unfairly affecting the trademark rights of the owner in trade	Right to prevent unauthorized copying, and reproductions
Body of Law	Federal	Federal and State	Federal and State	Federal
Major costs involved	Prosecution, application and maintenance fees	Implementation of security measures, training of employees	Advertisement and promotion	Reproductions in different media

NOTES

[1] This appendix is dedicated to Professor William Hennessey, who directed the MIP program at Pierce Law from 1983 to 2002. Today, the program offers around 40 IP and IP-related courses, and attracts participants from around 60 countries.

[2] Section 101 of the Patent Act.

[3] *Cochrane v. Deener,* 94 US 780 (1877).

[4] *American Fruit Growers Inc. v. Brogdex Co.,* 283 US 1 (1931).

[5] *Diamond v. Chakrabarty,* 447 US 303 (1980).

[6] Analogous fields of technology are those in which the same problem as that addressed by the invention arises. In one case, the art of detecting stars and rockets was found analogous to that of detecting glass impurities, since the same technology is used.

[7] Section 14 of the Uniform Trade Secrets Act, adopted by 48 states in 1989 with minor variations.

[8] The U.S. Congress enacted the Economic Espionage Act in 1996 making misappropriation of trade secrets a federal crime in certain circumstances. The crime is punishable by imprisonment terms up to 10 years and may include extensive financial fines. The Act prohibits acts amounting to unauthorized appropriation or communication of trade secrets where the actor intends to benefit a foreign government or agent, or intends to injure the owner of the trade secrets to the benefit of another.

[9] An exception is software programs in which only a part of the source code is revealed for copyright registration purposes and the more critical parts are not disclosed and kept as trade secrets. This, however, is a case peculiar to software programs.

[10] Section 1 of the Uniform Trade Secrets Act, Commissioner's Comment, 14 U.L.A. 439 (1990).

[11] These represent actual incidents that were committed and litigated in the United States.

[12] Article 43(c) of the Lanham Act.

[13] Section 102(a) of the Copyright Act.

Index